THE BIOLOGY OF
PLANT PARASITIC NEMATODES

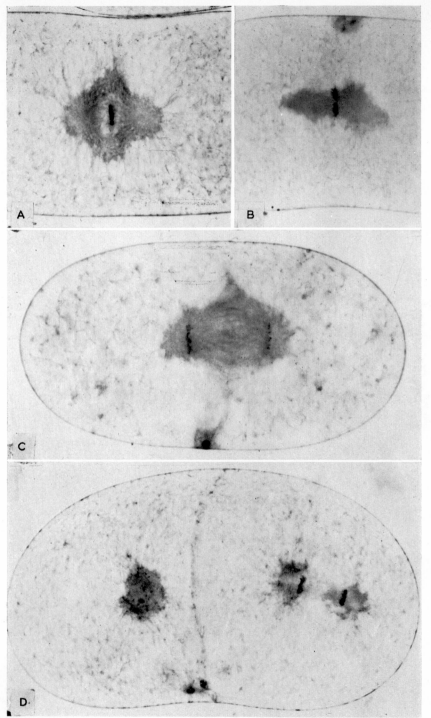

FRONTISPIECE.   Cleavage divisions in *Heterodera glycines*.   (A) Metaphase of first cleavage: the chromosomes form a single metaphase plate; (B) Metaphase of first cleavage: sperm and egg chromosomes form separate metaphase plates on a common plane; (C) Anaphase of first cleavage; (D) Second cleavage division: the two polar nuclei are still visible (×1200).   *See* page 12.
Triantaphyllou and Hirschmann, *Nematologica*, 1962.   E. J. Brill.   Reproduced by permission.

The Biology of Plant Parasitic Nematodes

by

H. R. WALLACE, D.Sc.

Rothamsted Experimental Station

LONDON

EDWARD ARNOLD (PUBLISHERS) LTD

First published 1963

186716

Made and printed in Great Britain by
William Clowes and Sons, Limited, London and Beccles

PREFACE

Plant nematology is a young subject, for it is only during the last ten to fifteen years that it has begun to emerge from the early descriptive stage into an experimental one. Previous books dealing with plant nematodes have been concerned mainly with the taxonomy or with the disease nematodes cause and this is the first attempt to draw together what is known of their biology. In addition to summarising current knowledge of their behaviour and of the ways that multiplication, movement and survival of nematodes are affected by changes in the environment, the book indicates some of the major gaps in knowledge and shows that some hypotheses, which have been widely accepted as fact, are of doubtful validity. It is now possible to indicate some general principles underlying nematode behaviour without too much speculation unsupported by experimental evidence.

I thank those who kindly gave me photographs for use in the text; acknowledgments for other illustrations are made where the figures occur. I am grateful for the discussion, criticism and advice given by my colleagues in the Nematology Department at Rothamsted, particularly Mr. F. G. W. Jones and Dr. Audrey Shepherd and to Mrs. Janet Cowland who drew the figures and helped a great deal with the typing and checking of the text.

Rothamsted Experimental Station   H. R. WALLACE

September 1963.

CONTENTS

vii

CHAPTER 1

Introduction

ECONOMIC IMPORTANCE

The impetus for the rapidly and steadily increasing amount of work on the biology of plant nematodes has largely come from the increasing awareness of the diseases nematodes cause to agricultural and horticultural crops. It is impossible to assess their economic importance even roughly, for in many parts of the world they have still to be sought, but it is probably safe to say that every country and every crop will be troubled by nematodes. Their importance is often evident enough without needing any precise tests to measure percentage losses of yield; a potato crop planted on land heavily infested with *Heterodera rostochiensis* or tobacco on land with root knot can be rendered worthless and in bush or tree crops such as tea and citrus, yields can be halved by the depredations of plant nematodes.

Some workers have attempted to express these losses in terms of money. Thus, *Pratylenchus vulnus* causes a loss of half a million dollars in walnuts in California alone (Lownsbery and Thomason, 1959), and the total annual losses from plant nematode attacks in that State are put at more than 90 million dollars (Allen and Maggenti, 1959). Over the U.S.A. as a whole, estimates of the annual loss in cultivated crops due to plant nematodes range from 250 million dollars (Hutchinson *et al.*, 1961) to 500 million dollars (Cairns, 1955). Comparable losses probably occur elsewhere in the world. An assessment in England and Wales in 1949, for example, showed that the annual loss of potatoes caused by *Heterodera rostochiensis* was of the order of 200,000 tons, representing £2 million (Southey and Samuel, 1954). Such figures must, however, be treated with caution because present methods of estimating crop losses are open to question. There are dangers in deriving figures from nematicide-treated plots, as Seinhorst (1960) has pointed out, and extrapolation from small experimental fields to areas as big as the U.S.A. is obviously liable to give results which may be well wide of the true figures. This does not necessarily mean that the figures quoted over-estimate the position, on the contrary, they may under-estimate the economic importance of plant nematodes. For example, losses in yield can occur without obvious symptoms of nematode attack and so the effects of the nematodes may easily be overlooked.

Economic importance is not the only stimulus for interest in plant nematodes, however. From the biological aspect they present many fundamental problems in the fields of animal behaviour, soil biology, plant pathology and pest control.

1

GENERAL CHARACTERISTICS

Plant nematodes are colourless and most have an elongated cylindrical shape (Fig. 1). In genera like *Heterodera* and *Meloidogyne*, however, the adult female is more or less spherical or lemon-shaped. In length, most lie in the range of 0·5 to 5 mm and in width from 20 to 100 μ.

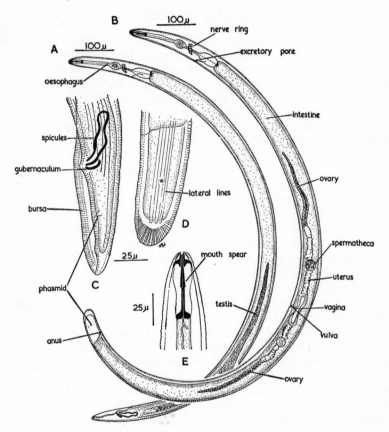

FIG. 1. General morphology of a plant parasitic nematode, *Tylenchorhynchus icarus*. (A) male, (B) Female; (C) male tail; (D) female tail; (E) head. (Wallace and Greet, 1963. Reproduced by permission of Rothamsted Experimental Station).

Plant nematodes occur chiefly in the soil, where they attack plant roots, but the genera *Aphelenchoides*, *Ditylenchus* and *Anguina* contain species that parasitize plants above soil level, in leaves, stems or flowers. The nematodes can be classified according to their parasitic habits. Some are ectoparasitic and feed by thrusting the mouth-spear into plant tissues without actually entering the plant. Others are endoparasitic and spend all or part of their life-cycle within the plant tissues. Of the endoparasites, some, like *Pratylenchus* spp., move freely within the tissues as larvae and adults and often emerge from the root into the soil. Species, which develop spherical or ovoid females, lose the power of locomotion and so remain immobile within the tissues. The distinction between ecto- and endoparasitism is not clear-cut, however; some species like *Aphelenchoides ritzemabosi* may be endoparasitic within the mature leaves of chrysanthemums but ectoparasitic on the young leaves. Some ectoparasites have also been observed with about half their body embedded in the plant tissues, whereas usually only the mouth spear penetrates the plant; *Tylenchorchynchus macrurus* on grass roots is an example.

The life-cycle of plant nematodes consists of the egg, four larval stages and the adult. There are, therefore, four moults, the first of which usually occurs within the egg. The larvae usually resemble the adults except in gonadal development. By definition the term larva is, therefore, incorrect, 'juvenile' would be more appropriate, but usage has now established the term 'larva' in plant nematology and there is no point in changing it now.

GENERAL MORPHOLOGY

The nematode body wall has an outer non-cellular cuticle which may have transverse, lateral or longitudinal thickenings giving characteristic striations. The cuticle is composed of three main layers, the cortex, matrix and fibre layers. Bird (1958) identified fifteen amino acids in the cuticle of *Meloidogyne hapla* and *M. javanica* and he suggested that the chemical reactions of the cuticle indicated the presence of collagen as well as phenolic compounds and polyphenol oxidase. Within the cuticle is a cellular syncytial layer, the hypodermis. The ventral, dorsal and lateral chords are merely thickenings of the hypodermis. The body muscles, which are responsible for the undulatory type of movement in nematodes, consist of a single layer of elongated cells attached to the hypodermis. The muscles are distributed in four longitudinal bands down the length of the body between the chords and so lie dorso- and ventro-laterally. During movement, contractions of these muscle cells bend the body in the dorso-ventral plane. There are no circular muscles. Between the body wall and the inner digestive tube is a fluid-filled cavity containing the reproductive system and some of the gland cells.

The digestive system consists of an anterior terminal mouth usually surrounded by six lips in which lie structures resembling sense-organs, but whose function has not yet been demonstrated. The most anterior part of the digestive tube is the cuticle-lined stoma which, in the plant nematodes, is in the form of a mouth spear which can be protruded from the mouth to penetrate plant tissues during feeding and invasion. The stoma leads into the oesophagus, which is muscular and has a triradiate lumen. Ducts of the oesophageal glands join the lumen of the oesophagus.

There then follows the intestine, a straight tube, one cell thick, ending, in females, in the rectum with a posterior, sub-terminal opening, the anus. In males, the vas deferens of the reproductive system joins the rectum to form a cloaca.

The female reproductive system consists of either one or two ovaries which connect with the ventral vaginal opening, the vulva, by tubular uteri. In species with two ovaries the branches are usually directed anteriorly and posteriorly and the vulva is more or less median except in *Heterodera* and *Meloidogyne* which have a terminal vulva and ovaries directed anteriorly. Where there is only one ovary the arrangement varies in different genera. Spermathecae are sometimes present in the uteri. The male reproductive system has one or two testes entering into the vasa deferentia which join with the rectum to form a cloaca. The male usually has a pair of cuticularised spicules dorsal to the cloaca and a single additional structure, the gubernaculum. These organs appear to function as a holding mechanism during copulation. Most plant nematodes are bisexual, but parthenogenesis and hermaphroditism also occur in some species.

The structure of the excretory system is very variable but often consists of a transverse canal leading from one or two excretory cells to the ventral excretory pore which is usually in the region of the oesophagus. Flame cells are absent.

Little is known of the nervous system in nematodes, but it is usually assumed that they possess the same organisation as the larger animal parasitic nematodes, which have been more closely studied. In many plant nematode species it is possible to see only the nerve-ring, which encircles the oesophagus. It seems likely that nerves from the nerve-ring extend anteriorly to innervate the amphids and other structures in the head region. The cephalids, deirids, phasmids and hemizonion are possibly sensory, but their relationships to the nervous system are not known. A clear area in the hypodermis on the ventral side of the nematode in the region of the nerve-ring has been described by J. B. Goodey (1959). This is the hemizonid and appears to be a ventro-lateral commisure of the nervous system; its function is unknown.

One of the striking features of nematodes is the lack of variation in form and organisation between different species with quite different habits and habitats. This uniformity has been attributed to the need to satisfy the rigorous requirements of mechanical strength and efficiency (Harris and Crofton, 1957). Thus, in animals that move by undulatory propulsion, there is little scope for modification of the characteristic elongated cylindrical shape. The organisation of the internal anatomy may also be correlated with the mechanical principles involved in locomotion. Harris and Crofton (1957) show that the cuticle, with its spiral basketwork of inextensible fibres and elastic layer, is an efficient system which gives at any given internal volume, a constant length against which the pull of the dorsal or ventral muscles can give a powerful bending movement of the body. The system functions, not only at a high internal turgor pressure, but over a wide range of pressures. They suggest that the triradiate pharynx provides a highly efficient pumping mechanism for keeping the alimentary canal open when localised increases in turgor pressure during movement tend to collapse it. Harris and Crofton take their arguments even further and suggest that the structural organisation of the excretory system and reproductive system is influenced by the mechanical features of nematodes.

Uniformity is also apparent in some aspects of behaviour. The pattern of locomotion in nematodes, for example, is very similar. In fact, in studying nematode movement I have found it useful to consider these animals in terms of simple mechanical models. Such an approach can be taken too far, of course, for there are many obvious differences between the behaviour of different species. However, at the functional and mechanical levels it appears to be a valid working hypothesis.

TAXONOMY

Nematodes include species that are saprophytic and those that are parasitic on many hosts of plants and animals. They occupy almost every conceivable habitat—freshwater, salt water and soil, in fact all situations where there is sufficient moisture and a source of organic food supply, and this includes such unlikely places as vinegar vats and beer mats.

There are at present conflicting views on the classification of the higher groups of nematodes. Thorne (1961) considers the group as a Phylum, Nemata, divided into two classes, the Secernentea and Adenophorea. J. B. Goodey (1963) considers the group to have the status of Class, the Nematodea, and he rejects the initial binary grouping. There are also differences at the Order level between these two classifications. Such differences are mostly a question of subjective opinion, however, and need not concern the experimentalist. Neither do they affect the general statements that the majority of plant-parasitic nematodes occur in the Order Tylenchida, with a few in the Dorylaimida, and that all of them are distinguished by the possession of a mouth spear. In the Tylenchida the spear is a hollow cuticular structure, usually with basal knobs. In the Dorylaimida the spear has a different origin, developing sub-ventrally from a tooth or teeth and is often asymmetrical; basal knobs are usually absent.

The primary concern of the experimentalist is to know the identity of the animal he is working with. Correct identification as distinct from taxonomy is therefore an essential prerequisite to research and, for this, accurate detailed descriptions of species are required. Such descriptions often give a range of dimensions of males and females, together with diagnostic morphological characters. In other words, the description is based on a sample from a population and the reliability of any measurements depends on the size of the sample. The number of individuals

Plant Parasitic Nematodes

which have to be measured to give a reliable indication of the degree of variability can be decided by a simple statistical procedure and I see no reason why morphometric descriptions of species should not be accompanied by a mean and standard error so that comparisons can be made between different populations. Furthermore, some indication of variation in morphological characters could be indicated by a series of drawings to show the range of variation. Thus, de Coninck (1962) has stressed the importance of intra-specific variability and Taylor and Jenkins (1957) and Coomans (1962) give statistical data in their descriptions of *Pratylenchus* spp. and *Rotylenchus goodeyi* respectively. By this approach descriptions of species become more objective and less the product of subjective opinion.

RELATIONSHIPS TO OTHER ORGANISMS

It is often useful in research to use techniques developed in other branches of biology and this has been done in plant nematology. Methods of culturing nematodes on plant tissues under aseptic conditions, the Baermann funnel technique for extracting nematodes from soil, histological studies of nematodes and infested plants are a few examples of techniques which originated in other biological fields. Furthermore, observations from experiments with other kinds of animals may suggest a useful approach to a problem in plant nematology, although it is dangerous to take such analogies too far. Nematodes occupy a distinct ecological niche in the soil, so much so that Haarløv (1960) considers that there is little direct competition between nematodes and micro-arthropods. Nematodes, unlike micro-arthropods and earthworms, are continually surrounded by water on which they are entirely dependent for their activities, i.e. they are hydrophilous as opposed to aerophilous. Nematodes, like protozoa and rotifers, move in the water films in the soil pore spaces without disturbing the soil particles, unlike the larger members of the soil fauna. These nematode characteristics present to the biologist problems which are in many ways distinct from those in other animal groups, hence it is often necessary to use new techniques and new concepts in studies on nematode biology.

The animal parasitic nematodes, as might be expected, have features in common with the plant parasitic species. There are close similarities between the two groups in their temperature, oxygen and osmotic requirements and in locomotion and orientation responses (Wallace, 1961). Although the biochemical aspects of the physiology of plant parasitic nematodes are little understood, Krusberg (1960) has shown that *Ditylenchus dipsaci* has a metabolism which follows the general pattern established for the animal parasitic nematodes. Rogers (1960) discusses the mechanisms controlling the hatching of eggs and moulting of larvae of nematodes. He suggests that, in parasitic species, part of the internal mechanism determining these processes has been lost, so that the parasite is dependent on the host to replace it. In animal nematodes the host appears to provide a stimulus which causes the infective stage to produce the internal secretions necessary for hatching and moulting. Rogers suggests that in plant nematodes the host may provide the missing internal secretions which initiate these processes. The mechanisms involved in hatching and moulting of plant nematodes are unknown, but there is no doubt that chemical exudates from plant roots do stimulate them. Here then is at least one example where both animal and plant nematodes should be considered as a whole.

Such a common approach would also be useful in the ecological field. Plant parasitic nematodes which leave the soil and ascend plants to invade leaves, stems or flowers are more active than the root parasites that stay in the soil. This increased activity is associated with the ability to swim upwards in water films, and I suggest, therefore, that plant nematodes can be divided into two groups; those which, by their inherent high activity, can escape from the soil and invade new habitats above soil level, and those which are confined to the soil because they are too inactive to swim upwards in the water films on the outside of plants. There is a similar division in the saprophytic nematodes between soil forms and those which occur in moss cushions, tree boles, etc. The fact that many species of animal parasitic nematodes ascend herbage which is then eaten by the host suggests that this group may have this ecological division as well.

The lack of interchange of experience which has existed up to the present between the animal and plant nematologists is certainly unfortunate for I think that each could learn from the other techniques and methods of approach to different problems. Seinhorst's ingenious sedimentation and elutriation techniques for the recovery of nematodes from soil could be used equally well for the soil-inhabiting stages of animal nematodes, and his mistifier method for extracting nematodes from plant tissues might be adapted for recovering animal nematodes from herbage or animal tissues. The influence of oxygen and carbon dioxide on the hatching of eggs in the centre of a *Heterodera* cyst and on the hatching of trichostrongyle eggs in the centre of faecal pellets seem to me to be similar problems; in fact one could compile many such examples.

The absence in this book of a chapter on physiology reflects the large gaps in our knowledge of the plant nematodes, but at least it is useful to know where the gaps exist. Work on the physiology of animal nematodes as described by von Brand (1952) and Rogers (1962) provides valuable information on which the plant nematologist can base his research.

REFERENCES

ALLEN, M. W. and MAGGENTI, A. R. (1959). Plant nematology in California. *Calif. Agric.* **13** (9), 2–3.
BIRD, A. F. (1958). The adult female cuticle and egg sac of the genus *Meloidogyne* Goeldi, 1887. *Nematologica*, **3** (3), 205–212.

VON BRAND, T. (1952). *Chemical physiology of ectoparasitic animals.* New York: Academic Press Inc.

CAIRNS, E. J. (1955). Nematodes—tiny but mighty. Research under way points to development of better and cheaper controls. *Highlights of Agricultural Research,* **2** (1).

DE CONINCK, L. (1962). Problems of systematics and taxonomy in nematology today. *Nematologica,* **7**, 1–7.

COOMANS, A. (1962). Morphological observations on *Rotylenchus goodeyi* Loof and Oostenbrink 1958. 1. Redescription and variability. *Nematologica,* **7**, 203–215.

GOODEY, J. B. (1959). The excretory system of *Paraphelenchus* and the identity of the hemizonid. *Nematologica,* **4**, 157–159.

GOODEY, T. (1963). *Soil and freshwater nematodes.* Revised edition, edited by J. B. Goodey. London: Methuen & Co. Ltd.

HAARLØV, N. (1960). Microarthropods from Danish soils. *Oikos,* suppl. **3**, 9–176.

HARRIS, J. E. and CROFTON, H. D. (1957). Structure and function in the nematodes: internal pressure and cuticular structure in *Ascaris. J. exp. Biol.* **34** (1), 116–130.

HUTCHINSON, M. T., REED, J. P., STREU, H. T., EDWARDO, A. A. and SCHROEDER, P. H. (1961). Plant parasitic nematodes of New Jersey. *New Jersey agric. exp. Sta. Rutgers,* Bull. **796**.

KRUSBERG, L. R. (1960). Hydrolytic and respiratory enzymes of species of *Ditylenchus* and *Pratylenchus. Phytopathology,* **50** (1), 9–22.

LOWNSBERY, B. F. and THOMASON, I. J. (1959). Progress in nematology related to horticulture. *Proc. Amer. Soc. hort. Sci.* **74**, 730–746.

ROGERS, W. P. (1960). The physiology of infective processes of nematode parasites; the stimulus from the animal host. *Proc. roy. Soc.* B. **152**, 367–386.

—— (1962). *The nature of parasitism.* New York and London: Academic Press.

SEINHORST, J. W. (1960). Over het bepalen van door aaltjes veroorzaakte opbrengstvermindering bij cultuurgewassen. *Meded. LandbHoogesch. Gent.* **25** (3/4), 1026–1039.

SOUTHEY, J. F. and SAMUEL, G. G. (1954). Potato root eelworm. 1. A review of the situation. 2. Research in progress. *Min. Agric. & Fish. N.A.A.S.* 12 pp.

SUIT, R. F. and DUCHARME, E. P. (1957). Spreading decline of citrus. *State Plant Board Florida* **2**, Bull. 2.

TAYLOR, D. P. and JENKINS, W. R. (1957). Variation within the nematode genus *Pratylenchus,* with the descriptions of *P. hexincisus* n.sp. and *P. sub-penetrans* n.sp. *Nematologica,* **2**, 159–174.

THORNE, G. (1961). *Principles of nematology.* New York: McGraw-Hill Book Company Inc.

WALLACE, H. R. (1961). The bionomics of the free-living stages of zoo-parasitic and phytoparasitic nematodes—a critical survey. *Helm. Abs.* **30** (1), 1–22.

WALLACE, H. R. and GREET, D. N. (1963). Observations on the taxonomy and biology of *Tylenchorhynchus macrurus* (Goodey, 1932) Filipjev, 1936 and *Tylenchorhynchus icarus* n.sp. *Parasitology* (in press).

CHAPTER 2

Reproduction, Development and Growth

REPRODUCTION

Reproduction in plant nematodes is mainly bisexual with no scarcity of males, although the sex ratio may vary considerably under different environmental conditions. Tyler (1933a), studying the reproduction of root knot nematodes (*Meloidogyne* sp.), found that although males were rare they were more frequent in old, unhealthy or heavily parasitised roots; 16·4 per cent of the population were males in primary infections but 56·5 per cent in secondary infections. Tyler suggested that the proportion of males increased under adverse conditions. Sex determination in *Heterodera rostochiensis* may depend on abundance of food (Den Ouden, 1960) for with high larval infestations competition for food might result in more males. This would account for the decrease in the rate of multiplication of this species with increasing initial infestation (Fenwick and Reid, 1953). Bird (1960) found that in nitrogen deficient plants, where there might be a scarcity of food, only males of *Meloidogyne javanica* were present. Similarly, a preponderance of males may occur in large populations of mermithids parasitising grasshoppers (Cobb *et al.*, 1927).

Changes in sex ratio may be caused by differential mortality rates of males and females but there is no evidence for this. Ellenby (1954) suggests that sex in *Heterodera rostochiensis* is determined by the environment and he discounts a differential death rate between the sexes (Fig. 2). Triantaphyllou (1960) studied sex determination in *Meloidogyne incognita* and found that when few larvae entered tomato roots, most or all of them developed into females. When large numbers entered the apical portions of the roots, however, galls were formed, rootlet growth ceased and the nematodes, which were crowded together, developed mostly into males. Triantaphyllou, like Tyler, concluded that unfavourable conditions for development induce maleness. Triantaphyllou, however, took the problem a stage further. He showed that, in incubated, galled tomato roots, all second stage male larvae developed into adult males with one testis. Furthermore, many second stage female larvae underwent sex reversal and developed into adult males with two testes. Anatomical examination of second stage larvae substantiated the hypothesis of sex reversal which, Triantaphyllou suggests, is caused chiefly by nutritional deficiencies.

Sex ratio is therefore density dependent and possibly controlled by nutrition but further research is needed before the specific factors are known. The influence of population size and environmental factors on the sex-ratio of plant nematodes other than *Meloidogyne* and *Heterodera* have not been studied, although disparity in numbers between the sexes has been recorded for several species. The fact that intersexes have been observed in *Ditylenchus triformis* (Hirschmann and Sasser, 1955; Hirschmann, 1962) suggests that environmental control of sex may also occur in this species.

Parthenogenesis has been recorded in the genera *Heterodera*, *Meloidogyne*, *Tylenchulus* and *Hemicycliophora*. Mulvey (1958a) found that

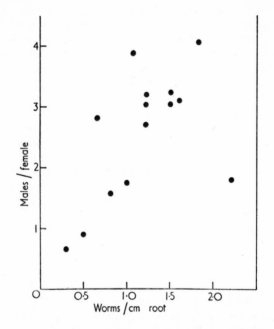

FIG. 2. The relationship between the ratio of males to females of *Heterodera rostochiensis* at different population levels. (After Ellenby, 1954.)

Heterodera trifolii reproduced in the absence of males. Adults, reared from single larvae, were diploid and parthenogenetic and no males were found. When *H. trifolii* females were impregnated by males of *H. schachtii*, a bisexual species, no males were produced (Mulvey, 1958b) although there were some giant eggs and larvae. Mulvey (1960b) suggests that these may have been tetraploid resulting from the fusion of an egg nucleus of *H. trifolii* (27 chromosomes) with a haploid gamete of the sperm of *H. schachtii* (9 chromosomes) giving a giant tetraploid progeny with 36 chromosomes. Onions (1953) also suggests that polyploidy is the cause of giant larvae in *H. rostochiensis*.

Dropkin (1953) reared populations of *Meloidogyne incognita acrita* and *M. arenaria* from single larva infections, thus demonstrating parthenogenesis in these species. However, Mulvey (1960a) found sperm in the oöcytes of *M. arenaria* as well as in the males which were numerous, so it is possible that the type of reproduction in this species depends on the presence of males.

Reproduction without males has also been observed in *Tylenchulus semipenetrans* (van Gundy, 1958), in *Hemicycliophora typica* (Kuiper, 1959) and in *Hemicycliophora arenaria* (van Gundy, 1959). There are several other species where males are rare or unknown, so further research may reveal that parthenogenesis is a more widespread phenomenon than was first thought. There appears to be a correlation between a naturally occurring scarcity of males and parthenogenesis and, conversely, parthenogenesis does not occur where males are abundant. Thus, attempts to

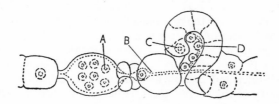

FIG. 3. Gonad of a hermaphroditic *Helicotylenchus* sp. (A) spermatheca with sperm, (B) oviduct, (C) primordial germ cell, (D) sperm in spermagonium. (After Perry, 1959.)

demonstrate parthenogenesis in *Heterodera rostochiensis* (Ellenby, 1957a; Williams, 1957; Fassuliotis, 1957) which produces many males, have failed. Males are also necessary for reproduction in *Ditylenchus dipsaci* (Yuksel, 1960; Palo, 1962), *Tylenchorhynchus claytoni* (Krusberg, 1959) and in *Aphelenchoides ritzemabosi* (French and Barraclough, 1961).

Perry (1959) examined thousands of specimens of *Helicotylenchus* species but found no males. The spermatheca in these species is adjacent to the entrance of the oviduct and usually contains well developed spermatozoa which originate in a spheroid structure, the spermagonium, dorsal to the oviduct near its junction with the spermatheca (Fig. 3). This sperm-producing organ contains a primordial cell (C) which produces primary spermatocytes by mitosis and then four spermatozoa by meiosis (D). These move through the oviduct (B) to the spermatheca (A), where fertilisation of the oöcytes occurs. Such structures were observed in *Helicotylenchus nannus* which is, therefore, a digonic hermaphrodite since it has a distinct reproductive organ in both reproductive systems. Subsequently, Perry *et al* (1959) named four species with a spermagonium and in which males were unknown. Other species of

Helicotylenchus which are bisexual have numerous males. *Pratylenchus crenatus*, a monosexual nematode, is also a digonic hermaphrodite (Dickerson, 1962).

OÖGENESIS AND SPERMATOGENESIS

Mulvey (1960a) studied oögenesis in species of *Heterodera* and *Meloidogyne*. At the anterior ends of both arms of the female reproductive tract in *Heterodera* spp., oögonia increase in number by mitotic division, increasing in size as they move down the ovary to the oviduct. Following reduction division, oöcytes are formed which move, first in double file and then in single file, into the spermatheca which contains the spermatozoa. The sperm enters one end of the oöcyte as it passes through the spermatheca and then it moves into the egg cytoplasm where its chromatin mass resolves into nine discrete chromosomes. Each oöcyte then passes into the uterus where further development produces the egg.

The egg nucleus is in the first metaphase when the oöcyte is penetrated by the sperm. Prior to this, the homologous chromosomes in the oöctye pair, and then align themselves at the metaphase plate where they split longitudinally to form bivalents. During the first metaphase the spindle fibres are distinct and one small and eight large bivalents are visible. After the entry of the sperm, the spindle and its chromosomes describe a 90-degree turn and separation of the members of each homologous pair to the poles now begins, followed by reduction division and formation of the first polar body. There are now nine chromosomes in the polar body and in the oöcyte. A second spindle quickly forms and the chromosomes divide again to form the secondary oöcyte and a further polar body. The oöcyte and sperm nuclei now form a nucleus with 18 chromosomes. Embryonic development then follows. A similar picture is given by Hirschmann (1960) for oögenesis in the animal parasitic nematode *Parascaris equorum*.

In *Heterodera trifolii*, which is parthenogenetic, there is no reduction in the chromosome number during maturation and only one polar body is produced. The chromosomes apparently do not pair, so only univalents are present at the first metaphase. There are 27 chromosomes suggesting that this species is triploid (Mulvey, 1960a).

In *Heterodera glycines* maturation of oöcytes occurs only in inseminated females. There are two meiotic divisions with the formation of two polar bodies (see Frontispiece) (Triantaphyllou and Hirschmann, 1962). Nine bivalents are present at the first metaphase and sperm enter the oöcytes at late prophase or early metaphase. Following the second maturation division sperm and egg pronuclei fuse to form the zygote nucleus.

Oögenesis in *Meloidogyne* spp. is similar to that in *Heterodera*, although the number of chromosomes in the nucleus is different. *M. hapla* and *M. incognita* have 20 chromosomes whereas *M. incognita acrita*, *M.*

javanica and *M. arenaria* have a variable number, usually about 27 or 18 to 20. Mulvey (1960a) suggests that the high chromosome numbers indicate polyploidy, parthenogenesis and possibly gynogenesis. Whatever the mechanism, there is clearly a great need for research into the reproduction of species like *M. arenaria* which are parthenogenetic but in which fusion between sperm and oöcyte can occur. If the parthenogenetic individuals are diploid as Mulvey suggests, are the progeny of bisexual reproduction triploid? And if so are there any morphological differences between diploid and triploid individuals?

Triantaphyllou (1962) studied oögenesis in several isolates of *Meloidogyne javanica* from different countries. The diploid chromosome number was preserved by suppression of chromosome pairing during meiotic prophase and lack of a second meiotic division. Maturation of the oöcytes consisted of one mitotic division giving one polar body and the egg pronucleus. At late prophase or early metaphase, chromosomes consisted of two discrete chromatids. Four egg mass isolates from the U.S.A. had 48 chromosomes, whereas an isolate from Greece and another from Rhodesia had 46. A population from England comprised individuals with 44 or 43 chromosomes and an Australian population consisted of two forms, one with 44 chromosomes and the other with 46 (see Plate I). Triantaphyllou suggests that these differences may become established during the evolution of the parthenogenetic mode of reproduction in association with polyploidy in different populations. When sex is controlled by the environment the difference in the number of chromosomes between males and females may give rise to females with variable chromosome numbers. Thus, females developing from genotypically male embryos will be different in this respect from individuals which are phenotypically and genotypically females. Mulvey's (1960a) chromosome counts for *M. javanica* are lower and more variable than Triantaphyllou's (1962), emphasising the need for more observations on this subject.

Mulvey (1960a) describes the sperm of *Heterodera* spp. as small, tailless and composed of a small nucleus surrounded by a clear area. They are also reputed to move in an amoeboid fashion in the uterus. Little is known of their development from spematogonia, although Cobb (1925) has described spermatogenesis in the free-living marine nematode *Spirina parasitifera*, and he suggests that the process may be similar in other species.

EMBRYONIC DEVELOPMENT

The most complete descriptions of nematode embryology are those by Hyman (1951) and Hirschmann (1960), both of whom referred to the work of Boveri (1899) on *Parascaris equorum*, a zoo-parasitic nematode. In this species, the first cleavage is transverse to the egg axis, producing two cells of equal size. The second cleavage gives four cells in a T-shape but these eventually rearrange themselves into a rhomboid shape. A series of mitotic cleavages results in a coeloblastula which is generally flattened dorso-ventrally and elongated in the antero-posterior direction. The coeloblastula is followed by the gastrula stage. The ectodermal sides of the embryo grow down and push the ventral surface into the interior. During gastrulation the previously flattened embryo becomes cylindrical and the three germ layers are well-defined. In cross section the embryo consists of an ectodermal epithelium enclosing a central column of endoderm in the middle, with a strand of mesoderm to either side. Further growth produces a recognisable larva within the egg membranes.

How far is this general description consistent with observations on the embryonic development of plant nematodes ? In *Radopholus similis* (van Weerdt, 1960) the first division results in a large posterior cell and a slightly smaller anterior one. During the second cleavage the anterior cell divides transversely into an anterior and a posterior cell of equal size. The posterior then divides transversely to give the four-cell stage embryo. These cells show some variation in arrangement; they usually lie in a single line but other arrangements were observed, including that already described for *Parascaris equorum*. Several rapid divisions now follow giving a group of small cells at the anterior end of the embryo. In the gastrula stage the ectoderm is distinguished by small angular cells surrounding an inner mass of larger cells, presumably endoderm and mesoderm (Fig. 4A).

In *Ditylenchus dipsaci* (Yuksel, 1960) the first cleavage is transverse and results in the formation of two cells of unequal size as in *Radopholus similis*. The large anterior cell then divides transversely and the outer cell of these two undergoes two further divisions, one transverse and one longitudinal, to give four cells at the anterior end of the embryo. The single cell at the posterior end, formed by the first cleavage, now divides. Further rapid and repeated cell division results in the formation of the blastula. Gastrulation was not observed. Yuksel then observed a withdrawal of cells near the anterior end into the interior of the embryo to form a curved head region. A curved tail region was formed by a similar process at the posterior end (Fig. 4B).

Maggenti (1961) briefly describes the embryonic development of *Plectus parietinus*, a free-living nematode. The first cleavage is transverse and the second longitudinal, both the anterior and posterior cells dividing to give the rhomboidal arrangement described by Hirschmann. Twenty-four hours after the single-cell egg is laid it has developed to an eight-celled form and after a further 48 hr. gastrulation is completed (Fig. 4C).

The early embryonic development of *Ditylenchus dipsaci* and *Radopholus similis* differs slightly from that of *Parascaris equorum*, particularly in the cell arrangement and the sequence of division to the four-cell stage but as yet there are not enough data to assess whether major differences occur.

In water, development from the single-cell stage to the larva took 5 days for *Paratylenchus projectus* (Rhoades and Linford, 1961), about 5 days for *Ditylenchus dipsaci* (Yuksel, 1960), 3 to 5 days for *Hemicycliophora arenaria* (van Gundy, 1959), 4 to 11 days for *Radopholus similis* (van Weerdt, 1960) and about 11 days for *Plectus parietinus* (Maggenti, 1961).

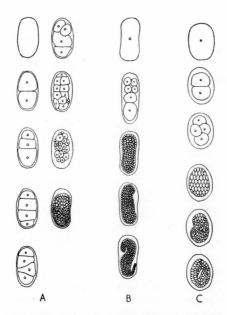

FIG. 4. Embryonic development of (A) *Radopholus similis*, (B) *Ditylenchus, dipsaci*, (C) *Plectus parietinus*. (After van Weerdt, 1960; Yuksel, 1960 and Maggenti, 1961 respectively.)

HATCHING

Two important questions arise in the study of hatching: What stimuli initiate the process? And how does the nematode break out of the egg membranes? Hatching in some *Heterodera* spp. is induced by root secretions. *Heterodera rostochiensis*, for example, shows hardly any hatch in water, but in root exudates of potato or tomato, which are its specific hosts, it hatches readily. *H. schachtii* is similar, except that the water hatch is greater and diffusates from many plant species induce hatching. This is correlated with the greater host range of this species. *H. göttingiana*, on the other hand, has a low hatch in water and in root exudates, although it hatches readily in soil in the presence of host plants. Within the genus *Heterodera* there is clearly a great variation between species in degree of host specificity, their reaction to root exudates of different plant species and their level of hatch in water. Although *H. rostochiensis* eggs are very specific to the diffusates in which they will hatch, cyst contents are reduced by about 50 per cent in a year in soil in the absence of a host plant. The root-secretion stimulus may, therefore, cause a rapid and localised hatching, supplementing the basic slow rate of hatch. This has been considered by many authors to be an example of adaptation of the parasite to the host.

Apart from *Meloidogyne hapla*, *M. incognita acrita* and *M. javanica* (Viglierchio and Lownsbery, 1960) there is no evidence among other genera of increased hatch in root diffusates. What stimuli induce hatch in other species? The fact that eggs of some species can develop in water from the one-cell stage and then hatch (page 15) suggests that the initiation of hatching, like moulting, might occur at a certain stage in development.

Just before hatching, the nematode moves vigorously inside the egg (Dropkin *et al.*, 1958; Edwardo, 1960; Rhoades and Linford, 1961; Shepherd, 1961), often causing bulging of the egg membranes. It then makes a series of rapid thrusts with the mouth spear against one end of the egg until the shell is pierced. *Meloidogyne arenaria* makes 70 to 90 thrusts a minute and repeatedly returns to the same spot on the shell (Dropkin *et al.*, 1958). In *Heterodera schachtii* the larva moves its head slowly back and forth in an arc round the egg making rhythmical stylet thrusts at a rate of 40/min., which is increased to 90/min. just before hatching (Shepherd, 1961). The nematode vacates the egg in a few seconds. In some zooparasitic nematodes the egg shell is pierced with the pointed tail (Silverman and Campbell, 1959).

Ellenby (1957b) was unable to detect any movement of larvae of *Heterodera rostochiensis* within the egg. He therefore suggested that the larvae, when stimulated by root exudates, increase their tension so bursting out of the egg. The unequivocal evidence of larval movement prior to hatching, recorded by various workers, seems to invalidate this hypothesis, although such a mechanism does occur in some zooparasitic nematodes. Rogers (1958) found that dissolved gaseous CO_2 at low redox potentials stimulated unhatched larvae of *Ascaris lumbricoides* to produce a hatching fluid containing an esterase, a chitinase and possibly a protease. He suggested that the esterase alters the vitelline membrane of the eggs so that the chitinase and protease hydrolyse the hard shell either generally or in a restricted area. The larvae finally escape by stretching and bursting through the weakened part of the membrane. Wilson (1958) also studied hatching in an animal parasitic nematode, *Trichostrongylus retortaeformis*. He concluded that larval movements, inside the egg help to emulsify the inner lipoid layer. Once this layer is broken down the larva takes up water from its surroundings and exerts pressure on the egg shell. An additional hatching factor then weakens the outer protein layer enabling the larva to hatch. There is no evidence that the physical and chemical properties of the egg membranes of phyto-

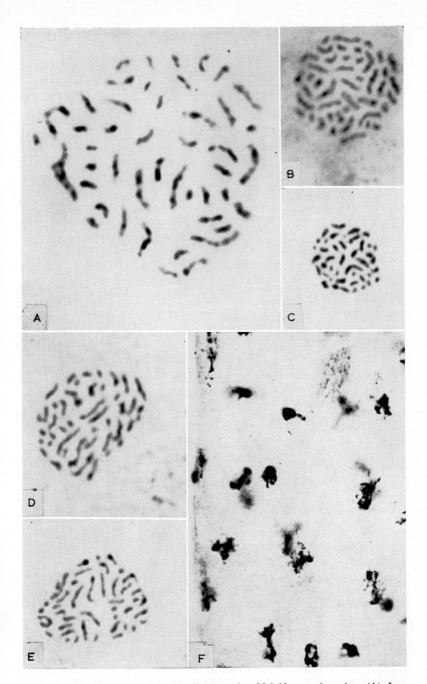

I. Photomicrographs of oögonial divisions in *Meloidogyne javanica*. (A) Late prophase in a Rhodesian population with 46 chromosomes (×5000); (B) and (C) Early and late metaphase in an English population with 44 chromosomes (×3700); (D) and (E) Early metaphase in a Greek and Australian population respectively (×3700); (F) Region of ovary adjacent to germinal zone with chromatic material of oöcytes condensed and stained heavily (×1500). *See* page 13. *Nematologica*, 1962. E. J. Brill. Reproduced by permission.

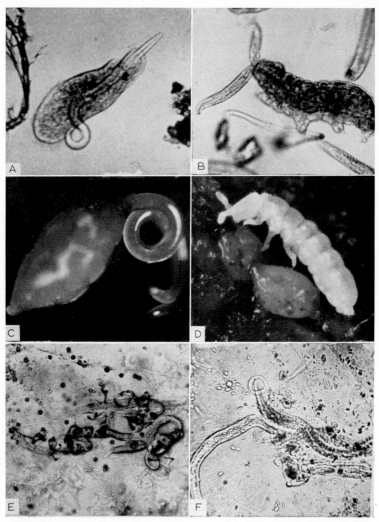

II. Parasites and predators of nematodes. (A) Protozoa, *Urostyla*; (B) Tardigrada, *Macrobiotus* sp.; (C) Dorylaim nematode feeding on a cyst of *Heterodera avenae*; (D) Collembola, *Onychiurus armatus* feeding on *Heterodera trifolii* cyst; (E) Predacious fungus, *Dactylaria thaumasia* with sticky traps; (F) Predacious fungus, *Dactylella doedecoides* with constricting ring trap. *See* page 79. (Reproduced by permission of C. C. Doncaster, 1962.)

parasitic nematodes are altered prior to hatching although Edwardo (1960) states that the egg shell of *Pratylenchus penetrans* becomes thin and plastic.

The use of the stylet during hatching, feeding and invasion of host plants (Chapter 6) appears to be very similar, so it may be valid to ask whether the stimuli which induce these processes are also similar. The piercing action may be induced by particular physical or chemical properties at certain localised regions of the egg or plant root.

Eggs of *Meloidogyne* and *Heterodera* occur in compact masses. This introduces a further complication into studies on hatching, for we have now to consider the egg mass as an entity and not just a collection of isolated units. The decrease in percentage hatch with increase in the number of eggs in the cysts of *Heterodera rostochiensis* (Hesling, 1959) and in egg masses of *Meloidogyne incognita acrita* (Ishibashi et al., 1960) may be caused by an inhibitor which accumulates as hatching proceeds (Ellenby, 1946). Such an inhibitor may arise from bacterial secretions which kill eggs within the cyst (Bergman and Duuren, 1959), but not invariably so. Eggs which fail to hatch in root exudates may do so the following year when fresh root exudates are used. Eggs within the mass may therefore influence each other by preventing the escape of inhibitors.

Onions (1955) showed that hatching of *Heterodera rostochiensis* eggs was not random within the cyst; eggs near the cyst wall hatched sooner than those in the middle. He suggests that an oxygen gradient might occur from the periphery to the centre of cysts, so that eggs at the centre are affected by low oxygen concentrations. It is also possible that accumulation of CO_2 inside cysts inhibits hatch (Gillard et al., 1958; Wallace, 1959).

Egg hatch within the cyst is distinct from larval emergence from the cyst, although in the literature the term hatch is often used instead of emergence. This may be misleading because it has been shown (Wallace, 1959) that the number of free larvae within cysts of *Heterodera schachtii* is almost always low. When the oral and vulval openings of the cyst are sealed, the newly hatched larvae do not accumulate within the cyst, even at the optimal temperature and moisture conditions for larval emergence. This suggests that the presence of free larvae within the cyst inhibits further hatch, and that rate of emergence is one of the limiting factors controlling the rate of egg hatch. Conversely, rate of emergence is obviously controlled by rate of hatch. Sealing one of the two natural openings in cysts of *Heterodera rostochiensis* does not affect the rate of emergence (Onions, 1957), so competition between larvae to escape from the cyst is probably not great.

It is evident from Shepherd's (1962) detailed review that hatching and emergence in *Heterodera* is greatly influenced by environmental factors but this subject will be discussed in Chapter 4, where the influence of the environment on phytoparasitic nematodes will be considered.

2

MOULTING

When a nematode moults, the entire cuticle, including the cuticular lining of the stoma, oesophagus, vulva, cloaca and rectum, is shed. Most plant parasitic nematodes have four moults, the first occurring in the egg, although Linford and Oliveira (1940) failed to detect the pre-hatch moult in *Rotylenchulus reniformis*. The pre-hatch moult may also be absent in the free-living nematode, *Plectus parietinus* (Maggenti, 1961). There are the usual four larval moults in *Hemicycliophora arenaria*, the first within the egg, but the adult female produces a sixth cuticle before shedding the fourth larval cuticle (van Gundy, 1959).

Just before moulting begins, the nematode stops feeding and becomes sluggish or inactive (Linford and Oliveira, 1940; van Gundy, 1958; Rhoades and Linford, 1961). The body contents may become more dense (Hooper, 1961). A space develops between the old and the new cuticle and folds may appear in the old cuticle as it enlarges and becomes loose (Linford and Oliveira, 1940). The basal part of the stylet now dissolves and slow, retractive movements disengage the head from the anterior part of the old stylet, which remains attached to the anterior part of the newly cast cuticle. A new stylet is then usually formed, but in adult males of *Hemicycliophora arenaria* a stylet is not developed after the fourth moult (van Gundy, 1959) and only the second stage larvae and adults of *Meloidogyne arenaria* have a stylet (Triantaphyllou and Hirschmann, 1960).

The formation of the stylet in newly moulted *Longidorus* spp. has been described by Hooper (1961). The stylet becomes detached from the stylet extension and is shed with the old cuticle. The new stylet develops in the oesophageal wall just behind the base of the stylet extension. On moulting, the guide ring and the linings of the exterior amphidial ducts and stoma are shed. The new stylet now passes into the lumen of the stylet extension and its posterior end becomes attached to the anterior end of the stylet extension. A similar picture has been given by Goodey and his colleagues (1960) for stylet formation in *Xiphinema diversicaudatum*.

Having completed the formation of the new cuticular structures, the nematode breaks out of the old cuticle. This, as Hooper (1961) suggests, may be achieved by piercing the old cuticle with the new stylet, but there is little evidence to corroborate this. The old cuticle may be discarded by simple abrasion against soil particles; van Gundy (1958), for example, showed that males of *Tylenchulus semipenetrans* which had developed in water, retained their moulted larval cuticles, whereas males recovered from soil did not. Males and females of *Rotylenchulus reniformis* may also retain their larval cuticles if they lack a rough substratum (Linford and Oliveira, 1940). The nematode's own movements in soil also probably help to get rid of the moulted cuticle. In *Meloidogyne, Heterodera, Rotylenchulus, Tylenchulus* and *Hemicycliophora*, one or more larval cuticles are retained. When this occurs the nematode cannot feed and there is little subsequent growth. This outer covering of larval cuticles may provide protection against adverse conditions (Hirschmann, 1960), but it may have no function at all.

Feeding is an essential prerequisite to moulting in some plant parasitic nematodes and there is probably a relationship between nematode size and the onset of moulting. Golden (1956), for example, suggests that *Rotylenchus buxophilus* moults when a certain size has been reached, hence the distinctive size groups of the larval stages (Fig. 5). The

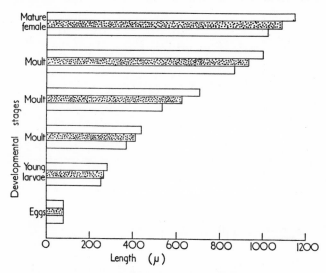

FIG. 5. Dimensions of stages of *Rotylenchus buxophilus*.
Stippled histograms show the mean length, white histograms the extreme lengths. (After Golden, 1956.)

factors which initiate moulting in plant nematodes are, however, largely unknown.

Rogers (1960) suggests that moulting and hatching of free living nematodes are controlled and coordinated by some internal mechanism in the animal. Internal secretions may regulate the time of production of substances which cause moulting and hatching. He further suggests that in parasitic species, part of this mechanism might be lost so that the parasite would depend on the host to replace it. The host might provide a stimulus which induces the nematode to produce the internal secretions or it might provide substances which replace the missing internal secretions. Experiments on trichostrongyle larvae (animal parasitic nematodes) showed that the activity of the host stimulus depended on the concentration of undissociated carbonic acid, on redox potential and on pH. The stimulus caused larvae to produce a fluid which enabled them to escape from the larval cuticle (exsheathment) and Rogers and Sommerville (1960) also showed that the reception of such stimuli and the site of production of the fluid were located between the base of the oesophagus and the excretory pore from which the fluid was released.

Is such a hypothesis relevant to moulting in phytoparasitic nematodes ? The work of Bird (1959) and Rhoades and Linford (1959, 1961) suggests that it may be.   Although Bird was unable to show any changes in the size of the oesophageal glands at the onset of moulting, there were obvious changes in the hypodermis, which became thicker and more clearly demarcated just before moulting began.   The excretory system

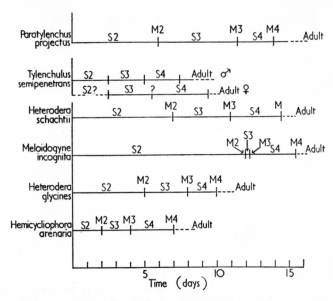

FIG. 6.   A comparison of the duration of developmental stages of six plant parasitic nematodes.   (S) stage, (M) moult.   These are only examples; development is greatly influenced by host plant and environment.

appeared to be connected with the hypodermis so Bird, like Rogers and Sommerville, suggests that the excretory system is involved in moulting. Rhoades and Linford found that pre-adults of *Paratylenchus projectus* accumulated in old pot cultures.   In the presence of young roots or root diffusate, however, the pre-adults moulted.   Rhoades and Linford suggest that old roots, having undergone secondary thickening, fail to provide the stimulus to moult.

There is some indication then, that in some species an external stimulus from the host is necessary to initiate moulting and that the excretory system may be connected in some way with this process.   On the other hand, the stimulus to moult may be related to nutrition and growth, as in some insects. Until there is more information on the stimuli which cause moulting and the source and identity of the moulting fluid, any hypothesis must be very tentative.

GROWTH AND DEVELOPMENT

Phytoparasitic nematodes usually have four moults, four larval stages and an adult stage. In the endoparasitic nematodes it is the second-stage larvae which are infective and the three subsequent moults occur within the host plant.

Some indication of the duration of the larval stages in parasitic species can be obtained from the six examples in Fig. 6. The duration of the second larval stage is very variable because in endoparasites it may be prolonged by inactivity in the soil, due to low temperature or moisture, or by delayed invasion. Once inside a suitable plant, however, feeding starts and the larvae grow and develop to adults in about 3–8 days in many species. The ectoparasitic nematodes such as *Paratylenchus* are exposed to environmental conditions for all of their life cycle, so the duration of the stages is even more variable.

Factors influencing development

Parasitic nematodes are less affected by the soil environment once they are within the host, when rate of development becomes related to conditions inside the plant. The most obvious factor influencing development is host specificity. This subject will be considered in a later chapter; at present it is sufficient to say that many parasitic nematodes will only reproduce on a limited range of host plants and, of these, some are more favourable than others for development. For example, development of *Meloidogyne incognita acrita* is rapid in tomato and slow in *Crotalaria* (Fig. 7).

The age of the plant also influences development. Ritter and Ritter (1958) infected plants of various ages with *Meloidogyne incognita acrita* at a constant temperature of 22°C. Development was quickest on plants which were 65 and 75 days old, slower on those 55 days old and slower still on those 35 days old.

Temperature fluctuations affect the environment within the plant as well as within the soil. The temperature requirements of different nematode species vary a great deal. Thus, the upper limit for development of *Heterodera rostochiensis* (Ferris, 1957) and *Meloidogyne* sp. (Tyler, 1933b) is about 30°C, whereas Thomason's (1957) results suggest that *Meloidogyne javanica* may need a higher temperature for reproduction than *M. hapla*; Bird (1959), however, found that these two species had a similar growth rate under conditions of Australian summer shade with temperatures ranging from 11 to 40°C. Bird suggests that higher temperatures may inhibit the invasion of *M. hapla* and not its rate of development.

Lower temperature limits for development are equally variable. *Heterodera glycines* (Ross, 1960) and root knot nematodes (Tyler, 1933b) cease development at temperatures below 10°C whereas a *Trichodorus* sp. (Rohde and Jenkins, 1957) only develops above 20°C. No generalisa-

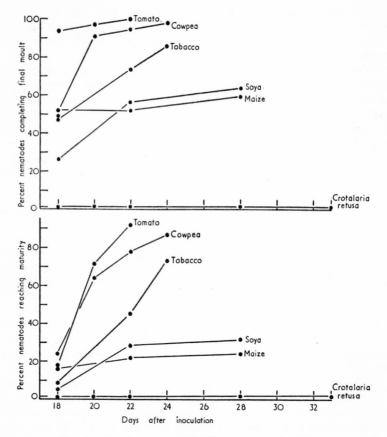

Fig. 7.   Development of *Meloidogyne* sp. on six plants.
(After Peacock, 1957.)

tions can be made about optimum temperatures for development. *Ditylenchus dipsaci* develops quickest at about 15°C (Blake, 1962) whereas *Hemicycliophora arenaria* (Baines *et al.*, 1959) has an optimum temperature in the region of 28 to 32°C. The optimum temperature for development may even depend on the host, for Krusberg (1959) showed that with *Tylenchorhynchus claytoni* on wheat it was 21 to 27°C whereas on tobacco it was 29 to 35°C.

Oxygen concentration in the soil may also affect nematode development within the host plant. Van Gundy and Stolzy (1961) used *Meloidogyne javanica* to infect roots of tomato plants, growing in soil, which were subjected to oxygen concentrations of 21, 5·5, 3·5, 2·0, 0·6 and 0 per cent. The plants were removed after 28 and 35 days to assess development of the nematode. The lowest oxygen concentration at which development of host and parasite occurred was 3·5 per cent; below this level, root growth, size of developing females and egg production were reduced.

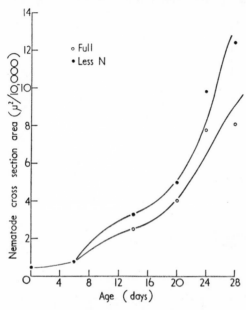

FIG. 8. The growth curves of *Meloidogyne java-nica* on tomato plants supplied with full nutrient and with a nitrogen deficiency. (After Bird, 1960.)

Whether the low oxygen levels influenced development directly or whether the nematodes were affected through reduced plant vigour is not known.

Triantaphyllou and Hirschmann (1960) suggest that the growth rate of larvae of *Meloidogyne incognita* is reduced by crowding and competition for food, and that, consequently, more males develop. Bird (1960), however, showed that in plants deficient in nitrogen, growth of *Meloidogyne javanica* was more rapid than in healthy plants on full nutrient (Fig. 8) and he suggested that in nitrogen deficient plants scarcity of food not only produces more males but also causes the females to grow more quickly. While there is unequivocal evidence that both crowding and nitrogen deficiency produce relatively more males, it does not necessarily follow that the effect of both of these factors is simply to reduce the amount of food available to the nematodes.   Bird's hypothesis that certain single element deficiencies cause a metabolic disturbance in the host plant thereby inducing increased nematode growth seems a more likely explanation.

Oteifa (1953) has also shown that plant nutrition may affect nematode development.   Plants were given potassium nutrient at three levels: deficient, optimum and excessive.   There was no difference between the rate of development of *Meloidogyne incognita* in plants grown at these three nutrient levels, but there was a considerable effect on the length of

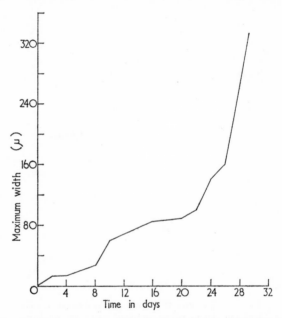

FIG. 9.   Mean growth curve of a mixed population of five *Meloidogyne* spp.   (After Tarjan, 1952.)

time between maturity and egg laying.   The first egg was laid after 40 days in plants with deficient potassium, after 24 days with optimum potassium and after 16 days with excess potassium.

Growth

Insect growth is often confined to a short period following moulting and, therefore, proceeds in a series of steps.   In plant nematodes, however, the body may continue to increase in length and width for several days after moulting.   Bird (1959) suggests that growth in *Meloidogyne javanica* is not achieved through the elasticity of the cuticle but by its growth. The cuticle, he suggests, is a living structure, not an inert exoskeleton and Bird's (1957) observations on the chemical composition of the cuticle of *Ascaris lumbricoides* support this hypothesis. Rhoades and Linford (1961) also observed marked growth in second stage larvae of *Paratylenchus projectus* during a five-day period of feeding on red clover roots. Thus the growth curve of an individual nematode is probably a sigmoid which is made up of a series of smaller sigmoidal curves corresponding to the different larval stages. It resembles the insect growth

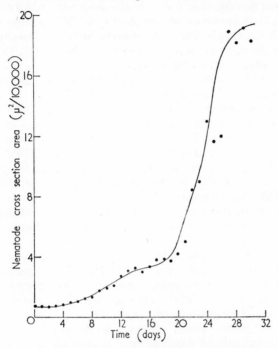

FIG. 10. The growth curve of *Meloidogyne javanica* females. Each point is the mean of eight measurements. Nematode size is expressed as cross-sectional area in sq. μ. (After Bird, 1959.)

curve except that the vertical and horizontal parts of each step are replaced by a sigmoid curve. Unfortunately, there are no data on the growth curves of individual nematodes to support this hypothesis. Tarjan (1952) plotted a mean growth curve for a mixed population of five species of *Meloidogyne* and obtained several steps (Fig. 9). Bird (1959), using a more critical technique, obtained the growth curve of *Meloidogyne javanica* which was sigmoidal in shape with a plateau in the middle (Fig. 10). He showed that the third and fourth moults in this species occur within the shed cuticle of the second stage. Thus, the plateau in the growth curve corresponds to this period, when there is neither feeding nor growth. Blake (1962) obtained a growth curve from measurements of body length in a population of *Ditylenchus dipsaci*.

Although the curve was roughly sigmoidal there was little indication of a series of gradual steps probably because the variation in moulting time of individuals obscured the steps in all but the last moult. There is obviously a need for information on the growth curves of individuals of different species and on the properties of the nematode cuticle. Not all species increase in size as they pass through the larval stages to maturity, there may even be a decrease. *Tylenchulus semipenetrans*, for example, has the following measurements: second stage male, 307 μ; third-stage male, 281 μ; fourth-stage male, 290 μ; adult male, 370 μ. Similarly measurements for the females are: second stage, 323 μ; third stage, 342 μ; fourth stage, 326 μ; adult female, 290 μ increasing to 375 μ (van Gundy, 1958). In *Rotylenchulus reniformis* also, there is little indication of growth until the adult stage is reached (Linford and Oliveira, 1940).

The size of any particular stage in a species might be expected to vary widely under different environmental conditions, whereas in a uniform environment, this variability would not be present to obscure any size differences which might exist between stages. Golden (1956) found no evidence of overlapping in *Rotylenchus buxophilus* (Fig. 5) and Yuksel (1961) came to a similar conclusion about *Ditylenchus dipsaci*. van Weerdt's (1960) measurements of *Radopholus similis* and Blake's (1962) of *Ditylenchus dipsaci*, however, show clear evidence of overlapping. To base the identification of the stage of a nematode solely on measurement may, therefore, be misleading.

Most newly-hatched nematodes are fully developed except for body size and differentiation of the gonads. In *Ditylenchus dipsaci*, growth is sigmoidal in shape, but once gonad development has started, the rate of increase in size remains fairly constant until the nematodes attain maturity. Cell differentiation and organisation accompany increase in gonad length (Blake, 1962). Gonad development may, therefore, proceed independently of moulting but, as with increase in body size, there are no data for individual nematodes, so it is impossible to be definite on this aspect. The ratio of body length to gonad length in *Ditylenchus dipsaci* is the same for nematodes feeding in either susceptible or resistant plants. This ratio, however, may be different before and after the early fourth stage. Thus in the early larval stages the ratio of gonad growth to body growth is less than in the later stages. Blake (1962) suggests that these results indicate that gonad growth is allometric and independent of the environment, thus supporting Huxley's (1932) hypothesis on growth. Further observations on other species are needed, however, before any generalisation can be made on this subject.

The ratio of ovary length to body length between different species may be related to the rate of reproduction. Sedentary tylenchs like *Meloidogyne*, *Heterodera*, *Nacobbus*, *Tylenchulus* and *Rotylenchulus* have rapid reproduction and an ovary-body length ratio greater than one. Migratory tylenchs and aphelenchs have ratios of 0·35 and 0·28 respectively and a moderate rate of reproduction. *Dorylaimus* and *Xiphinema* have ratios of 0·18 and 0·17 and a low reproductive rate (Hollis and Fielding, 1956). It is also possible that if gonad length is related to body length, the reproduction in a species may be related to the size of the adult female. For example, small females of *Heterodera* spp. produce fewer eggs than large females.

Gonad development

Gonad development starts in the first larval stage before hatching. The genital primordium which consists of either two central germinal cells as in *Radopholus similis* (van Weerdt, 1960) or one large central cell as in *Ditylenchus triformis* (Hirschmann, 1962), is bordered by two smaller somatic cells. Subsequent development of the male and female gonads have been described in detail for *Heterodera schachtii* (Raski, 1950), *Radopholus similis* (van Weerdt, 1960), *Meloidogyne incognita* (Trianta-phyllou and Hirschmann, 1960), *Ditylenchus dipsaci* (Yuksel, 1960) and *Ditylenchus triformis* (Hirschmann, 1962). The mode of development in these species is so different that it is impossible to discuss post-embryonic development in general terms.

Fecundity

Meloidogyne and *Heterodera* species usually produce about 500 eggs and Tyler (1938) observed as many as 2,882 in an individual of a *Meloidogyne* sp. *Rotylenchulus reniformis* may lay as many as 196 eggs in a mass (Linford and Oliveira, 1940). *Aphelenchoides ritzemabosi* appears to lay few eggs, only 20 to 30 (French and Barraclough, 1961; Wallace, 1960) but this may be an underestimate because, unless the female is observed throughout its life, the total egg production will not be recorded. Yuksel (1960) studied *Ditylenchus dipsaci* in onion seedlings over 47 to 73 days, the life-span of the species. During this time each female laid from 207 to 498 eggs, thus approaching the figures for *Heterodera*.

The rate of egg-laying has been observed in the following species: *Meloidogyne* sp., 24 eggs per day at 22°C and 12 eggs per day at 16°C (Tyler, 1933b); *Aphelenchoides ritzemabosi*, 2 per day (French and Barra-clough, 1961); *Paratylenchus projectus*, 3 per day (Rhoades and Linford, 1961); *Ditylenchus dipsaci*, 8 to 10 per day (Yuksel, 1960), and *Radopholus similis*, about 4 per day (Loos, 1962).

While egg production in the sedentary species can be easily assessed, the migratory species present a more difficult problem because eggs are often laid in batches in different places over a period of several weeks. Until there is more information on the total eggs produced during the life of plant nematodes it seems unwise to assume that the sedentary species lay more eggs than migratory species.

Rate of reproduction

Some of the factors influencing the rate of reproduction of plant nematodes, such as rate of embryonic development, fecundity, rate of egg laying, hatching, moulting, and rate of post embryonic development, have now been considered. To this list may be added movement, and attraction to and invasion of the host; these will be discussed in Chapters 5 and 6. All of these phases in the life-history are influenced by environmental factors and by the plant itself. It is possible to assess the net effect of all these factors by comparing the length of life cycle of different species (Table 1).

TABLE 1. *The length of life cycle of plant parasitic nematodes*

Species	Length of life cycle (days)	Temperature (°C)	Author
Anguina agrostis	21–28	–	Courtney and Howell, 1952
Aphelenchoides ritzemabosi	14	—	Stewart, 1921
A. ritzemabosi	11–12	17–23	French and Barraclough, 1961
A. ritzemabosi	13–14	13–18	,, ,,
A. ritzemabosi	10–13	14	Wallace, 1960
Ditylenchus dipsaci	19–23	15	Yuksel, 1960
Hemicycliophora arenaria	15–18	30	van Gundy, 1959
Heterodera glycines	21	23	Skotland, 1957
H. glycines	24	—	Ichinohe, 1953
Heterodera trifolii	31	20	Mulvey, 1959
H. trifolii	45	15	,, ,,
Heterodera schachtii	31	19	Raski, 1950
Meloidogyne incognita acrita	28–33	26–31	Peacock, 1957
M. incognita acrita	25–90	—	Ritter and Ritter, 1958
Meloidogyne sp.	19–35	—	Godfrey and Oliveira, 1932
Meloidogyne sp.	25	27	Tyler, 1933b
Meloidogyne sp.	87	16·5	,, ,,
Paratylenchus projectus	30–31	25–28	Rhoades and Linford, 1961
Pratylenchus pratensis	45–48	—	Gadd and Loos, 1941
Radopholus similis	20–25	24–32	Loos, 1962
Trichodorus sp.	16–17	30	Rohde and Jenkins, 1957
Trichodorus sp.	21–22	22	,, ,,
Tylenchorhynchus claytoni	33	24	Krusberg, 1959
Tylenchulus semipenetrans	42–56	—	van Grundy, 1958

There are two main conclusions to be drawn from these results. First, in spite of all the different environmental conditions under which phyto-parasitic nematodes have been studied, the time for completion of the life cycle is of the order of 20 to 40 days. Second, the environment has such a profound influence on development, that unless life cycles are studied at the optimum conditions for each species, no precise comparisons can be made.

REFERENCES

BAINES, R. C., VAN GUNDY, S. D. and SHER, S. A. (1959). Citrus and avocado nematodes. *Calif. Agric.* **13** (9), 16–18.

BERGMAN, B. H. H. and VAN DUUREN, A. J. (1959). Sugar beet eelworm and its control. 7. The action of metabolic products of some micro-organisms on the larvae of *Heterodera schachtii*. *Meded. Inst. Suikerbeit. Bergen-o-Z.* **29** (2), 27–52.

BIRD, A. F. (1957). Chemical composition of the nematode cuticle. Observations on individual layers and extracts from these layers in *Ascaris lumbricoides* cuticle. *Exp. Parasitol.* **6**, 383–403.

—— (1959). Development of the root-knot nematodes *Meloidogyne javanica* (Treub) and *Meloidogyne hapla* Chitwood in the tomato. *Nematologica*, **4** (1), 31–42.

—— (1960). The effect of some single element deficiencies on the growth of *Meloidogyne javanica*. *Nematologica*, **5** (2), 78–85.

BLAKE, C. D. (1962). The etiology of tulip-root disease in susceptible and resistant varieties of oats infested by the stem nematode, *Ditylenchus dipsaci* (Kühn) Filipjev. II. Histopathology of tulip root and development of the nematode. *Ann. appl. Biol.* **50**, 713–722.

BOVERI, T. (1899). Die Entwicklung von *Ascaris* Festschrift für Kupffer.

COBB, N. A. (1925). Nemic spermatogenesis. *J. Hered.* **16** (10), 357–359.

COBB, N. A., STEINER, G. and CHRISTIE, J. R. (1927). When and how does sex arise? *Official record U.S.D.A.* **6** (43), 1–4.

COURTNEY, W. D. and HOWELL, H. B. (1952). Investigations on the bent grass nematode, *Anguina agrostis* (Steinbuch, 1799) Filipjev 1936. *Plant Dis. Reptr.* **36** (3), 78–83.

DICKERSON, O. J. (1962). Gonad development in *Pratylenchus crenatus* and observations on the female genital structure of *P. penetrans*. *Proc. helm. Soc. Wash.* **29**, 173–176.

DROPKIN, V. H. (1953). Studies on the variability of anal plate patterns in pure lines of *Meloidogyne* spp., the root-knot nematode. *Proc. helm. Soc. Wash.* **20**, 32–39.

DROPKIN, V. H., MARTIN, G. C. and JOHNSON, R. W. (1958). Effect of osmotic concentration on hatching of some plant parasitic nematodes. *Nematologica*, **3**, 115–126.

EDWARDO, A. A., DI (1960). Time-lapse studies of movement, feeding and hatching of *Pratylenchus penetrans*. *Phytopathology*, **50** (8), 570.

ELLENBY, C. (1946). Nature of the cyst wall of the potato root eelworm, *Heterodera rostochiensis* Wollenweber and its permeability to water. *Nature, Lond.* **157**, 302–303.

ELLENBY, C. (1954). Environmental determination of the sex ratio of a plant parasitic nematode. *Nature, Lond.* **174**, 1016.

—— (1957a). An investigation into the possibility of parthenogenesis in the potato root eelworm (*Heterodera rostochiensis* Wollenweber). *Nematologica,* **2** (3), 250–254.

—— (1957b). Some physiological aspects of the hatching mechanism of the potato root eelworm, *Heterodera rostochiensis* Wollenweber. *Symposium: Insect and Foodplant, Wageningen,* 1957, 95–102.

FASSULIOTIS, G. (1957). Role of the male in reproduction of the golden nematode. *Phytopathology,* **47**, 11.

FENWICK, D. W. and REID, E. (1953). Population studies on the potato root eelworm (*Heterodera rostochiensis,* Woll.). *J. Helminth.* **27** (3/4), 119–128.

FERRIS, J. M. (1957). Effect of soil temperature on the life cycle of the golden nematode in host and non-host species. *Phytopathology,* **47**, 221.

FRENCH, N. and BARRACLOUGH, R. M. (1961). Observations on the reproduction of *Aphelenchoides ritzema-bosi* (Schwartz). *Nematologica,* **6** (2), 89–94.

GADD, C. H. and LOOS, C. A. (1941). Observations on the life history of *Anguillulina pratensis. Ann. appl. Biol.* **28**, 39–51.

GILLARD, A., D'HERDE, J. and VAN DEN BRANDE, J. (1958). Invloed van koolzuur op het uitkomen der larven van *Heterodera rostochiensis* Woll. *Meded. LandbHoogesch. Gent.* **23** (3/4), 689–694.

GODFREY, G. H. and OLIVEIRA, J. (1932). The development of the root-knot nematode in relation to root tissues of pineapple and cowpea. *Phytopathology,* **22**, 325–348.

GOLDEN, A. M. (1956). Taxonomy of the spiral nematodes (*Rotylenchus* and *Helicotylenchus*) and the developmental stages and host-parasite relationships of *R. buxophilus* n.sp. attacking boxwood. *Univ. Md. agric. Exp. Sta. Bull.* **A-85**, 1–28.

GOODEY, J. B., PEACOCK, F. C. and PITCHER, R. S. (1960). A re-description of *Xiphinema diversicaudatum* (Micoletzky, 1923 and 1927) Thorne 1939 and observations on its larval stages. *Nematologica,* **5**, 127–135.

GUNDY, S. D., VAN (1958). The life history of the citrus nematode *Tylenchulus semipenetrans* Cobb. *Nematologica,* **3**, 283–294.

—— (1959). The life history of *Hemicycliophora arenaria* Raski (Nematoda, Criconematidae). *Proc. helm. Soc. Wash.* **26** (1), 67–72.

GUNDY, S. D., VAN and STOLZY, L. H. (1961). Influence of soil oxygen concentrations on the development of *Meloidogyne javanica. Science,* **134** (3480), 665.

HESLING, J. J. (1959). The emergence of larvae of *Heterodera rostochiensis* Woll. from single cysts. *Nematologica,* **4**, 126–131.

HIRSCHMANN, H. (1960). Reproduction of nematodes. In: *Nematology, fundamentals and recent advances with emphasis on plant parasitic and soil forms.* Edited by J. N. Sasser and W. R. Jenkins. Chapter 12. Chapel Hill: Univ. North Carolina Press.

—— (1962). The life cycle of *Ditylenchus triformis* (Nematoda: Tylenchida) with emphasis on post-embryonic development. *Proc. helm. Soc. Wash.* **29** (1), 30–43.

HIRSCHMANN, H. and SASSER, J. N. (1955). On the occurrence of an intersexual form in *Ditylenchus triformis* n.sp. (Nematoda, Tylenchida). *Proc. helm. Soc. Wash.* **22** (2), 115–123.

HOLLIS, J. P. and FIELDING, M. J. (1956). Relatedness of ovary length and rate of reproduction in plant nematodes. *Phytopathology,* **46** (1), 15.

HOOPER, D. J. (1961). A re-description of *Longidorus elongatus* (deMan, 1876) Thorne and Swanger, 1936 (Nematoda; Dorylaimidae) and descriptions of five new species of *Longidorus* from Great Britain. *Nematologica,* **6,** 237–257.

HUXLEY, J. S. (1932). *Problems of relative growth.* London: Methuen & Co. Ltd.

HYMAN, L. H. (1951). *The invertebrates,* vol. 3, pp. 254–260. New York: McGraw-Hill.

ICHINOHE, M. (1953). On the parasitism of the soybean nematode, *Heterodera glycines. Hokkaido Nat. agric. Expt. Sta.* Res. Bull. **64,** 1–80.

ISHIBASHI, N., KEGASAWA, K. and KUNII, Y. (1960). Studies on hatching of the root-knot nematode *Meloidogyne incognita* var. *acrita* Chitwood. 1. The relation between hatching and the original egg content of egg mass. *Jap. J. appl. Ent. Zool.* **4** (4), 249–255.

KRUSBERG, L. R. (1959). Investigations on the life cycle, reproduction, feeding habits and host range of *Tylenchorhynchus claytoni* Steiner. *Nematologica,* **4,** 187–197.

KUIPER, K. (1959). Inoculatieproeven met *Hemicycliophora typica. Meded. LandbHoogesch. Gent.* **24** (3/4), 619–627.

LINFORD, M. B. and OLIVEIRA, J. M. (1940). *Rotylenchulus reniformis* nov.-gen. n.sp., a nematode parasite of roots. *Proc. helm. Soc. Wash.* **7** (1), 35–42.

LOOS, C. A. (1962). Studies on the life-history and habits of the burrowing nematode, *Radopholus similis,* the cause of black-head disease of banana. *Proc. helm. Soc. Wash.* **29** (1), 43–52.

MAGGENTI, A. R. (1961). Morphology and biology of the genus *Plectus* (Nematoda, Plectidae). *Proc. helm. Soc. Wash.* **28** (2), 118–130.

MULVEY, R. H. (1958a). Parthenogenesis in a cyst forming nematode, *Heterodera trifolii* (Nematoda; Heteroderidae). *Can. J. Zool.* **36,** 91–93.

—— (1958b). Impregnation of *Heterodera trifolii* by males of *H. schachtii* (Nematoda Heteroderidae). *Can. J. Zool.* **36,** 839–841.

—— (1959). Susceptibilities of plants to the clover cyst nematode, *Heterodera trifolii* and the period required to complete a life cycle. *Nematologica,* **4** (2), 132–135.

—— (1960a). Oögenesis in some species of *Heterodera* and *Meloidogyne.* In: *Nematology, fundamentals and recent advances with emphasis on plant parasitic and soil forms.* Edited by J. N. Sasser and W. R. Jenkins. Chapter 33. Chapel Hill: Univ. North Carolina Press.

—— (1960b). Parthenogenesis and the role of the male in reproduction. In: *Nematology, fundamentals and recent advances with emphasis on plant parasitic and soil forms.* Edited by J. N. Sasser and W. R. Jenkins. Chapter 34. Chapel Hill: Univ. North Carolina Press.

ONIONS, T. G. (1953). Giant larvae of the potato root eelworm, *Heterodera rostochiensis* Wollenweber. *Nature, Lond.* **172,** 249.

—— (1955). The distribution of hatching within the cyst of the potato-root eelworm, *Heterodera rostochiensis. Quart. J. Micr. Sci.* **96** (4), 495–513.

—— (1957). Emergence of larvae from sealed cysts of the potato root eelworm, *Heterodera rostochiensis* Wollenweber. *Nature, Lond.* **179,** 323–324.

OTEIFA, B. A. (1953). Development of the root-knot nematode, *Meloidogyne incognita*, as affected by potassium nutrition of the host. *Phytopathology*, **43** (4), 171–174.

OUDEN, H. DEN (1960). A note on parthenogenesis and sex determination in *Heterodera rostochiensis* Woll. *Nematologica*, **5**, 215–216.

PALO, A. V. (1962). Translocation and development of stem eelworm, *Ditylenchus dipsaci* (Kühn) in lucerne, *Medicago sativa* L. *Nematologica*, **7**, 122–132.

PEACOCK, F. C. (1957). Studies on root-knot nematodes of the genus *Meloidogyne* in the Gold Coast. Part I. *Nematologica*, **2** (1), 76–84.

PERRY, V. G. (1959). A note on digonic hermaphroditism in spiral nematodes, *Helicotylenchus* sp. *Nematologica*, **4**, 87–88.

PERRY, V. G., DARLING, H. M. and THORNE, G. (1959). Anatomy, taxonomy and control of certain spiral nematodes attacking blue-grass in Wisconsin. *Res. Bull. Wis. agric. Exp. Sta.* **207**, 1–24.

RASKI, D. J. (1950). The life history and morphology of the sugar-beet nematode, *Heterodera schachtii* Schmidt. *Phytopathology*, **40**, 135–151.

RHOADES, H. L. and LINFORD, M. B. (1959). Molting of preadult nematodes of the genus *Paratylenchus* stimulated by root diffusates. *Science*, **130** (3387), 1476–1477.

—— —— (1961). Biological studies on some members of the genus *Paratylenchus*. *Proc. helm. Soc. Wash.* **28** (1), 51–59.

RITTER, M. and RITTER, R. (1958). Influence de l'âge de la plante-hôte sur le développement de *Meloidogyne incognita*, nématode phytoparasite. *C.R. Acad. Sci. Paris*, **246** (13), 2054–2056.

ROGERS, W. P. (1958). Physiology of the hatching of eggs of *Ascaris lumbricoides*. *Nature, Lond.* **181**, 1410.

—— (1960). The physiology of infective processes of nematode parasites; the stimulus from the animal host. *Proc. roy. Soc. B.* **152**, 367–386.

ROGERS, W. P. and SOMMERVILLE, R. I. (1960). The physiology of the second ecdysis of parasitic nematodes. *Parasitology*, **50**, 329–348.

ROHDE, R. A. and JENKINS, W. R. (1957). Effect of temperature on the life cycle of stubby root nematodes. *Phytopathology*, **47** (1), 29.

ROSS, J. P. (1960). The effect of soil temperature on development of *Heterodera glycines* in soybeans. *Phytopathology*, **50** (9), 652.

SHEPHERD, A. M. (1961). (Hatching and hatching factors.) In: Jones, F. G. W., Nematology Department. *Rep. Rothamst. exp. Sta.*, 127–128.

—— (1962). *The emergence of larvae from cysts in the genus Heterodera.* Comm. agric. Bur., Farnham Royal, England.

SILVERMAN, P. H. and CAMPBELL, J. A. (1959). Studies on parasitic worms of sheep in Scotland. 1. Embryonic and larval development of *Haemonchus contortus* at constant conditions. *Parasitology*, **49**, 23–38.

SKOTLAND, C. B. (1957). Biological studies of the soybean cyst nematode. *Phytopathology*, **47**, 623.

STEWART, F. H. (1921). The anatomy and biology of the parasitic *Aphelenchi*. *Parasitology*, **13** (2), 160–179.

TARJAN, A. C. (1952). Comparative studies of some root-knot nematodes infecting the common snapdragon, *Antirrhinum majus* L. *Phytopathology*, **42**, 641–644.

THOMASON, I. J. (1957). Influence of soil temperature on reproduction of *Meloidogyne spp. Phytopathology*, **47**, 34.

TRIANTAPHYLLOU, A. C. (1960). Sex determination in *Meloidogyne incognita* Chitwood, 1949 and intersexuality in *M. javanica* (Treub, 1885) Chitwood, 1949. *Ann. Inst. Phytopath. Benaki*, N.S. **3**, 12–31.

—— (1962). Oögenesis in the root knot nematode *Meloidogyne javanica*. *Nematologica*, **7**, 105–113.

TRIANTAPHYLLOU, A. C. and HIRSCHMANN, H. (1960). Post infection development of *Meloidogyne incognita* Chitwood, 1949. *Ann. Inst. Phytopath. Benaki*, N.S. **3**, 3–11.

—— (1962). Oögenesis and mode of reproduction in the soybean cyst nematode, *Heterodera glycines*. *Nematologica*, **7**, 235–241.

TYLER, J. (1933a). Reproduction without males in aseptic root cultures of the root-knot nematode. *Hilgardia*, **7** (10), 389–392.

—— (1933b). Development of the root-knot nematode as affected by temperature. *Hilgardia*, **7**, 392–415.

—— (1938). Egg output of the root-knot nematode. *Proc. helm. Soc. Wash.* **5** (2), 49–54.

VIGLIERCHIO, D. R. and LOWNSBERY, B. F. (1960). The hatching response of *Meloidogyne* species to the emanations from the roots of germinating tomatoes. *Nematologica*, **5**, 153–157.

WALLACE, H. R. (1959). Further observations on some factors influencing the emergence of larvae from cysts of the beet eeelworm *Heterodera schachtii* Schmidt. *Nematologica*, **4**, 245–252.

—— (1960). Observations on the behaviour of *Aphelenchoides ritzema-bosi* in chrysanthemum leaves. *Nematologica*, **5**, 315–321.

WEERDT, L. G., VAN (1960). Studies on the biology of *Radopholus similis* (Cobb, 1893) Thorne, 1949. Part 3. Embryology and post embryonic development. *Nematologica*, **5** (1), 43–52.

WILLIAMS, T. D. (1957). Development of isolated female larvae of the potato root eelworm (*Heterodera rostochiensis* Woll.). *Nature, Lond.* **180**, 1000.

WILSON, P. A. G. (1958). The effect of weak electrolyte solutions on the hatching rate of the eggs of *Trichostrongylus retortaeformis* (Zeder) and its interpretation in terms of a proposed hatching mechanism of strongyloid eggs. *J. exp. Biol.* **35**, 584–601.

YUKSEL, H. S. (1960). Observations on the life cycle of *Ditylenchus dipsaci* on onion seedlings. *Nematologica*, **5** (4), 289–296.

CHAPTER 3

The Soil Environment

Soil science is a heterogeneous subject embracing several disciplines. Consequently, there is a wealth of information on the influence of soil conditions on plant growth which is relevant to plant nematology because any factor which affects plant growth also affects the population dynamics of the nematodes. There are several text-books describing the relationship between the plant and soil (Russel, 1950; Shaw, 1952; Lyon, Buckman and Brady, 1952; Baver, 1956; Millar, Turk and Foth, 1958) and some on soil zoology (Kevan, 1955, 1962; Kuhnelt, 1961), but there is very little information on the effect of the environment on the nematode. It may be useful, therefore, to start from first principles and examine those physical and chemical properties of the soil which might be expected to influence the activities of nematodes and then to see what effect the incursion of the plant has on the soil environment. This chapter, therefore, aims at describing the sort of environment nematodes are likely to experience in soil, while in later chapters we will see how they respond to such surroundings.

Before the different soil factors are discussed it will be useful to set down some general principles. First, nematodes are entirely dependent on water for their activities; some species can survive dry conditions but they cannot move, feed, lay eggs, etc., until moisture is restored to the soil and they become active again. Second, they do not disturb the soil during movement as earthworms do; so, like the protozoa and rotifiers, they are confined to existing pore spaces. Third, they cannot squeeze through spaces much narrower than their own body width, so their movement through pores is related to their body size.

In soil, the nematode moves through a labyrinth of pore spaces, the size and distribution of which depend on the size of the soil crumbs. Crumb formation is in turn dependent on weathering, cultivation, presence of roots, amount of colloids, etc. In a well-tilled seed-bed, for example, crumb structure is clearly evident but the soil appears more clod-like in a heavy pasture soil. The arrangement of crumbs or aggregates in a soil is referred to as structure which is distinct from its texture (percentage of sand, silt and clay). In considering the soil pore spaces in which the nematode lives, we must, therefore, think in terms of soil structure, although texture is not irrelevant. Sandy soils, for example, usually contain larger pores and drain more quickly than heavy clay soils. Furthermore, although it is possible for a sandy and a clay soil to have similar sized crumbs and therefore pores of similar size, the water relationships are different because the clay crumbs are themselves made up of smaller units and are therefore permeable to water, unlike the sand particles which may be solid quartz.

The principal soil factors in the nematode's environment are pore size, water, aeration, temperature and the chemistry of the soil solution.

PORE SIZE AND WATER

By considering a hypothetical system of identical spheres it is possible to obtain some idea of the complex arrangement of soil pores and their interconnecting necks. In a close-packed system there are twelve points of contact per sphere and each pore has four or eight pore necks depending on whether the pores are tetrahedral or rhombohedral. In the open-packed system there are six points of contact and each pore has six pore necks. The shape and size of pores is, therefore, influenced by the arrangement of the soil crumbs. In the soil, crumbs vary greatly in size and shape, consequently, the size and shape of pores and necks are also extremely variable. However, the pore necks are always smaller than the pore itself, so a water-filled pore can only be emptied if the air-water interface can pass through the neck. To do this the meniscus must be sucked through the neck against the surface tension forces acting there. Although the necks are irregular in shape they can be considered to have an equivalent radius r (cm). Then the area on which the suction acts is πr^2 and the perimeter on which the surface tension acts is $2\pi r$. If T is the surface tension (73 dynes/cm for water) the suction S to empty a pore is given by

$$S \times \pi r^2 = 2\pi r \times T$$

or

$$S = \frac{2T}{r} \tag{1}$$

It is convenient to express the suction in terms of the equivalent height (h cm) to which it could raise a column of water. Thus

$$S = h\rho g \tag{2}$$

where g is the acceleration due to gravity, 981 cm/sec^2 and ρ is the density of water (1 g/cc).

So substituting in equation (1)

$$h\rho g = \frac{2T}{r} \tag{3}$$

and if the diameter of the pore, $d = 2r$ and is measured in microns, then simplifying equation (3)

$$h\rho g = \frac{4T}{d} \tag{4}$$

and so

$$hd = 3,000 \tag{5}$$

For initially saturated soil it is possible to measure the residual water content over a range of applied suctions and, by plotting these two variables, to obtain a graph which is called the moisture characteristic. A full account of the properties of the moisture characteristic and how it is obtained is given by Childs (1940).

Figure 11 shows such a curve for a hypothetical soil. As suction

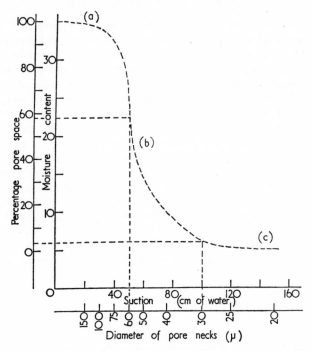

Fig. 11. The moisture characteristic of a hypothetical soil sample. (a) pores full of water, (b) pores emptying, (c) pores empty. (After Wallace, 1958.)

increases from zero there is, at first, little decrease in moisture content. At about 40 cm suction the moisture content drops as the pores begin to empty and this process continues up to about 100 cm suction when the pores are more or less empty. At 40 cm suction the pores which empty have a mean neck diameter of about 75 μ (equation 5) and at 100 cm suction the neck diameter is 30 μ. Thus in this hypothetical soil the majority of pores have neck diameters of 30 to 75 μ. Defining the effective pore space as the volume of water withdrawn between complete saturation ($h=0$) and the stage when the pores are 'empty' ($h=100$), the moisture content scale can be converted into a percentage pore space scale. Furthermore, as the suction scale can be converted to a neck diameter scale it is possible to estimate from the curve the fraction of the pore space occupied by pores having neck diameters in any specified range. For example, in Fig. 11 pores with neck diameters between 30 and 60 μ occupy about 52 per cent of the pore space. The shape of the moisture characteristic of a soil reflects its pore size distribution. Thus, the point of inflexion of the curve will occur at a much lower suction in a coarse soil with large pores, than in a fine soil.

Moisture characteristics like that shown in Fig. 11 are usually only obtained with sandy soils. In other soil types the curve may lose its sigmoid shape and become flattened and for a system of crumbs a double sigmoid may result as with increasing suction, first the inter-crumb pores and later the pores within the crumbs are drained.

The moisture characteristic is an invaluable tool in assessing pore size and water distribution in a soil, two important factors influencing nematode activity and behaviour. It also gives the observer a mental picture of the sort of conditions a nematode might encounter in soil. Such an approach might be anthropocentric but it is undoubtedly useful in this complex subject.

The pore size distribution of undisturbed soil samples can also be determined and related to nematode activity, although interpretation of environmental conditions in the field by measurements of moisture and suction are difficult because the moisture characteristic shows a hysteresis effect. The shape of the curve depends on whether the soil is wetting or drying and there is, therefore, no unique relationship between suction and moisture content. It is not feasible, for example, to determine the pore size distribution of a soil sample and then, by measurements of soil moisture in the field, to deduce suctions. Descriptions of water relations of different soils in terms of percentage moisture alone are even less reliable for there is no clear relationship between moisture content and percentage saturation of pores. Moreover, such observations give no indication of the distribution of water in the pores. The interpretation of soil moisture data obtained by tensiometer or porous block techniques have, therefore, to be treated with caution.

Soil moisture may also be expressed in terms of the permanent wilting point of plants and field capacity but these are rather arbitrary soil constants. The suction at which a plant wilts varies with transpiration rate, root density, root depth and the osmotic pressure of the soil solution but is of the order of 15 atmospheres. Field capacity, which corresponds to the suction at which gravitational water has drained away from the soil is equally variable and depends on soil type (Browning, 1941; Smith and Browning, 1947) but it is usually stated to be about 100 to 150 cm of water. Both of these constants are, therefore, explicable in terms of more or less understood factors but, as Childs and Collis-George (1948) point out, they cannot be defined precisely.

Some indication of how the water is distributed in soil pores at various suctions during the draining cycle has been described (Wallace, 1958). At zero suction the pores are full of water; as suction increases, pores empty in order of decreasing size. Thus pores are either full or empty and the water remaining in a drained pore is confined to the points of contact between particles in the form of lenses. Reduction in the lens water occurs by evaporation and by drainage through the permeable crumbs themselves at high suctions.

The body width of nematodes is of the order of 20 μ or larger, except in the early larval stages. Consequently, nematodes are confined to pores with necks of this diameter. Such pores empty at a suction of about 150 cm of water or about field capacity, so it follows that nematodes are confined to the so-called macropores which for most of their time are filled with air. Such a habitat is distinct from that within the crumb where many microorganisms and plant roots occur. Currie (1961) has discussed the properties of the intra-crumb habitat but this may not be very important from the nematological aspect.

An indication of the vertical distribution of water in a field soil can be obtained from Penman's (1961) description. Initially the soil is considered to be thoroughly wetted and then to drain for 2 days or so until equilibrium is reached. At this stage there is uniform water and air content for part of the depth and then a gradual transition to a water-logged pore space which corresponds to the water table. The soil then dries at the surface, the water is replaced by air and further drying penetrates more deeply. Following rain the surface is flooded, but after a few days all the water distributes itself to bring a surface layer to field capacity. There is now a wet layer of soil at the surface with a dry layer below and the front between the two is very sharp and static. Water can only move down if more water falls on the surface as rain. Gradients of moisture in the soil are obviously complex and depend a great deal on soil structure, rainfall, season etc. Thus, it will be evident from this discussion that the practice of adding water to pots to maintain a constant moisture content has serious disadvantages because of undefined variations at various parts of the pot. By using the sintered funnel method (Parry, 1954; Wallace, 1958; Collis-George and Blake, 1959) moisture conditions can be controlled and measured.

So far, in this discussion, soil moisture has been described chiefly in static terms. We have now to consider the movement of water in soil. The rate at which soil permits water to flow through it is called permeability, and is primarily dependent on pore size and the continuity of the pores. The permeability of sandy soils is therefore greater than that of heavy clay soils, where pores are smaller and where swelling may close channels. In soils with a low permeability, water may collect on the surface and if the land is sloping this may result in a surface run off, an important factor in the passive distribution of some plant parasitic nematodes (page 129).

In the absence of soil temperature gradients, movement of water occurs primarily in the liquid phase through pore channels. When temperature gradients occur, however, there is a transfer of water vapour from high to low temperature regions, that is, from regions of high to low vapour pressure. There is also a transfer of water vapour from the soil to the atmosphere by evaporation. The rate of this water loss is controlled by such weather factors as temperature, solar energy, wind velocity and relative humidity, and by soil factors such as moisture content, particle size and topography. When the rate of evaporation is high the surface layers of the soil dry out, thereby inhibiting nematode activity completely. In discussing the drying effect of soils on nematodes it is probably better to think in terms of the free energy of the soil solution than the relative humidity of the air spaces, for relative humidity in soil is difficult to measure accurately. The free energy of the soil solution is the sum of its osmotic potential and suction potential. In dry soils the nematodes will tend to lose water until the osmotic pressure of their body fluids equals the free energy of the soil solution. Under such conditions some nematode species die, some become quiescent and are resistant to desiccation and some migrate downwards to zones where there is enough moisture to permit activity.

SOIL AERATION

The concentration of oxygen in the soil air is controlled by the rates at which oxygen is consumed and is replaced by diffusion from the atmosphere. Similarly the amount of carbon dioxide is controlled by its rate of production and the rate at which it diffuses upwards to the atmosphere. For a gaseous movement to occur there must be a partial pressure gradient of both gases in the soil. Consumption of oxygen and production of carbon dioxide in the soil by biological and chemical activity produce such gradients, the slopes of which vary according to the type of soil. The rate of diffusion is then controlled by the physical properties of the soil itself.

The mathematical relationship between the rate of diffusion of gases and the air-filled pore spaces in soil is complex and there is, as yet, no complete solution to this problem. However, it is known that the shape of the pores and especially the amount of water in a soil have important influences. Thus, a small amount of water in a sandy soil may decrease the diffusion rate considerably because larger pores are filled. In a system of soil crumbs, however, the water enters the small spaces within the crumbs first, so permitting diffusion through the larger air-filled pores. When the crumb pores are saturated, further addition of water tends to fill the larger pores, hence, diffusion is reduced. The ratio of carbon dioxide to oxygen increases with depth and with decrease in the amount of air in the soil, the sum of their concentrations remaining almost constant at 21 per cent. Thus, in wet soils where the amount of air is reduced, diffusion is also reduced and the CO_2/O_2 ratio increases. Badly drained or compacted soils will clearly be badly aerated and conversely, any soil treatment such as cultivation or ploughing which increases the volume of air in the soil, will give increased aeration. It is not surprising, therefore, that there are seasonal fluctuations in the concentrations of oxygen and carbon dioxide in the soil (Fig. 12).

It has already been pointed out that soil nematodes live in the water films within the soil pore spaces, consequently the soil atmosphere is not the real nematode environment. This is an important distinction

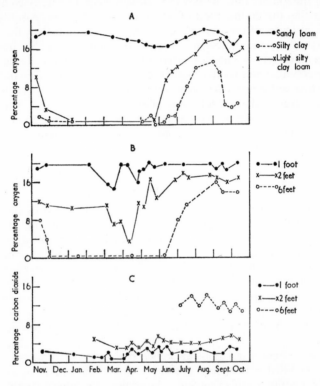

Fig. 12. Seasonal variations of oxygen and carbon dioxide in orchard soils. (A) Oxygen per cent at 5 ft depth as affected by temperature. (B) Oxygen per cent at three depths in a light silty clay loam. (C) Carbon dioxide per cent at three depths in a silty loam. (After Boynton and Reutner, 1939.)

because gaseous concentrations in the soil water may be different from those in the soil atmosphere. Diffusion of gas molecules is slower in water than in gases, hence, if oxygen is being consumed faster than it can be replaced by diffusion through the water, the nematode may suffer an oxygen lack; excess of CO_2 will also occur under such conditions. Furthermore, any changes in the concentrations of oxygen and carbon dioxide in the soil air may not be reflected in the soil water because oxygen has a much lower solubility in water than carbon dioxide.

The thickness of the soil water film between the nematode cuticle and the air-water interface is, therefore, important especially where the nematodes occur within soil crumbs. Measurements of oxygen and carbon dioxide concentration in the soil water are difficult, although some success has been achieved with the platinum electrode technique in assessing oxygen supplying power. It seems likely from practical measurements and on theoretical grounds that anaerobic conditions may occur commonly in soils with a high moisture content and within soil crumbs at about field capacity. Currie (1961), for example, suggests that soil aeration is not only a function of soil depth and the rate of diffusion through the larger pores, but is also a function of the crumbs themselves. He shows that the centres of crumbs greater than 1 mm in diameter may become anaerobic at about field capacity and that the anaerobic zone increases with crumb size.

TEMPERATURE

Soil temperature is determined largely by those factors which control the transference of heat into, and out of, the soil.

The specific heat of most dry soils is about $0 \cdot 2$ cal/g and for water 1 cal/g. Thus as the moisture content of a soil increases there is also an increase in its thermal capacity (specific heat × mass). By definition, the thermal capacity of a body is the amount of heat needed to raise its temperature 1°C. Hence, a wet soil has a smaller rise in temperature than when it is dry for the same heat input at the surface. The thermal conductivity of a soil also increases with moisture content, so temperature gradients are steeper in dry soils than wet soils. In other words, heat from the sun penetrates deeper in wet than in dry soils but there is a smaller rise in temperature. Thus well drained sandy soils tend to be warmer in the upper layers in the spring than heavy soils.

Heat will flow down into a soil as long as the surface is at a higher temperature than the subsurface layers. This happens in the daytime in summer when the sun is shining. If the soil surface becomes cooler at night, however, there is a flow of heat in the opposite direction. There is, therefore, a diurnal change in the temperature gradient which is greatest at the soil surface (Fig. 13).

A seasonal fluctuation in temperature also occurs and Smith (1932) has measured this in Californian soils where temperature increases with depth in February but decreases with depth in July (Fig. 14). During autumn and winter heat tends to move upward from the warmer soil to the colder atmosphere but in spring and summer the direction of flow is reversed.

SOIL SOLUTION

The chemical composition of the soil solution has a profound effect on plant growth and so influences the plant parasitic nematodes indirectly.

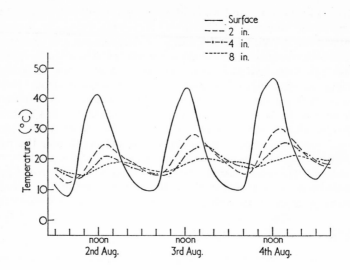

Fig. 13.   The daily variation in temperature at different
soil depths.   (After Russell, 1950.)

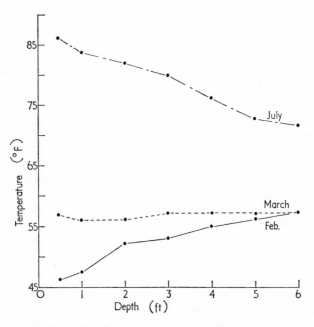

Fig. 14.   Variation in temperature with depth in February,
March and July in California.   (After Smith, 1932.)

It is unlikely that the nematodes themselves derive any nutrients from the soil solution although factors such as pH and osmotic pressure may influence their activities.

An acid reaction in a soil indicates that there is an excess of hydrogen ions over hydroxyl ions in the soil solution. Any process which removes the dissociated hydrogen ions results in further dissociation of hydrogen ions in the soil to restore equilibrium. There is, therefore, a reserve of hydrogen ions in the soil which may be increased by the leaching out of bases especially on farm soils where there are no cover crops to protect the soil. Lime is therefore used to replace the loss of exchangeable bases and to neutralise the soil acidity.

The hydrogen ion concentration or pH of a soil may show seasonal fluctuations associated with rainfall and drought, and the vertical distribution of colloidal material in the soil profile may also cause variations in pH with soil depth. In agricultural soils, pH seldom falls below 4 or exceeds 8 and mostly lies between 5·0 to 7·0.

The osmotic pressure of the soil solution depends on the amount of salts and water present in the soil. Hence, with decreasing moisture content the osmotic pressure increases but this seldom exceeds 2 atmospheres at the wilting point, except in arid regions or in soil which has received heavy applications of fertiliser (Russell, 1950).

THE INFLUENCE OF THE PLANT

The plant takes up water from the soil close to its roots until the free energy and hydraulic conductivity of the soil becomes limiting. At this stage the root cannot take up enough water to replace that lost by transpiration, and the plant wilts. Plants tend to dry out the surface layer of a soil but wilting may not occur if water is still available to deeply growing roots. Furthermore, the surface layer of dry soil reduces the upward flow of water to the surface, hence water loss is reduced in spite of transpiration from leaves. Thus, the plant chiefly influences soil moisture by producing gradients in the soil profile and around its roots.

Plant root respiration tends to reduce the oxygen and increase the carbon dioxide content of the soil atmosphere and soil solution, so producing gradients of oxygen and carbon dioxide close to the roots. There are also large seasonal fluctuations in the proportions of oxygen and carbon dioxide in the soil associated with plant growth and development. For example, as plants age and die at the end of the season there is a high carbon dioxide output from the soil which is probably associated with increased activity of micro-organisms.

Plants also affect soil temperature by intercepting radiation from the sun, thereby reducing the amount of heat falling on the soil surface. In the colder seasons plants reduce the amount of heat lost by the soil so their net effect is to damp diurnal and seasonal fluctuations of soil temperature.

The uptake of ions and the liberation of carbon dioxide by plant roots produce changes in the pH of the soil solution which in turn produce changes in the numbers and kind of microorganisms around the root. Amino acids and reducing compounds may also be liberated from the roots and Katznelson and his colleagues (1955) have suggested that the occurrence of certain kinds of bacteria is associated with the chemicals in the rhizosphere.

It is now possible to visualise the sort of environment that a plant nematode will experience during its free-living stage in the soil. The first concept is one of change. The pores in the soil contain air for most of the time but following rain, water percolates downwards into the pores in sudden surges as the surface tension at the pore necks is overcome; there is no smooth flow of water except through pores already full of water. After rain there follows a more leisurely redistribution of water by diffusion through the narrow pores inside the crumbs and by movement of water vapour. In clay soils, the pore spaces may shrink and necks may close as water enters. After drainage has finished the soil pores will once again contain air and the water will be confined to thin films over the surface of crumbs and to pockets where crumbs touch. As the soil dries the water pockets decrease and the free energy increases. The soil surface layers may become so dry that the nematode is unable to move and the free energy may be so great that water is sucked out of the nematode's body. The pH, osmotic pressure, oxygen and carbon dioxide concentrations in the soil solution change with the fluctuations in moisture, and anaerobic conditions may occur where the soil moisture is high. The diurnal rise and fall of temperature is superimposed on a seasonal fluctuation as the weather changes. Gradients of moisture, temperature, oxygen, carbon dioxide, pH and osmotic pressure are present throughout the soil profile as well as lateral gradients due to topography, height of water table, proximity to rivers and vegetation, etc. The incursion of the plant into the environment introduces further complexities. Localised physical and chemical gradients occur near the roots and there is a corresponding change in the population of microorganisms. The influence of the plant also changes as it grows to maturity and then dies. The soil environment is therefore in a constant state of change.

The second concept of the soil environment is interdependence. Moisture influences temperature, aeration, pH and osmotic pressure; soil structure affects suction, water percolation, aeration and temperature; in fact, the whole physical-chemical environment is a complex of inter-related factors. Some idea of this can be obtained from Fig. 15, where the influence of one factor on another is indicated by an arrow.

The two concepts just discussed emphasise the difficulty of interpreting cause and effect in soil biology. Experimental data may suggest that the occurrence of a particular species in a habitat is related to soil moisture but is this because of aeration, pH or temperature, or because the host crop happens to grow well in the soil? The problem is in fact insoluble, although further research may reveal close correlations between environmental factors and nematode activity. By accumulating knowledge of how nematodes behave under controlled conditions, hypotheses can be put forward to explain their reactions in the natural environment. Such hypotheses will then stand or fall in the light of future work.

Physical — chemical environment

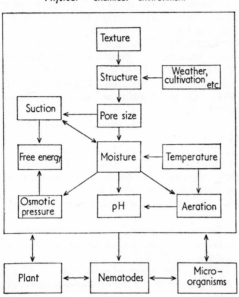

FIG. 15. A diagrammatic representation of the interrelationship of physical, chemical and biological factors in the soil and their influence on nematodes.

REFERENCES

BAVER, L. D. (1956). *Soil physics* (3rd edition). New York: John Wiley and Sons Inc.

BOYNTON, D. and REUTNER, W. (1939). Seasonal variation of oxygen and carbon dioxide in three different orchard soils during 1938 and its possible significance. *Proc. Amer. Soc. hort. Sci.* **36**, 1–6.

BROWNING, G. M. (1941). Relation of field capacity to moisture equivalent in soils of West Virginia. *Soil Sci.* **52**, 445–450.

CHILDS, E. C. (1940). The use of soil moisture characteristics in soil studies. *Soil Sci.* **50**, 239–252.

CHILDS, E. C. and COLLIS-GEORGE, N. (1948). Soil geometry and soil water equilibria. *Disc. Faraday Soc.* **3**, 78–85.

COLLIS-GEORGE, N. and BLAKE, C. D. (1959). The influence of the soil moisture regime on the expulsion of the larval mass of the nematode *Anguina agrostis* from galls. *Aust. J. Biol. Soc.* **12** (3), 247–256.

CURRIE, J. A. (1961).   Gaseous diffusion in the aeration of aggregated soils. *Soil Sci.* **92** (1), 40–45.

KATZNELSON, H., ROUATT, J. W. and PAYNE, T. M. B. (1955).   The liberation of amino acids and reducing compounds by plant roots.   *Plant and Soil*, **7**, (1), 35–48.

KEVAN, D. K. McE. (1955).   S*oil Zoology*.   London: Butterworths Scientific Publications.

—— (1962).   *Soil Animals*.   London: H. F. and G. Witherby Ltd.

KÜHNELT, W. (1961).   *Soil biology with special reference to the animal kingdom.* London: Faber and Faber.

LYON, T. L., BUCKMAN, H. O. and BRADY, N. C. (1952).   *The nature and properties of soils* (5th edition).   New York: The Macmillan Company.

MILLAR, C. E., TURK, L. M. and FOTH, H. D. (1958).   *Fundamentals of soil science* (3rd edition).   New York: John Wiley and Sons Inc.

PARRY, D. A. (1954).   On the drinking of soil capillary water by spiders.   *J. exp. Biol.* **31**, 218–227.

PENMAN, H. L. (1961).   Weather, plant and soil factors in hydrology. *Weather*, **16** (7), 207–219.

RUSSELL, Sir E. J. (1950).   *Soil conditions and plant growth* (8th edition recast and rewritten by E. W. Russell).   London: Longmans, Green and Co.

SHAW, B. T. (1952).   *Agronomy*.   Volume 2. *Soil physical conditions and plant growth*.   New York: Academic Press Inc.

SMITH, A. (1932).   Seasonal subsoil temperature variations.   *J. agric. Res.*, **44**, 421–428.

SMITH, R. M. and BROWNING, D. R. (1947).   Soil moisture tension and pore space relations for several soils in the range of the 'Field Capacity'.   *Proc. Soil Sci. Soc. Amer.* **12**, 17–21.

WALLACE, H. R. (1958).   Movement of eelworms.   1. The influence of pore size and moisture content of the soil on the migration of larvae of the beet eelworm, *Heterodera schachtii* Schmidt.   *Ann. appl. Biol.* **46**, 74–85.

CHAPTER 4

The Influence of the Environment

Some examples of the influence of the environment on plant parasitic nematodes are given in the chapters on movement, behaviour, growth, development and reproduction, and distribution. Discussion in this chapter will, therefore, include topics which do not come under these headings.

WATER

Nematodes appear to be well adapted to living in the soil pores. Their small size permits them to move through most of the soil cavities and because their undulatory type of locomotion is along a sinusoidal path of the same width as the nematode body, little space is required for movement. The general elongate shape of the nematode is obviously suited to moving through small openings. It also enables the nematode to bridge the gaps between isolated water pockets in soil and so obtain maximum coverage of water along its body; the elongate body and hydrophilic cuticle ensure that any water in contact with the nematode is distributed in a film over its body. These properties are important because nematodes are entirely dependent on water for most of their activities.

Extreme moisture conditions in a soil do not favour nematodes. Flooding, for example, may kill root knot nematodes (Brown, 1933) and is used as a method of control in some countries. Drying out of the soil also reduces root knot nematode populations and in warm countries a bare fallow may be useful in controlling this pest (Crittenden, 1953; Peacock, 1957). Tolerance to drying out and saturation vary greatly between species; root knot nematodes appear to be susceptible to desiccation whereas *Ditylenchus dipsaci* is particularly resistant. Most species are adversely affected by high soil moisture but some, like *Radopholus oryzae* and *Ditylenchus angustus*, inhabit paddy fields where they are parasitic on rice, so they are probably more tolerant of saturated conditions. In spite of these variations, however, it is likely that, somewhere between these extremes, each species has an optimum soil moisture for activity. Let us first consider, however, some of the general evidence that nematodes are influenced by moisture.

Damage to oats by *Heterodera avenae* (Kort and s'Jacob, 1956) and to tobacco by *Ditylenchus dipsaci* (Cairaschi, 1954) is governed to a large extent by soil moisture. At high soil moistures *Heterodera glycines* produces a high proportion of white cysts on soy bean roots but the rate of

47

larval emergence is low. As the soil moisture decreases the proportion of white cysts decreases as does the rate of larval emergence (Hamblen and Slack, 1959). The life cycle of *Tylenchulus semipenetrans* is influenced by frequency of irrigation because, as van Gundy (1958) suggests, free water is necessary to flush the larvae from the egg mass into the soil where they can invade other roots. The geographical distribution of *Xiphinema americanum* is related to soil type, but Ward (1960) considers that extremes of soil moisture are the chief factors limiting population increase.

Dolichodorus heterocephalus (Perry, 1953) and *Radopholus gracilis* (Golden, 1957) are chiefly found in wet localities and can live and thrive in saturated soil. High soil moisture content also favours population increase of *Ditylenchus dipsaci* (Barker, 1959; Barker and Sasser, 1959). The population growth of some species is inhibited by excessive moisture, however. Root knot nematode attacks on crops following rice are reduced if the rice crop is flooded as in paddy fields (Thames, 1952) and population growth of *Tylenchorhynchus martini* on rice and *Tylenchorhynchus acutus* on soybeans is inhibited if the crop receives excessive water (Hollis and Johnston, 1957). The viability of cysts of *Heterodera rostochiensis* declines more rapidly in flooded and moist soil, although some encysted larvae can survive for 8 months under such conditions (Lewis and Mai, 1960). The longevity of *Paratylenchus amblycephalus* is reduced in soils with a high moisture content (Reuver, 1959).

Dry conditions may also depress nematode activity. *Heterodera rostochiensis* develops more rapidly on potato roots in plots receiving regular irrigation than on non-irrigated plots (Mai and Harrison, 1959) and Couch and Bloom (1960) consider that low moisture conditions reduce the mobility of *Meloidogyne hapla*. Although dry conditions may inhibit activity, it does not follow that the nematodes are killed. Although hatching of *Heterodera rostochiensis*, *Meloidogyne arenaria* and *Ditylenchus dipsaci* may be reduced in drying conditions, the eggs survive and are able to hatch when moisture increases (Dropkin *et al.*, 1958). Similarly, preadults of *Paratylenchus projectus* are tolerant to low soil moisture and Rhoades and Linford (1961) conclude that drying-out in the field is not a practicable control measure for this species. *Paratylenchus amblycephalus* is also resistant to desiccation in the soil (Reuver, 1959).

The influence of soil moisture is sometimes evident in the relationship between rainfall and nematode population changes. Minton and his colleagues (1960) found that rainfall and population size were not closely correlated for *Meloidogyne incognita acrita*, *Trichodorus christiei*, *Pratylenchus brachyurus* and *Criconemoides curvatum* but there was some correlation for *Hoplolaimus tylenchiformis*, a migratory ectoparasite. Populations of *Paratylenchus projectus*, *Tylenchorhynchus brevidens* and *Aphelenchus avenae* increased after rainfall and Norton (1959) suggests that this is caused by increased hatching when the soil is moist (Fig. 16). Increased galling on potatoes by root knot nematodes is associated with rainfall during the growing season (Parris, 1948) whereas numbers of *Tylenchorhynchus martini* in a soybean crop decrease with increase in the amount of rain (Hollis and Johnston, 1957). Numbers of *Ditylenchus dipsaci* in the soil in an oat plot rose following rain but declined to a low level in a subsequent dry period (Wallace, 1962). It seems likely that the increased hatching of *Heterodera* spp. in the spring and early summer

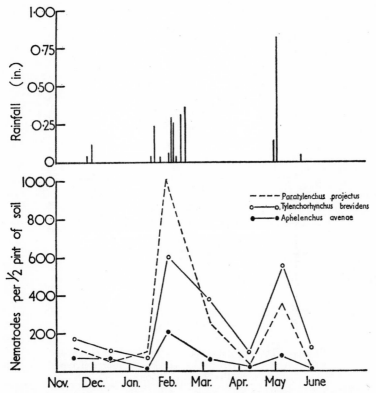

FIG. 16. The relationship between rainfall in Texas and population fluctuations of three species of plant parasitic nematodes. (After Norton, 1959.)

is chiefly a combined effect of moisture and temperature. Andersen (1961), for example, found a peak of hatching for *H. avenae* in the spring. A high rate of larval emergence from cysts of *H. schachtii* during April and May is often followed by a low emergence rate from June to September in England and it has been suggested (Wallace, 1956b) that low soil moisture is probably the chief factor inhibiting emergence in the summer months (Fig. 17).

These general observations illustrate the effect of moisture on nematode activity and the wide differences between species in tolerance to extreme

4

conditions.   The wide diurnal and seasonal fluctuations in soil moisture probably impose a cycle of activity on plant nematodes while they are in the soil.   Nielsen (1949) suggests that, in moist soils, nematodes are probably constantly active whereas in dry habitats they must be periodically inactive.   But how active, how moist, and for how long?   These are questions which can only be answered when we have examined more

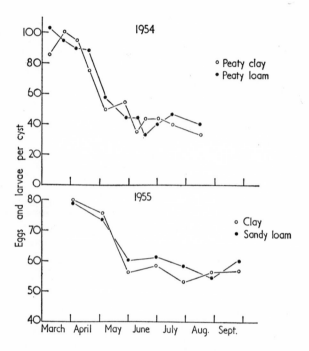

FIG. 17.   The seasonal variation in the numbers of eggs and larvae in cysts of *Heterodera schachtii* in four soil types. (After Wallace, 1956b.)

precise data on the influence of soil moisture on the activity of phyto-parasitic nematodes.

Godfrey (1926) used jars of sandy loam to give a series of moisture levels expressed in terms of percentage field capacity.   He adjusted the moisture content by adding water to the soil or by allowing it to dry to a predetermined level and then he studied the degree of infestation of tomato plants by root knot nematodes at the various moisture contents. His results (Fig. 18) show clearly that there is an optimum soil moisture content for nematode gall formation somewhere between 50 and 80 per cent field capacity.   As the tomato plants themselves grew best between these moisture levels the degree to which the nematode infestation was influenced by moisture or plant vigour is not clear but Godfrey thought that plant growth was the chief factor.

Peacock (1957) used similar criteria for measuring soil moisture in his studies on survival of root knot nematode larvae in soil. In a naturally occurring infestation the larvae did not survive 2 to 5 days at 10·7 per cent of field capacity, and there was a considerable reduction in numbers at field capacity. Most nematodes survived in soil at 29 per cent field

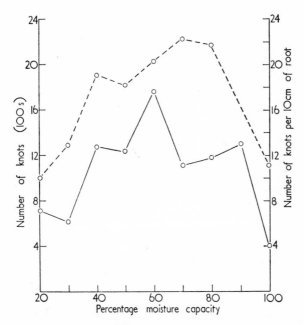

Fig. 18. The influence of soil moisture on the development of *Meloidogyne* sp. in tomato. Continuous line indicates number of knots, the broken line the number of knots per 10 cm of root. (After Godfrey, 1926.)

capacity. Although Peacock's main objective was to examine the tolerance of root-knot nematodes to desiccation in soil, his results show clearly that there is an optimum soil moisture level for survival (Fig. 19).

Johnston (1958) incubated *Tylenchorhynchus martini* in a rice field soil at moisture levels of 11, 25, 30, 75 and 100 per cent field capacity and at saturation. Survival was greatest between 40 and 60 per cent and lowest at 11 per cent and at saturation (Fig. 20). These results are, therefore, more or less in agreement with those of Godfrey and Peacock.

In experiments on the influence of soil moisture on the expulsion of larvae of *Anguina agrostis* from galls, Collis-George and Blake (1959) found that the numbers of larvae ejected increased with soil moisture. They also showed that the nematode gall could only overcome a limited

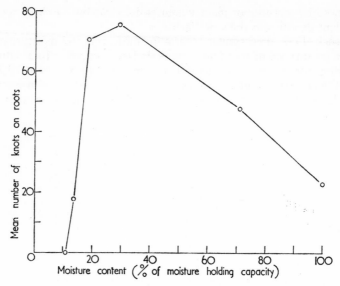

FIG. 19.   The influence of soil moisture on the development of knots
of *Meloidogyne* sp. on tomato roots.   (After Peacock, 1957.)

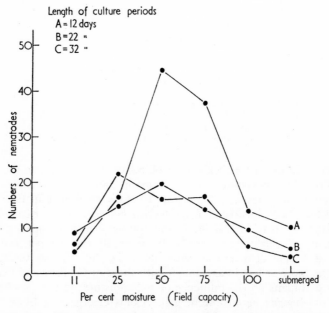

FIG. 20.   The influence of soil moisture on the survival of *Tylenchorhynchus martini*.   (After Johnston, 1958.)

soil moisture stress to obtain its moisture requirements; consequently, the potential gradient moving water from the soil to the gall could only be small.   Hence, if the hydraulic conductivity of the soil is low, owing to emptying of pores, the rate of supply of water to the gall is too small to satisfy its requirements.   Collis-George and Blake suggest that, in the field, the environmental conditions for maximum expulsion and movement of larvae occur only during the period when the soil is at about field

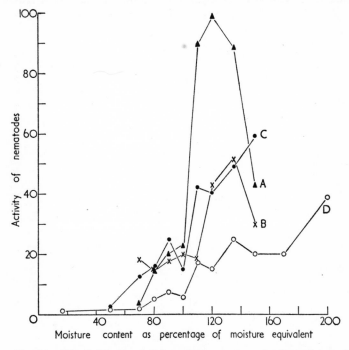

FIG. 21.   The influence of soil moisture content on the activity of *Ditylenchus dipsaci*.   (A) partially sterilised loam, (B) silty soil, (C) loam soil, (D) sandy soil with fairly high humus content.   (After Seinhorst, 1950.)

capacity and that these same conditions appear to be optimum for most seedling germination.

Seinhorst (1950) found that activity of *Ditylenchus dipsaci* was inhibited at the moisture equivalent of soil.   His data also show that there is maximum activity in some soil types when the moisture content is about 120 to 135 per cent of the moisture equivalent (Fig. 21).   The term moisture equivalent is used to express the moisture content after a saturated sample of the soil has been centrifuged at 1,000 g and is equivalent to a suction of about 500 cm of water.   Although the moisture equivalent is sometimes used as a measure of field capacity, 500 cm of water suction is rather high compared with other estimates of 100 to 150 cm of water. Thus the suction for maximum activity of *Ditylenchus dipsaci* in Seinhorst's experiments and the suctions corresponding to percentage field capacity quoted by Godfrey, Peacock and Johnson earlier in the chapter, are probably of the same order.

There is also an optimum suction for the emergence of larvae of *Heterodera schachtii* from cysts (Wallace, 1954). At low suctions, when the medium is saturated, emergence is low but as suction increases and

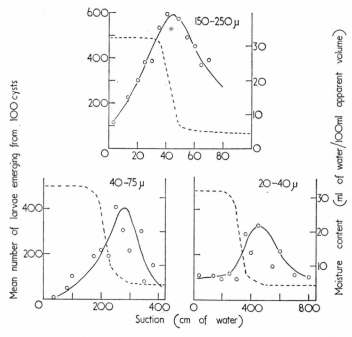

FIG. 22. The influence of soil suction on the emergence of larvae from cysts of *Heterodera schachtii* in three size grades of sand. The dotted curves indicate the moisture characteristic. (After Wallace, 1959.)

the soil pores empty, there is a corresponding increase in emergence until at higher suctions there is a decrease in emergence. Maximum emergence occurred when most of the pores were emptied of water and subsequently it was shown that this was true irrespective of the different particle size of the medium (Fig. 22 and Wallace, 1955a, 1959). Thus, the optimum conditions for larval emergence from cysts are related to the distribution of water in the pores. The fact that the suction at which maximum emergence occurs depends on the hysteresis curve of the moisture characteristic, emphasises the importance of moisture distribution in the pores (Fig. 23).

The invasion of the host plant roots by *Heterodera schachtii* and *Heterodera göttingiana* reaches a maximum when most of the pores are empty (Shepherd and Wallace, 1959) and Blake (1962) found that the invasion of oat plants by *Ditylenchus dipsaci* followed a similar pattern. Furthermore, the mobility curves of several species of phytoparasitic nematodes bear a similar relationship to soil moisture. In fact, the relationships between the moisture characteristic and the curves for larval emergence, invasion and mobility are very similar.

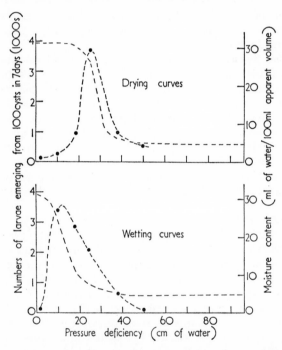

FIG. 23. The influence of the hysteresis effect on the emergence of larvae from cysts of *Heterodera schachtii* at different suctions (or pressure deficiency). (After Wallace, 1956c.)

It is probable, therefore, that any nematode activity in the soil which involves bodily movement will be at a maximum when the soil pores are empty but where water still remains at the points of contact of soil crumbs. Such conditions probably occur at moisture contents a little below field capacity.

Collis-George and Blake (1959) point out that field capacity is about the optimum moisture content for movement of *Anguina agrostis* and expulsion of larvae from the gall and also for germination of the host seedling. In some species of *Heterodera* hatching is stimulated by exudates from the host plant root and it has been shown that the production of such hatching factors is greatest when the soil pores are emptying (Shepherd and Wallace, 1959). Furthermore, the diffusion of such chemicals increases with moisture content, so soil moisture may influence egg hatch and larval attraction by its influence on the diffusion of root exudates. The close relationship between plant, nematode activity and soil moisture is another example of an efficient host-parasite association.

Nematode activity is not influenced by soil moisture alone because many other factors vary simultaneously with moisture. This is when the problem becomes difficult, for to relate cause and effect in such a complex environment as the soil is nearly impossible. Some attempts have been made, however.

Ditylenchus dipsaci and *Heterodera schachtii* tolerate osmotic pressures up to about 10 atmospheres (Wallace, 1956d; Blake, 1961a). Consequently, increase in osmotic pressure with decreasing soil moisture has little effect on nematodes, for in most agricultural soils the osmotic pressure seldom exceeds 2 atmospheres, even at the wilting point. Although aeration is not a limiting factor in dry soils, nematode activity is greatly inhibited by desiccation as the free energy (osmotic potential plus suction potential) increases. Resistance to desiccation is a form of quiescence and is discussed in Chapter 6. Reduction in moisture content may also inhibit nematode activity by producing very thin films in which the nematode cannot move.

In saturated soils, the air spaces are reduced and so lack of aeration probably reduces nematode activity (Wallace, 1954, 1955b, 1956c). Other factors such as pore size, depth and oxygen consumption in the soil also affect aeration and, with it, the rate of larval emergence from cysts of *Heterodera schachtii* (Wallace, 1956c). Johnston (1957), however, has shown that in saturated rice-field soil, a bacterium, *Clostridium* sp., appears which produces chemicals toxic to *Tylenchorhynchus martini*. Thus the decline in population of some phytoparasitic nematode species in very wet soil may be caused by factors other than soil aeration (Johnston, 1958).

In *Meloidogyne* and *Heterodera* spp. the eggs are protected from drying out by being parcelled together in egg masses. Godfrey and Hoshino (1933) studied the survival of an unidentified species of *Meloidogyne* at different humidities; at 50 per cent relative humidity, larvae survived for $3\frac{1}{2}$ min., eggs in a mass for $2\frac{1}{4}$ hr., free eggs $1\frac{1}{4}$ hr. and eggs in root gall tissue $1\frac{1}{2}$ days. At 90 per cent humidity, larvae survived for 25 minutes, eggs in masses $8\frac{1}{2}$ hr., free eggs $5\frac{1}{2}$ hr. and eggs in gall tissue more than 20 days. *Heterodera* spp. vary widely in their tolerance to desiccation. *H. rostochiensis* cysts were viable after being stored dry in a bottle at room humidity for several months, although subsequent hatch did increase as the humidity of the air, in which they were stored, increased (Lewis and Mai, 1960). Emergence of *H. schachtii* larvae, however, is greatly decreased when the cysts are previously exposed to atmospheres below saturation (Wallace, 1955a). Viglierchio (1961) suggests that while desiccation of *H. schachtii* cysts decreases the subsequent hatch, the effect may be related to rate of drying rather than the degree of dryness. Larvae of *Heterodera* spp. are more susceptible to drying out than the eggs, and Kämpfe (1959b) showed that the mortality of larvae of *H. schachtii* and *H. rostochiensis* decreased as the relative humidity decreased. Of the two, *H. schachtii* appeared to be the more resistant at humidities below 50 per cent. *H. glycines* also does not tolerate desiccation very well (Epps, 1958; Slack and Hamblen, 1961). At a relative humidity of 3·2 per cent, larvae, in cysts mixed with soil, survived for up to 5 months, but only for 2 months when the cysts were not in soil. Larvae in free eggs survived this humidity for 1 to 4 days whereas free larvae were dead after 10 min. (Endo, 1962). Larval emergence from cysts of *H. avenae* ceased after they had been stored in air dried soil for longer than 6 months although there was an appreciable emergence after 3 months storage (Duggan, 1960). When *H. avenae* cysts are removed from soil and exposed to the atmosphere, however, emergence is inhibited in a matter of hours (Winslow, 1955; Hesling, 1956).

Egg masses, cysts and root galls clearly protect eggs from desiccation as does the soil itself. Formation of a dry surface layer reduces the loss of water from a soil. Even in soils at the wilting point for plants, the relative humidity is still as high as 98·5 per cent, so that in a temperate climate such as in England, death of nematodes by desiccation is probably confined to the soil surface.

SOIL PORE SIZE

Nielsen (1949) suggests that nematodes are so small that soil pore size is probably insignificant in determining their distribution. Seinhorst (1950) also concluded that pore size was unimportant in the control of *Ditylenchus dipsaci*. There is little doubt, however, of its importance in nematode movement in soil (Chapter 5) and there is evidence that the rate of larval emergence from cysts of *Heterodera schachtii* increases with pore size at the optimum suction for emergence (Fig. 22). The addition of clay to a sand reduces its porosity and also reduces the rate of hatching of *Heterodera schachtii*. This effect has been explained in terms of reduced aeration with decreasing porosity (Wallace, 1956c); in fact, it is likely that the major effect of pore size on nematode activity is in its influence on soil moisture and aeration.

AERATION

The content of oxygen and carbon dioxide in the soil water varies between wide limits. In fact it is probably safe to assume that in some heavy wet soils nematodes experience anaerobic conditions, whereas in dry sandy soils the gaseous composition of the soil water may resemble that of the atmosphere. Nielsen (1949) showed that there was no change in nematode oxygen consumption when the oxygen tension was decreased by 10 per cent from atmospheric and he concluded that, within the variations of oxygen tensions occurring in normal soils, the oxygen consumption of nematodes is independent of oxygen tension. This hypothesis is untenable because it underestimates the range of fluctuations of oxygen in the soil water. Consequently, the influence of the full range of oxygen and carbon dioxide concentrations on nematode activity must be determined before the effects of soil aeration can be assessed.

Several authors have suggested that nematode activity increases with aeration. Hastings and Newton (1934) found that more quiescent individuals of *Ditylenchus dipsaci* became active when they were placed in shallow dishes than in deep tubes with the same volume of water. They showed that recovery decreased with increasing depth of water and that when the air over the water was replaced by carbon dioxide there was no recovery. Twenty hours exposure to carbon dioxide appeared to kill the nematodes. Chapman (1957) increased the number of *Pratylenchus* spp. emerging from roots in a Baermann funnel by bubbling air through or shaking the water. More larvae of *Heterodera schachtii* emerged from cysts placed in a thin film of root diffusate than in watchglasses where the solution is several mm. deep (Shepherd, 1959). Similarly, it was shown (Wallace, 1955a) that the number of larvae emerging in 7 days from five lots of 100 *H. schachtii* cysts in watchglasses was 363 in tap water and 1,249 in beet diffusate; in moist sand where most of the pores were empty of water, however, 10,079 larvae emerged. The low level of emergence in watchglasses was attributed to lack of oxygen. In moist sand, the thin film of water and air-filled pores give good aeration and so induce rapid emergence (Wallace, 1954). The importance of aeration in larval emergence from cysts of *H. schachtii* has been stressed (Wallace, 1956a) and the influence of moisture content, pore size, depth and oxygen consumption of the soil is probably related to their influence on soil aeration (Wallace, 1956c). The ratio of numbers of larvae emerging from cysts of *Heterodera glycines* in a thin film of water, in a $\frac{1}{2}$ in. (1·27 cm) depth of water and in an 8 in. (20·3 cm) depth of water was 35:15:1 (Slack and Hamblen, 1961).

There is, therefore, some evidence that conditions which reduce aeration also decrease the activity of nematodes but whether this is due to decreased oxygen, high carbon dioxide concentration or the accumulation of toxic chemicals is unknown.

Stolzy, van Gundy and Letey (1960) maintained different oxygen levels in containers of soil and studied the tolerance of different species of plant parasitic nematodes to low oxygen concentrations. Partial pressures of oxygen of 152, 50, 15 and 0 mm of Hg corresponding to 21, 7, 2 and 0 per cent oxygen were used. Nitrogen was the other constituent of the atmosphere and there was no carbon dioxide. A Beckman oxygen meter was used to measure the gaseous oxygen in the soil pore spaces and a platinum electrode to assess the oxygen diffusion rates in the water films. Populations of *Meloidogyne incognita*, *Trichodorus christiei* and *Tylenchulus semipenetrans* were significantly reduced at zero oxygen but there was no change at the other three oxygen levels over 10 days. The number of *Xiphinema americanum* decreased as oxygen concentration decreased and they were apparently killed or inactivated after 3 days at zero oxygen. Hatching of eggs of *Tylenchulus semipenetrans* was also reduced after 3 days without oxygen. There is, therefore, good evidence

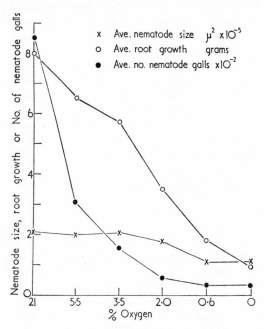

FIG. 24. The influence of oxygen concentration on tomato root growth, number of galls of *Meloidogyne javanica* and size of female nematodes. (After van Gundy and Stolzy, 1961.)

here that lack of oxygen may reduce nematode numbers in soil but what is perhaps more important, all the species studied appeared to tolerate low oxygen concentration for several days. Using similar techniques van Gundy and Stolzy (1961) studied the influence of oxygen concentration on the development of *Meloidogyne javanica* in tomato roots in soil. Oxygen concentrations of 21, 5·5, 3·5, 2·0, 0·6 and 0 per cent were used and the plants were examined after 28 and 35 days. The lowest oxygen concentration allowing development of host and parasite was 3·5 per cent; below this level plant root growth, size of developing females and egg production were reduced (Fig. 24). Nematode activity, as measured by the number of galls on the roots of treated plants, was sharply reduced at

5·5 per cent oxygen. The results show clearly the influence of oxygen lack on nematode infestation but whether this is an indirect effect through inhibition of plant growth or a direct effect on nematode activity is hard to assess. Later work by van Gundy and his colleagues (1962) showed that there was a critical rate of oxygen supply of about 30×10^{-8} g cm^{-2} min^{-1} for survival in soil of *Meloidogyne incognita, Paratylenchus elachistus, Trichodorus christiei, Tylenchulus semipenetrans* and *Xiphinema americanum. Trichodorus christiei* and *Xiphinema americanum* were more sensitive to length of exposure than the other species. This work also established that the availability of oxygen to nematodes decreased with depth and was profoundly affected by soil moisture content.

Feldmesser and Feder (1954) used sealed tubes containing water in which oxygen tension was varied by the inclusion of sodium sulphite which was oxidised to sulphate. At an oxygen tension equivalent to 400 p.p.m. of sodium sulphite, *Aphelenchoides* sp. ceased to move after 4 min., *Meloidogyne* sp. after 15 min. and *Heterodera rostochiensis* after 20 min., but they all resumed activity after 2 min. aeration, even after 20 hr. inactivity. Although the actual oxygen concentrations at which activity ceased in these nematodes is not known, the results do illustrate the effect of low oxygen concentrations and, furthermore, they indicate that different species may have different tolerance levels. Subsequent work by Feder and Feldmesser (1955) substantiates this.

Triffitt (1930) showed that larvae of *Heterodera rostochiensis* did not emerge from cysts in the absence of oxygen. *H. schachtii* larvae behave similarly (Wallace, 1955a). Cysts were placed in sealed tubes containing distilled water at different oxygen concentrations and the larvae emerging in 7 days were counted. Emergence increased as the initial oxygen concentration increased. The effect of pre-treating cysts to a low oxygen concentration of 0 to 0·5 mg of oxygen per litre for different times was also studied. Subsequent larval emergence in beet diffusate was lessened after exposure to such conditions for a few hours, nevertheless it was still appreciable after 22 days at the low oxygen level. Emergence of *H. schachtii* larvae increases as the oxygen concentration of air over the water increases (Wallace, 1955b, Fig. 25). Although this appears to show the effect of oxygen it does not provide any information on the oxygen requirements of the nematodes because the level of oxygen concentration within the cyst is unknown and is undoubtedly a fraction of that applied in the experiments.

What effect has carbon dioxide on plant nematodes? Steiner (1952) has pointed out that the soil air has a greater amount of carbon dioxide than the atmosphere and that the respiratory needs of plant nematodes are unknown. Saturated carbon dioxide solutions completely inhibit larval emergence from cysts of *Heterodera rostochiensis* and the subsequent rate of emergence decreases with the time of exposure to such conditions (Gillard *et al.*, 1958). The activity of *H. rostochiensis, H. schachtii* and *Aphelenchoides ritzemabosi* is also reduced by exposure to carbon dioxide

(Kämpfe, 1959b). It has been suggested that accumulations of carbon dioxide in cysts of *H. schachtii* may be the cause of the incomplete hatch (Wallace, 1959). The activity of *Pratylenchus penetrans* and *Hoplolaimus uniformis* is inhibited by carbon dioxide concentrations above atmospheric but low concentrations appear to have a stimulatory effect (Rohde, 1960). The mobility of *H. rostochiensis* and *H. schachtii* was increased by previous exposure to carbon dioxide and 6 days storage in carbon dioxide caused no damage to larvae, which quickly became active when oxygen was reintroduced (Kämpfe, 1959a).

There seems little doubt that the activity of many plant nematodes is increased by increased oxygen concentration and decreased by increasing

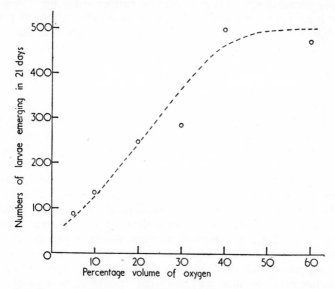

FIG. 25.   The influence of oxygen concentration on the emergence of larvae from cysts of *Heterodera schachtii*. (After Wallace, 1955b.)

carbon dioxide. However, there is no evidence that carbon dioxide is toxic; it may even be stimulatory at low concentrations or short exposure times. Carbon dioxide and oxygen occur together in the soil water and the relative proportions of each vary widely. Although the oxygen and carbon dioxide in the air together amount to about 21 per cent, this does not occur in the soil water because of the different solubilities and diffusion rates of the two gases. The data just discussed do not, therefore, give any indication of the effects of different proportions of carbon dioxide, oxygen and nitrogen on nematode activity. The only information on this topic is that of Shepherd (*in litt.*) who measured the effect of different proportions of oxygen, carbon dioxide and nitrogen on larval emergence from cysts of *Heterodera schachtii*. Shepherd found that (*a*) at a constant concentration of nitrogen, emergence increased as the ratio of oxygen to carbon dioxide increased; (*b*) at constant oxygen there was a decrease in emergence as carbon dioxide concentration increased, with a possible optimum at 10 per cent; (*c*) at constant carbon dioxide, emergence increased with oxygen concentration. There was no evidence from these data of an optimum carbon dioxide-oxygen ratio. Consequently it seems possible that there is no complicated interaction between carbon dioxide inhibition and oxygen stimulation but further research along these lines is needed, especially using low oxygen concentrations. The possible optimum at 10 per cent carbon dioxide supports Kämpfe's (1959a) and Rohde's (1960) observations that at low concentrations this gas may stimulate nematodes. This also calls for further study for if nematode activity is related to carbon dioxide concentration then it may be possible to explain, for example, the orientation of nematodes in concentration gradients of this gas, in terms of a speed kinesis (Chapter 5).

TEMPERATURE

The influence of temperature on plant nematodes can be divided into five arbitrary phases: (1) non-lethal low temperatures at which activity is inhibited, (2) optimum temperatures, (3) non-lethal high temperatures at which activity is inhibited, (4) lethal low temperatures, (5) lethal high temperatures. Theoretically, every species should have a temperature range corresponding to each of these categories, but complete data on any one species are lacking. Examples of categories (1), (2) and (3) are given in Table 2, but before any conclusions are drawn it is imperative to understand the limitations of such data. First, different nematode activities (hatching, reproduction, movement, development, etc.) may have different temperature requirements; second, where nematode activity is associated with the host plant (development, reproduction, etc.) temperature relations may vary with the species of host plant; third, individuals of different age or at different degrees of starvation, may behave differently; fourth, different populations of the same species may have different temperature characteristics. For example, populations of *Meloidogyne javanica* from Georgia, U.S.A., North Carolina and Southern Rhodesia each have differences in their tolerance to high and low temperatures (Daulton and Nusbaum, 1962). Consequently, each of the five categories is a temperature range. Similarly, the temperature limits at which a species is killed (categories (4) and (5)) are very variable and depend on time of exposure.

There is probably enough data from observations on such species as *Heterodera rostochiensis* and *Ditylenchus dipsaci* to define these categories, but can any generalisations be made on the phytoparasitic nematodes as a whole? Examination of Table 2 suggests that the low temperature range over which most phytoparasitic nematodes become inactive is about 5 to 15°C, the optimum range is about 15 to 30°C and the high

TABLE 2.   *Inhibition of plant nematodes at low temperatures (°C)*

Aphelenchoides ritzemabosi	reproduction	8	Dolliver *et al.*, 1962
Ditylenchus dipsaci	activity	15	Courtney and Latta, 1934
D. dispaci	infestation	7–13	Cairns, 1954
Heterodera glycines	emergence	16	Slack and Hamble, 1959
H. glycines	development	10	Ichinohe, 1955
H. glycines	development	10	Ross, 1960
H. rostochiensis	development	11	Chitwood and Buhrer, 1946
H. rostochiensis	activity	5–10	Kämpfe, 1958
H. rostochiensis	,,	16	Mai and Harrison, 1959
H. rostochiensis	,,	9	Chitwood and Buhrer, 1945
H. schachtii	,,	5–10	Kämpfe, 1958
H. schachtii	emergence	10	Wallace, 1955a
Meloidogyne spp.	reproduction	15–16	Thomason and Lear, 1961
Meloidogyne sp.	reproduction	9	Tyler, 1933
Meloidogyne sp.	infestation	10–12	Godfrey, 1926
Paratylenchus projectus	moulting	10	Rhoades and Linford, 1959

Optimum temperature for plant nematodes (°C)

Criconemoides xenoplax	reproduction	26	Lownsbery, 1961
Ditylenchus dipsaci	reproduction	18	Barker, 1959
D. dipsaci	activity	10–20	Seinhorst, 1950
D. dipsaci	activity	21	Sayre and Mountain, 1962
D. dipsaci	mobility	15–20	Wallace, 1958, 1961
D. dipsaci	mobility	15–20	Blake, 1962
D. myceliophagus	infestation	18	Cairns, 1954
Hemicycliophora arenaria	reproduction	30–33	van Gundy and Rackham, 1961
H. arenaria	development	28–32	Baines *et al.*, 1959
Heterodera glycines	emergence	24	Slack and Hamblen, 1959
H. glycines	development	23	Ichinohe, 1955
H. avenae	reproduction	20	Winslow, 1955
H. rostochiensis	invasion	15–16	Chitwood and Buhrer, 1946
H. rostochiensis	emergence	21	Lownsbery, 1950
H. rostochiensis	activity	25	Kämpfe, 1955
H. rostochiensis	emergence	25	Fenwick, 1951a
H. rostochiensis	development	18–24	Ferris, 1957
H. schachtii	reproduction	21–27	Raski and Johnson, 1959

TABLE 2—*continued*

Optimum temperature for plant nematodes (°C)

H. schachtii	reproduction	27·5	Thomason and Fife, 1962
H. schachtii	activity	25	Kämpfe, 1955
H. schachtii	mobility	15	Wallace, 1958
H. schachtii	emergence	25	Wallace, 1955a
Meloidogyne spp.	reproduction	25–32	Thomason and Lear, 1961
Meloidogyne sp.	reproduction	27	Tyler, 1933
Meloidogyne sp.	infestation	20–35	Godfrey, 1926
M. incognita acrita	hatching	27	Bergeson. 1959
Paratylenchus amblycephalus	infestation	16–21	Reuver, 1959
P. projectus	moulting	19–30	Rhoades and Linford, 1959
Tylenchorhynchus claytoni	reproduction (in tobacco)	29–35	Krusberg, 1959
T. claytoni	reproduction (in wheat)	21–27	Krusberg, 1959
Tylenchulus semipenetrans	development	25–31	Baines et al., 1959

Inhibition of plant nematodes at high temperatures (°C)

Ditylenchus dipsaci	activity	38	Courtney and Latta, 1934
Heterodera glycines	emergence	36	Slack and Hamblen, 1959
H. rostochiensis	development	32	Fenwick, 1951b
H. rostochiensis	emergence	30	Fenwick, 1951a
H. rostochiensis	—	37	Mai, 1952
H. rostochiensis	activity	30–35	Kämpfe, 1958
H. rostochiensis	development	29	Mai and Harrison, 1959
H. rostochiensis	development	29	Ferris, 1957
H. schachtii	emergence	35	Wallace, 1955a
H. schachtii	activity	30–35	Kämpfe, 1958
H. schachtii	development	32·5	Thomason and Fife, 1962
Paratylenchus projectus	moulting	35	Rhoades and Linford, 1959
Trichodorus sp.	development	35	Rohde and Jenkins, 1957

temperature range for inactivity is 30 to 40°C. Outside this range temperatures are often lethal. These ranges are, of course, very similar to those for many other organisms (Allee *et al.*, 1949). To the plant nematologist, however, it is the factors which cause the wide variation in temperature requirements that are important.

The development of *Heterodera rostochiensis* within the host plant is inhibited at 29 to 32°C (Fenwick, 1951b; Ferris, 1957; Mai and Harrison, 1959) but emergence of larvae from the cyst may continue until 36 to 37°C (Mai, 1952; Slack and Hamblen, 1959). The optimum temperature for invasion in this species is 15 to 16°C (Chitwood and Buhrer, 1946), for emergence from the cyst 21 to 25°C (Lownsbery, 1950; Fenwick, 1951a) and for development 18 to 24°C (Ferris, 1957). The optimum temperature for emergence of larvae from cysts of *Heterodera schachtii* is about 25°C but for movement it is 15°C (Wallace, 1958). These examples indicate that in giving the optimum temperature for a species the particular nematode activity must be defined and this probably explains why such a complex phenomenon as population increase has a wide optimum temperature range.

Studies on the temperature relations of nematode reproduction in plants are complicated because the plant itself is often affected by temperature. Godfrey (1926), for example, showed that the number of root galls on lettuce plants was greatest at 20°C and fell steeply at 23°C. On celery and potatoes, however, the number of galls increased with temperature up to 27°C. Reduced gall formation at 23°C on lettuce roots was attributed to the poor root growth of the plant. Krusberg (1959) found that the optimum temperature for reproduction of *Tylenchorhynchus claytoni* was 21 to 27°C on wheat and 29 to 35°C on tobacco. Blake (1962) showed that reproduction of *Ditylenchus dipsaci* in oats was greater at 8°C than at 15°C. Furthermore, in carrot callus tissue cultures Blake found that the slow growth of the tissue at 8°C favoured reproduction whereas at 15°C the tissue grew quickly and inhibited reproduction. Reproduction is, therefore, related not only to temperature but also to growth of the host. This may explain why infestations of *D. dipsaci* are more severe in autumn sown oats than in spring sown oats in England. These observations emphasise the danger of relating nematode distribution to climatic temperature. Winslow (1960) states that *D. dipsaci* occurs chiefly in cooler climates. While this may be true, it is not clear whether distribution is determined by the nematodes' or by the plants' temperature requirements.

There is little information on the influence of age, starvation, etc., on temperature relations of plant nematodes. The tolerance of *Ditylenchus dipsaci* to low temperatures (Bosher and McKeen, 1954) and high temperatures (Courtney and Latta, 1934) is greater when the fourth stage larvae are in the dry quiescent state. Similarly, fourth stage larvae of *Paratylenchus projectus* can survive sudden exposure to low temperatures better than other stages (Rhoades and Linford, 1961).

The influence of alternating temperatures

The study of nematode activity at constant temperatures is obviously artificial because, in the soil, temperatures fluctuate. Bishop (1953,

5

1955) showed that the rate of emergence of larvae from cysts of *Heterodera rostochiensis* increased with alternating temperature. After 13 days at 25°C about 45 per cent of the larvae emerged. When the temperature was lowered from 25 to 15°C for 5 hr twice a week, about 63 per cent emerged and when lowered five times a week, 82 per cent emerged. Emergence of larvae from cysts of *H. schachtii* also increased when temperatures fluctuated between 24 and 15°C (Fig. 26) although the amount

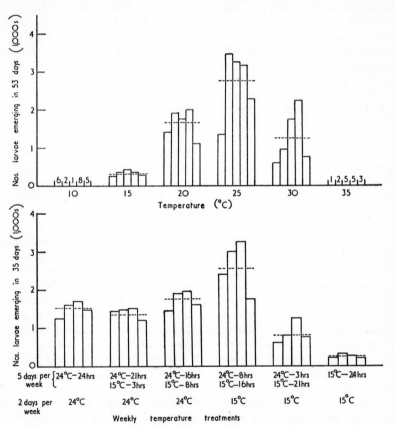

FIG. 26.   The influence of fluctuating temperature on the emergence of larvae from cysts of *Heterodera schachtii*. (After Wallace, 1955a.)

of heat received was less than that for the optimum constant temperature. Slack and Hamblen (1961) exposed cysts of *H. glycines* to similar temperature fluctuations as those just described for *H. schachtii*, but they found no increase in the rate of larval emergence. Lewis and Mai (1957) showed that in moist soil, viability of eggs and larvae within cysts of *H. rostochiensis* decreased more with alternating than with constant temperature. In dry soil, fluctuating temperature had no effect. More information is clearly needed on the influence of alternating temperatures on plant nematode activity before its importance can be assessed or any attempt can be made to express quantitatively the relationship between temperature and development, hatching, movement, etc. For similar reasons, the correlation between nematode population dynamics and the diurnal and seasonal cycles of temperature in the soil must also await further research. Expressing soil temperature in terms of daily means is clearly inadequate.

An attempt was made by Tyler (1933) to relate temperature and rate of development in root knot nematodes. She plotted the reciprocal of time of development ('rate') against temperature and obtained a straight line, although there was variation at the extremes of the temperature range. The line cut the 'rate' axis at about 10°C, the lower temperature threshold for development, so Tyler computed the number of heat units for development to the egg laying stage in terms of hour-degrees above 10°C. Ichinohe (1955) calculated the number of day-degrees for the completion of one generation of *Heterodera glycines* in a similar way. He took 10°C to be the lower threshold and added up the total temperature above this level at 5 cm and 30 cm soil depth from June 1st to October 10th, the developmental period of the nematode. The number of day-degrees above 10°C over this period divided by the number of day-degrees for development came to about 3·5, so Ichinohe concluded that three generations of *H. glycines* were possible in a season in Hokkaido, Japan. Field observations supported this hypothesis. The heat summation method may, therefore, be valid over the straight part of the development curve, although its value in interpreting field data is largely unproven.

Low lethal temperatures

Bosher and McKeen (1954) found that *Ditylenchus dipsaci* in the dried quiescent state, survived −80°C for 20 min. but the nematodes were killed if they were subjected to this temperature when wet. In Hokkaido, Japan, cysts of *Heterodera glycines* still contained living eggs after 7 months at −40°C (Ichinohe, 1955) and Slack and Hamblen (1961) found that some eggs in cysts of the same species could withstand −24°C for 18 months. Larvae of *H. glycines* were killed, however, as soon as they became frozen (Slack and Hamblen, 1959). Resistant fourth stage larvae of *Paratylenchus projectus* survived −19°C for 4 days whereas second and third stage larvae and adults were killed (Rhoades and Linford, 1961). Temperatures of 0 to 5°C kill larvae of *Meloidogyne incognita acrita* but the eggs were more resistant (Bergeson, 1959). Egg masses of *Meloidogyne hapla* tolerated −6°C for 5 days and −8°C for 2 days (Gillard, 1961). Plant parasitic nematodes in the quiescent stage may, therefore, withstand very low temperatures whereas the active stages are probably killed at or just below freezing point, although the time of exposure is obviously important.

High lethal temperatures

Hot water treatment of infested plant material is a useful method of control for some plant nematode species (Chapter 10). Research on such methods has also provided information on the lethal effects of high temperatures. When the thermal death curves of different species are plotted on the same graph (Fig. 27) it is clear that there is a wide variation

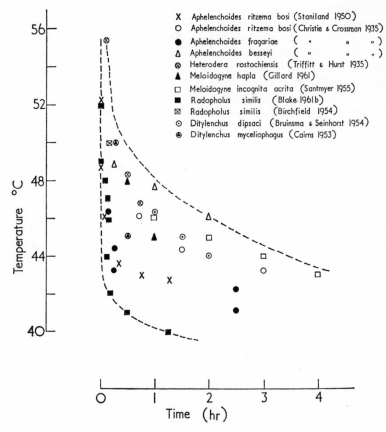

Fig. 27. The relationship between temperature and the time needed to kill different nematode species.

between species. This variation is probably caused by several factors other than inherent differences between species. For example, the techniques used to determine the thermal death time are very important. Thus, if the nematodes are immersed in a large quantity of water there will be a considerable time lag between the application of heat and its reaching the nematode. For this reason, Staniland (1950) and Blake (1961b) placed nematodes in fine capillaries and it is perhaps significant that their results show the quickest kills at any one temperature. A time lag will also occur where nematodes are enclosed within the host plant tissues, or where eggs are grouped together in cysts (*Heterodera* spp.) or in egg masses (*Meloidogyne* spp.). The experimental criterion of death may introduce further variation. Many authors diagnose death when the nematode shows no signs of movement 2 days or so after treatment. Santmyer (1955) introduced heat treated larvae of *Meloidogyne incognita acrita* into soil containing tomato plants and assessed kill by subsequent infections. Such a method assumes that absence of infection denotes complete kill, but many larvae may be uninfective without being killed and not all untreated nematodes invade the host. This may explain why, in Santmyer's experiments, long exposure times were needed to give complete kill at any one temperature.

The lower the temperature, the greater the variation and this is clearly shown in Fig. 27. Although it is dangerous to generalise from such data, two tentative conclusions can be drawn: (1) nematodes are probably killed in a few seconds at about 52°C; this is sometimes called the instantaneous death point. Egg masses of *Heterodera* and *Meloidogyne* may have a higher death point however; (2) temperatures above 40°C may be lethal if nematodes are exposed for long enough.

Different species of the same genus may have different thermal death curves. Christie and Crossman (1935) showed that different strains of *Aphelenchoides fragariae* needed different exposure times at any particular temperature (Fig. 28). At 42°C, for example, the strawberry strain from North Carolina (=*A. besseyi*) took 15 hr. to kill, the chrysanthemum strain (=*A. ritzemabosi*) 5 hr. and the begonia strain and the Massachusetts strawberry strain (=*A. fragariae*) each took about 1 hr. to kill. Walker (1960) found that the times required to kill 50 per cent of the larvae of different *Meloidogyne* spp. at 44°C were: *M. arenaria*, 35 min.; *M. javanica*, 26·6 min.; *M. incognita acrita*, 21·6 min.; *M. incognita*, 18·3 min.; and *M. hapla*, 8·3 min. Thus *M. arenaria*, the southern root knot nematode is more resistant to high temperatures than the northern species, *M. hapla*.

OSMOTIC PRESSURE

Differences in osmotic potential between the nematode's body fluids and the soil solution occur with changes in concentration of dissolved salts in the soil water. In such conditions, water and salts tend to move through the cuticle to restore osmotic equilibrium. Increase in osmotic potential occurs as the soil dries, so water is drawn out of the nematode. In considering this process, however, it should be remembered that suction potential as well as osmotic potential is acting on the nematode; together they constitute the free energy of the soil which has already been discussed in the section on soil water.

Stephenson (1942) observed that a *Rhabditis* sp., a free-living nematode, shrank in concentrated saline solutions. The alimentary canal showed less change in size than the body as a whole, so Stephenson concluded that water passed out of the nematode through the body wall and not through the gut. Unhatched larvae of *Heterodera schachtii* shrink in concentrated solutions of sodium chloride, sucrose and urea (Wallace, 1956d). At concentrations greater than 0·01 M there was marked

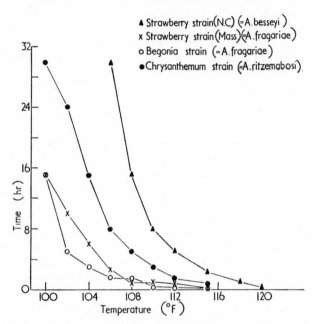

FIG. 28. The time required to kill different species of *Aphelenchoides ritzemabosi* at different temperatures. (After Christie and Crossman, 1935.)

reduction in length. Cysts of *H. schachtii* exposed to molar solutions for 5 weeks recovered completely although immersion in 3 to 4 M solutions was lethal. Larval emergence from cysts was very low at about 0·6 M which is equivalent to the free energy of the soil water at the permanent wilting point for plants (Fig. 29). Dropkin and his colleagues (1958) made similar observations on *H. rostochiensis* and *Meloidogyne arenaria*. The hatch in these species was assessed at five concentrations of sodium chloride, calcium chloride, potassium chloride and dextrose (0·1, 0·2, 0·3, 0·4 and 1 M). Hatching decreased as concentration increased and was markedly reduced between 0·3 and 1 M. The unhatched larvae were undamaged by the high osmotic pressures and hatching recommenced on transference to water. Inhibition of hatching occurred at osmotic pressures equivalent to 15 atmospheres, the permanent wilting point for plants in soil.   Blake (1961a) found that fourth stage larvae of *Ditylenchus dipsaci* were killed in 1 and 2 M urea; larvae recovered after immersion in 0·3 M urea.   Feder (1960) increased the osmotic potential of the soil water by adding dextrose or sucrose at the rate of 1 to 5 per cent by weight.   He found that 1,000 p.p.m. of dextrose was lethal to nematodes.

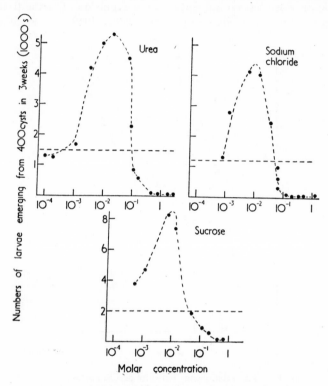

FIG. 29.   The influence of the osmotic pressure of urea, sodium chloride and sucrose solutions on the emergence of larvae from cysts of *Heterodera schachtii*.   The horizontal dotted line indicates the rate of larval emergence in water.   (After Wallace, 1956d.)

In vitro tests showed that parasitic and free-living nematodes were killed in 1 hr. in 30 to 40 per cent sucrose and in 10 per cent glucose.   Immersion for 10 to 15 min., however, was not lethal.   Feder suggests that the nematodes were killed by exosmosis at osmotic pressures of 22·4 atmospheres in sucrose and 12·3 atmospheres in glucose, values which are close to the permanent wilting point of plants in soil (Fig. 30).

It seems likely, therefore, that plant nematodes can tolerate osmotic pressures up to about 10 atmospheres; beyond this level, activity may be inhibited although the nematodes may not be killed. At higher concentrations the nematodes shrivel, become distorted and eventually die (Kämpfe, 1959b).

In most agricultural soils the osmotic pressure of the soil solution rarely exceeds 2 atmospheres even at the wilting point of plants, so it is clear that osmotic pressure alone is unlikely to be an inhibitory factor. Osmotic pressure has no influence on the expulsion of larvae from galls of *Anguina agrostis* (Collis-George and Blake, 1959). The galls were

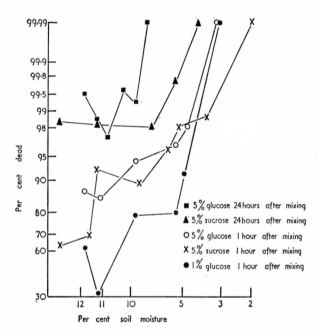

FIG. 30. The relationship between percentage soil moisture and percentage nematodes killed 1 hr. and 24 hr. after mixing the soils with either 1 per cent or 5 per cent dextrose or sucrose. (After Feder, 1960.)

immersed in sodium chloride solutions at osmotic pressures from 5×10^{-4} to 100 atmospheres, but there was no difference in the expulsion pattern, although at high concentrations the larvae were inactive and shrivelled. Collis-George and Blake conclude that the larvae play no active part in expulsion, and that the soil moisture suction is the most important factor (Fig. 31).

So far, only the inhibitory effect of osmotic pressure has been discussed. There is some evidence, however, that osmotic pressure may have a stimulatory influence. Machmer (1958), for example, states that *Tylenchulus semipenetrans* and *Meloidogyne incognita acrita* not only survived but showed greater population increase than controls in high salinities in soil containing host plants. The nematodes tolerated the high salt concentrations although plant growth was impaired. Bird (1959) found that the attractiveness of reducing agents to *Meloidogyne javanica* was greatest at concentrations of 0·02 to 0·04 M. The rate of larval emergence from cysts of *Heterodera schachtii* was studied in various concentrations of organic and inorganic chemicals (Wallace, 1956d). Many substances stimulated emergence above that in water, the optimum

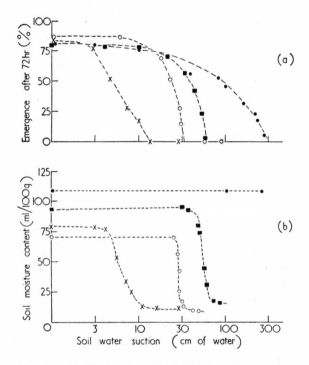

Fig. 31. (a) The influence of soil suction on the emergence of larvae from galls of *Anguina agrostis*, (b) moisture characteristics of soils used in (a). Crosses—1 to 2 mm sand; open circles—300 to 400 μ sand; squares—150 μ alumina; closed circles—25 μ alumina. (After Collis-George and Blake, 1959.)

concentration being about 0·01 M. In beet diffusate the osmotic pressure of the optimum concentration for emergence was 0·48 atmospheres, which is equivalent to about 0·01 M sodium chloride. Although there is little data from which to generalise on isotonic values for nematodes, the possibility of this factor should not be overlooked in experiments where chemical concentration is involved.

Osmotic pressure appears to exert very little influence on nematode activity in soil because salt concentrations rarely rise to inhibitory levels. In very dry soils where osmotic pressure is at its highest, the desiccatory effect may even aid survival. Thus, *Ditylenchus dipsaci* can survive temperatures as low as $-80°C$ if water is removed from the body by previous immersion in concentrated salt solutions (Bosher and McKeen, 1954). Unhatched larvae of *Heterodera rostochiensis* and *Meloidogyne arenaria* become quiescent at high salt concentrations so enabling them to survive dry soil conditions (Dropkin *et al.*, 1958).

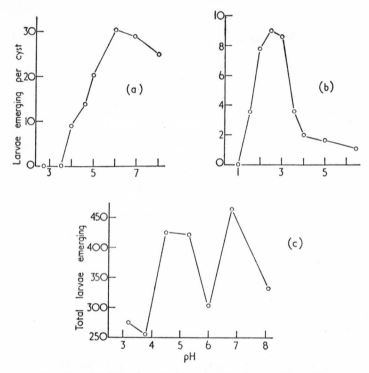

Fig. 32. The influence of pH on the emergence of larvae from cysts of *Heterodera rostochiensis* (a) after Ellenby, 1946, (b) after Robinson and Neal, 1956, (c) after Fenwick, 1951.

HYDROGEN ION CONCENTRATION

Evidence for the influence of pH on plant nematodes is contradictory. Ellenby (1946) soaked cysts of *Heterodera rostochiensis* for 24 hr. in a series of acetate buffers; they were then washed, soaked in distilled water for a further 24 hr and placed in potato root diffusate. Emergence of larvae from the cysts decreased as pH fell from 6·7 to 4·0; at pH 3·4 and below there was no emergence at all. There was an apparent optimum for emergence at pH 6 and Ellenby concluded that marked disturbance of pH on the alkaline as well as the acid side of neutrality might inhibit emergence (Fig. 32a). Fenwick (1951a) measured larval emergence from cysts of *H. rostochiensis* in root diffusate containing different proportions of N/10 sodium carbonate and N/10 hydrochloric acid solutions. There appeared to be no difference in total emergence or rate of emergence over the range of pH 3·0 to 8·0 (Fig. 32c). Robinson and Neal (1956) studied the influence of pH on larval emergence from *H. rostochiensis* cysts in glass distilled water containing hydrochloric acid. Emergence reached a maximum at pH 2·5 over the range 1 to 6·5 and similar results were obtained with citric and fumaric acids (Fig. 32b). In root diffusate, however, the results were conflicting and emergence appeared to vary with the source of the cysts and the concentration of the diffusate.

Such conflicting results do not permit any generalisations to be made and field observations do not clarify the picture. Peters (1926), for example, found little correlation between pH and cyst concentration of *H. rostochiensis* in soil from various districts of South Lincolnshire, England. Ahlberg (1951) states that there is no difference between the rate of reproduction of *H. rostochiensis* in acid and alkali soils in Sweden and Mai and Harrison (1959) conclude that in the range in which potatoes are normally grown, pH appears to have little influence on the susceptibility of potatoes to attack by *H. rostochiensis*.

Simon (1955) states that there is a close correlation between soil pH and the level of *Heterodera schachtii* infestations in Belgium. Simon divided the levels of infestation into three categories: light (< 10 viable cysts/100 g of soil), medium (10–19) and heavy (> 20). About 24,000 soil samples were examined over 5 years and results from 1952–53 clearly show this correlation (Fig. 33) but, once again, it is difficult to relate cause and effect. Sugar beet grows best on alkaline soils so nematode infestation may be correlated with host plant growth rather than pH. Petherbridge and Jones (1944), for example, state that *Heterodera schachtii* is absent from areas in the Fen district of England where the soil is markedly acid, probably because such soils are unsuitable for sugar beet growing. Oostenbrink (1958) also found that some cases of poor beet growth could be cured by treating the soil with chalk, heat or with the nematicide DD. He attributed the subsequent improvement in sugar beet growth to increased pH caused by these treatments rather than to nematode control.

The hatch of *Meloidogyne incognita incognita* and larval survival reaches a maximum at about pH 6·5 in Heller's nutrient solution (Fig. 34). Godfrey and Hagan (1933), however, found that soils at a range of pH from 4·0 to 8·5 had little influence on the infestation of pineapple by a *Meloidogyne* sp. The tests were conducted in two ways: (*a*) with soils adjusted to different pH values by the addition of sulphuric acid and sodium hydroxide; and (*b*) the collection of pineapple and sugar cane field soils of known pH, through a wide range.

Other information on the influence of pH is of a negative kind.

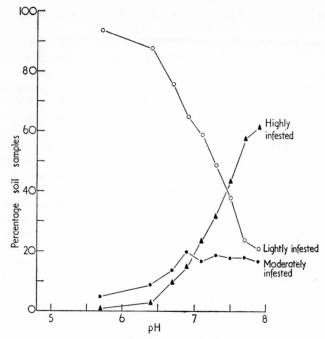

FIG. 33. The relationship between pH and the population density of *Heterodera schachtii* in soil. (After Simon, 1955.)

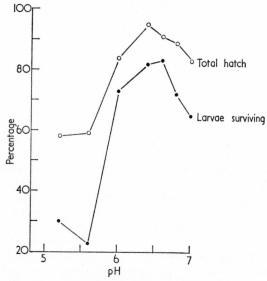

FIG. 34. The influence of pH on the hatch and larval survival of *Meloidogyne incognita incognita*. (After Loewenberg *et al.*, 1960).

Lownsbery (1961) found no difference between population levels of *Criconemoides xenoplax* on peach soil at pH 5 and 7. Bird (1959), in studies on the attraction of *Meloidogyne javanica* to roots, concluded that pH played only a secondary role although larvae were repelled at pH 3 and 10·6 at either end of the range.

The scarcity and conflicting nature of data on effects of pH emphasise the need for further research. pH may be unimportant in nematode ecology (Steiner, 1952) but there are not enough observations as yet to support such a view.

CHEMICALS

Chemicals in the soil solution may affect plant nematodes indirectly through plant growth (Chapter 3) or directly by acting as orientation stimuli (Chapter 5). There may also be a direct metabolic effect and it is this aspect which will be discussed here. The relationship between the numbers of free-living nematodes and chemical concentration in the soil can be explained in terms of food supply, for the microorganisms on which the nematodes feed are susceptible to chemical change. Bassus (1960), for example, found that when calcium carbonate or calcium oxide was added to pine humus, the free-living nematode population increased by 25 to 100 per cent. Lime never caused decreases in population density.

Seinhorst (1950) suggests that in some Dutch soils, a factor is present which inhibits the activity of *Ditylenchus dipsaci*. The factor, presumably chemical, was eliminated by partial heat sterilisation, treatment with mercuric chloride solution, organic mercury compounds and the vapour of chloroform, ether and carbon bisulphide; it could also be extracted and introduced into other soils where it inhibited nematode activity. Soils heated to 100°C lost their inhibitive properties. Bacteria may be the source of such an inhibitor, for Johnston (1957) showed that, in water saturated soils, a bacterium, *Clostridium* sp., produced a toxic principle which killed *Tylenchorhynchus martini*. Chemical inhibitors may also be given out by plant roots. Luc (1961) showed that millet roots produced a factor which inhibited the migration of *Hemicycliophora paradoxa*. The identity of these chemicals, however, is unknown.

Henderson and Katznelson (1961) found that the number of nematodes in the rhizosphere of several crops was much greater than in the adjacent root-free soil and they suggest that the population growth of such plant nematodes as *Pratylenchus* and *Paratylenchus* spp. is governed directly or indirectly by the amino acid concentration in the rhizosphere. Whether this distribution is caused by attraction of the nematodes to the roots or by some other process is not known.

Larval emergence from cysts of *Heterodera rostochiensis* may be influenced by the type of ions in the hatching solution (Ellenby and Gilbert, 1958). Emergence in root diffusate, diffusate plus calcium chloride and diffusate plus potassium chloride were compared at different concentrations. Concentration had little effect, but emergence with calcium chloride was about twice as high, and with potassium chloride about half as high as that in diffusate alone. Ellenby and Gilbert state that, in general, chlorides of monovalent ions depress emergence whereas chlorides of divalent ions stimulate emergence. Differences in the emergence behaviour of cysts from different sources may therefore be related to their previous ionic environment. Robinson (1956) found that zinc and cadmium salts strongly inhibited larval emergence of *Heterodera rostochiensis*. Robinson and Neal (1959) showed that larval emergence in this species was influenced by the kind and concentration of cations in solution. A mixture of sodium, potassium, magnesium and calcium chlorides caused increased emergence in tomato root diffusate. Individual salts and various combinations of them failed to produce a larval emergence equivalent to the complete mixture. Potassium appeared to stimulate emergence more than any other single component, contrary to the findings of Ellenby and Gilbert.

The absence of calcium chloride, magnesium sulphate or chelated iron in solution reduced the survival of larvae of *Meloidogyne incognita incognita* and the omission of sodium or potassium chloride depressed emergence (Loewenberg *et al.*, 1960). These investigations also emphasised the importance of balance of ions on larval emergence.

Chemical inhibition and stimulation of nematode activity and the concentration and balance of ions are factors which call for more research.

LIGHT

The emergence of larvae from cysts of *Heterodera rostochiensis* was unaffected by exposure to the dark and to diffuse light but in bright sunlight at the same temperature there was no emergence and the same cysts produced no larvae when they were transferred to the dark (Fenwick, 1951a). Lownsbery (1950) also found that emergence in *Heterodera rostochiensis* was inhibited by light. Irradiation with ultraviolet light is lethal to larvae and eggs of *Meloidogyne* sp. (Godfrey and Hoshino, 1933). The ultra-violet from the mid-day sun on a clear day in April in Hawaii killed the larvae in about 22·5 min., eggs in egg masses in 4·5 hr. and free eggs in 75 min.

Slack and Hamblen (1961) exposed *Heterodera glycines* cysts to a constant light from two 4-watt fluorescent-light tubes placed 6 in. away; a second group of cysts were excluded from the light but kept at the same temperature. There was no difference in the emergence of larvae from the two groups. Winslow (1955) also found that light had no influence on larval emergence from *H. major* cysts. Kämpfe (1959a) exposed larvae of *H. rostochiensis* and *H. schachtii* to darkness, white artificial light and infra red light for 20 min. but could detect no differences in mobility;

heat was excluded by placing a water cell between the larvae and the light source.

Light, especially in the ultra-violet range, may be lethal to nematodes but information on times of exposure, intensity and wavelength is lacking. Light may affect those nematode species which occur above ground level, e.g. *Ditylenchus* and *Aphelenchoides*, but it is doubtful whether it has any influence on nematodes in the soil, except through its indirect effect on the host plant.

PARASITES AND PREDATORS

Up to now this chapter has emphasised the importance of physical factors on plant nematodes. Let us now consider the influence of the soil fauna and flora. There are a variety of ways in which nematodes can be affected by other organisms. Chemicals may accumulate in soil by the secretions or break-down products of organisms and so influence the distribution and numbers of nematodes by their toxic or attractive properties. This aspect is discussed in the sections on soil water (page 56), chemicals (page 77) and movement (page 125). These may be considered as indirect effects; what will be discussed now is the direct effect on nematode mortality of parasites and predators. That steam sterilisation of soil increases the pathogenicity of some plant nematodes suggests that soil organisms exert some control on nematode numbers. Linford (1954) demonstrated this for *Heterodera trifolii* on white clover, but what sort of organisms are responsible for this effect? Observations suggest that viruses, protozoa, tardigrades, nematodes, enchytraeids, arthropods and fungi are the most important groups (see Plate II).

Viruses

Loewenberg, Sullivan and Schuster (1959) found that in some of their cultures, larvae of *Meloidogyne incognita incognita* were very sluggish. Fungi did not appear to be the cause of this effect and when a suspension of the affected nematodes was mixed with a suspension of surface steri-lised eggs, the larvae which subsequently hatched showed slow and jerky movements; the posterior portion of the body lost power of locomotion first and many nematodes died. Having demonstrated the transmissi-bility of the unknown disease, the contents of several dishes were filtered through Seitz filters and aliquots of the filtrate were added to sterile nutrient agar. This test failed to show bacteria or visible micro-organisms. Other aliquots were added to surface sterilised eggs, and the larvae which hatched had reduced activity, for they failed to reach tomato roots grown in agar culture, or took more than 3 hr. to do so compared with 1 hr. for the controls. A Seitz filtrate, prepared from the suspension in which the latter nematodes had emerged, spread the disease to another sample of healthy eggs. The disease was therefore self-propagating and Loewenberg and his colleagues concluded that these observations indicated that the disease was caused by a virus.

Protozoa

Doncaster and Hooper (1961) observed that a species of *Urostyla* ingested nematodes. The protozoan was often ruptured by the nematode, however, and there was no indication of digestion. The authors, therefore, concluded that *Urostyla* should not be considered as a predator. Doncaster (1956) also records that the ciliate, *Stylonichia pustulata* fed on nematodes.

An amoeboid organism was seen attacking *Heterodera rostochiensis* larvae to which it adhered near the head or tail (Weber *et al.*, 1952). The larva became motionless and was engulfed in 20 min. to 2 hr. A cyst wall then developed around the organism and the nematode was digested. *Meloidogyne* sp., *Ditylenchus dispsaci*, *Hemicycliophora* sp. and *Pratylenchus pratensis* were also attacked. Zwillenberg (1953) later described the organism as *Theratromyxa weberi*. Winslow and Williams (1957) observed a similar organism attacking, *in vitro*, larvae of *Heterodera rostochiensis* in England and *Heterodera schachtii* in Ontario, Canada, but the myxomycetous networks as described by Weber and colleagues were rarely formed and the parasitised nematodes occurred in small, not large clumps.

Thorne (1940) found that *Pratylenchus pratensis* was sometimes parasitised by a sporozoon *Duboscquia penetrans*. Thorne described the life cycle of the parasite and suggested that it was possibly specific to this nematode species. *Kuiper* (1958), however, found the same parasite in *Pratylenchus pratensis*, *Pratylenchus penetrans*, *Rotylenchus robustus*, *Tylenchorhynchus dubius* and *Meloidogyne arenaria*. Williams (1960) states that females of *M. javanica* and *M. incognita acrita* are sometimes filled with a sporozoon which may be a haplosporidian or micro sporidian and may resemble *Duboscquia penetrans* as described by Thorne although Williams' description of the life cycle differs from Thorne's. Of 174 female *Meloidogyne* removed from sugar cane roots at least 34 per cent were infected by the sporozoon. The spores, which completely filled the body, were probably passively dispersed and transmitted in the percolating soil water.

Tardigrades

Hutchinson and Streu (1960) observed unidentified tardigrades attacking nematodes, including *Trichodorus aequalis* and *Tylenchus* sp. The tardigrade stylets made distinct tears in the nematodes, which were eventually immobilised. Doncaster and Hooper (1961) made similar observations on a tardigrade, *Macrobiotus* sp. It is possible that a toxic secretion passes into the nematode causing immobilisation.

Nematodes

Early records of the predatory habits of *Mononchus* spp. are given by Steiner and Heinly (1922) and by Thorne (1927), who observed *Mononchus papillatus* feeding on *Heterodera schachtii* larvae and males; other species appeared to attack rotifiers and other microorganisms. Thorne also states that the *Mononchus* spp. were themselves parasitised by sporozoons. Not all predatory nematodes attack other nematodes; *Nygolaimus* and *Sectonema* spp. for example were not seen to attack nematodes but they did attack oligochaetes (Thorne, 1930). Furthermore, the occurrence of *Cephalobus*, *Acrobeles*, *Dorylaimus*, *Tylenchus* and *Plectus* spp. in cysts of *Heterodera schachtii* does not necessarily mean that they are predators (Thorne, 1928). There is good evidence, however, that other species are predatory. Linford and Oliveira (1937) observed ten species of *Dorylaimus*, two of *Discolaimus* and one of *Actinolaimus* feeding on other nematodes and they considered that predation by these hollow stylet nematodes was more important than that of *Mononchus*. Two species of *Aphelenchoides*, attacking *Pratylenchus pratensis* and root knot larvae, appeared to paralyse the prey, presumably by the injection of saliva. Linford and Oliveira's description of the feeding of the predatory *Aphelenchoides* is very similar to that of root feeding by plant nematodes.

Enchytraeids

Larvae of *Heterodera schachtii* within the host plant are sometimes destroyed by enchytraeid larvae which enter the roots (Schaerffenberg, 1951; Schaerffenberg and Tendl, 1951). The enchytraeids secrete digestive enzymes which dissolve the nematode larvae and these are then sucked up. Nematodes outside the root are not attacked and enchytraeid adults do not, themselves, attack nematodes. Schaerffenberg suggests that in rich humus soils (e.g. those which are green manured) there is a high population of enchytraeids and that it is unlikely that heavy nematode infestations will occur there; such soils are therefore suitable for sugar beet growing. There is no quantitative data, however, to support such an optimistic outlook. Doncaster (1962) also observed the enchytraeid, *Fridericia* sp. feeding on *Heterodera cruciferae* cysts.

Arthropods

Murphy and Doncaster (1957) showed that in a plot of rape 30 per cent of *Heterodera cruciferae* cysts on the roots had large, irregular perforations and the body contents had disappeared. Collembola, recovered from the soil, and cysts of *H. cruciferae* were placed together on damp sintered glass plates and observed. *Onychiurus armatus*, *Isotoma viridis*, *Achorutes* sp., and *Orchesella villosa* fed on the cysts. In a pot experiment where the mean number of *Onychiurus armatus* per g of soil and roots was 1·0 and of *H. cruciferae* cysts 5·3, Murphy and Doncaster estimated that

6

about 6·9 per cent of the cysts were damaged by Collembola. Brown (1954) also observed the collembolan, *Isotoma* sp. feeding on nematodes which were ingested in 2 to 3 sec. Doncaster (1962) observed several arthropods on sintered glass plates and found that the collembolans *Achorutes*, *Folsomia* and *Isotoma* spp., *Symphylids*, the predacious mite *Pergamasus crassipes*, larvae of several Staphylinid beetles (*Philonthus*, *Omalium* and *Trechus*) and a centipede *Lithobius duboscqui* all fed on *Heterodera* cysts. Doncaster also used glass-fronted observation boxes containing soil and plants to observe the feeding habits of predatory arthropods in near-natural surroundings.

Fungi

The biology of the predacious fungi has been described by Duddington (1956, 1960) so there is no need to discuss it in detail here.

The predacious fungi capture nematodes by trapping mechanisms which are of two main types, sticky traps and ring traps. The sticky traps, as occur in *Arthrobotrys oligospora*, consist of a system of loops from the parent hypha which form an anastomosing network. The loops are sticky and nematodes, wandering into the net, are held there by the adhesive fluid secreted by cells of the loops. The trapped nematode becomes immobile within about 2 hr, by which time fine outgrowths from the loop have penetrated the nematode cuticle. An infection bulb swells within the nematode and from this, trophic hyphae grow out, fill the body and absorb its contents. In some species, for example *Dactylella lobata* the mycelium forms short lateral branches of one, two or three cells that are sticky and on which nematodes are trapped by adhesion, while in others, like *Dactylella ellipsospora*, an adhesive knob is formed on a short stalk of two cells.

Ring traps are of two kinds, non-constricting and constricting. In *Dactylaria candida*, a branch from the mycelium forms a three-celled ring, attached to the parent hypha by a slender stalk. Nematodes become wedged in the rings and hyphae growing out from the ring cells, penetrate the nematode and absorb its body contents. With this trap, the size of the nematode is critical because those having a diameter less than that of the ring can slip through. This does not happen with the constricting ring which is formed in a similar way, but in which the inside surface of the ring is sensitive to touch. When a nematode enters, the ring cells suddenly inflate to about three times their original volume, closing the opening. The nematode is firmly held in the ring and trophic hyphae from the ring cells absorb the body contents.

Some fungi are internal parasites of nematodes. They usually have a sticky spore which adheres to the cuticle of the nematode, sends a germ tube into it and forms a mycelium which ramifies through the interior of the host until the body contents have disappeared. The genus *Acrostalagmus* is a common example. Hyphae then emerge from the nematode to produce further spores. Van der Laan (1953) frequently found a parasite in the cyst contents of *Heterodera rostochiensis* in Holland; pycnidia were formed on the cyst surface. Van der Laan (1956) also observed that the fungus *Phialophora heteroderae* parasitised eggs of *H. rostochiensis*. Hyphae entered the cysts through the oral and vulval openings and penetrated the egg shell. When added to pots this fungal parasite reduced the number of *H. rostochiensis* cysts formed on the plant roots and the density of larvae within the roots.

Little is known of the geographical distribution or the soil factors which influence distribution of nematode trapping fungi. Gorlenko (1956), for example, found that predacious fungi were widespread in soils of the Soviet Union and he suggested that soil conditions determined feeding habits of the fungi. Some species were predatory in alkaline or neutral soils, but in acid soils they were mainly saprophytic. Shepherd (1956) found that *Arthrobotrys oligospora* was widely distributed in Danish agricultural soils and she concluded that its occurrence was not affected by variations in pH, organic content of the soil or soil structure.

Although studies of predacious fungi in agar cultures are necessary and useful, it is obviously unwise to extrapolate from such observations and suggest what might happen in the soil. Capstick, Twinn and Waid (1957) have confirmed that predacious fungi are active in nematode populations in the soil, although Mankau (1962) has shown that in some soils there are factors which are fugistatic to conidia of some nematode-trapping fungi. Cooke (1962) studied the behaviour of predacious fungi during the decomposition of organic matter in soil and reached the important conclusion that populations of the fungi and free-living nematodes are not in equilibrium. However, quantitative data are still lacking. The relationship between nematodes and their fungal predators appears to be complex. There is evidence that nematode secretions may induce trap formation (Pramer and Stoll, 1959; Tarjan, 1960). On the other hand ring formation may also be genetically controlled, as it is in *Dactylella doedycoides*, so that the ability of a fungus to produce constricting rings may be variable because of nuclear heterogeneity (Feder *et al.*, 1960).

Information on the effects of predacious fungi on nematodes in soil occurs chiefly in the literature on biological control (Chapter 10). However, a few examples at this point will illustrate the nature of the problem. Linford (1937) added chopped pineapple to soil and obtained an effective reduction of root-knot nematode larvae. He attributed this to the activities of nematode-destroying fungi, arguing that an increase in the total population of soil nematodes would be followed by an even greater increase in the numbers of their natural enemies. Linford and Yap (1939) also suggested that *Dactylella ellipsospora* reduced root knot nematode injury to pineapple in pot experiments. Duddington, Everard and Duthoit (1961) studied the influence of *Dactylaria thaumasia* and green manuring (grass mowings) on *Heterodera avenae* in soil plots containing oats. The plots received four treatments: fungus and green manure, fungus only, green manure only and untreated control. The number of nematode cysts was significantly reduced in the first two treatments, although green manure alone also caused a reduction but to a lesser extent. A second, similar experiment indicated that nematode control was greatest in the fungus plus manure treatment, whereas green manure alone failed to produce any effect on nematode numbers. These statistically designed and controlled experiments provide good evidence that predacious fungi may reduce nematode populations. The fact that other attempts to control plant parasitic nematodes by this means have failed (Duddington, Jones and Williams, 1956; Duddington, Jones and Moriarty, 1956; Hutchinson and Mai, 1954; Mankau, 1960; Hams and Wilkin, 1961) do not invalidate this conclusion; they only emphasise the difficulties inherent in the problem.

Although numerous authors, especially Dollfus, Drechsler, Duddington, Muller, Deschiens and Roubaud, have contributed a great deal of information on the taxonomy and biology of nematode trapping fungi, there are many questions still unanswered: What mechanisms control ring constriction? Are the nematode trapping fungi chiefly saprophytic in soil or are they more or less dependent on nematodes for nutrition? How much do these fungi contribute to the nematode mortality rate in soil? What is the relationship between the population dynamics of the fungi and of the nematodes? What soil factors determine their distribution and behaviour? As Duddington (1956) remarks, this is a subject which offers great opportunities for further research. The same can be said of the soil fauna generally. More quantitative data are needed on the population dynamics of nematodes and their parasites and predators in soil before we can begin to discuss such aspects as nematode mortality and biological control.

SOIL TYPE

The influence of soil type on plant parasitic nematodes is a highly complex problem because the physical and chemical factors vary so much between localities, even where the textural composition of the soil is more or less similar. For example, a clay soil under cultivation may have a good crumb structure and be well drained whereas, in an adjacent locality, the same soil type may be lacking in crumb structure and may even be waterlogged because of a high water table and absence of field drains.

In view of this the association between soil type and nematodes in Table 4 must be considered critically. Furthermore, there are several observations where no such association has been found. Hollis and Fielding (1958) found that in Louisiana the distribution of commonly occurring species in the genera *Pratylenchus*, *Trichodorus*, *Tylenchorhynchus*, *Xiphinema*, *Hoplolaimus* and *Helicotylenchus* was independent of soil type. Caveness (1957) studied the nematodes associated with sugar beet production in some northwest and north central states of the U.S.A. He found no evidence that any genus or species of plant parasitic nematode was associated with any particular soil type. A survey of the incidence of *Heterodera schachtii* in California, Colorado and Michigan (Anon, 1957) showed that dense populations were widely distributed. Similarly, in Alabama root knot nematodes were found in soils ranging from light sand to heavy clay (Minton, 1957). The distribution of *Heterodera göttingiana* in the eastern counties of England gives a similar picture. Brown (1958) found that this species occurred on both heavy and light soils. In East Suffolk many attacks occurred in the middle of the county on heavy clay soils and also in coastal areas where the soil was a sandy loam.

Several authors, however, suggest that there is an association between soil type and the distribution of some nematode species. Sasser (1954) states that infestations of *Meloidogyne incognita*, *M. incognita acrita* and *M. hapla* are more severe in the sandy loam soils than in the heavy clay soils of Eastern Maryland. Root knot nematodes (*Meloidogyne* spp.) are a relatively minor problem in the non-irrigated vineyards of the Californian coastal areas, where heavy mineral soils occur (Raski and Lider, 1959). In the major cotton growing areas of California, the greatest infestations of *M. incognita acrita* occur in the coarse textured soils of the San Joaquin Valley; they are less common in the fine textured loams and the clay loams (Thomason and Lear, 1959). In Arizona, too, the heaviest infestations of *M. incognita acrita* occur on the coarse textured soils (O'Bannon and Reynolds, 1961). *Nacobbus batatiformis* is also more common in sandy coarse soils in Nebraska (Thorne and Schuster, 1956). Oostenbrink (1954) examined the roots of several crops of maize and beet in a heterogeneous agricultural area in Holland. He found that *Pratylenchus pratensis* and *P. penetrans* were more abundant in sand and sandy peat soils whereas *P. minyus* occurred chiefly in clay soils. Sol and Seinhorst (1961) state that *Trichodorus pachydermus* occurs most commonly on sandy soils in Holland whether in arable, pasture, woodland or in soil not under cultivation; it is rare in clay soils.

What sort of factors are responsible for these variable and sometimes conflicting observations? The answer probably lies in the wide variation of the biotic, physical and chemical environment within textural categories. Such factors have a profound influence on the general activities of plant nematodes, as the previous part of this chapter has shown and would therefore influence their abundance in a particular area.

But this is not the whole story. Several other factors must also be taken into account. For instance, cropping practice and history may be important in determining distribution, although their effects are often speculative and cannot be measured precisely. Then, too, the vigour of the host plant may vary with differing soil conditions and, with it, the size of the nematode population it can support. A third factor is the degree of tolerance to nematode attack exhibited by a host plant under different soil conditions.   For example, a crop may show few symptoms with a high level of infestation when growing on a fertile peat soil, but succumb to quite low infestations on an infertile sandy soil.   Southey (1956) found that of the fields carrying cereals in England and Wales, a greater percentage was damaged by *Heterodera avenae* on light soils than on medium or heavy soils, although districts with a high proportion of infested fields were not always those where the most serious damage occurred.   Again, Mai and Harrison (1959) suggested that potato plants with nematode-damaged roots may suffer more from lack of water when grown on sandy soils.   This effect on plant tolerance is reflected, once more in the final populations which can be supported, for if the host is seriously damaged, many of the parasites are likely to die before reaching maturity.

Ideally, an association between soil type and nematode distribution can only be reliably established if the survey covers areas of widely differing soil types all carrying similar crops.   The previous cropping history of the areas and the suitability of the soil for crop growth should also be known.   On this basis, Norton (1959) considers that the distribution of some plant nematode species in Texas is influenced chiefly by geological derivation of soils, past natural vegetation, cropping practice and climate.

The moisture-retaining properties of different soil types may also influence nematode distribution.   Clay soils usually retain more water than sandy soils and Ward (1960) suggests that while there are fewer *Xiphinema americanum* in clay soils than in other soil types the chief factor limiting the population increase is soil moisture.   Ahlberg (1951) considers that reproduction of *Heterodera rostochiensis* is low in sandy soils because of their high permeability which tends to produce dry conditions and, that, in spite of this, the nematode is more common and serious on sandy soils in Sweden because of intensive potato growing in these districts.   *Dolichodorus heterocephalus* is encountered more in heavy soils because, Christie (1952) suggests, this species is associated with wet soil conditions.   Overgaard Nielsen (1949) found that some nematodes occurred in all soil types but he considered that the distribution of the others was related to moisture content.   Seinhorst (1950) showed that in Holland, infestations of *Ditylenchus dipsaci* were more frequent on clay soils and he suggested that the high moisture content in such soils favoured infection and movement.   Seinhorst also showed that there was some factor in the sandy soils which inhibited activity.   A survey of the island of Goeree-Overflakkee (Seinhorst, 1956) indicated that there was a very close correlation between high population levels of *D. dipsaci* and the clay soils (Fig. 35).   Cropping practice was not the cause of this distribution because susceptible crops (rye and onions) are grown more on the lightly infested sandy soils.   It is possible, therefore, that the higher moisture levels of clay soils may influence the incidence of some nematode species but whether this is caused directly by moisture, by reduced aeration or by toxic chemicals is unknown.

The cultivation of a crop on a certain soil type and the close association of a nematode species with the crop might produce an apparent nematode-soil-type relationship. Thus, Kleyberg and Oostenbrink (1959) found marked quantitative and qualitative differences in nematode distribution between various farms and nurseries in Holland. Sandy soils were

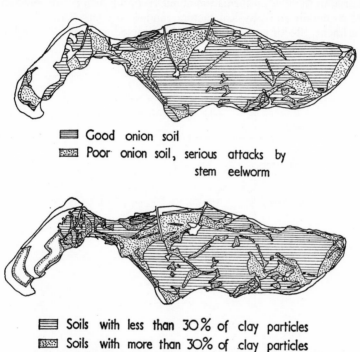

≡ Good onion soil

▒ Poor onion soil, serious attacks by
                 stem eelworm

≡ Soils with less than 30% of clay particles

▒ Soils with more than 30% of clay particles

FIG. 35. Maps of Goeree-Overflakkee in Holland, showing relationship between soil type and occurrence of serious attacks on onions by *Ditylenchus dipsaci*. (After Seinhorst, 1956.)

characterised by the occurrence of *Pratylenchus penetrans* and *Tylenchorhynchus dubius*; clay soils contained *Pratylenchus minyus*, *Pratylenchus thornei* and certain *Tylenchorhynchus* spp. The principle factor influencing populations, however, was the last grown crop. Similarly, in Germany Kemper (1958) compared the distribution of *Heterodera rostochiensis* on two farms. He concluded that infestations were heavier on sandy soils where potatoes were grown more frequently. Petherbridge and Jones (1944) found *Heterodera schachtii* in most soil types, but not in heavy soils where beet is grown less frequently. A survey of cherry orchards in New York State showed that *Pratylenchus penetrans* caused most damage in light soils, and the nematode was rare in heavy soils. However, few orchards were grown in heavy soils because these were unsuitable for tree growth.

When all the factors associated with soil type are considered together, it is not surprising that there is so much variation and contradiction in the field observations. Controlled experiments are probably the only means of assessing the influence of soil type on nematode numbers and activity because, in the field, information about cropping history and practice are hard to obtain and physical factors cannot be controlled. In such an experiment, Sleeth and Reynolds (1955) mixed a loamy sand and a clay

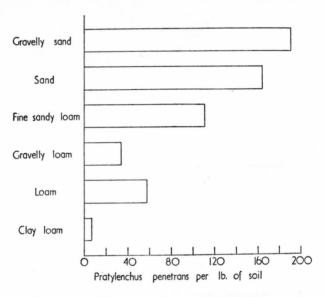

FIG. 36. The relationship between soil type and soil populations of *Pratylenchus penetrans* in peach nursery soils in Canada. (After Mountain and Boyce, 1958.)

loam to give five mixtures. The level of infestation of *Sesbania exaltata* by *Meloidogyne javanica* was then measured in each soil texture. Infestations were very light in the clay loam soil and increased as the proportion of loamy sand increased. Sleeth and Reynolds suggest that a physical analysis of the soil should indicate whether root knot infestations will be serious. This seems to be an over-optimistic appraisal of the situation, as subsequent field observations have shown (Minton, 1957). To determine whether numbers of *Pratylenchus penetrans* were related to general soil types in Ontario peach orchards, soil samples were taken and the nematode populations assessed (Mountain and Boyce, 1958). The results (Fig. 36) showed that the coarse soils contained larger populations of *P. penetrans* than the finer soils. A greenhouse experiment was then done to test this association. Peach seedlings were grown in coarse and fine textured soils infested with *P. penetrans*. Seedling growth in the coarse textured soil was markedly suppressed whereas, in the fine soil, there was little effect compared with seedling growth in uninfested controls. There was no significant difference in seedling growth between the two soil types without nematodes. Although equal numbers of nematodes were introduced into both soil types at the beginning of the experiment, there was a much greater population increase in the coarse textured soil. Endo (1959) grew strawberry and cotton plants in four soil types: sand, sandy loam, loam and clay loam. A suspension of about 500 adults and larvae of *Pratylenchus brachyurus* were added to the different soil types and after 3 months the infestation levels were determined by counting the nematodes in the roots. Infestations were greatest in the sandy loam and least in the sand and clay loam. No controls were run to test the effect of soil type on plant growth so it is difficult to assess the direct influence of the soils on the nematodes. Van Gundy and Rackham (1961) found that the population increase of *Hemicycliophora arenaria* on tomatoes was greater in sandy soil than in a loam soil or a mixture of equal parts of the two. Thomason (1959) compared the development of *Trichodorus christiei* on sudan grass in three soil types: silty clay loam, loam and sandy loam. While this nematode increased most rapidly and reached the highest concentration in the sandy loam, survival was also lowest in this soil type.

In general, clay soils often have a lower permeability to water than sandy soils because their pores are smaller. Consequently clay soils tend to be wetter and less well aerated than sandy soils under the same climatic conditions. During periods of drought, therefore, the surface layers of sandy soils may become very dry and inhibit nematode activity. There are, of course, wide variations within soil types depending on the degree of cultivation and the application of farmyard manure and lime which influence soil structure or crumb formation. When different soil types were sieved to give a uniform crumb structure, the rate of larval emergence from cysts of *Heterodera schachtii* was greatest in the light sandy soils and least in the heavy clays; the emergence rate also tended to be higher among larger than among smaller crumbs in each soil type (Wallace, 1956c). Thus, pore size may influence emergence and measurements of the oxygen consumption of the different soils suggested that in clays there was great competition for oxygen which also reduced emergence. The mobility of *Heterodera rostochiensis* in clay and sandy soils was similar when the soils had the same crumb size (Wallace, 1960). These results emphasise that soil structure as well as texture (per cent clay, silt and sand) should be taken into account when soil type and nematode activity are being studied. Thus, Caveness (1958) suggests that the dense populations of *Heterodera schachtii* in clay soils in the U.S.A. may be related to soil structure.

It is also interesting to note that the migration of zooparasitic nematodes is greater in sandy than in clay soils (Payne, 1923; Lucker, 1936, 1938; Bruns, 1937), whereas *Ascaris* eggs survive longer in heavy clay soils (Beaver, 1953; Seitz, 1953).

Laboratory experiments on the influence of soil type on nematode activity, movement, reproduction, etc., can only be satisfactory if pore size, moisture and temperature are controlled. Even then, interpretation of the results in terms of field conditions is difficult. Nevertheless, the experiments of Mountain and Boyce (1958) on the distribution of *Pratylenchus penetrans* in Ontario soils indicate the value of such an approach. Laboratory experiments may, however, be misleading if the ecology of the nematode is not taken into account. For example, the mobility of *Heterodera rostochiensis* is highest in peat soils and it has been suggested that this may have some bearing on the fact that this nematode is particularly abundant and active in the Fen peat soils of England (Wallace, 1960). Experiments with *Ditylenchus dipsaci* showed that mobility was higher in sandy than in clay soils (Wallace, 1962), although Seinhorst (1950, 1956) found that this nematode was more abundant and destructive on clay soils. At first sight, these results may appear to conflict but *Ditylenchus dipsaci* invades the host plant at or above the soil surface so, in sandy soils, the nematodes probably disperse down through the soil away from the infection sites at the surface. With a root invader, like *Heterodera*, the situation is different, for high mobility in soil increases infestation.

Experimental data, together with field observations (Table 4), suggest that most plant nematode species cause greater crop damage on light sandy soils than on heavy clay soils. This may be due to poor crop growth on the sandy soils, but there is some evidence that such soils have a direct influence on nematode numbers.

The problem has now gone full circle, for to explain the reactions of nematodes to different soil types, the whole complex of physical and biotic soil factors must be considered. It is to this consideration that this chapter has been devoted.

REFERENCES

AHLBERG, O. (1951). *Heterodera rostochiensis*: Distribution in relation to climatic and geographical conditions. *Proc. Int. Nemat. Symp. & training course R.E.S.* Sept. 1951.

ALLEE, W. C., PARK, O., EMERSON, A. E., PARK, T. and SCHMIDT, K. P. (1949). *Principles of animal ecology.* Philadelphia: W. B. Saunders Company.

ANDERSEN, S. (1961). Resistens mod Havreal. *Heterodera avenae. Medd. VetHøjsk. Landb. Plantenkultur. Kbh.* **68**, 1–179 pp.

ANON. (1957). A study of the incidence of nematodes in sugar beet production. *Beet Sugar Development Foundation, Fort Collins, Colorado.*

BAINES, R. C., VAN GUNDY, S. D. and SHER, S. A. (1959). Citrus and avocado nematodes. *Calif. Agric.* **13** (9), 16–18.

BARKER, K. R. (1959). Studies on the biology of the stem nematode. *Phytopathology*, **49** (5), 315.

BARKER, K. R. and SASSER, J. N. (1959). Biology and control of the stem nematode, *Ditylenchus dipsaci*. *Phytopathology*, **49** (10), 664–670.

BASSUS, W. (1960). Die Nematodenfauna des Fichtenrohhumus unter dem Einfluss der Kalkdungung. *Nematologica*, **5**, 86–91.

BEAVER, P. C. (1953). Persistence of hookworm larvae in soil. *Amer. J. trop. Med. Hyg.* **2**, 102–108.

BERGESON, G. B. (1959). The influence of temperature on the survival of some species of the genus *Meloidogyne*, in the absence of a host. *Nematologica*, **4**, 344–354.

BIRCHFIELD, W. (1954). The hot water treatment of nematode infested nursery stock. *Proc. Fla. State hort. Soc.* **67**, 94–96.

BIRD, A. F. (1959). The attractiveness of roots to the plant parasitic nematodes *Meloidogyne javanica* and *M. hapla*. *Nematologica*, **4** (4), 322–335.

BISHOP, D. D. (1953). Hatching the contents of cysts of *Heterodera rostochiensis* with alternating temperature conditions. *Nature, Lond.* **172**, 1108.

—— (1955). The emergence of larvae of *Heterodera rostochiensis* under conditions of constant and alternating temperature. *Ann. appl. Biol.* **43** (4), 525–532.

BLAKE, C. D. (1961a). Importance of osmotic potential as a component of the total potential of the soil water on the movement of nematodes. *Nature, Lond.* **192**, (4798), 144–145.

—— (1961b). Root rot of bananas caused by *Radopholus similis* (Cobb) and its control in New South Wales. *Nematologica*, **6**, 295–310.

—— (1962). Some observations on the orientation of *Ditylenchus dipsaci* and invasion of oat seedlings. *Nematologica*, **8**, 177–192.

BOSHER, J. E. and McKEEN, W. E. (1954). Lyophilisation and low temperature studies with the bulb and stem nematode *Ditylenchus dipsaci* (Kuhn, 1858) Filipjev. *Proc. helm. Soc. Wash.* **21** (2), 113–117.

BROWN, E. B. (1958). Pea root eelworm in the eastern counties of England. *Nematologica*, **3**, 257–268.

BROWN, F. N. (1933). Flooding to control root-knot nematodes. *J. Agric. Res.* **47**, 883–888.

BROWN, W. L. (1954). Collembola feeding upon nematodes. *Ecology*, **35**, 421.

BRUINSMA, F. and SEINHORST, J. W. (1954). Warmwaterbehandeling van sjalotten tegen aantasting door stengelaaltjes (*Ditylenchus dipsaci* (Kühn) Filipjev). *Meded. Directeur van Tuinbouw*, **17**, 437–446.

BRUNS, W. (1937). Das Verhalten der invasionsfähigen Larven der Pferdestrongyliden in verschiedenen Bodenarten. *Inaugural Dissertation, Berlin.* 31 pp.

CAIRASCHI, E. A. (1954). Observations sur une maladie vermiculaire du tabac en Alsace. *C. R. Acad. Agric. Fr.* **40** (2), 75–77.

CAIRNS, E. J. (1953). Moisture conditions and control by heat of the mushroom spawn nematode, *Ditylenchus* spp. *Phytopathology*, **43**, 404.

—— (1954). Effects of temperature upon pathogenicity of the mushroom spawn nematode, *Ditylenchus* sp. *Proc. Int. Conf. Sci. aspects of mushroom growing.* 11. *Gembloux, June 16–20 1953*, 164–167.

CAPSTICK, C. K., TWINN, D. C. and WAID, J. S. (1957). Predation of natural populations of free-living nematodes by fungi. *Nematologica*, **2** (3), 193–201.

CAVENESS, F. E. (1957). A study of nematodes associated with sugar beet production in selected Northwest and North Central states. *Beet Sugar Development Foundation, Fort Collins, Colorado.*

—— (1958). The incidence of *Heterodera schachtii* soil population densities in various soil types. *J. Amer. Soc. Sugar Beet Technol.* **10** (2), 177–180.

CHAPMAN, R. A. (1957). The effect of aeration and temperature on the emergence of species of *Pratylenchus* from roots. *Plant Dis. Reptr.* **41**, 836.

CHITWOOD, B. G. and BUHRER, E. M. (1945). The life history of the golden nematode of potatoes, *Heterodera rostochiensis* Wollenweber, under Long Island, New York, conditions. *Phytopathology*, **36** (3), 180–189.

—— —— (1946). Further studies on the life history of the golden nematode of potatoes, *Heterodera rostochiensis* Wollenweber. *Proc. helm. Soc. Wash.* **13** (2), 54–56.

CHRISTIE, J. R. (1952). Some new nematode species of critical importance to Florida growers. *Proc. Soil Sci. Soc. Fla.* **12**, 30–39.

CHRISTIE, J. R. and CROSSMAN, L. (1935). Water temperatures lethal to begonia, chrysanthemum and strawberry 'strains' of the nematode *Aphelenchoides fragariae* (Anguillulinidae). *Proc. helm. Soc. Wash.* **2** (2), 98–103.

COLLIS-GEORGE, N. and BLAKE, C. D. (1959). The influence of the soil moisture regime on the expulsion of the larval mass of the nematode *Anguina agrostis* from galls. *Aust. J. Biol. Sci.* **12** (3), 247–256.

COOKE, R. C. (1962). Behaviour of nematode-trapping fungi during decomposition of organic matter in the soil. *Trans. Brit. mycol. Soc.* **45**, 314–320.

COUCH, H. B. and BLOOM, J. R. (1960). Influence of soil moisture stresses on the development of the root-knot nematode. *Phytopathology*, **50** (4), 319–321.

COURTNEY, W. D. and LATTA, R. (1934). Some experiments concerning the revival of quiescent *Anguillulina dipsaci*. *Proc. helm. Soc. Wash.* **1** (1), 20.

CRITTENDEN, H. W. (1953). Effect of clean fallow in root-knot development in soybeans. *Phytopathology*, **43**, 405.

DAULTON, R. A. and NUSBAUM, C. J. (1962). The effect of soil temperature on the survival of the root knot nematodes *Meloidogyne javanica* and *M. hapla*. *Nematologica*, **6**, 280–294.

DOLLIVER, J. S., HILDEBRANDT, A. C. and RIKER, A. J. (1962). Studies of reproduction of *Aphelenchoides ritzemabosi* (Schwartz) on plant tissues in culture. *Nematologica*, **7**, 294–300.

DONCASTER, C. C. (1956). Electronic flash in photomicrography. *Nematologica*, **1** (1), 51–55.

—— (1962). Natürliche Feinde wirtschaftlich bedeutsamer Schadnematoden. *Die Umschau in Wissenschaft und Technik.* **14**, 443–446.

DONCASTER, C. C. and HOOPER, D. J. (1961). Nematodes attacked by protozoa and tardigrades. *Nematologica*, **6** (4), 333–335.

DROPKIN, V. H., MARTIN, C. G. and JOHNSON, R. W. (1958). Effect of osmotic concentration on hatching of some plant parasitic nematodes. *Nematologica*, **3**, 115–126.

DUDDINGTON, C. L. (1956). The predacious fungi: zoopagales and moniliales. *Biological Reviews*, **31**, 152–193.

—— (1960). Biological control—Predacious fungi. In: *Nematology fundamentals and recent advances with emphasis on plant parasitic and soil forms.* Edited by J. N. Sasser and W. R. Jenkins. Chapter 45. Chapel Hill: Univ. North Carolina Press.

DUDDINGTON, C. L., EVERARD, C. O. R. and DUTHOIT, C. M. G. (1961). Effect of green manuring and a predacious fungus on cereal root eelworm in oats. *Plant Pathology*, **10** (3), 108–109.

DUDDINGTON, C. L., JONES, F. G. W. and MORIARTY, F. (1956). The effect of predacious fungus and organic matter upon the soil population of beet eelworm, *Heterodera schachtii* Schm. *Nematologica*, **1** (4), 344–348.

DUDDINGTON, C. L., JONES, F. G. W. and WILLIAMS, T. D. (1956). An experiment on the effect of a predacious fungus upon the soil population of potato root eelworm, *Heterodera rostochiensis* Woll. *Nematologica*, **1** (4), 341–343.

DUGGAN, J. J. (1960). Effect of soil drying on the viability of *Heterodera major* cysts. *Nature, Lond.*, **185**, 554–555.

ELLENBY, C. (1946). Ecology of the eelworm cyst. *Nature, Lond.*, **157**, 451.

ELLENBY, C. and GILBERT, A. B. (1958). Influence of certain inorganic ions on the hatching of the potato root eelworm, *Heterodera rostochiensis* Wollenweber. *Nature, Lond.* **182** (4628), 121–122.

ENDO, B. Y. (1959). Responses of root-lesion nematodes, *Pratylenchus brachyurus* and *P. zeae* to various plants and soil types. *Phytopathology*, **49** (7), 417–421.

—— (1962). Survival of *Heterodera glycines* at controlled relative humidities. *Phytopathology*, **52** (1), 80–88.

EPPS, J. E. (1958). Viability of air dried *Heterodera glycines* cysts. *Plant Dis. Reptr.* **42** (5), 594–596.

FEDER, W. A. (1960). Osmotic destruction of plant parasitic and saprophytic nematodes by the addition of sugars to soil. *Plant Dis. Reptr.* **44** (12), 883–885.

FEDER, W. A. and FELDMESSER, J. (1955). Further studies on plant parasitic nematodes maintained in altered oxygen tensions. *J. Parasitol.* **41**, 47.

FEDER, W. A., EVERARD, C. O. R. and DUDDINGTON, C. L. (1960). Heterocaryotic nature of ring formation in the predacious fungus *Dactylella doedycoides*. *Science*, **131** (3404), 922–924.

FELDMESSER, J. and FEDER, W. A. (1954). Some effects of altered oxygen tensions on certain plant parasitic and soil inhabiting nematodes *in vitro*. *J. Parasitol.* **40**, 18.

FENWICK, D. W. (1951a). Investigations on the emergence of larvae from the cysts of the potato root eelworm, *Heterodera rostochiensis*. 4. Physical conditions and their influence on larval emergence in the laboratory. *J. Helminth.* **25** (1/2), 37–48.

—— (1951b). The effect of temperature on the development of the potato root eeelworm, *Heterodera rostochiensis*. *Ann. appl. Biol.* **38** (3), 615–617.

FERRIS, J. M. (1957). Effect of soil temperature on the life cycle of the golden nematode in host and non-host species. *Phytopathology*, **47**, 221.

GILLARD, A. (1961). Onderzoekingen omtrent de biologie, de verspreiding en de bestrijding van wortelknobbelaaltjes (*Meloidogyne* spp.). *Meded. LandbHoogesch. Gent.* **26** (2), 515–646.

GILLARD, A., D'HERDE, J. and BRANDE, J., VAN DEN (1958). Invloed van koolzuur op het uitkomen der larven van *Heterodera rostochiensis*. *Meded. LandbHoogesch. Gent.* **23** (3/4), 689–694.

GODFREY, G. H. (1926). Effect of temperature and moisture on nematode root knot. *J. agric. Res.* **33** (3), 223–254.

GODFREY, G. H. and HAGAN, H. R. (1933). Influence of soil hydrogen-ion concentration on infection by *Heterodera radicicola* (Greeff) Muller. *Soil Science,* **35**, 175–184.

GODFREY, G. H. and HOSHINO, H. M. (1933). Studies on certain environmental relations of root knot nematode *Heterodera radicicola*. *Phytopathology,* **23**, 41–62.

GOLDEN, A. M. (1957). Occurrence of *Radopholus gracilis* (Nematoda: Tylenchidae) in the United States. *Plant Dis. Reptr.* **41** (2), 91.

GORLENKO, M. V. (1956). Predatory fungi and their utilisation in nematode control. *Nematologica,* **1** (2), 147–150.

GUNDY, S. D., VAN (1958). The life history of the citrus nematode, *Tylenchulus semipenetrans* Cobb. *Nematologica,* **3** (4), 283–294.

GUNDY, S. D., VAN and RACKHAM, R. L. (1961). Studies on the biology and pathogenicity of *Hemicycliophora arenaria*. *Phytopathology,* **51** (6), 393–397.

GUNDY, S. D., VAN and STOLZY, L. H. (1961). Influence of soil oxygen concentrations on the development of *Meloidogyne javanica*. *Science,* **134** (3480), 665.

GUNDY, S. D., VAN, STOLZY, L. H., SZUSZKIEWICZ, T. E. and RACKHAM, R. L. (1962). Influence of oxygen supply on survival of plant parasitic nematodes in soil. *Phytopathology,* **52** (7), 628–632.

HAMBLEN, M. L. and SLACK, D. A. (1959). Factors influencing the emergence of larvae from cysts of *Heterodera glycines* Ichinohe. Cyst development, condition and variability. *Phytopathology,* **49** (5), 317.

HAMS, A. F. and WILKIN, G. D. (1961). Observations on the use of predacious fungi for the control of *Heterodera* spp. *Ann. appl. Biol.* **49**, 515–523.

HASTINGS, R. J. and NEWTON, W. (1934). The influence of a number of factors upon the activation of dormant or quiescent bulb nematodes, *Anguillulina dipsaci* (Kuhn, 1858) Gerv. and v. Ben., 1859 (Anguillulinidae). *Proc. helm. Soc. Wash.* **1** (2), 52–54.

HENDERSON, V. E. and KATZNELSON, H. (1961). The effect of plant roots on the nematode population of the soil. *Canad. J. Microbiol.* **7**, 163–167.

HESLING, J. J. (1956). Some observations on *Heterodera major*. *Nematologica,* **1** (1), 56–63.

HOLLIS, J. P. and FIELDING, M. J. (1958). Population behaviour of plant parasitic nematodes in soil fumigation experiments. *La. State Univ. agric. Exp. Sta.* Bull. **515**, 1–30.

HOLLIS, J. P. and JOHNSTON, T. (1957). Microbiological reduction of nematode populations in water saturated soils. *Phytopathology,* **47** (1), 16.

HUTCHINSON, M. T. and STREU, H. T. (1960). Tardigrades attacking nematodes. *Nematologica,* **5** (2), 149.

HUTCHINSON, S. A. and MAI, W. F. (1954). A study of the efficiency of the catching organs of *Dactylaria endermata* (Drechs) in relation to *Heterodera rostochiensis* (Wr.) in soil. *Plant Dis. Reptr.* **38** (3), 185–186.

ICHINOHE, M. (1955). Studies on the morphology and ecology of the soybean nematode. *Hokkaido Agr. Exp. Sta. Rept.* **48**, 1–64. (In Japanese.)

JOHNSTON, T. (1957). Further studies on microbiological reduction of nematode population in water saturated soils. *Phytopathologist*, **47** (9), 525–526.

—— (1958). The effect of soil moisture on *Tylenchorhynchus martini* and other nematodes. *Proc. La. Acad. Sci.*, **20**, 52–55.

KÄMPFE, L. (1955). Die Aktivität von Kartoffel-und Rübennematoden bei verschiedenen Temperaturen und ihre Bedeutung für die Mittelprüfung. *Mitt. Biol. Zent. Anst. Berlin*, **83**, 139–142.

—— (1958). Physiologische Befunde zur Arttrennung und zum Herkunftsnachweis in der Gattung *Heterodera* Schmidt (Nematodes). *Ver. Deutsch. Zool. Ges. Frankfurt.* **25**, 383–391.

—— (1959a). Zur Physiologie von *Heterodera* larven unter Laboratoriumsbedingungen als Testobjekte für Nematizidprufungen. *Verh. IV Int. Pflz. Kongresses Hamburg* (1957), **1**, 605–611.

—— (1959b). Über Möglichkeiten der physiologisch-ökologischen Arbeitsweise in der Nematodenforschung. *Verh. d. Deutsch Zool.* (1959), **25**, 378–386.

KEMPER, A. (1958). Kann eine weitere Ausbreitung des Kartoffelnematoden verhindert werden? *Anz. Schadlingsk.* **31** (11), 165–170.

KLEYBURG, P. and OOSTENBRINK, M. (1959). Nematodes in relation to plant growth. 1. The nematode distribution pattern of typical farms and nurseries. *Neth. J. agric. Sci.* **7** (4), 327–343.

KORT, J. and S'JACOB, J. J. (1956). Een orienterend onderzoek naar het voorkomen van en de Schade veroorzaakt door het Havercystenaaltje. *T. Pl. ziekten.* **62**, 7–11.

KRUSBERG, L. R. (1959). Investigations on the life cycle, reproduction, feeding habits and host range of *Tylenchorhynchus claytoni* Steiner. *Nematologica*, **4**, 187–197.

KUIPER, K. (1958). Parasitering van aaltjes door protozoen. *T. Pl. ziekten.* **64**, 122.

LAAN, P. A., VAN DER (1953). Een schimmel als parasiet van de cysteinhoud van het aardappelcystenaaltje (*Heterodera rostochiensis* Wollenw). *T. Pl. ziekten.* **59** (3), 101–103.

—— (1956). Onderzoekingen over schimmels, die parasiteren op de cysteinhoud van het aardappelcystenaaltje (*Heterodera rostochiensis* Wollenw.). *T. Pl. ziekten.* **62** (6), 305–321.

LEWIS, F. J. and MAI, W. F. (1957). Survival of encysted eggs and larvae of the golden nematode to alternating temperatures. *Phytopathology*, **47**, 527.

—— —— (1960). Survival of encysted and free larvae of the golden nematode in relation to temperature and relative humidity. *Proc. helm. Soc. Wash.* **27** (1), 80–85.

LINFORD, M. B. (1937). Stimulated activity of natural enemies of nematodes. *Science*, **85** (2196), 123–124.

—— (1954). Pathogenicity tests with the clover root nematode. *Phytopathology*, **44**, 496.

LINFORD, M. B. and OLIVEIRA, J. M. (1937). The feeding of hollow spear nematodes on other nematodes. *Science*, **85** (2203), 295–297.

LINFORD, M. B. and YAP, F. (1939). Root-knot nematode injury restricted by a fungus. *Phytopathology*, **29** (7), 596–609.

LOEWENBERG, J. R., SULLIVAN, T. and SCHUSTER, M. L. (1959). A virus disease of *Meloidogyne incognita incognita*, the southern root knot nematode, *Nature, Lond.* **184** (4702), 1896.

—— —— —— (1960). The effect of pH and minerals on the hatching and survival of *Meloidogyne incognita* larvae. *Phytopathology*, **50** (3), 215–217.

LOWNSBERY, B. F. (1950). Stimulation of golden nematode larvae by root leachings. *Phytopathology*, **40**, 18.

—— (1961). Factors affecting population levels of *Criconemoides xenoplax*. *Phytopathology*, **51** (2), 101–104.

LUC, M. (1961). Note préliminaire sur le déplacement de *Hemicycliophora paradoxa* Luc (Nematoda, Criconematidae) dans le sol. *Nematologica*, **6**, 95–106.

LUCKER, J. T. (1936). Extent of vertical migration of horse strongyle larvae in soils of different types. *J. agric. Res.* **52**, 353–361.

—— (1938). Vertical migration, distribution and survival of infective horse strongyle larvae developing in feces buried in different soils. *J. agric. Res.* **57**, 335–348.

MACHMER, J. H. (1958). Effect of soil salinity on nematodes in citrus and papaya plantings. *J. Rio Grande Valley hort. Soc.*, **12**, 57–60.

MAI, W. F. (1952). Temperature in relation to retention of viability of encysted larvae of the golden nematode of potato, *Heterodera rostochiensis* Wollenweber. *Phytopathology*, **42** (2), 113.

MAI, W. F. and HARRISON, M. B. (1959). The golden nematode. *Cornell Ext.* Bull. **870**.

MANKAU, R. (1960). The use of nematode trapping fungi to control root-knot nematodes. *Phytopathology*, **50** (9), 645.

—— (1962). Soil fungistasis and nematophagus fungi. *Phytopathology*, **52**, 611–615.

MINTON, N. A. (1957). Distribution of root knot nematode in Alabama. *J. Alabama Acad. Sci.* **29**, Oct. 1st, 1957.

MINTON, N. A., CAIRNS, E. J. and SMITH, A. L. (1960). Effect on root knot nematode populations of resistant and susceptible cotton. *Phytopathology*, **50** (11), 784–787.

MOUNTAIN, W. B. and BOYCE, H. R. (1958). The peach replant problem in Ontario. 5. The relation of parasitic nematodes to regional differences in severity of peach replant failure. *Canad. J. Bot.* **36**, 125–134.

MURPHY, P. W. and DONCASTER, C. C. (1957). A culture method for soil meiofauna and its application to the study of nematode predators. *Nematologica*, **2** (3), 202–214.

NIELSEN, C. O. (1949). Studies on the soil microfauna. 11. The soil inhabiting nematodes. *Natura Jutlandica*, **2**, 1–131.

NORTON, D. C. (1959). Relationship of nematodes to small grains and native grasses in north and central Texas. *Plant Dis. Reptr.* **43** (2), 227–235.

O'BANNON, J. H. and REYNOLDS, H. W. (1961). Root knot nematode damage and cotton yields in relation to certain soil properties. *Soil Sci.* **92**, 384–386.

OOSTENBRINK, M. (1954). Over de betekenis van vrijlevende wortelaaltjes in land-en tuinbouw. *Versl. Pl. Ziekt. Dienst Wageningen*, **124**, 196–233.

—— (1958). Grondontsmetting en pH. *Meded. LandbHoogesch. Gent*, **23** (3/4), 628–635.

PARRIS, G. K. (1948).   Influence of soil moisture on the growth of the potato plant and its infection by the root knot nematode.   *Phytopathology*, **38**, 480–488.

PAYNE, F. K. (1923).   Investigations on the control of hookworm disease. XXX. Studies on factors involved in migration of hookworm larvae in soil.   *Amer. J. Hyg.* **3**, 547–583.

PEACOCK, F. C. (1957).   Studies on root-knot nematodes of the genus *Meloidogyne* in the Gold Coast.   Part 2.   *Nematologica*, **2** (2), 114–122.

PERRY, V. G. (1953).   The awl nematode, *Dolichodorus heterocephalus*, a devastating plant parasite.   *Proc. helm. Soc. Wash.* **20** (1), 21–27.

PETERS, B. G. (1926).   *Heterodera schachtii* (Schmidt) and soil acidity.   *J. Helminth.* **4** (3), 87–114.

PETHERBRIDGE, F. R. and JONES, F. G. W. (1944).   Beet eelworm (*Heterodera schachtii* Schm.) in East Anglia, 1934–1943.   *Ann. appl. Biol.* **31** (4), 320–332.

PRAMER, D. and STOLL, N. R. (1959).   Nemin: a morphogenic substance causing trap formation by predacious fungi.   *Science*, **129** (3354), 966–967.

RASKI, D. J. and JOHNSON, R. T. (1959).   Temperature and activity of the sugar beet nematode as related to sugar beet production.   *Nematologica*, **4**, 136–141.

RASKI, D. J. and LIDER, L. (1959).   Nematodes in grape production.   *Calif. Agric.* **13** (9), 13–15.

REUVER, I. (1959).   Untersuchungen uber *Paratylenchus amblycephalus* n. sp. (Nematoda, Criconematidae).   *Nematologica*, **4** (1), 3–15.

RHOADES, H. L. and LINFORD, M. B. (1959).   Molting of pre-adult nematodes of the genus *Paratylenchus* stimulated by root diffusates.   *Science*, **130** (3387), 1476–1477.

———— (1961).   Biological studies on some members of the genus *Paratylenchus*.   *Proc. helm. Soc. Wash.* **28** (1), 51–59.

ROBINSON, T. (1956).   Factors influencing emergence of larvae of the golden nematode (*Heterodera rostochiensis* Wollenweber).   *Diss. Abstr.* **16** (8), 1335–1336.

ROBINSON, T. and NEAL, A. L. (1956).   The influence of hydrogen ion concentration on the emergence of golden nematode larvae.   *Phytopathology*, **46**, 665.

———— (1959).   The influence of certain mineral elements on emergence of golden nematode larvae.   *Proc. helm. Soc. Wash.* **26** (1), 60–64.

ROHDE, R. A. (1960).   The influence of carbon dioxide on respiration of certain plant parasitic nematodes.   *Proc. helm. Soc. Wash.* **27** (2), 160–164.

ROHDE, R. A. and JENKINS, W. R. (1957).   Effect of temperature on the life cycle of stubby root nematodes.   *Phytopathology*, **47** (1), 29.

ROSS, J. P. (1960).   The effect of soil temperature on development of *Heterodera glycines* in soybeans.   *Phytopathology*, **50** (9), 652.

SANTMYER, P. H. (1955).   A comparison of the thermal death time of two dissimilar species of nematodes: *Panagrellus redivivus* (Linn. 1767) Goodey, 1945, and *Meloidogyne incognita* var. *acrita* Chitwood, 1949.   *Proc. helm. Soc. Wash.* **22** (1), 22–25.

SASSER, J. N. (1954).   Identification and host-parasite relationships of certain root-knot nematodes (Meloidogyne sp.).   *Univ. Md. agric. Expt. Sta. Bull.* **A-77**.

SAYRE, R. M. and MOUNTAIN, W. B. (1962). The bulb and stem nematode (*Ditylenchus dipsaci*) on onion in Southwestern Ontario. *Phytopathology*, **52** (6), 510–516.

SCHAERFFENBERG, B. (1951). Untersuchungen über die Bedeutung der Enchytraeiden als Nematodenfeinde. *Mitt. biol. Zent. Anst. Berl.* **70**, 55–58.

SCHAERFFENBERG, B. and TENDL, H. (1951). Untersuchungen über das Verhalten der Enchytraeiden gegenuber dem Zuckerrubennematoden, *Heterodera schachtii* (Schm.) *Z. angew. Ent.* **32** (3), 476–488.

SEINHORST, J. W. (1950). De betekenis van de toestand van de grond voor het optreden van aantasting door het stengelaaltje (*Ditylenchus dipsaci* (Kuhn) Filipjev). *T. Pl. ziekten*, **56** (5/6), 289–348.

—— (1956). Population studies on stem eelworms (*Ditylenchus dipsaci*). *Nematologica*, **1** (2), 159–164.

SEITZ, K. (1953). Über Zusammenhänge Zwischen Askaridiasis und Bodenbeschaffenheit. *Medizinische, Stuttgart* (1953), **9**, 287–288.

SHEPHERD, A. M. (1956). A short survey of Danish nematophagous fungi. *Friesia, Copenhagen*, **5** (3/5), 396–408.

—— (1959). Increasing the rate of larval emergence from cysts in hatching tests with beet eelworm, *Heterodera schachtii* Schmidt. *Nematologica*, **4**, 161–164.

SHEPHERD, A. M. and WALLACE, H. R. (1959). A comparison of the rates of emergence and invasion of beet eelworm, *Heterodera schachtii* Schmidt and pea root eelworm *Heterodera göttingiana* Liebscher. *Nematologica*, **4**, 227–235.

SIMON, M. (1955). L'étude du rapport entre le pH du sol et les nématodes. *Publ. Inst. belge Amelior. Better.* **22** (3), 85–89.

SLACK, D. A. and HAMBLEN, M. L. (1959). Factors influencing emergence of larvae from cysts of *Heterodera glycines* Ichinohe. Influence of constant temperature. *Phytopathology*, **49** (5), 319–320.

—— —— (1961). The effect of various factors on larval emergence from cysts of *Heterodera glycines*. *Phytopathology*, **51** (6), 350–355.

SLEETH, B. and REYNOLDS, H. W. (1955). Root-knot nematode infestation as influenced by soil texture. *Soil Science*, **80** (6), 459–461.

SOL, H. H. and SEINHORST, J. W. (1961). The transmission of rattle virus by *Trichodorus pachydermus*. *T. Pl. ziekten*, **67**, 307–311.

SOUTHEY, J. F. (1956). National survey work for cereal root eelworm (*Heterodera major* (O. Schmidt) Franklin). *Nematologica*, **1** (1), 64–71.

STANILAND, L. N. (1950). Experiments on the control of chrysanthemum eelworm (*Aphelenchoides ritzema-bosi*, Schwartz) by hot water treatment. *Ann. appl. Biol.* **37**, 11–18.

STEINER, G. (1952). The soil in its relationship to plant nematodes. *Proc. Soil Sci. Soc. Fla.* **12**, 24–29.

STEINER, G. and HEINLY, H. (1922). The possibility of control of *Heterodera radicicola* and other plant injurious nemas by predatory nemas, especially by *Mononchus papillatus* Bastian. *J. Wash. Acad. Sci.* **12** (16), 367–386.

STEPHENSON, W. (1942). Resistance of a soil nematode to changes in osmotic pressure. *Nature, Lond.* **149** (3783), 500.

STOLZY, L. H., GUNDY, S. D., VAN and LETEY, J. (1960). Oxygen tolerances of four plant parasitic nematodes. *Phytopathology*, **50**, 656.

TARJAN, A. C. (1960). Induction of traps of nematophagous fungi using *Panagrellus redivivus*. *Nature, Lond.* **185** (4715), 779–780.

THAMES, W. H. (1952). The benefits of flooding in the control of nematodes. *Proc. Soil Sci. Soc. Fla.* **76**, 77.

THOMASON, I. J. (1959). Influence of soil texture on development of the stubby root nematode. *Phytopathology*, **49** (9), 552.

THOMASON, I. J. and FIFE, D. (1962). The effect of temperature on development and survival of *Heterodera schachtii* Schm. *Nematologica*, **7**, 139–145.

THOMASON, I. J. and LEAR, B. (1959). Field and vegetable crops. *Calif. Agric.* **13** (9), 8–12.

—— —— (1961). Rate of reproduction of *Meloidogyne* spp. as influenced by soil temperatures. *Phytopathology*, **51** (8), 520–524.

THORNE, G. (1927). The life history, habits and economic importance of some *Mononchs*. *J. agric. Res.* **34** (3), 265–286.

—— (1928). Nematodes inhabiting the cysts of the sugar-beet nematode (*Heterodera schachtii* Schmidt). *J. agric. Res.* **37** (10), 571–575.

—— (1930). Predacious nemas of the genus *Nygolaimus* and a new genus *Sectonema*. *J. agric. Res.* **41** (6), 445–466.

—— (1940). *Dubosquia penetrans* n.sp. (Sporozoa; Microsporidia, Nosematidae) a parasite of the nematode *Pratylenchus pratensis* (de Man) Filipjev. *Proc. helm. Soc. Wash.* **7** (1), 51–53.

THORNE, G. and SCHUSTER, M. L. (1956). *Nacobbus batatiformis* n.sp. (Nematoda: Tylenchidae) producing galls on the roots of sugar beets and other plants. *Proc. helm. Soc. Wash.* **23** (2), 128–134.

TRIFFITT, M. J. (1930). Observations on the life cycle of *Heterodera schachtii*. *J. Helminth.* **8** (4), 185–196.

TRIFFITT, M. J. and HURST, R. H. (1935). On the thermal death point of *Heterodera schachtii*. *J. Helminth.* **13** (4), 219–223.

TYLER, J. (1933). Development of the root knot nematode as affected by temperature. *Hilgardia*, **7**, 392–415.

VIGLIERCHIO, D. R. (1961). Effects of storage environment on '*in vitro*' hatching of larvae from cysts of *Heterodera schachtii* Schmidt 1871. *Phytopathology*, **51** (9), 623–625.

WALKER, J. T. (1960). The effect of hot water at different temperatures on larvae of various species of *Meloidogyne*. *Phytopathology*, **50** (9), 658.

WALLACE, H. R. (1954). Hydrostatic pressure deficiency and the emergence of larvae from cysts of the beet eelworm. *Nature, Lond.* **173**, 502.

—— (1955a). Factors influencing the emergence of larvae from cysts of the beet eelworm, *Heterodera schachtii* Schmidt. *J. Helminth.* **29**, 3–16.

—— (1955b). The influence of soil moisture on the emergence of larvae from cysts of the beet eelworm, *Heterodera schachtii* Schmidt. *Ann. appl. Biol.* **43**, 477–484.

—— (1956a). The effect of soil structure on the emergence of larvae from cysts of the beet eelworm. *Nematologica*, **1**, 145–146.

—— (1956b). The seasonal emergence of larvae from cysts of the beet eelworm, *Heterodera schachtii* Schmidt. *Nematologica*, **1**, 227–238.

—— (1956c). Soil aeration and the emergence of larvae from cysts of the beet eelworm, *Heterodera schachtii* Schmidt. *Ann. appl. Biol.* **44**, 57–66.

—— (1956d). The emergence of larvae from cysts of the beet eelworm,

Heterodera schachtii Schmidt in aqueous solutions of organic and inorganic substances. *Ann. appl. Biol.* **44**, 274–282.

—— (1958). Movement of eelworms. 2. A comparative study of the movement in soil of *Heterodera schachtii* Schmidt and of *Ditylenchus dipsaci* (Kühn) Filipjev. *Ann. appl. Biol.* **46**, 86–94.

—— (1959). Further observations on some factors influencing the emergence of larvae from cysts of the beet eelworm, *Heterodera schachtii* Schmidt. *Nematologica*, **4**, 245–252.

—— (1960). Movement of eelworms. 6. The influence of soil type, moisture gradients and host plant roots on migration of the potato root eelworm, *Heterodera rostochiensis* Wollenweber. *Ann. appl. Biol.* **48**, 107–120.

—— (1961). The orientation of *Ditylenchus dipsaci* to physical stimuli. *Nematologica*, **6**, 222–236.

—— (1962). Observations on the behaviour of *Ditylenchus dipsaci* in soil. *Nematologica*, **7**, 91–101.

WARD, C. H. (1960). Dagger nematodes associated with forage crops in New York. *Phytopathology*, **50** (9), 658.

WEBER, A. P., ZWILLENBERG, L. O. and LAAN, P. A., VAN DER (1952). A predacious amoeboid organism destroying larvae of the potato root eelworm and other nematodes. *Nature, Lond.* **169** (4307), 834–835.

WILLIAMS, J. R. (1960). Studies on the nematode soil fauna of sugarcane fields in Mauritius. 5. Notes upon a parasite of root-knot nematodes. *Nematologica*, **5** (1), 37–42.

WINSLOW, R. D. (1955). The hatching responses of some root eelworms of the genus *Heterodera*. *Ann. appl. Biol.* **43** (4), 19–36.

—— (1960). Some aspects of the ecology of freeliving and plant parasitic nematodes. In: *Nematology fundamentals and recent advances with emphasis on plant parasitic and soil forms.* Edited by J. N. Sasser and W. R. Jenkins. Chapter 36. Chapel Hill: Univ. North Carolina Press.

WINSLOW, R. D. and WILLIAMS, T. D. (1957). Amoeboid organisms attacking larvae of the potato root eelworm (*Heterodera rostochiensis* Woll.) in England and the beet eelworm (*H. schachtii* Schm.) in Canada. *T. Pl. ziekten.* **63**, 242–243.

ZWILLENBERG, L. O. (1953). *Theratromyxa weberi* a new proteomyxean organism from soil. *Anthonie v. Leeuwenhoek*, **19**, 101–116.

CHAPTER 5

Movement

Most species of plant nematodes have a freeliving stage when they move through the soil or on the surface of plants above ground. This may involve a migration towards a host plant after hatching in the soil or from one feeding site to another. Migration is, therefore, a prerequisite to invasion or to external feeding and any inhibition of such movement will be reflected in the population dynamics of the species. The importance of nematode movement is related to localised activities near the host plant rather than to the spread of the nematode over large areas. Figures have been quoted for the rate of spread of nematodes in soil but in general these seldom exceed 1 to 2 m a year. Fuch's (1911) claim that *Heterodera schachtii* larvae could travel 15 to 24 m a year is probably an overestimate. Of course, nematodes may be carried passively over large distances by water, wind or animals, especially man, but the nematodes own activities are of little importance here.

UNDULATORY PROPULSION

Nematodes are entirely dependent on water for movement. In the absence of water some species dry out and die whereas others survive but become quiescent; no nematodes can move without water. Like snakes, eels, spermatozoa, ceratopogonid larvae and many other animals, nematodes form bending waves which pass antero-posteriorly along the body. Such waves are seen most distinctly when the nematodes are moving in thin water films or between soil particles; in fact, undulatory propulsion is, with few exceptions, a characteristic of nematodes. Thus the locomotion of nematodes in soil and of *Ascaris* in the bile duct (Akimoto, 1950) is essentially similar. The bending waves are formed by coordinated contraction and relaxation of the longitudinal muscles on opposite sides of the body in a dorso-ventral plane to give a draconian type of movement. In thin water films, therefore, nematodes move along on their sides, unlike snakes which crawl on their ventral surface with a serpentine movement. However, the fundamental principles of undulatory propulsion are the same for snakes and nematodes as well as for other organisms which move in this way.

To form bending waves the body must be subjected to bending couples. In snakes the rigid vertebrae prevent any compression of the longitudinal axis of the body and so any muscular tension developed on one side of the axis induces compression of the vertebral axis. Equal and opposite bending couples are thereby developed in the vertebrae concerned. In nematodes, bending couples are formed by the action of the longitudinal muscles opposed by the forces exerted by the internal hydrostatic pressure on the cuticle, and the organisation of the nematode body is well adapted to provide such a system. The cuticle has at least two component parts one of which consists of a system of inextensible diagonal or spiral

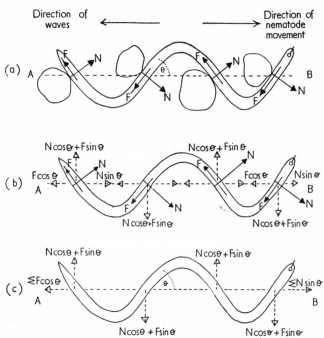

FIG. 37. A diagram showing the forces acting on a nematode moving by undulatory propulsion in a rigid environment. (a) The normal reaction N and the friction force F are shown where the body touches external resistances such as soil particles. θ is the angle between the axis AB and the nematode. (b) The forces F and N are resolved along and at right angles to the axis AB (the resolved forces are only shown at the ends of the nematode). (c) The resultant of all the forces is zero at right angles to the axis AB, and when $\sum F \cos \theta = \sum N \sin \theta$, steady motion occurs. (Based on data of Gray, 1953.)

fibres and the other is elastic. This system allows anisometric extension and shortening of the cuticle giving a constant length at any given internal volume (Harris and Crofton, 1957).

How does a train of bending waves passing posteriorly along the body propel a nematode forward? Before answering this question it is necessary to distinguish between locomotion in a more or less rigid environment (crawling) and locomotion in deep water (swimming).

In a rigid environment such as the soil or in thin water films, nematodes form symmetrical bending waves in which each part of the body follows the part in front. Ciné film of moving nematodes (Wallace, 1959c) and photographs of nematode tracks (Rode and Staar, 1961) illustrate this point well (see Plate III). The propulsive thrust necessary to maintain motion is derived from the external forces acting at right angles to the surface of the nematode. During steady motion these forces are equal and opposite to the tangential drag. Gray's (1946, 1951) detailed studies of the mechanics of undulatory locomotion enable nematode locomotion to be described in the following simplified manner.

A nematode moving through soil touches soil particles at different points on its body (Fig. 37a). The thrust of the nematode at each point is opposed by an equal but opposite force N acting at right angles to the body. Also acting through this point is a tangential force F, due to friction, along the axis of the body and opposed to the direction of motion. When the forces F and N are resolved parallel and at right angles to the direction of the nematode track AB (Fig. 37b) the sum of the forces at right angles to the track, $\sum N \cos \theta + \sum F \sin \theta$, is zero and during steady motion the forces acting parallel to the track are equal but opposite, i.e. $N \sin \theta = F \cos \theta$ or $F = N \tan \theta$, where θ is the angle between AB and the nematode body. The magnitude of F will depend on the coefficient of friction (μ) of the substratum and with an increase in F the nematode would have to increase θ to move. Thus waves of larger amplitude would have to be formed. Friction also acts at the points of contact between the body and the external resistances and so the forward tangential thrust (P) becomes $P - \mu N$ (Fig. 37c). Since $\tan \theta = P/N$ the forward thrust becomes $P - \mu P / \tan \theta$ or $P(1 - \mu \cot \theta)$. If $\mu = \tan \theta$ the forward thrust is zero and the nematode cannot move, so it would have to increase θ. Thus an increase in both types of friction induces waves of greater amplitude and shorter wavelength. The wave formation giving maximum speed is one of long wavelength and short amplitude and this occurs when friction between the nematode and the environment is low. This type of movement can readily be seen in nematodes moving through water filled pore spaces in soil (Fig. 38), in fact with optimum conditions for movement it is often difficult to detect any waves at all as the nematodes glide between the particles.

In soil and on the surface of plants, water drains away or evaporates leaving only films or drops of water in which the nematode can move. In such an environment the external forces acting on the nematode are somewhat different from those for soil particles but the mechanical principles for movement are the same. In thin films the nematode derives its propulsive force from the surface tension of the water. Thus, the forces acting on a nematode at rest in a horizontal thin film are $2T \cos \theta_1 + mg$ acting at right angles to the substratum where T is the surface tension of water, m is the mass of the nematode, g is the acceleration due to gravity and θ_1 is the angle between the surface tension force and the

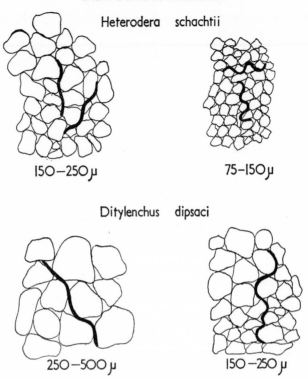

FIG. 38.   The form of body waves in *Heterodera schachtii* and
Ditylenchus dipsaci in different fractions of Woburn soil.
(After Wallace, 1958b.)

vertical (Fig. 39a).   The surface tension force acts along the whole
length of the worm but it is convenient to consider its effect on the nematode in transverse section.   As the film gets thinner θ_1 decreases and so
$2T \cos \theta_2$ increases, i.e. the nematode is pressed more firmly on to the
substratum (Fig. 39b).   When the nematode begins its undulatory movements the body tends to move laterally, so distorting the water film.
This motion is opposed by the horizontal component of the surface
tension force $R \cos \alpha$ plus the friction force F (Fig. 39c).   If P is the
thrust of the nematode against the film, then when $P = F + R \cos \alpha$ there
is no lateral slip, the nematode leaving a sinusoidal track of the same
thickness as its body.   Under these conditions it is likely that the maximum propulsive thrust is being obtained from the film.   The water film
behaves like a rigid environment and the arguments developed previously
for movement in soil are valid here.   As the film becomes thinner the
reaction of the forces at right angles to the substratum (N) increases and
since $F = \mu N$ the friction force (F), acting along the longitudinal axis of
the nematode opposing motion, also increases.   The response of the

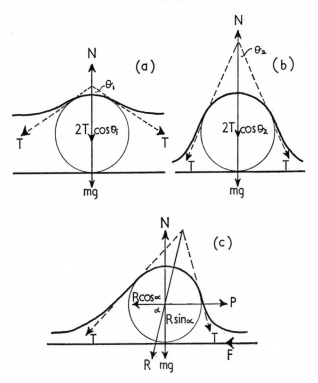

FIG. 39. The external forces acting on an eelworm at rest and moving in a water film. (After Wallace, 1959c.)

nematode to increased friction is to form waves of greater amplitude and small wavelength, as has been shown previously. The differences in wave form of tracks on agar (Plate III) are possibly due to variation in thickness of the water film. A clear indication of the areas of thrust developed by nematodes moving in thin water films are apparent from ciné films using indirect lighting. The posterior edge of each wave pushes against the water film which exerts an equal, but opposite, thrust on the nematode (Fig. 40).

As the film becomes thicker there is lateral slip and a wide track is left. Under these conditions the propulsive thrust is not at a maximum and the speed is decreased accordingly. Eventually, in a film of the same diameter as the nematode, surface tension ceases to act and movement can only occur by swimming or by using the friction forces of the substratum to obtain a propulsive thrust. From these arguments it is clear that nematodes probably have an optimum film thickness for movement, which for *Heterodera schachtii* is about 2 to 5 μ and also the form of the waves will be determined by the thickness of the film (Wallace, 1958a).

The relationship between speed and the form of the waves has been studied in water droplets (Wallace, 1958b) where maximum speeds are associated with waves of small amplitude and long wavelength, as in soil.

In a rigid environment the external resistances prevent the body moving at right angles to its own longitudinal axis and the nematode moves forward at the same speed as the waves travel backwards along the body. When swimming in water, however, forces acting at right angles to the body can only arise when a section of it is moving with its surface

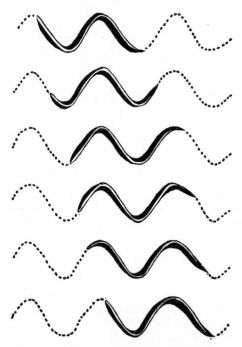

FIG. 40. Wave formation and distribution of water along the body of a chrysanthemum eelworm adult moving in a thin water film. The drawings were taken from ciné film. (After Wallace, 1959c.)

inclined at an angle to the path of motion, in much the same way as propulsion is developed by a ship's propeller. Thus, with a swimming nematode the waves move back relative to the ground, unlike those in a rigid environment where they are stationary. This backward movement is in fact a measure of the extent to which each element of the wave has a component of motion at right angles to its own longitudinal axis and can thereby develop a propulsive thrust from the surrounding water (Gray, 1951). The speed of the nematode through the water is equal to the speed of propagation of the waves back along the body minus the speed of the waves relative to the ground. This point can be clarified by comparing swimming to gliding through a close fitting glass tube which slips back relative to the ground as the nematode moves forward. The same analogy can also be used for crawling in a rigid environment except that the glass tube is stationary. The balance of the forces required to enable a nematode to swim in water are fundamentally the same as those for a rigid environment, namely the retarding effect of all the tangential forces must be balanced by the propulsive effect of the forces acting at right angles to the body (Gray, 1951). A solution to the problem of expressing speed of swimming in terms of wave frequency and form is difficult, although G. I. Taylor (1951, 1952) and Hancock (1953) have made an attempt from mathematical and aerodynamical principles. Unfortunately, in nematodes and other organisms, an understanding of the mechanics of swimming is made more difficult by the fact that waves change in length and amplitude as well as speed as they pass down the body (Wallace, 1959c).

Few species of plant nematodes can swim because they have not the required wave frequency or sufficient speed of waves relative to the ground to develop the necessary propulsive thrust. In deep water most nematodes sink and even when they touch the substratum lateral slip is often too great for crawling. Some genera such as *Aphelenchoides* and *Ditylenchus* can swim well enough to overcome gravity, but only just, because when a number of these nematodes is placed in deep water they eventually sink to the bottom.

MOVEMENT OF *CRICONEMOIDES*

Criconemoides spp., unlike other plant nematodes, have a different type of locomotion. This was described by Stauffer (1924), Taylor (1936) and Thomas (1959) as an alternate lengthening and shortening of the body assisted by the retrorse edges of the annules which inhibited backward slipping. A new interpretation of this type of movement has recently been suggested by Streu, Jenkins and Hutchinson (1961) with the aid of ciné film. They show conclusively that *Criconemoides curvatum* in water on slides moves forward by wave-like contractions passing along the body from the posterior to the anterior end. Only one such wave passed along the body at a time propelling the nematode forward by about 20 μ (Fig. 41). This type of locomotion is different from undulatory movement in three respects. First, the waves pass from the posterior to the anterior end, second it is probable that contractions of the longitudinal muscles occur simultaneously in any one sector of the body and third, the body changes in length during passage of the waves. The principles involved in this type of locomotion still await analysis, moreover some species of *Criconemoides* appear to move by undulatory propulsion without showing the wave-like contractions just described

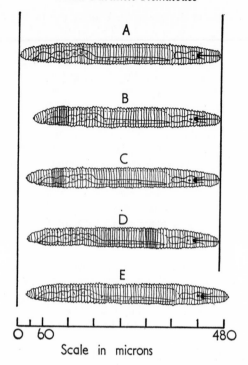

A

B

C

D

E

O   60   480

Scale in microns

Fig. 41. Diagrammatic representation of the
movement of *Criconemoides curvatum* in
water, showing a contractile wave moving
forward along the nematode body. The
nematode is moving from left to right.
(After Streu *et al.*, 1961.)

(Wallace, unpublished). The movement of *Criconemoides*, which so
closely resembles that of snails, clearly warrants further study.

PASSIVE MOVEMENT

Water percolating down through the soil may transport algae, bacteria
and fungal spores from the surface to deeper layers (Burges, 1958).
Although nematodes are much larger than fungal spores there is some
evidence that their movements in soil may also be affected by percolating
water. Peters (1953), for example, observed that larvae of *Heterodera
rostochiensis* tended to move down further in soil columns when water
was allowed to percolate down from the top than when it was allowed to
rise from the bottom. Streu and his colleagues (1961) suggest that the
distribution of *Criconemoides curvatum* is caused mainly by percolating
water. Ducharme (1955) found that, in the sandy soils of citrus groves
in central Florida, the downward movement of water was rapid. The

flow of water influenced the direction and speed of movement of *Radopholus similis* to such an extent that nematodes introduced at the top of a 42 in. column of citrus grove soil appeared at the bottom after 30 hr. with intermittent watering and there was further evidence that this nematode moved down as far as 8 ft to the water table. Ducharme also noted that inactive nematodes did not move down in percolating water; he therefore concluded that movement of water did not carry the nematodes passively through the soil. It has also been suggested that vertical movements of water in the soil are responsible for the migration of animal parasitic nematodes to the soil surface (Payne, 1923a, 1923b) and the transport of *Ascaris* eggs into the soil (Legler, 1950).

An empirical approach to the problem has shown that there is a relationship between the rate of flow of water in soil, particle size, nematode length and nematode speed (Wallace, 1959a). For rates of flow greater than 500 cm/hr.

$$V = 0.052R\left(\frac{4D}{L} - 1\right)$$

where V is the speed of the nematodes, R the speed of water, D the mean diameter of the soil pores and L the length of the nematode. It is apparent from this equation that nematode speed (*a*) increases as the pore diameter increases, (*b*) approaches zero when the nematode length exceeds four times the pore diameter, (*c*) increases with decrease in length. Species of widely different habit, activity and length were used in the experiments and it was shown that nematode speed was independent of its own activity. At slower flow rates, however, the speed increased with activity and the nematodes passed through smaller pores. Ducharme's (1955) observation, that inactive nematodes do not move very far even with very fast flow rates, was also confirmed.

It is clear from direct observation of nematodes in percolating water in soil columns that although movement is purely passive, the nematodes' own activity is essential in orientating the body with the flow stream so that they are not trapped across pore necks.

There seems a distinct possibility that given a soil with large pore spaces and adequate rainfall or irrigation, nematodes may be transported downwards. Furthermore, the vertical size distribution of nematodes in soil may be affected under such conditions to give a picture resembling that for Collembola and Acarina (Salt *et al.*, 1948). Carried a stage further it is even possible that if parasitic nematodes and especially their eggs are carried far enough down in the soil the chances of invading a host plant root would be diminished, but apart from Ducharme's (1955) observations there is no evidence to support such ideas.

Plant nematodes which crawl over the surface of plants are also liable to be carried down to the soil by water percolating over the plant surface. The chrysanthemum eelworm, *Aphelenchoides ritzemabosi*, for example, emerges in large numbers from chrysanthemum leaves after rain and wanders over the stems and leaves. Further rain washes the nematodes down and the rate at which they are transported increases with the flow rate of the water down the plant (Wallace, 1959b).

FACTORS AFFECTING MOVEMENT IN THE SOIL

Temperature

Although there is plenty of information on the influence of temperature on different activities of plant nematodes, its effect on movement has hardly been studied at all. The optimum temperature for movement of the beet eelworm, *Heterodera schachtii,* is about 15°C (Wallace, 1958b), for *Ditylenchus dipsaci* 15 to 20°C (Wallace, 1958b, Blake, 1962) and for *Tylenchorhynchus icarus* about 20°C (Wallace and Greet, 1963). Movement of each of these three species is markedly reduced at 30°C and at 10°C.

Moisture and pore size

The relationship between soil moisture and pore-size is so close that, in studies of their influence on nematode movement, it is necessary to consider them together. Before proceeding any further, however, two important facts must be stressed: nematodes are wholly dependent on water for movement (Wallace, 1956) and, unlike earthworms which burrow through the soil, they are confined to the soil pore spaces (Wallace, 1958a; Nielsen, 1949). The problem then resolves itself into the question—how do changes in the amount and distribution of water in pores of different sizes affect the undulatory movement of nematodes?

It is clear from Seinhorst's (1950) work that the movement of *Ditylenchus dipsaci* is inhibited in soils drier than the moisture equivalent and there is also evidence of an optimum moisture content (Fig. 21). Couch and Bloom (1960) suggest that high moisture stress inhibits migration and motility of root knot nematodes. What are the factors which influence nematodes in this way? Because nematodes do not disturb the environment one factor is immediately obvious; movement will be inhibited when the pore spaces are too narrow to allow the nematodes to squeeze through them. Thus, *Heterodera schachtii* larvae, migrating downwards through vertical saturated columns of sand, are greatly impeded where the sand particle diameter is less than 150 to 250 μ, because the mean pore diameter is about the same as the nematode width (Wallace, 1958a). It follows from this that the particle or pore size at which movement is inhibited depends on the size of the nematode.

Mobility is influenced by both particle size (and pore size) and suction. Thus larvae of *Heterodera schachtii* in three different particle sizes of Woburn soil, subjected to a range of suctions, moved further in the 150 to 250 μ fraction, whereas *Ditylenchus dipsaci* had greater mobility in the

250 to 500 μ fraction (Fig. 42). The different particle size optima for these species is probably related to nematode size; the length of *Ditylenchus dipsaci* is about 1 mm whereas *Heterodera schachtii* measures just over ½ mm. Another important fact emerges from these results; the optimum suction for movement for both species corresponds to the

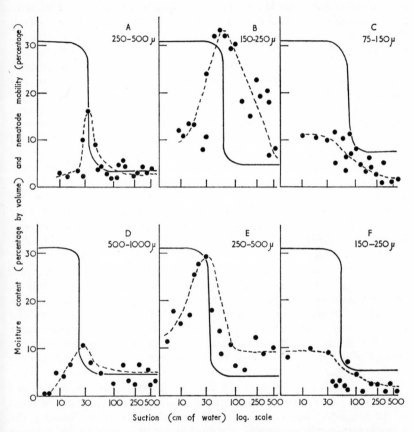

FIG. 42. Horizontal migration of *Heterodera schachtii* (a, b and c) and *Ditylenchus dipsaci* (d, e and f) through different fractions of Woburn soil at different suctions. Values on the ordinates refer both to moisture content and mobility. Each point is the mean of two replicates. (After Wallace, 1958b.)

point of inflexion of the moisture characteristic except in the smallest fractions where pore-width is limiting.

It would be unwise to base any hypotheses relating mobility to particle size, suction and nematode length on this one result. Fortunately there is more confirmatory evidence. The optimum suction for movement corresponds to the flex point of the moisture characteristic in the following species. *Ditylenchus dipsaci* (Blake, 1961, 1962; Wallace, 1958b),

Heterodera schachtii (Wallace, 1958a), *Heterodera rostochiensis* (Wallace, 1960), *Aphelenchoides ritzemabosi* (Hesling and Wallace, 1961) and *Tylenchorhynchus icarus* (Wallace and Greet, 1963). These plant parasitic nematodes are of widely different habit, activity and size so it is probably valid to generalise on this aspect of movement. What about the relationship between nematode length, particle size and movement? Estimates of the mobility of several nematode species in different particle sizes at the suction corresponding to the flex point of the moisture characteristic, indicate that the size of the particles (or pore size) for maximum mobility increases as the nematode length increases, and that for maximum mobility the ratio of particle diameter to nematode length is about 1:3 (Wallace, 1958c).

These criteria form the basis for the interpretation of nematode movement in soil. The argument can be taken a stage further, however, because the speed of a nematode is probably a function of its length and activity or wave frequency. This point is illustrated in studies of the movement of nematodes on agar where speed and wave form can easily be measured. The product of length and activity bears a linear relationship to speed (Wallace, 1958c).

Whether this hypothesis applies to movement in soil was tested by plotting the product of length and activity against mobility for several nematode species moving among sand particles of different sizes (Fig. 43). In the two larger fractions, 250 to 500 μ and 500 to 1,000 μ, a linear relationship exists but not in the two smaller fractions, 75 to 150 μ and 150 to 250 μ. The reason for this is that in the two larger fractions all the nematode species had a length *less* than three times the particle diameter. In such an environment with most of the moisture confined to the points of contact between particles, as would commonly occur after free drainage in the soil, the nematodes move in thin films over the surface of the particles. Thus, their movement is similar to that on the surface of agar, particle and pore size having little influence on locomotion. The similarity between the two graphs is, consequently, not surprising. In the two smaller size fractions, where the length of most of the nematodes equals or exceeds three times the particle diameter, the particle size–nematode length relationship now has an effect and a linear graph is not obtained.

The original question on how moisture and pore size influence movement can, therefore, be answered as follows. A nematode of given body length and width (1) cannot move between soil particles when the pore diameters are less than the nematode width; (2) has an optimum particle size for movement which is about one third the nematode length; (3) has maximum mobility at a suction corresponding to the point of inflexion of the moisture characteristic of the soil; (4) moves in soil at about field capacity with a speed which is a function of its length and activity, provided the body length is less than three times the particle diameter.

We have now developed some broad and probably oversimplified generalisations about nematode movement but there are several aspects which need elucidation. It is easy to see why nematodes cannot squeeze through holes smaller than their own width, but why do they move best at a suction corresponding to the flex point of the moisture characteristic and why do they move more quickly among particles of a certain characteristic size? There are no quantitative data to provide answers to these

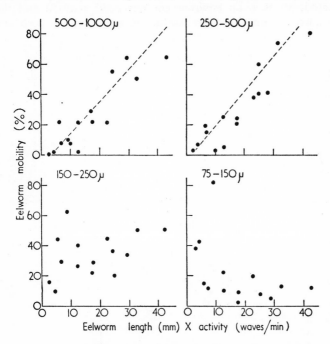

FIG. 43. The relationship between eelworm length, activity and mobility in four particle-size fractions of soil. (After Wallace, 1958c.)

questions but direct observation on nematodes moving in a single layer of particles has helped. For example, the wave form of nematodes is determined by particle size (Fig. 38). *Heterodera schachtii* and *Ditylenchus dipsaci* in sub-optimal size particles move slowly with many waves of short wavelength and large amplitude whereas in optimum size particles they glide through the spaces at high speed with waves of long wavelength and short amplitude. Such behaviour is clearly related to the mechanics of undulatory propulsion described in a previous section and measurements relating speed to wave form support this hypothesis (Wallace, 1958b).

The relationship between mobility and suction can be explained as follows. At low suctions the pores are full of water and aeration is low

8

and, as is explained in Chapter 4, nematodes become inactive when deprived of oxygen. In addition, if the pore spaces are large, the soil particles do not give the optimal external resistances for undulatory movement, in fact, the nematode has to swim, an inefficient type of locomotion for most nematode species. As the suction increases to the flex point of the moisture characteristic of the soil most of the pores are empty and water is in the form of small lenses where the particles touch. A nematode in such an environment has good aeration and there is enough water to form thin films in which it can move. At high suctions,

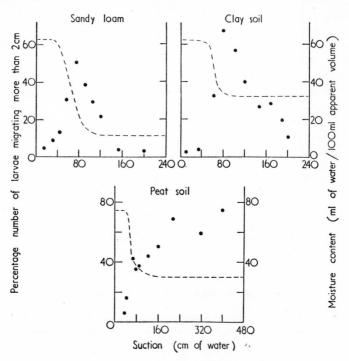

FIG. 44. Mobility of larvae of *Heterodera rostochiensis* in three soil types of crumb size 150 to 250 μ. The dotted line indicates the moisture characteristic. (After Wallace, 1960.)

although there is good aeration, there is not enough water to form films thick enough for movement. Thus, an intermediate soil moisture content between saturated and dry is necessary for migration.

Soil type

Any attempt to elucidate the effect of soil type is difficult, because a particular soil sample consists of numerous unknown and variable factors. To understand the factors responsible for differences in movement between soil types, crumb size and suction have to be controlled. When this is done (Fig. 44) it is apparent that movement in such widely different types as sandy loam and heavy gault clay are closely similar whereas in the organic peat soil relationships are different. It looks as though soil texture, i.e. the percentage of sand, silt and clay, has little relation to movement; what really matters is crumb and pore size. Sandy soils usually have larger pores, i.e. they are coarse-textured, so there are more channels through which the nematodes can penetrate and aeration is also higher. Thus, *Pratylenchus zeae* and *Pratylenchus brachyurus* move further in sandy loam than in clay and Kincaid (1946) suggests that porous sandy soils favour movement of root knot nematodes. *Heterodera rostochiensis* migrate further in sandy soils, less in loamy soils and least in clay soils (Rode, 1962). In some soils chemical factors may affect activity and movement (Seinhorst, 1950; Luc, 1961) so the problem is not always a simple question of pore size relationships.

The lack of an optimum suction in the peat soil suggests that nematodes can migrate here at much higher suctions than in other soil types. The reason for this is obscure but it is possible that on peat crumbs the hydrophobic properties of the organic matter produce different angles of contact between the nematode and the water films, thus affecting the surface tension forces which in turn control the external resistances for undulatory propulsion. It has also been suggested that friction between the nematode's body and the peat crumb is less than that between clay and sand crumbs (Wallace, 1960). This would enable the nematode to overcome restraining forces of the very thin films at much higher suctions in the peat soil than in the other two soil types. Although these views are somewhat speculative it is known that nematodes move between particles with smooth surfaces better than between rough particles, thus friction may be important (Wallace, 1960).

Although the influence of soil type is still obscure, it is quite clear that the practice of relating the behaviour of nematodes to soil texture may lead to erroneous conclusions unless the soil structure (pore size relationships) is also taken into account.

Osmotic pressure

Blake (1961) compared the migration of *Ditylenchus dipsaci* in sand at various suctions with and without an osmotic potential. No difference was found between these two treatments and he concluded that movement depends only on moisture content and is independent of osmotic potential until the solute concentration causes incipient plasmolysis of the nematode (Fig. 45). In most fertile soils the salt concentration of the soil water does not exceed two atmospheres and because nematodes are probably unaffected by osmotic pressures up to about 10 atmospheres, it seems likely that the effect of osmotic pressure on movement in soil is unimportant.

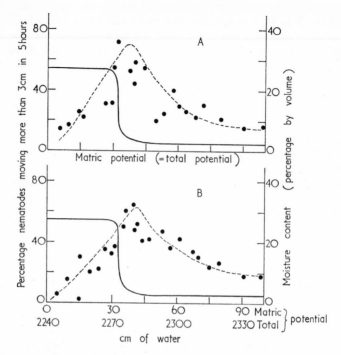

FIG. 45. Horizontal migration of *Ditylenchus dipsaci* through sand at different total potentials. Each point is the mean of two replicates. In A the sand is wetted by distilled water (osmotic potential = 0) and in B by 0·1 M urea solution (osmotic potential = 2,240 cm water). The moisture characteristic of the sand is shown as a solid curve. (After Blake, 1961.)

FACTORS AFFECTING MOVEMENT ABOVE SOIL LEVEL

At first sight the environmental factors affecting migration of plant nematodes on plants above ground would appear to be radically different from those in the soil, but this is not so. Such species as *Aphelenchoides ritzemabosi*, *Ditylenchus dipsaci*, *Anguina agrostis* and *A. tritici* still require water films in which to move. Climatic factors, which affect the rate of evaporation and the deposition of water on plants, are therefore important in this respect. The upward migration of *A. ritzemabosi* on chrysanthemum plants (Wallace, 1959b) and the movement of *Ditylenchus dipsaci* from the host plant (Wallace, 1962) is greatest after rainfall or mists, when excess water has drained off the plants. This is comparable to soil conditions where maximum migration occurs after drainage of water to the field capacity level. The density of hairs on leaves also controls the mobility of *A. ritzemabosi* in much the same way as particle size influences nematode movement in soil. Soil particle size controls pore size and density of leaf hairs controls their spacing, causing differences in the external resistances which are so important for undulatory movement. Similarly, the length and activity of nematodes influences their ability to migrate over the surface of plants; larvae of *A. ritzemabosi* which are both shorter and less active than the adults, migrate to a much lesser extent than the adults. Water, percolating down the plant stems carries nematodes to soil level in much the same way as nematodes are transported passively in the soil by percolating water, the density of hairs on the stem determining the rate of downward movement.

The nature of the micro-environment on plant surfaces and its influence on nematode movement has received more attention from zoo-nematologists (Crofton, 1948a, 1948b, 1954; Rees, 1950; Tarshis, 1958). This is understandable because the infection of animal hosts by nematodes is often dependent on the ability of the parasite to migrate up on to the leaves of herbage which the host eats. The aerial phase of the freeliving stages is therefore a very important aspect of the epidemiology of nematode infection. Similar studies on the influence of microclimatic conditions on the plant surface would obviously provide valuable information about the etiology of those plant nematodes which live above soil level.

ORIENTATION

In a complex environment like the soil many factors may influence the directed movement of nematodes and when plants are present the situation is even more complex. There is plenty of evidence that nematodes are attracted to plants but the factors which control such movements and the mechanisms of orientation are little understood. There are at least two lines of approach to this problem. The behaviour of nematodes can be studied under artificial conditions, such as on agar plates, with as close a control as possible of the environmental conditions. Having built up a picture of the influence of individual factors on nematode orientation, then it is possible to erect hypotheses explaining the behaviour of nematodes under natural conditions. Another approach is to study nematodes in an environment as close as possible to natural conditions, e.g. pot experiments, in which only a few environmental factors can be controlled. From such observations tentative conclusions can be drawn about the factors which most influence orientation. Both of these methods of approach have their merits and both depend on a knowledge of the micro-environment, especially in the proximity of plant roots.

In recent years there has been much speculation and disagreement about this subject, so generalisations are difficult. In separating speculation from fact and in assessing the validity of experimental interpretation, the question of the negative result arises. If one observer's experiments fail to show the influence of a certain factor on nematode orientation but a second observer succeeds, then it seems prudent to treat the first observer's results with caution.   If, however, several observers obtain the same negative results then from sheer weight of numbers it may be necessary to admit that a positive result may not be forthcoming.   Thus, failure to demonstrate a reaction by *Ditylenchus dipsaci* to light (Wallace, 1961) does not mean that light has no effect on this species.   Another observer with a different technique may later succeed.   Experimental

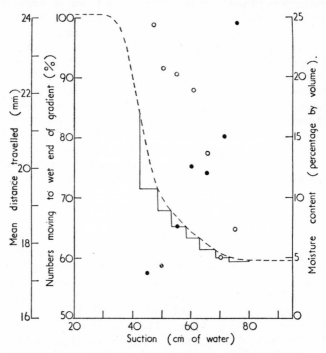

FIG. 46.   Relationship between (*a*) suction and larval mobility of *Heterodera rostochiensis* and (*b*) moisture gradient and movement to the wet end.   The dotted line indicates the moisture characteristic and the horizontal and vertical lines show the steepness of the moisture gradient at different suctions.   Open circles indicate numbers moving to wet end of the gradient. Closed circles show the mean distance travelled.   (After Wallace, 1960.)

technique is, therefore, very important in the study of nematode orientation and if several different methods can be used in the investigation of a particular aspect, so much the better.

In a previous section, generalisations about the movement of nematodes in soil have emphasised the similarity between species.   Orientation does not permit such generalisations, for there is ample evidence to show that different species may behave differently under the same conditions.

ORIENTATION TO PHYSICAL AND CHEMICAL FACTORS

Soil moisture and gravity

Larvae of *Heterodera rostochiensis*, introduced into the centre of a 5 cm cube containing 150 to 250 μ sand, migrate upwards or downwards to the wet end of a vertical moisture gradient (Wallace, 1960). By varying the suction between the top and bottom of the cube, different moisture gradients are obtained, the degree of migration to the wet end varying directly as the difference in moisture content between the ends of the gradient (Fig. 46).

Pore size also influences the ability of *Heterodera rostochiensis* to respond to moisture gradients, orientation only occurring when the pore-size is optimal for locomotion (Wallace, 1960). Similar results have been found for *Tylenchorhynchus icarus* (Wallace and Greet, 1963) and *Ditylenchus dipsaci* (Wallace, 1961) which responds to moisture gradients as low as 1 per cent moisture content over a length of 10 cm. *Hemicycliophora paradoxa* in vertical columns of soil also migrates to the wet end of a moisture gradient (Luc, 1961).

It is difficult to visualise how *Heterodera rostochiensis* manages to move downwards under gravity in an environment such as sand or soil where the intercrumb pathways are relatively small and tortuous. It is possible that in addition to a simple falling effect there is some orientation because the centre of gravity of the larvae is anterior to the mid-point. Thus in water the larvae tend to become orientated with their heads downwards and so move downwards. The same phenomenon has been recorded for vinegar eelworm (*Turbatrix aceti*) which, because it is tail-heavy, tends to swim to the surface (Peters, 1952). The relationship between pore size, nematode size and water distribution may also shed some light on behaviour in soil or sand. Figure 47 shows diagrammatically a larva of *Heterodera rostochiensis* in different sized pore spaces which are either full of water or have just been emptied. The geometrical relationship between nematode diameter, minimum pore diameter and distribution of water gives some idea of the conditions in the experiments just described. In the largest pores (55 μ and 110 μ) the nematode lies in a large volume of water whether the pore is empty or not and so the nematode is more likely to fall under gravity. In the 31 μ pores, gravity only affects the nematode in the full pores; in the empty pores the body is in contact with the air–water interface and surface tension overcomes any gravity effect. In the finest pores (19 μ), the larvae have just enough room to move, consequently neither water nor gravity affect them. Such a hypothetical picture helps to explain why a response to moisture gradients only occurs when the nematode is in contact with the air–water interface in the pores, in which condition it also moves fastest.

Although much work has been done on geotaxis in animal-parasitic nematodes, Crofton (1954) discounts the evidence for such behaviour on the basis of his results with *Trichostrongylus retortaeformis* which moves at random on vertical surfaces. Nothing in the plant nematology field contradicts Crofton's opinion that nematodes do not have an inherent

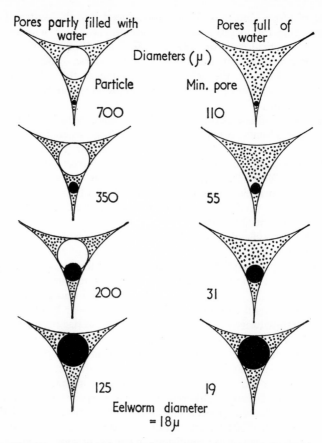

FIG. 47. Relationship of eelworm diameter to pore size and moisture content in sand. To facilitate drawing, the relative size of pore and larva is changed in each drawing. As drawn, pore size appears constant but in fact varies from 110 to 19 μ while the larval diameter which appears to increase is constant at 18 μ. Equivalent particle sizes are also given and vary with pore size from 700 to 125 μ. An eelworm is represented by a solid black circle and stippling indicates water. (After Wallace, 1960.)

selective behaviour pattern which produces orientation to gravity. Suggestions that zoo-parasitic nematodes migrate upwards to higher moisture levels in the soil (Spindler, 1936; Bruns, 1937; Beaver, 1953) have been opposed by Lane (1930, 1933) and Reesal (1951) on the grounds that because nematodes are always surrounded by water they cannot detect differences in soil moisture. The fact that phyto-parasitic nematodes do respond to moisture gradients casts doubt on this criticism; exception can also be taken to interpretations of vertical movement in the soil, where factors such as temperature and aeration are probably just as important as moisture in the movement of nematodes.

Light

There is no known evidence that plant nematodes respond to light. This is not surprising because most species spend their life in total darkness in the soil, and so the ability to respond to light would have doubtful survival value. Orientation to light might have a possible value for those nematodes living above soil level, but so far this has not been demonstrated (Wallace, 1961). Even information on phototaxis by zoo-parasitic nematodes is contradictory and Parker and Haley (1960), in showing that *Nippostrongylus muris* moves to the heat produced by a light source, cast some doubt on much of the previous work on this subject.

Temperature

Ditylenchus dipsaci, in a temperature gradient of 2° to 30°C in horizontal tubes of saturated sand, aggregates at about 10°C (Fig. 48). The nematodes were introduced into the gradient at the 20°C point, the optimum temperature for locomotion. With a simple speed orthokinesis, aggregation would occur at both ends of the gradient where mobility was low. In fact, there was a generalised movement to the cold end suggesting some behavioural response to temperature, such as differences in adaptation to rising and falling temperature in a gradient. Whether other species of nematodes behave similarly or have different aggregation temperatures remains to be seen. Apart from the observation of Parker and Haley (1960) that larvae of *Nippostrongylus muris* are positively thermotactic, there is little critical work on the orientation of zoo-parasitic nematodes to temperature.

Water currents

Orientation in water currents or rheotaxis is defined as follows: if an animal is in a fluid velocity gradient and the long axis of its body is aligned parallel to the direction of flow with the head pointing consistently in one direction, the animal is said to exhibit rheotaxis (Bretherton and Rothschild, 1961). When the animal's head points upstream it is positively rheotactic. Thus, simple alignment with the direction of flow, regardless of the orientation of the body, is not rheotaxis but flow orientation. Weischer's (1959) claim that larvae of *Heterodera rostochiensis* are rheotactic because they move with a stream of water through particles of 200 to 500 μ diameter is, therefore, not substantiated. A more likely interpretation, that the larvae were carried passively by the water, is supported by the fact that the much longer *Ditylenchus dipsaci* did not move in this way. As we have seen previously nematode length and particle size are closely related to speed of passive movement in percolating water. Direct observation of *Ditylenchus dipsaci* in water moving through sand also failed to detect either rheotaxis or flow orientation (Wallace, 1961). Voss (1930) suggested that the upward migration

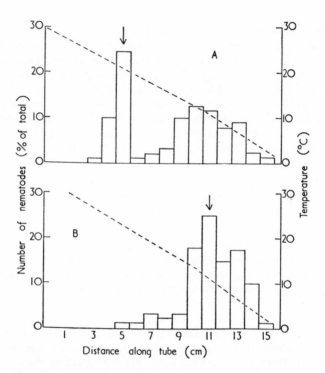

FIG. 48. Distribution of *Ditylenchus dipsaci* in a 15 cm tube of saturated sand after 5 hr. in a temperature gradient. The dotted line shows the temperature gradient and the arrow the point where the nematodes were inoculated into the sand at (A) 20°C and (B) 10°C. (After Wallace, 1961.)

of *Aphelenchoides ritzemabosi* on chrysanthemum stems was a rheotaxis in response to downwardly percolating water. Although this species tends to move up rather than down stems, water running down the plant only inhibits this migration (Wallace, 1959b), thus, in the absence of direct observation, there is no evidence for rheotaxis. The observation that *Ancylostoma* and *Strongyloides* larvae, both zoo-parasitic nematode genera, tend to face a water current (Fulleborn, 1932) seems to be the only evidence of a nematode rheotaxis.

Texture

The aggregation of *Ditylenchus dipsaci* in the fine particles at one end of a particle size gradient is probably a simple orthokinesis or trapping effect (Wallace, 1961) and, therefore, hardly comes under the heading of orientation. Such a mechanism, however inefficient, might lead to aggregation and may be important in some soil profiles.

Electrical fields and redox potential

Panagrellus redivivus, a free-living nematode, moves to the cathode when a current greater than 0·02 milliamps is passed. *Tylenchus* sp., *Pratylenchus* sp., *Aphelenchoides* sp., *Dorylaimus* sp. and other freeliving nematodes behave similarly (Caveness and Panzer, 1960). Such an orientation is termed galvanotaxis. Jones (1960) found that when simple platinum electrodes were placed in a petri dish containing vinegar or water, the vinegar eelworm, *Turbatrix aceti*, collected around the cathode. This response depended on the potential gradient rather than on the current passed and a minimum threshold value of 30 mV/mm was detected. In a sand–water system *Heterodera schachtii* moved to the anode whereas *Ditylenchus dipsaci* moved to the cathode, both having a minimum threshold value of 20 mV/mm (Fig. 49). Direct observation of *Ditylenchus dipsaci* in water showed that there was an immediate response to a reversal of the current as far as 2·5 cm from the electrodes. There was no suggestion of orthokinesis; the nematodes showed distinct directional movements more in the nature of a klinokinesis. As Jones has pointed out, plant roots are negatively charged and potential differences of 60 mV are known to occur, so it is possible that nematodes are attracted to roots galvanotactically. This contradicts the view of Fraenkel and Gunn (1940) that stimulation of animals by electrical currents is rarely a natural phenomenon.

The hypothesis that nematodes are attracted to roots in gradients of electrical potential gains some support from Bird's (1959) observations that *Meloidogyne hapla* and *M. javanica* are strongly attracted to reducing agents, especially sodium dithionite. Bird suggests that these species are attracted along electrical potential gradients caused by lower redox potentials, other factors such as moisture and temperature playing only a secondary rôle. Bird (1960) later modified his views in the light of further work which showed that, although low redox potential was an important attractant for *M. javanica* and *Heterodera schachtii*, it did not affect other species he examined, thus redox potential was not as important as he first thought. Klingler (1961) showed that reducing agents which lowered the redox potential and oxidising agents which raised it, both attracted *Ditylenchus dipsaci*. He was unable to demonstrate any attraction to either anode or cathode, however, unlike Jones (1960). Klingler, therefore, disagrees with Bird's redox potential hypothesis and proposes that attraction at a distance is to CO_2, with more specific orientation to other root exudates near the root.

The significance of electrical potentials in nematode orientation is clearly in doubt. Nevertheless, there is good evidence that such orientation does occur in artificial media and it is also known that electrical potential gradients of the order of magnitude necessary to elicit nematode

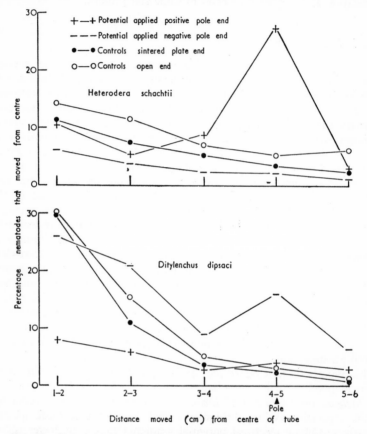

FIG. 49. Response to an electric current passed through a sand-tap water system at 40 cm suction. *Heterodera schachtii* is attracted to the anode, *Ditylenchus dipsaci* is attracted to the cathode. (After Jones, 1960.)

orientation, do occur near plant roots. The point in doubt is how much this factor contributes to the complex of stimuli attracting nematodes to plants.

pH

A range of pH from 3·0 to 10·6 has no effect on the orientation of *Meloidogyne hapla* or *M. arenaria* (Bird, 1959) and Johnson and Viglierchio

(1961) found no correlation between pH and the aggregation of *M. javanica, M. hapla, Heterodera schachtii* and *Ditylenchus dipsaci.* There is, therefore, no evidence as yet that pH affects orientation.

Chemicals

It will now be evident that there are many factors influencing the orientation of nematodes in the vicinity of plant roots. To this complex picture must now be added the multitude of chemical substances emanating from the plant itself.

There is unequivocal evidence that some species of plant nematodes are attracted to CO_2. Thus, *Ditylenchus dipsaci* (Klingler, 1959, 1961), *Meloidogyne javanica, M. hapla* and *Heterodera schachtii* (Johnson and Viglierchio, 1961) aggregate at a source of CO_2. Bird (1959) was unable to demonstrate any such effect with *M. javanica* and *M. hapla* but he later (1960) showed that not only was *M. javanica* attracted to CO_2, but so also were larvae of *Heterodera schachtii, Pratylenchus minyus, Paratylenchus* sp. and rhabditids. Bird, like Klingler (1961), thinks that CO_2 acts as a long range rather than a root surface attractant. A different view is held by Rohde (1960) who, having shown that CO_2 concentrations above atmospheric inhibit nematode movement, suggested that nematodes would collect at roots by an orthokinetic stimulus because of the high CO_2 concentrations at the root surface. Peacock (1961) opposes this hypothesis with data on the invasion of tomato roots by *M. incognita.* The invasion of the roots was much less when charcoal was mixed with the vermiculite or sand in which the plants were growing. This result could be interpreted as a removal either of attractant CO_2 or of root exudate. When, however, exchange resins were used to absorb the CO_2 there was no reduction in the invasion, so Peacock concludes that if CO_2 is an important attractant its extraction by the resins would have inhibited invasion. In view of the conflicting evidence it would be unwise to suggest that CO_2 is the chief chemical factor responsible for the orientation of plant nematodes to roots.

Other chemicals which are known to attract some species of nematodes are the reducing agents sodium dithionite, cysteine, glutathione and ascorbic acid (Bird, 1959), the oxidising agent potassium permanganate (Klingler, 1961), oxygen (Johnson and Viglierchio, 1961) and tyrosine (Oteifa and Elgindi, 1961). In addition, Luc (1961) and Weischer (1959) suggest that some root exudates may have attractive properties.

From all these observations it is difficult to avoid the somewhat obvious conclusion that the chemical substances exuded by plants form a complex which acts as a source of attraction to nematodes. If this is true, it follows that there is little likelihood of particular plant species having a specific attractant or, conversely, that particular nematode species are attracted to specific plant species. Such a view has been expressed by Lownsbery and Viglierchio (1961) who suggest that the accumulation of *Meloidogyne hapla* around germinating tomato seeds is a composite effect of random nematode movement, directed movement to secreted substances and retention at the root surface; secreted substances may increase the intensity of nematode attack but they do not govern host selection rigorously. Shibuya (1952) is dogmatic on this point. He states that chemicals secreted by plant roots are not selective; nematodes are attracted to and invade many different plant species. Whether the plant will act as an efficient host is only determined inside the root. Observations such as those of Shepherd (1959), recording the invasion of non-host plants by nematode parasites, tend to support this hypothesis.

ORIENTATION TO PLANT ROOTS

The much quoted observations of Linford (1939) that root knot nematode larvae congregate around roots, especially in the region of the root cap, emphasises the value of direct observation in the study of nematode orientation. Since Linford's paper there has been plenty of confirmatory evidence that plant roots attract nematodes. Larvae of *Heterodera rostochiensis* may even anticipate the production of new rootlets by collecting at particular loci on the tomato root (Widdowson *et al.*, 1958). *Meloidogyne hapla* is attracted to roots of tomato seedlings but only when these are growing. The apical 2 mm of excised root tips are repellent whereas the next 6 mm are attractive (Wieser, 1955). On the basis of these results, Wieser (1956) puts forward the hypothesis that plants possess a repellent and an attractant agent, the balance between the two determining whether or not a plant attracts a nematode. Thus he claimed that tomato is attractive, bean repellent and egg plant and soybean neutral to *M. hapla*. Loewenberg and colleagues (1960) oppose this hypothesis on the grounds that their observations show distinct attraction of *M. incognita* to the terminal centimetre of intact roots and they suggest that Wieser's root tips might have been repellent because he used excised roots. Peacock (1959) found nothing to support Wieser's theory of repellent areas; larvae of *M. incognita* were attracted to a closely defined area immediately behind the apical meristem. When apical dominance diminished, the lateral root buds became active and larvae were strongly attracted to them and not to the root apex. However, Peacock did confirm Wieser's observation that when linear root growth ceased, larval attraction also ceased.

Bergman and van Duuren (1959a, b) suggest that bacteria in the rhizosphere may be responsible for the attraction of nematodes. They isolated bacteria some of which were attractive and some repellent to *Heterodera schachtii* on rape and sugar beet. Under sterile conditions *H. schachtii* was not attracted to roots or to root diffusate. They question the statement by Widdowson and colleagues (1958) that *H. rostochiensis* is attracted to tomato roots in sterile conditions, interpreting the observations as a trapping of larvae at the root tips in agar which had been softened by root secretions and Sandstedt and Schuster (1962) support this view. Nematodes *are* attracted to roots in the absence of bacteria, however (Peacock, 1959; Blake, 1962), so without discounting the importance of attraction by bacteria there is no reason to underestimate the attractive properties of root exudates. Thus, Henderson and Katznelson (1961) suggest that amino acid concentration in the rhizosphere may govern the numbers of plant parasitic nematodes there.

Whatever the factors responsible, there is little doubt that nematodes tend to accumulate around the roots of plants in soil, but how does this occur?

There are two rival hypotheses to explain this phenomenon. The first supposes that nematodes move at random in the vicinity of plant roots, reaching the root by chance and they are then detained there by attraction near the root surface. Kühn (1959) and Sandstedt and colleagues (1961) support such a hypothesis. Kühn suggests that attraction of *H. rostochiensis* at a distance from the roots does not occur and that root exudates only influence the rate of movement of nematodes but do not attract them. Kühn further states that diffusion gradients of an attractant substance in soil do not exist. Rode (1962) found no evidence substantiating the hypothesis that larvae of *H. rostochiensis* were attracted to roots at distances greater than 5 cm.

The second hypothesis explains attraction in terms of the orientation of nematodes in concentration gradients of some stimulus emitted by the root and acting at a distance. Kämpfe (1960) working with *H. schachtii* supports this hypothesis. Several workers (Peacock, 1959; Lownsbery and Viglierchio, 1960; Wallace, 1960; Viglierchio, 1961; Blake, 1962) have shown that nematodes are attracted to roots when access to the root itself is prevented by a permeable membrane of cellophane or by sintered glass. They may even be attracted to the site where plants had originally been growing (Wallace, 1958d; Blake, 1962). Thus contact between nematode and root surface is not necessary for attraction.

Let us now examine these two hypotheses. Experimental data purporting to show that nematodes move at random in the vicinity of plant roots may only express the limitations of the technique. The same nematodes may show orientation behaviour under different experimental conditions. On the other hand, although nematodes are attracted to plants when separated from them by a permeable barrier, it can be argued that they, nevertheless, move at random but become more or less stationary at the surface of the membrane under the influence of some diffusible factor which extends from the root to the membrane. The difference between the two hypotheses now depends on the distance from the root at which exudates can influence nematodes and whether behaviour responses enable the nematode to orientate itself to such chemical gradients.

Theoretically, if the plant is emitting some chemical which diffuses away then concentration gradients will be set up whose range will depend on the concentration at the root surface, the rate of diffusion and the rate of breakdown of the chemical. Soil conditions, especially moisture and crumb structure, will influence diffusion and the physiology of the plant will affect the rate of production of the chemical. That gradients of CO_2 and oxygen occur in the soil is well known, so there seems no reason why such gradients should not exist around roots. The fact that exudates from cress roots grown in sand stimulate hatch of *Heterodera schachtii* 3 cm away and attract the larvae over a distance of 4·5 cm (Wallace, 1958d) suggests that concentration gradients of root exudates may extend over at least 3 or 4 cm. Luc (1961) goes even further and suggests that factors produced by millet roots can stimulate larvae of *Hemicycliophora paradoxa* as far away as 20 to 40 cm.

Blake's (1962) observations on the behaviour of *Ditylenchus dipsaci* near oat plants show that the rate of turning of the nematodes increases in the vicinity of the plants producing aggregation. Jones (1960) states that this species exhibits somewhat similar movements in an electrical field. These results both point to the klino-tactic behaviour discussed by Fraenkel and Gunn (1940).

The evidence for both hypotheses is obviously tenuous but there is enough to suggest that they are only dealing with different aspects of the same phenomenon. The range of influence of root exudates, being dependent on soil and plant physiological factors, may be expected to vary over wide limits. Thus, at one time nematodes may reach a plant root by random movement and at other times they may be attracted from a distance. To try to substantiate one or other of the hypotheses seems rather pointless. A more useful approach would be to obtain further evidence to test the hypothesis that nematodes accumulate at plant roots by behaviour responses which produce orientation in a gradient of stimuli originating at the root surface; where the gradient is too small to be detected, nematodes may reach roots by random movement and collect there by attractant stimuli at the root surface.

The concept of attraction from a distance may be unrealistic with crops such as cereals or grass where the soil in the root zone has a high concentration of roots. In such surroundings any chemical gradients would probably intercross and nematodes would always be close to a root anyway so the benefits of orientation are doubtful. Nevertheless there might be a vertical attraction to the root zone from deeper soil layers. With root crops and deeply rooting plants, however, attraction from a distance would ensure increased invasion of the host.

The approach to the problem is now more clearly defined. Information is needed on the physics and chemistry of chemical gradients near roots and their occurrence under natural conditions. The physiology of the plant in relation to the production of attractant exudates is also relevant. The mechanism of orientation of nematodes and the threshold values of different chemical stimuli need investigation. Such work would inevitably lead to research on sensory-physiology of nematodes for, although the anatomy of such structures as the amphids strongly suggests a sensory function, there is no evidence for this (Hirschmann, 1959).

SPREAD

The spread of plant nematodes can be considered under three headings: (1) short range—within a small area such as a field, (2) medium range—between fields or farms and (3) long range—from one county, state or country to another. This subdivision is purely arbitrary, for some factors may cause spread over all these ranges.

Short range spread

Within a field the spread of a nematode population by active migration is influenced by any factors which produce directed movements. In the absence of these factors the rate of spread is probably small, 1 or 2 m a year seems to be a fair estimate. When plant roots are present the rate of spread may increase (Endo, 1959). Thus, *Radopholus similis* moves from infested soil into clean soil at about 6 to 8·5 in. (15·2 to 21·6 cm) per month when the roots of adjacent citrus seedlings are in contact (Feldmesser *et al.*, 1960). Records on the spreading decline of citrus show that the disease spreads at the rate of about two trees per year although eight trees per year has been recorded (Suit and Ducharme, 1957). If the primary pathogen for this disease is *R. similis*, it is hard to visualise how the nematodes could spread at such rates unless some other factor such as water drainage passively transported the nematodes. For example, Ducharme (1955) states that in a citrus grove on a hillside, spreading decline spreads 25 ft uphill compared with 200 ft downhill in one year and he suggests that this is caused by the influence of percolating water on the direction and rate of movement of *R. similis*. There is certainly plenty of evidence that this phenomenon occurs with other species. Nematode diseased patches, elongated in a downhill direction, have been recorded for *Heterodera schachtii* in sugar beet (Steiner *et al.*, 1951), *Aphelenchoides besseyi* in soybean (Tamura and Kegasawa, 1958) and *Heterodera glycines* in soybean (Ichinohe, 1955). Similar crop symptoms are seen where surface run-off water has carried *Ditylenchus dipsaci* downhill (Beaumont and Staniland, 1941; Seinhorst, 1950; Brown, 1955; Bingefors, 1957). Brown (1957) records elongated patches, 50 to 60 yd (45·8 to 54·9 m) long, caused by this phenomenon.

Ploughing and harrowing also spread nematodes. Chitwood (1951) records a spread of *Heterodera rostochiensis* of 400 ft in a season in the direction of cultivation and opposite to the direction of water drainage. *Heterodera schachtii* (Petherbridge and Jones, 1944; Golden and Jorgenson, 1961b) and *Ditylenchus dipsaci* (Beaumont and Staniland, 1941; Seinhorst, 1950) are also considered to be spread in this way. In fact, anything which disturbs or moves over the soil is a possible means of spread in a field.

9

Medium range spread

The spread of nematodes from one farm or field to another is really a process of passive transportation in which Man is probably the chief agent.   The use of farm machinery in different fields means that infested soil is often transported about the farm and, where machinery is used on a cooperative basis, nematodes may be carried from one farm to another (Courtney and Howell, 1952; Reynolds, 1958; Mai and Harrison, 1959; Baines *et al.*, 1959; Bingefors, 1960).   Similarly, the introduction of infested nursery stock into uninfested land and the movement of soil to new sites can cause fresh nematode problems.   Factors such as wind (Chitwood, 1951; White, 1953) and floods (Petherbridge and Jones, 1944; Thompson *et al.*, 1949) rarely cause any great dispersal of nematodes, although there is little doubt that the flow of irrigation water is important in this respect.

Long range spread

Plant nematodes such as *Pratylenchus* spp. may be carried over long distances in soil on nursery stock (Oostenbrink, 1957) or in the roots themselves (Mountain and Boyce, 1958).   Some nematodes which can resist desiccation are well adapted to seed-borne dispersal.   Thus *Ditylenchus dipsaci* (Goodey, 1950; Brown, 1955; Lewis, 1956; Bingefors, 1960; Diercks and Klewitz, 1962) and *Aphelenchoides* spp. (Cralley, 1949; Brown, 1956) are carried on seed which may be exported from one country to another.   Godfrey (1924) suggests that the widespread occurrence of *Ditylenchus dipsaci* on the Pacific Coast of the U.S.A. is due to windblown infested seed of such plants as the false dandelion, *Hypochaeris radicata*.

The cyst-forming nematodes are often carried in soil around roots of plants which are exported to other countries.   One of the jobs of the plant quarantine authorities is to try to intercept such introductions to obviate subsequent nematode problems.   Thus the new species *Heterodera leptonepia* was found by the plant quarantine authorities in soil imported with potatoes taken on as ship's stores at Callaeo, Peru and landed in Oakland, California (Cobb and Taylor, 1953).   Cysts of different *Heterodera* spp. were found in this way in soil on the roots of plants exported from Israel to the U.S.A. (Minz, 1956).   Southey (1957) also reports *Heterodera cacti* on imported cactus plants.   The American quarantine authorities have found *Heterodera* spp. in flower pots in crew's quarters of ships, in vegetable bins in ships' stores and in material used to pack plants brought in as baggage on ships and aircraft (Steiner *et al.*, 1951).   Burlap bags and packing material are also possible sources of *Heterodera* cysts (Chitwood, 1951; Mai and Harrison, 1959).

AGGREGATION AND SWARMING

Aggregation is well known throughout the animal kingdom (Allee, 1931) and the clumping together of suspensions of *Ditylenchus*, *Anguina* and *Aphelenchoides* offer good examples of this phenomenon. These three genera contain species which for at least part of their life cycle live on the host plant above ground level, so it is possible that aggregation has some survival value in resisting desiccation. The formation of 'eelworm wool' on bulbs and migrating nematode masses on sugar beet roots (Goffart, 1956) are caused by aggregations of *Ditylenchus dipsaci*. The possibility that such behaviour occurs in a drying environment needs investigating; in fact, the whole subject bristles with unanswered questions.

The factors which cause aggregation and then keep the nematodes together are little understood. Hollis (1960) extracted *Tylenchorhynchus* and *Hemicycliophora* spp. from soil and observed aggregations in suspension. The reaction was density dependent, species specific, non-sexual and independent of the original soil population density and purity. Hollis states that aggregation is caused by stickiness of the cuticle and may be related to the state of polysaccharide, lipid or protein substances of the cuticle. Whether such behaviour occurs in soil remains to be seen but it is known that males of *Heterodera schachtii* collect in clumps on sugar beet roots (Shepherd, private communication); it is possible that the males attract each other chemically or else collect by random movement.

The swarming of *Rhabditis* sp. on the surface of peat castings in mushroom houses (Staniland, 1957) and of other freeliving nematodes on the surface of cow faeces is usually thought to be related to dispersal by flies, beetles, acarina, etc., to which the nematodes attach themselves. Aggregations of the animal parasitic nematodes *Strongyloides* and *Ancylostoma* may be a similar phenomenon.

Plant nematodes are not distributed at random throughout the soil; in addition to physical and chemical factors, the nematodes themselves may cause mutual aggregation. Possible survival value of such behaviour may be related to host finding, increased chance of sexual reproduction in low-density populations and resistance to unfavourable environmental factors. The field of physiology and behaviour of nematode aggregations is virtually untouched and offers many problems for research.

REFERENCES

AKIMOTO, T. (1950). (On the motion of the *Ascaris lumbricoides* in a small tube. Report 1). *Hirosaki Medical Journal*, **1** (3), 53–56 (in Japanese).

ALLEE, W. C. (1931). *Animal aggregations*. Chicago: University of Chicago Press.

BAINES, R. C., GUNDY, S. D. VAN and SHER, S. A. (1959). Citrus and avocado nematodes. *Calif. Agric.* **13** (9), 16–18.

BEAUMONT, A. and STANILAND, L. N. (1941). The spread of eelworm in commercial narcissus plantings. *Ann. appl. Biol.* **28** (2), 135–141.

BEAVER, P. C. (1953). Persistence of hookworm larvae in soil. *Amer. J. trop. Med. Hyg.* **2**, 102–108.

BERGMAN, B. H. H. and DUUREN, A. J., VAN (1959a). Sugar beet eelworm and its control. VI. The influence of host plant roots and their secretion products on the orientation of *Heterodera schachtii* larvae *in vitro*. *Meded. Inst. Suikerbiet., Bergen-o-Z.* **29** (1), 1–24.

—— —— (1959b). Sugar beet eelworm and its control. VII. The action of metabolic products of some micro-organisms on the larvae of *Heterodera schachtii*. *Meded. Inst. Suikerbiet., Bergen-o-Z.* **29** (2), 27–52.

BINGEFORS, S. (1957). *Studies on breeding red clover for resistance to stem nematodes.* Uppsala: Almquist & Wiksells Boktryckeri AB.

—— (1960). Stem nematode in lucerne in Sweden. 1. A survey of the stem nematode in lucerne growing areas. *Kungl. Lantbrukshogskolans Annaler*, **26**, 317–322.

BIRD, A. F. (1959). The attractiveness of roots to the plant parasitic nematodes *Meloidogyne javanica* and *M. hapla*. *Nematologica*, 4 (4), 322–335.

—— (1960). Additional notes on the attractiveness of roots to plant parasitic nematodes. *Nematologica*, **5** (3), 217.

BLAKE, C. D. (1961). Importance of osmotic potential as a component of the total potential of the soil water on the movement of nematodes. *Nature, Lond.* **192** (4798), 144–145.

—— (1962). Some observations on the orientation of *Ditylenchus dipsaci* and invasion of oat seedlings. *Nematologica*, (3), 177–192.

BRETHERTON, F. P. and ROTHSCHILD, LORD (1961). Rheotaxis of spermatozoa. *Proc. roy. Soc.* B, **153**, 490–502.

BROWN, E. B. (1955). A seed-borne nematode infestation in annual asters. *Nature, Lond.* **175**, 178.

—— (1956). A seed-borne attack of chrysanthemum eelworm (*Aphelenchoides ritzema-bosi*) on the annual aster (*Callistephus chinensis*). *J. Helminth.* **30** (2/3), 145–148.

—— (1957). Lucerne stem eelworm, a serious threat to lucerne growing. *Agriculture, Lond.* **63**, 517–520.

BRUNS, W. (1937). Das Verhalten der invasionsfähigen Larven der Pferdestrongyliden in verschiedenen Bodenarten. *Inaugural Dissertation, Berlin*

BURGES, A. (1958). *Micro-organisms in the soil.* London: Hutchinson.

CAVENESS, F. E. and PANZER, J. D. (1960). Nemic galvanotaxis. *Proc. helm. Soc. Wash.* **27** (1), 73–74.

CHITWOOD, B. G. (1951). The golden nematode of potatoes. *U.S. Dept. Agric. Circ.* **875**.

COBB, G. S. and TAYLOR, A. L. (1953). *Heterodera leptonepia* n.sp., a cystforming nematode found in soil with stored potatoes. *Proc. helm. Soc. Wash.* **20** (1), 13–15.

COUCH, H. B. and BLOOM, J. R. (1960). Influence of soil moisture stresses on the development of the root-knot nematode. *Phytopathology*, **50** (4), 319–321.

COURTNEY, W. D. and HOWELL, H. B. (1952). Investigations on the bent grass nematode, *Anguina agrostis* (Steinbuch 1799) Filipjev 1936. *Plant Dis. Reptr.* **36** (3), 75–83.

CRALLEY, E. M. (1949). White tip of rice. *Phytopathology*, **39**, 5.

CROFTON, H. D. (1948a). The ecology of the immature phases of trichostrongyle nematodes. 1. The vertical distribution of infective larvae of *Trichostrongylus retortaeformis* in relation to their habitat. *Parasitology*, **39**, 17–25.

—— (1948b). The ecology of the immature phases of trichostrongyle nematodes. II. The effect of climatic factors on the availability of the infective larvae of *Trichostrongylus retortaeformis* to the host. *Parasitology*, **39**, 26–38.

—— (1954). The vertical migration of infective larvae of strongyloid nematodes. *J. Helminth.* **28**, 35–52.

DIERCKS, R. and KLEWITZ, R. (1962). Zur Samenubertragbarkeit einer an Ackerbohnen vorkommenden herkunft des Stengelälchens *Ditylenchus dipsaci* (Kühn). *Nematologica*, **7**, 155–163.

DUCHARME, E. P. (1955). Sub-soil drainage as a factor in the spread of the burrowing nematode. *Proc. Fla. State Hort. Soc.* **68**, 29–31.

ENDO, B. Y. (1959). Responses of root-lesion nematodes, *Pratylenchus brachyurus* and *P. zeae* to various plants and soil types. *Phytopathology*, **49** (7), 417–421.

FELDMESSER, J., CETAS, R. C., GRIMM, G. R., REBOIS, R. V. and WHIDDEN, R. (1960). Movement of *Radopholus similis* into rough lemon feeder roots and in soil and its relation to *Fusarium* in the roots. *Phytopathology*, **50** (9), 635.

FRAENKEL, G. S. and GUNN, D. L. (1940). *The orientation of animals.* Oxford: Clarendon Press.

FUCHS, P. (1911). Beitrage zur Biologie der Rübennematoden, *Heterodera schachtii. Z. Landw. Verswes. Öst.* **14**, 923–949.

FÜLLEBORN, F. (1932). Über die Taxen und das sonstige Verhalten der infektionsfähigen Larven von *Strongyloides* und *Ancylostoma. Zbl. Bakt. Abt. 1 Originale*, **126**, 161–180.

GODFREY, G. H. (1924). Dissemination of the stem and bulb infesting nematode *Tylenchus dipsaci* in seeds of certain composites. *J. agric. Res.* **28** (5), 473–478.

GOFFART, H. (1956). Über Nematodensukzessionen bei zucker-und Futterrüben. *Nematologica*, **1** (4), 349–352.

GOLDEN, A. M. and JORGENSON, E. C. (1961). The sugar beet nematode and its control. *U.S. Dept. Agric. Leaflet*, **486**.

GOODEY, T. (1950). Stem eelworm and clover. *Ann. appl. Biol.* **37** (2), 324–327.

GRAY, J. (1946). The mechanism of locomotion in snakes. *J. exp. Biol.* **23**, 101–120.

—— (1951). Undulatory propulsion in small organisms. *Nature, Lond.* **168**, 929–930.

HANCOCK, G. J. (1953). The self propulsion of microscopic organisms through liquids. *Proc. roy. Soc.* A **217**, 96–121.

HARRIS, J. E. and CROFTON, H. D. (1957). Structure and function in the nematodes: internal pressure and cuticular structure in *Ascaris. J. exp. Biol.* **34** (1), 116–130.

HENDERSON, V. E. and KATZNELSON, H. (1961). The effect of plant roots on the nematode population of the soil. *Canad. J. Microbiol.* **7**, 163–167.

HESLING, J. J. and WALLACE, H. R. (1961). Observations on the biology of chrysanthemum eelworm *Aphelenchoides ritzema-bosi* (Schwartz) Steiner in florists' chrysanthemums. 1. Spread of eelworm infestation. *Ann. appl. Biol.* **49**, 195–203.

HIRSCHMANN, H. (1959). Histological studies on the anterior region of *Heterodera glycines* and *Hoplolaimus tylenchiformis* (Nematoda: Tylenchida). *Proc. helm. Soc. Wash.* **26** (2), 73–90.

HOLLIS, J. P. (1960). Mechanism of swarming in *Tylenchorhynchus* species (Nematoda: Tylenchida). *Phytopathology*, **50**, 639.

ICHINOHE, M. (1955). (Survey on the 'Yellow Dwarf' disease of soybean plant caused by *Heterodera glycines* occurring in the peat soil in Hokkaido.) *Jap. J. Ecol.* **5** (1), 23–26 (in Japanese).

JOHNSON, R. N. and VIGLIERCHIO, D. R. (1961). The accumulation of plant parasitic nematode larvae around carbon dioxide and oxygen. *Proc. helm. Soc. Wash.* **28** (2), 171–174.

JONES, F. G. W. (1960). Some observations and reflections on host finding by plant nematodes. *Meded. LandbHoogesch. Gent.* **25** (3/4), 1009–1024.

KÄMPFE, L. (1960). Die Raumliche verteilung des primärbefalls von *Heterodera schachtii* Schmidt in den Wirtswurzeln. *Nematologica*, **5**, 18–26.

KINCAID, R. R. (1946). Soil factors affecting incidence of root knot. *Soil Science*, **61** (1), 101–109.

KLINGLER, J. (1959). Anziehung von Collembolen und Nematoden durch Kohlendioxyd-quellen. *Mitt. schweiz. ent. Ges.* **32** (2/3), 311–316.

—— (1961). Anziehungsversuche mit *Ditylenchus dipsaci* unter Berücksichtigung der Wirkung des Kohlendioxyds, des Redoxpotentials und anderer Faktoren. *Nematologica*, **6** (1), 69–84.

KUHN, H. (1959). Zum Problem der Wirtsfindung phytopathogener Nematoden. *Nematologica*, **4** (3), 165–171.

LANE, C. (1930). Behaviour of infective hookworm larvae. *Ann. trop. Med. Parasit.* **24**, 411–421.

—— (1933). The taxies of infective hookworm larvae. *Ann. trop. Med. Parasit.* **27**, 237–250.

LEGLER, F. (1950). Zur Frage der Infiltrationsweite von Ascarideneiern im Erdboden bei Abwasserversickerung. *Zbl. Bakt. Abt. 1 Originale*, **155**, 294–299.

LEWIS, G. D. (1956). An outbreak of onion bloat in southern New York. *Plant Dis. Reptr.* **40** (4), 271.

LINFORD, M. B. (1939). Attractiveness of roots and excised shoot tissues to certain nematodes. *Proc. helm. Soc. Wash.* **6** (1), 11–18.

LOEWENBERG, J. R., SULLIVAN, T. and SCHUSTER, M. L. (1960). Gall induction by *Meloidogyne incognita incognita* by surface feeding and factors affecting the behaviour pattern of the second stage larvae. *Phytopathology*, **50** (4), 322.

LOWNSBERY, B. F. and VIGLIERCHIO, D. R. (1961). Importance of response of *Meloidogyne hapla* to an agent from germinating tomato seeds. *Phytopathology*, **51** (4), 219–222.

LUC, M. (1961). Note préliminaire sur le déplacement de *Hemicycliophora paradoxa* Luc (Nematoda, Criconematidae) dans le sol. *Nematologica*, **6**, 95–106.

MAI, W. F. and HARRISON, M. B. (1959). The Golden Nematode. *Cornell Extension*, Bull. **870**.

Minz, G. (1956). Cyst forming nematodes in Israel. *Plant Dis. Reptr.* **40** (11), 971–973.

Mountain, W. B. and Boyce, H. R. (1958). The peach replant problem in Ontario. VI. The relation of *Pratylenchus penetrans* to the growth of young peach trees. *Canad. J. Bot.* **36**, 135–151.

Nielsen, C. O. (1949). Studies on the soil microfauna. II. The soil inhabiting nematodes. *Natura Jutlandica*, **2**, 1–131.

Oostenbrink, M. (1957). Der Transport von *Pratylenchus penetrans* (Nematoda) mit Pflanzgut. *Z. Pfl. Krankh.* **64** (7/10), 484–490.

Oteifa, B. A. and Elgindi, D. M. (1961). Physiological studies on host parasite relationship of the root knot nematode, *Meloidogyne javanica*. *Plant Dis. Reptr.* **45** (12), 928–929.

Parker, J. C. and Haley, A. J. (1960). Phototactic and thermotactic responses of the filariform larvae of the rat nematode *Nippostrongylus muris*. *Exp. Parasit.* **9**, 92–97.

Payne, F. K. (1923a). Investigations on the control of the hookworm disease. XIV. Field experiments on vertical migration of hookworm larvae. *Amer. J. Hyg.* **3**, 46–58.

——(1923b). Investigations on the control of hookworm disease. XXX. Studies on factors involved in migration of hookworm larvae in soil. *Amer. J. Hyg.* **3**, 547–583.

Peacock, F. C. (1959). The development of a technique for studying the host-parasite relationship of the root-knot nematode *Meloidogyne incognita* under controlled conditions. *Nematologica*, **4**, 43–55.

——(1961). A note on the attractiveness of roots to plant parasitic nematodes. *Nematologica*, **6**, 85–86.

Peters, B. G. (1952). Toxicity tests with vinegar eelworm. 1. Counting and culturing. *J. Helminth.* **26** (2/3), 97–110.

——(1953). Vertical migration of potato root eelworm. *J. Helminth.* **27**, (3/4), 107–112.

Petherbridge, F. R. and Jones, F. G. W. (1944). Beet eelworm (*Heterodera schachtii* Schmidt) in East Anglia, 1934–1943. *Ann. appl. Biol.* **31** (4), 320–332.

Rees, G. (1950). Observations on the vertical migrations of the third stage larvae of *Haemonchus contortus* (Rud.) on experimental plots of *Lolium perenne* S24, in relation to meteorological and micro-meteorological factors. *Parasitology*, **40**, 127–143.

Reesal, M. R. (1951). Observations on the biology of the infective larvae of *Strongyloides agoutii*. *Canad. J. Zool.* **29**, 109–115.

Reynolds, H. W. (1958). Control of the cotton root-knot nematode on extra-long-staple cotton. *Plant Dis. Reptr.* **42** (8), 944–947.

Rode, H. (1962). Untersuchungen über das Wandervermögen von Larven des Kartoffelnematoden (*Heterodera rostochiensis* Woll.) in Modellversuchen mit verschiedenen Bodenarten. *Nematologica*, **7**, 74–82.

Rode, H. and Staar, G. (1961). Die photographische Darstellung der Kriechspuren (ichnogramme) von Nematoden und ihre Bedeutung. *Nematologica*, **6**, 266–271.

Rohde, R. A. (1960). The influence of carbon dioxide on respiration of certain plant parasitic nematodes. *Proc. helm. Soc. Wash.* **27** (2), 160–164.

Salt, G., Hollick, F. S. J., Raw, F. and Brian, M. V. (1948). The arthropod population of pasture soil. *J. anim. Ecol.* **17**, 139.

SANDSTEDT, R. and SCHUSTER, M. L. (1962). Liquid trapping of *Meloido-gyne incognita incognita* about roots in agar medium. *Phytopathology*, **52** (2), 174–175.

SANDSTEDT, R., SULLIVAN, T. and SCHUSTER, M. L. (1961). Nematode tracks in the study of movement of *Meloidogyne incognita incognita*. *Nematologica*, **6** (4), 261–265.

SEINHORST, J. W. (1950). De betekenis van de toestand van de grond voor het optreden van aantasting door het stengelaaltje (*Ditylenchus dipsaci* (Kühn) Filipjev). *Tijdschr. PlZiekt.* **56** (5/6), 289–348.

SHEPHERD, A. M. (1959). The invasion and development of some species of *Heterodera* in plants of different host status. *Nematologica*, **4** (4), 253–267.

SHIBUYA, M. (1952). Studies on the varietal resistance of sweet potato to the root-knot nematode injury. *Mam. Fac. agric. Kagoshima Univ.* **1** (1), 1–22.

SOUTHEY, J. F. (1957). Observations on *Heterodera cacti* Filipjev et Sch. Stekhoven and *Meloidogyne spp.* on imported cactus plants with a list of new host records. *Nematologica*, **2** (1), 1–6.

SPINDLER, L. A. (1936). Effects of various physical factors on the survival of eggs and infective larvae of the swine nodular worm, *Oesophagostomum dentatum*. *J. Parasit.* **22**, 529.

STANILAND, L. N. (1957). The swarming of *Rhabditid* eelworms in mushroom houses. *Plant Pathology*, **6** (2), 61–62.

STAUFFER, H. (1924). Die Lokomotion der Nematoden. Beiträge zur Kausalmorphologie der Fadenwürmer. *Zool. Jahrb. Syst.* **49**, 1–118.

STEINER, G., TAYLOR, A. L. and COBB, G. S. (1951). Cyst-forming plant parasitic nematodes and their spread in commerce. *Proc. helm. Soc. Wash.* **18** (1), 13–18.

STREU, H. T., JENKINS, W. R. and HUTCHINSON, M. T. (1961). Nematodes associated with carnations. *New Jersey Agric. Exp. Sta. Rutgers*, Bull. **800**.

SUIT, R. F. and DUCHARME, E. P. (1957). Spreading decline of citrus. *State Plant Board of Florida*, **2**, Bull. 2.

TAMURA, I. and KEGASAWA, K. (1958). (II. On the parasitic ability of rice nematodes and their movement into hills.) *Jap. J. Ecol.* **8** (1), 37–42 (in Japanese.)

TARSHIS, I. B. (1958). A preliminary study of lateral migration by infective larvae of some cattle nematodes on experimentally contaminated forage plots. *Proc. helm. Soc. Wash.* **25**, 99–106.

TAYLOR, A. L. (1936). The genera and species of the Criconematinae, a subfamily of the Anguillulinidae (Nematoda). *Trans. Amer. Micro. Soc.* **55** (4), 391–421.

TAYLOR, G. I. (1951). Analysis of the swimming of microscopic organisms. *Proc. roy. Soc. A*, **209**, 447.

—— (1952). Analysis of the swimming of long and narrow animals. *Proc. roy. Soc. A*, **214**, 158.

THOMAS, H. A. (1959). On *Criconemoides xenoplax* Raski, with special reference to its biology under laboratory conditions. *Proc. helm. Soc. Wash.* **26** (1), 55–59.

THOMPSON, H. W., ROEBUCK, A. and COOPER, B. A. (1949). Floods and the spread of potato root eelworm. *J. Minist. Agric.* **56**, 109–114.

VIGLIERCHIO, D. R. (1961). Attraction of parasitic nematodes by plant root emanations. *Phytopathology*, **51** (3), 136–143.

VOSS, W. (1930). Beiträge zur Kenntnis der Älchenkrankheit der Chrysanthemen. *Z. Parasitenk.* **2**, 310–356.

WALLACE, H. R. (1956). Migration of nematodes. *Nature, Lond.*, **177**, 287–288.

—— (1958a). Movement of eelworms. I. The influence of pore size and moisture content of the soil on the migration of larvae of the beet eelworm. *Heterodera schachtii* Schmidt. *Ann. appl. Biol.* **46** (1), 74–85.

—— (1958b). Movement of eelworms. II. A comparative study of the movement in soil of *Heterodera schachtii* Schmidt and of *Ditylenchus dipsaci* (Kühn) Filipjev. *Ann. appl. Biol.* **46** (1), 86–94.

—— (1958c). Movement of eelworms. III. The relationship between eelworm length, activity and mobility. *Ann. appl. Biol.* **46** (4), 662–668.

—— (1958d). Observations on the emergence from cysts and the orientation of larvae of three species of the genus *Heterodera* in the presence of host plant roots. *Nematologica*, **3**, 236–243.

—— (1959a). Movement of eelworms. IV. The influence of water percolation. *Ann. appl. Biol.* **47** (1), 131–139.

—— (1959b). Movement of eelworms. V. Observations on *Aphelenchoides ritzema-bosi* (Schwartz, 1912) Steiner, 1932 on florists' chrysanthemums. *Ann. appl. Biol.* **47** (2), 350–360.

—— (1959c). The movement of eelworms in water films. *Ann. appl. Biol.* **47** (2), 366–370.

—— (1960). Movement of eelworms. VI. The influence of soil type, moisture gradients and host plant roots on the migration of the potato-root eelworm *Heterodera rostochiensis* Wollenweber. *Ann. appl. Biol.* **48** (1), 107–120.

—— (1961). The orientation of *Ditylenchus dipsaci* to physical stimuli. *Nematologica*, **6**, 222–236.

—— (1962). Observations on the behaviour of *Ditylenchus dipsaci* in soil. *Nematologica*, **7**, 91–101.

WALLACE, H. R. and GREET, D. N. (1963). Observations on the taxonomy and biology of *Tylenchorhynchus macrurus* (Goodey, 1932) Filipjev, 1936, and *Tylenchorhynchus icarus* n.sp. *Parasitology* (in press).

WEISCHER, B. (1959). Experimentelle Untersuchungen über die Wanderung von Nematoden. *Nematologica*, **4** (3), 172–186.

WHITE, J. H. (1953). Wind-borne dispersal of potato-root eelworm. *Nature, Lond.* **172**, 686–687.

WIDDOWSON, E., DONCASTER, C. C. and FENWICK, D. W. (1958). Observations on the development of *Heterodera rostochiensis* Woll. in sterile root cultures. *Nematologica*, **3**, 308–314.

WIESER, W. (1955). The attractiveness of plants to larvae of root-knot nematodes. 1. The effect of tomato seedlings and excised roots on *Meloidogyne hapla* Chitwood. *Proc. helm. Soc. Wash.* **22** (2), 106–112.

—— (1956). The attractiveness of plants to larvae of root-knot nematodes. II. The effect of excised bean, eggplant and soybean roots on *Meloidogyne hapla* Chitwood. *Proc. helm. Soc. Wash.* **23** (1), 59–64.

CHAPTER 6

Some Aspects of Behaviour

The study of nematode behaviour can be approached either by direct observation of the nematode under near-natural conditions or by experimentation. The two approaches are complementary but, unfortunately, little experimental work has been done on the stimuli which evoke behaviour responses. This lack of balance makes difficult any interpretation of cause and effect in the topics to be discussed in this chapter. Furthermore, in the absence of such information, it is tempting to describe the responses of nematodes in terms of directive behaviour, as though there was some innate drive to a final goal. It is probably wise to avoid such a teleological explanation of behaviour and confine discussion to objective observation.

FEEDING

Soil nematodes may be arbitrarily classified into the following three groups, according to their feeding habits: saprobes which ingest particulate matter, bacteria, etc., predators which feed on larger organisms and finally the plant and animal parasites. The plant parasitic nematodes are characterised by their mouth spear or stylet with which they pierce the host plant cells in much the same way that such sucking insects as aphids penetrate plants with their mouthparts (see Plate IV).

The orientation of nematodes to plant roots has already been discussed. We have now to consider what happens when they reach the root. The nematode first probes cells in its near vicinity without actually puncturing them (Krusberg, 1959; Zuckerman, 1960, 1961); at the same time the head may move from side to side (Thomas, 1959; Standifer and Perry, 1960). It is possible that, when the lip region touches a suitable spot on the root surface, sensory receptors are stimulated to initiate the feeding process (Thomas, 1959). Factors associated with the root surface which induce penetration may be chemical or physical. Dickinson (1959), for example, suggests that suberisation and the curvature of roots may be important.

Before penetrating the cell the body is arched, so bringing the head and stylet down at right angles to the root (Rohde and Jenkins, 1957; Sledge, 1959; Krusberg, 1959; Zuckerman, 1960; Standifer and Perry, 1960; Streu *et al.*, 1961). Penetration then starts (see Plate V). When the nematode exerts pressure with its spear, an equal but opposite force (in mathematical terms, a normal reaction) is exerted by the cell surface.

Thus, unless there is some additional force pushing the nematode against the root, penetration cannot occur. This additional force may be provided by the surface tension of the water film in which the nematode lies, by the normal reactions at points of contact between the body and soil particles or by friction between the nematode and the substratum. Dickinson (1959) also suggests that suction developed by the fused lips enables the nematode to adhere to hydrophobic surfaces such as suberised plant roots. It is likely that all these factors work together; in a well-drained soil, for example, the surface tension of the water films probably provides sufficient force to assist penetration. When there is more water in the soil pores the surface tension forces acting on the nematode decrease, so adhesion by the lips, the normal reactions from the soil particles and friction play an important role. The arched position that nematodes adopt, prior to penetration, orientates the stylet at right angles to the root, thus giving maximum thrust and simultaneously provides for the additional thrust from the water films and soil particles.

The fact that larvae of the animal parasitic nematodes *Necator americanus* and *Ancylostoma caninum* can only penetrate the host skin when in a thin film of water, whereas *Strongyloides* larvae penetrate in deep water in both an upward and a downward direction (Goodey, 1922, 1925) suggests that adhesion by the lips prior to host penetration may also occur in species of animal parasitic nematodes such as *Strongyloides*.

The nematode now starts to penetrate the plant cell wall. The stylet pierces the cell wall but only part of it penetrates into the cell (Linford, 1942; Krusberg, 1959; Rohde and Jenkins, 1957). The head may move from side to side to give a rasping action to the stylet (Rohde and Jenkins, 1957; Thomas, 1959), the extent of the thrust being short at the beginning of penetration but usually increasing as the stylet moves further into the cell (Thomas, 1959; Krusberg, 1959). Some nematode species push the stylet into the cell at a rate of about two to six thrusts per second (Edwardo, 1960; Zuckerman, 1960, 1961) whereas others are much slower (Rhoades and Linford, 1961a).

Following penetration there is a period of immobility when enzymes are probably secreted into the cell. Linford (1937a) observed the secretion of saliva from the stylet of *Aphelenchoides tenuicaudatus* and Sledge (1959) made a similar observation with *Helicotylenchus nannus*. The internal flow of saliva to the stylet tip was observed in root knot larvae (Linford, 1937b) and in *Paratylenchus projectus* and *Paratylenchus dianthus* (Rhoades and Linford, 1961a). Krusberg and Sasser (1956) suggest that staining reactions in sections of roots parasitised by the lance nematode *Hoplolaimus coronatus* may indicate the presence of nematode secretions. Dickinson (1959), while studying the attachment of larvae of *Heterodera schachtii* to nitrocellulose membranes, observed globules at the site where the larvae had penetrated the membrane. He suggested that these might be a nematode secretion. Experiments by Goffart and Heiling (1962) showed that the salivary secretions of *Ditylenchus destructor*,

Ditylenchus dipsaci, Heterodera rostochiensis and *Heterodera schachtii* contained amylase, invertase and pectin-dissociating enzymes. It seems possible then that *extra-corporeal* digestion by nematode enzymes may occur within the host cell.

Following saliva secretion, the median bulb of the oesophagus pulsates and the cell contents are ingested (Linford, 1941; Rohde and Jenkins, 1957; Zuckerman, 1960, 1961). The median bulb probably acts as a pumping mechanism as in the free-living nematodes. Thus, Doncaster (1962) showed that in *Rhabditis oxycerca* and *Pelodera lambdiensis*, food particles were drawn into the fore-end of the gut by a sudden dilation of the procorpus and metacorpus. Closure of the lumen in these regions expelled excess water and the accumulation of food was passed steadily backward by a wave of contraction of the radial muscles in the isthmus. Food particles were then forced back to the intestine by dilation and closure of the lumen of the posterior oesophageal bulb. Similar studies are needed to determine the feeding mechanism in plant nematodes and to see whether the turgor pressure of the plant cell contributes by forcing the cell contents up the stylet as occurs during the feeding of aphids (Kennedy and Mittler, 1953).

The time spent in feeding on a particular cell varies widely according to the species. *Trichodorus christiei* may feed for only 1 to 4·5 min. on one cell (Zuckerman, 1961) whereas females of *Paratylenchus* spp. may spend several days at the same cell (Rhoades and Linford, 1961b). The use of radioactive isotopes may be a useful technique for studying feeding times. Thus, Sprau and Süss (1962) were able to show that *Longidorus maximus* fed on sugar beet roots by spraying the plant leaves with NaH_2PO_4 labelled with radioactive phosphorus (P^{32}). The radioactivity of the nematodes near the treated plants was greater than those from the untreated plants.

There are, of course, variations in this pattern of feeding behaviour; van Gundy (1959), for example, did not observe any rest period after penetration, the oesophageal bulb pulsating all the time. Nevertheless, as Linford (1941) suggests, the general sequence of events is consistent enough to demonstrate the coordination between the action of the stylet and pulsation of the median bulb. Linford (1937a) states that the bulb pulsates only when the stylet is protruded. Nevertheless, during enzyme secretion, pulsation ceases even though the stylet is still protruded. It is possible that secretion of saliva is evoked by contact with cell contents following penetration. The termination of salivary flow down the stylet may then allow the cell contents to move up the stylet and so induce the pulsations of the median bulb. On the other hand, penetration of the cell wall may be a necessary precursor to saliva secretion and ingestion.

The elucidation of such behaviour sequences may provide answers to several questions. Are there any particular stimuli at the root surface which evoke nematode feeding? What is the chemical nature of nematode saliva and what stimuli evoke its secretion? What is the function of the median bulb? Is it possible to culture plant parasitic nematodes in media of known composition if the feeding responses do not occur, or must the nutrients be supplied in a membrane to simulate a plant cell, as Hollis (1957) suggests?

INVASION

Invasion is closely linked to feeding, for both require the penetration of the outer cell layer of the host. Some nematodes feed on the plant by inserting the stylet into cells and then they migrate to another part of the plant to feed; these are the browsing forms. Other species, called inter-mittent feeders by Goodey (1943), push the head and oesophageal region of the body into the cortex to feed before moving to another site. Finally, in some nematode species, the whole of the body enters the plant where growth, development and reproduction occur; these are usually called endoparasites, whereas the other two groups are ectoparasites.

In plant nematology the term invasion is often used loosely to cover the whole field of infestation of the host plant. Movement and orienta-tion may play an important role in this process, so in the present context invasion is defined as the entry of endoparasitic species into the host plant.

To invade, as well as to feed on a host plant, a nematode must use external resistances to give it the required thrust. Thus, nematodes can invade plant roots when they are in thin films or in agar but not when the plant is immersed in water. The vigour of the nematode itself may also decide whether invasion can occur. Dropkin (1957) showed that after larvae of *Heterodera rostochiensis* had been kept for 21 days after hatching only 19 per cent invaded the host plant compared with 71 per cent for newly hatched larvae. The energy needed by nematodes for invasion is not known, but it may be large enough to cause a shrinkage in the nematode by using up food reserves (Bird, 1959). The physical and chemical properties of the plant itself may also affect invasion. Sasser and Taylor (1952) suggest that resistance in plants to root knot nematodes may be caused in part by decreased invasion. Resistant varieties of clover may be invaded by *Ditylenchus dipsaci* to a lesser degree than susceptible varieties (Bingefors, 1957), but Blake (1962) was unable to show this for *Ditylenchus dipsaci* on oats, invasion bearing no relation to resistance.

We have already seen that many species of plant nematodes orientate to and aggregate at particular sections of the root. The question now arises whether the nematodes influence each other during invasion. Larvae of *Meloidogyne incognita* simultaneously invade the plant through a hole made by the first larva to enter (Peacock, 1959). The observation suggests that the number of nematodes invading the plant might be higher where there is aggregation and invasion through the same aperture. However, Dropkin (1957) did not find this for *Heterodera rostochiensis*. He used inocula of one, two and twenty-five larvae of *Heterodera rostochiensis* per plant, but no difference was found in the percentage of larvae that invaded. However, this may only be the result of using low levels of nematode inocula. Similarly, Blake (1962) showed that there was a linear relationship between the numbers of *Ditylenchus dipsaci* invading oat plants and the number introduced on to the plant, until the inoculum reached a level when the number of nematodes invading remained constant. He attributed this to competition between individuals for invasion sites or by the nematodes themselves rendering the root repellent to other nematodes. Apel and Kämpfe (1957) also demonstrated that there is an upper limit to the number of nematodes in a root.

The evidence so far suggests, then, that nematodes probably have little influence on each other during invasion, except at high population levels when inhibition may occur.

Observations on the behaviour of nematodes invading plants are chiefly confined to the genus *Meloidogyne*. The larvae collect in a localised region immediately behind the apical meristem (Godfrey and Oliveira, 1932; Peacock, 1959). Here, a nematode may stay for as long as 12 to 24 hr. at one spot (Loewenburg *et al.*, 1960), repeatedly penetrating the epidermal cells with the stylet. Eventually, the cell wall collapses and the head is pushed through the aperture (Linford, 1942). The larva takes up to 6 hr. to enter the plant (Godfrey and Oliveira, 1932), averaging about 3 to 4 hr. (Loewenburg *et al.*, 1960). Movement through the epidermis is halting as though there are periods when the nematode feeds on different cells. The stylet also separates cells along the middle lamella, thereby enabling freer movement (Linford, 1942). Once inside, the larva pushes its way between the cells as it moves about in the root. Other larvae then follow through the same hole (Godfrey and Oliveira, 1932; Peacock, 1959) which becomes enlarged and surrounded by necrotic cells.

The invasion of citrus roots by *Radopholus similis* is different in some respects. Penetration takes longer, 24 to 72 hr., and there is little indication on the root surface of the point of entry. The nematode penetrates the epidermis and underlying cortex of young roots by dissolving the cells. There is no mechanical forcing apart, but a digestion of successive cells as the nematode moves through the tissues. As a result, tunnels and irregular cavities are formed (Ducharme, 1959).

In addition to invasion by digestion and by mechanical destruction of cells, some species enter the host through natural openings. Root knot nematode larvae may invade potato tubers through enlarged lenticels which sometimes occur on tubers grown in wet soil (Parris, 1948). *Ditylenchus dipsaci* may invade clover seedlings via the stomata (Bingefors, 1957) and *Heterodera rostochiensis* may enter host plants at root junctions as the lateral roots break through the cortex of the primary root (Widdowson *et al.*, 1958). *Aphelenchoides ritzemabosi* invades the chrysanthemum leaf through the stomata which occur chiefly on the undersurface. The nematodes swim actively in the water films on the surface of the leaf but invasion only occurs when the films have evaporated and become so thin that the nematodes can only crawl slowly. At this stage they glide through the stomatal apertures in 3 or 4 sec. (Wallace, 1959). This is a good example of the influence of the environment, in this case water, affecting the ability to invade. There seems to be a similar situation with the hookworm larvae of *Ancylostoma caninum* which also requires thin films for invasion (Goodey, 1922, 1925).

Further research is clearly needed on nematode invasion, particularly variations in behaviour of particular species on different hosts and of different species on the same host. Direct observation of nematodes in observation boxes or on agar would be the first step towards this goal, and by using time-lapse photography and cinematography, some of the disadvantages of subjective interpretation could be overcome.

QUIESCENCE

Plant nematodes which become inactive under certain environmental conditions such as low temperatures or absence of water, and are capable of reactivation, are said to be in a dormant, anabiotic or quiescent state. Quiescence is probably an adaptation for survival in fluctuating environmental conditions.

Several species of nematodes become quiescent in a dry environment. Fourth stage larvae of *Ditylenchus dipsaci* aggregate into masses under drying conditions. The mushroom spawn nematode, *D. myceliophagus* behaves similarly and Cairns (1952, 1953a) suggests that such behaviour is important for the survival of this species in mushroom beds where dry conditions often occur. In the dried state nematodes are also more resistant to high temperatures (Cairns, 1953b; Courtney and Latta, 1934). Nematodes can remain alive for long periods in a quiescent state. Observations by Fielding (1951) on *D. dipsaci*, *D. phyllobius*, *Tylenchus balsamophilus*, *Anguina agrostis*, and *A. tritici* showed that all these species were capable of surviving for many years in the dried state. At the time the observations were made the various species had been stored dry for periods ranging from 4 years for *A. agrostis* to 28 years for *A. tritici*. The longest period of quiescence recorded is 39 years for *Tylenchus polyhypnus* (Steiner and Albin, 1946). The stage in the life cycle when quiescence occurs varies between species. For example, it is the fourth stage larvae in *Ditylenchus dipsaci*, the second stage larvae in *Anguina* spp. and the adult in *Aphelenchoides ritzemabosi*.

While it is interesting to know that some species of nematodes can resist drying for such long periods, the relevance of this in terms of survival under natural conditions is questionable, for they are unlikely to meet with conditions of such prolonged drought. *Aphelenchoides ritzemabosi*, for example, can be recovered from dried leaves and stored alive for up to two years, but in the field the nematode is only subjected to desiccation for a matter of days, the time in fact between mists or rain showers when the nematodes migrate actively over the plant surface (Hesling and Wallace, 1961).

Quiescence may also be induced by low temperatures. Bosher and McKeen (1954) showed that *Ditylenchus dipsaci* could survive freezing for 20 min. at $-80°C$, followed by vacuum dehydration and storage *in vacuo* for 28 days. The nematodes were killed and large vacuoles formed in the body, however, if they were subjected to such a temperature without dehydration, although mortality was reduced if the nematodes were in a solution of high osmotic pressure. Under these conditions, the water in the body would be in a bound state. Bosher and McKeen suggest that in the soil, organic matter would have a similar effect, protecting the nematodes in cold winter periods. *Ditylenchus dipsaci* also lives longer at low temperatures in the quiescent state (Bosher, 1960).

Quiescence in species of *Heterodera* has been studied by several workers. It is an interesting subject because it raises the question of whether there is some inherent physiological factor in the nematodes causing a type of quiescence analogous to true diapause in insects.

Lownsbery (1951) states that few larvae of *Heterodera rostochiensis* emerged from cysts collected in July, stored at $25°C$ and then placed in potato root diffusate in December. The larval emergence from cysts collected in November, after freezing temperatures in the soil, was also low. Lownsbery concluded that exposure to winter conditions, particularly temperature, are not necessary to induce quiescence, which is a part of the nematodes' physiology. Reinmuth (1929), Triffitt (1930), Calam, Raistrick and Todd (1949) and Winslow (1956) also concluded that variation in hatchability of *H. rostochiensis* cysts is a seasonal effect. Fenwick and Reid (1953), Dunn (1954) and Ellenby (1955) suggest that quiescence in this species is caused by environmental factors earlier in the year. Cunningham (1960) showed conclusively that cysts of *H. rostochiensis* collected from soil in midsummer and stored under laboratory conditions gave an abundant larval emergence in winter, whereas emergence from cysts of the same population was very low when they were allowed to remain in the soil out of doors until late autumn. Cunningham concludes that quiescence is not inherent in the seasonal hatch cycle of *H. rostochiensis*, but is induced by the soil conditions in the previous autumn or late summer. Although this seems to be the best hypothesis so far, further confirmation is necessary, together with information on the factors which induce quiescence.

It is often stated that plant nematodes become quiescent under adverse environmental conditions. While there is unequivocal evidence that nematodes can resist desiccation and low temperatures there is no evidence at present that they become quiescent at low oxygen or high CO_2 concentrations or at high temperatures. Although quiescent nematodes are always inactive, the converse, that inactive nematodes are quiescent, is

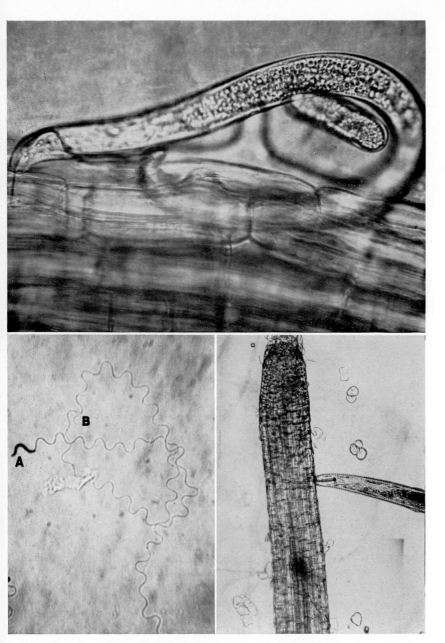

III. *Lower left:* Tracks of a larva of *Meloidogyne incognita* on the surface of agar. Length of larva ⅓ mm; A, nematode; B, track. *See* page 103. Sandstedt *et al.*, *Nematologica*, 1961. E. J. Brill. Reproduced by permission.

IV. *Top:* Female *Paratylenchus projectus* feeding on epidermal cell of tobacco root. One egg has been laid. *See* page 138. (Reproduced by permission of Rhoades and Linford, 1961a.)

V. *Lower right: Hemicycliophora similis* feeding on a root of *Vaccinium macrocarpon* showing penetration of mouth spear. *See* page 138. Zuckerman, *Nematologica*, 1961. E. J. Brill. Reproduced by permission.

VI. *Top:* Chrysanthemum variety Pennine Snow severely attacked by *Aphelenchoides ritzemabosi*. Other adjacent varieties show no apparent symptoms. *See* page 163.

VII. *Bottom:* The edge of a grove of 30-year-old orange trees in Florida showing margin of area with spreading decline caused by *Radopholus similis*. *See* page 166. (Reproduced by permission of R. F. Suit, photographed by Harriet Long.)

obviously not true. Thus, extreme environmental conditions often induce inactivity but whether the nematodes become quiescent depends on their physiological make-up. Ability to survive long periods of low temperature, low moisture, low oxygen concentration, etc., varies between species and between races and individuals of the same species but how this occurs is still unanswered.

At present, information on quiescence is chiefly confined to those species in which it is well marked, but the phenomenon may be more widespread than this. Rhoades and Linford (1961b), for example, have shown that preadult larvae of *Paratylenchus projectus* are more tolerant to desiccation and low temperatures than other stages and that they persist in soil without feeding until secretions from a host plant stimulate moulting to the adult stage. Is it possible that quiescence is widespread among soil inhabiting plant parasitic nematodes when conditions of moisture, temperature, food and oxygen are suboptimal?

LONGEVITY

As we have just seen, some nematodes which become quiescent in a dry environment are capable of living for many years; *Ditylenchus dipsaci*, for example, can survive desiccation for at least 23 years (Fielding, 1951) although longevity decreases with increasing humidity (Palo, 1962). In the soil, in the absence of host plants, however, this species may only persist for $1\frac{1}{2}$ years (Goodey, 1931) and with host plants present, when feeding and reproduction occur, longevity may be as short as 45 to 73 days (Yuksel, 1960). Under different environmental conditions, therefore, a nematode's life-span may vary between wide limits.

Data from laboratory experiments and field studies have given some idea of the time nematodes can live and the factors which cause such wide variation. Sub-zero temperatures may be fatal to some species (Reuver, 1959; Rhoades and Linford, 1961b) but with *Ditylenchus dipsaci* low temperatures may prolong longevity if the nematode is in a solution of high osmotic pressure (Bosher and McKeen, 1954; Bosher, 1960), or in dry soil (Sayre and Mountain, 1962). Low temperatures above zero increase the longevity of many nematodes. *Meloidogyne hapla* and *Pratylenchus penetrans* survive longer at 1 to 4·5°C than at 18 to 24°C but *Helicotylenchus nannus* survived equally well at both temperature ranges (Ferris, 1960). As temperature rises there is generally a decrease in longevity. Krusberg (1959) found that over the range of 2 to 24°C, the number of *Tylenchorhynchus claytoni* recovered from soil decreased with increase in temperature. The survival of *Aphelenchoides besseyi* decreased as the temperature increased from 20 to 30°C (Tamura and Kegasawa, 1958). The optimum temperature for survival of many species probably lies within the range 2 to 10°C; Bergeson (1959), for example, gives 10°C for eggs and larvae of *Meloidogyne acrita*. At this temperature the nematode lived for more than a year in the absence of a

TABLE 3. *Longevity of plant parasitic nematodes in fallow soil*

Species	Survival Time	Author
Anguina agrostis	1 year	Courtney and Howell, 1952
A. tritici	1 year	Leukel, 1957
Aphelenchoides ritzemabosi	3 months	Hesling and Wallace, 1961
A. ritzemabosi	17 weeks	French and Barraclough, 1962
Ditylenchus dipsaci	2 years	Lewis and Mai, 1960
D. dipsaci	1½ years	Goodey, 1931
Helicotylenchus buxophilus	8 months	Golden, 1956
H. nannus	6 months*	Ferris, 1960
Heterodera rostochiensis larvae	9 months	Franklin, 1937a
H. rostochiensis cysts	7 years	Miles and Miles, 1942
H. schachtii larvae	1 year	Golden and Shafer, 1960
H. schachtii cysts	6 years	Thorne, 1923
Hoplolaimus coronatus	6 months*	Tarjan, 1960
Meloidogyne sp.	16 months	Franklin, 1937b
M. hapla	6 months*	Ferris, 1960
Paratylenchus dianthus	4 years 7 months	Rhoades and Linford, 1961b
P. projectus	4 years 7 months	Rhoades and Linford, 1961b
Pratylenchus brachyurus	6 months*	Tarjan, 1960a
P. brachyurus	1 year 9 months	Feldmesser et al., 1960
P. penetrans	6 months*	Ferris, 1960
Radopholus similis	3 months	Feldmesser et al., 1960
R. similis	4 months	Birchfield, 1957
R. similis	6 months	Tarjan, 1960
R. similis	3 months	Ducharme, 1955
Tylenchorhynchus claytoni	10 months	Krusberg, 1959
T. icarus	9 months	Wallace and Greet, 1963
Tylenchulus semipenetrans	10 years	Baines et al., 1959

* No observations made beyond 6 months.

host, while at 10 to 15°C longevity was 6 months, at 15 to 20°C, 4 to 5 months and at 20 to 32°C, 3 to 4 months. Similarly Baines and his colleagues (1959) showed that *Tylenchulus semipenetrans*, the citrus nematode, stayed alive for more than a year at 9°C and 15°C, but for only a year at 21°C, 6½ months at 27°C and 2½ months at 33°C. At temperatures of 2 to 10°C many plant parasitic nematodes are slow moving or even inactive, so it is possible that quiescence, induced by low temperature, increases longevity.

Although many plant nematode species are incapable of surviving desiccation they may be tolerant of low soil moisture levels. *Paratylenchus dianthus*, *P. projectus* (Rhoades and Linford, 1961b) and *P. amblycephalus* (Reuver, 1959) survive such conditions and *Anguina tritici* lives longer in the absence of a host plant when the soil is dry rather than wet (Leukel, 1957). We have seen in Chapter 4 that high soil moisture may kill nematodes through increased microbial action or possibly lack of oxygen or excess CO_2, so it is perhaps not surprising that longevity is decreased in wet soils.

It is necessary to know how long nematodes will persist in soil if they are to be controlled by crop rotation or by leaving land fallow. Some examples of survival in fallow soil are given in Table 3.

From these few examples it is evident that the longevity of many nematode species in soil is of the order of several months and long enough in most cases to enable at least some of the nematodes to survive from one year to the next in the absence of a host crop. The figures quoted in Table 3 are only approximate times, future work will undoubtedly extend the survival time of many of the species.

Although plant parasitic nematodes may survive for several months or even years in fallow soil, this does not mean that they are necessarily capable of infesting a host plant at the end of this time. During their period of starvation food reserves are used up (Golden, 1956; Krusberg, 1959; Golden and Shafer, 1960) and their vigour may be reduced. On the other hand, the longevity of a species in a particular soil may be curtailed by predators and parasites or by some detrimental physical factor.

Experimental data suggest that soil factors such as low temperature and moisture induce quiescence, thereby prolonging the life of plant parasitic nematodes. Longevity is, therefore, an expression of physiological age rather than of time. Research into the physiology of ageing and quiescence in phytoparasitic nematodes may elucidate this point.

REFERENCES

APEL, A. and KÄMPFE, L. (1957). Beziehungen zwischen Wirt und Parasit im Infektionsverlauf von *Heterodera schachtii* Schmidt in kurzfristigen Topfversuchen. II. Haupt. und Nebenwurzelbefall, Geschlechtsverhältnis der Adulten und Lagerichtung der Larven. *Nematologica*, 2 (3), 215–227.

BAINES, R. C., VAN GUNDY, S. D. and SHER, S. A. (1959). Citrus and Avocado nematodes. *Calif. Agric.* 13 (9), 16–18.

BERGESON, G. B. (1959). The influence of temperature on the survival of some species of the genus *Meloidogyne* in the absence of a host. *Nematologica*, 4, 344–354.

BINGEFORS, S. (1957). *Studies on breeding red clover for resistance to stem nematodes.* Uppsala: Almquist & Wiksells Boktryckeri AB.

BIRCHFIELD, W. (1957). Observations on the longevity without food of the burrowing nematode. *Phytopathology*, 47 (3), 161–162.

BIRD, A. F. (1959). Development of the root-knot nematodes *Meloidogyne javanica* (Treub) and *Meloidogyne hapla* Chitwood in the tomato. *Nematologica*, 4 (1), 31–42.

BLAKE, C. D. (1962). The etiology of tulip-root disease in susceptible and resistant varieties of oats infested by the stem nematode, *Ditylenchus dipsaci* (Kühn) Filipjev. I. Invasion of the host and reproduction of the nematode. *Ann. appl. Biol.* **50**, 703–712.

BOSHER, J. E. (1960). Longevity *in vitro* of *Ditylenchus dipsaci* (Kühn) Filipjev from narcissus. *Proc. helm. Soc. Wash.* **27** (2), 127–128.

BOSHER, J. E. and McKEEN, W. E. (1954). Lyophilization and low temperature studies with the bulb and stem nematode *Ditylenchus dipsaci* (Kühn) 1858) Filipjev. *Proc. helm. Soc. Wash.* **21** (2), 113–117.

CAIRNS, E. J. (1952). Anabiotic survival of a new species of *Ditylenchus* nematode. *Phytopathology*, **42**, 464.

—— (1953a). Moisture conditions and control by heat of the mushroom spawn nematode *Ditylenchus* spp. *Phytopathology*, **43**, 404.

—— (1953b). Relationship of the environmental moisture conditions of the mushroom-spawn nematode, *Ditylenchus* sp., to its control by heat. *Mushroom Science II. Gembloux*, 161–164.

CALAM, C. T., RAISTRICK, H. and TODD, A. R. (1949). The potato eelworm hatching factor. I. The preparation of concentrates of the hatching factor and a method of bioassay. *Biochem. J.* **45**, 513–519.

COURTNEY, W. D. and HOWELL, H. B. (1952). Investigations on the bent grass nematode, *Anguina agrostis* (Steinbuch 1799) Filipjev 1936. *Plant. Dis. Reptr.* **36** (3), 75–83.

COURTNEY, W. D. and LATTA, R. (1934). Some experiments concerning the revival of quiescent *Anguillulina dipsaci. Proc. helm. Soc. Wash.* **1** (1), 20.

CUNNINGHAM, P. C. (1960). An investigation of winter dormancy in *Heterodera rostochiensis. Sci. Proc. R. Dublin Soc.*, Series B, **1**, 1–4.

DICKINSON, S. (1959). The behaviour of larvae of *Heterodera schachtii* on nitrocellulose membranes. *Nematologica*, **4** (1), 60–66.

DONCASTER, C. C. (1962). Nematode feeding mechanisms. I. Observations on *Rhabditis* and *Pelodera. Nematologica*, **8**, (4), 313–320.

DROPKIN, V. H. (1957). A method for determination of the infectivity of *Heterodera rostochiensis* larvae. *Nematologica*, **2**, 72–75.

DUCHARME, E. P. (1955). Sub-soil drainage as a factor in the spread of the burrowing nematode. *Proc. Fla. State hort. Soc.* **68**, 29–31.

—— (1959). Morphogenesis and histopathology of lesions induced on citrus roots by *Radopholus similis. Phytopathology*, **49** (6), 388–396.

DUNN, E. (1954). Factors influencing the emergence of *Heterodera rostochiensis* larvae. *Nature, Lond.*, **173** (4408), 780.

EDWARDO, A. A., DI (1960). Time-lapse studies of movement, feeding and hatching of *Pratylenchus penetrans. Phytopathology*, **50** (8), 570.

ELLENBY, C. (1955). The seasonal response of the potato-root eelworm, *Heterodera rostochiensis* Wollenweber: Emergence of larvae throughout the year from cysts exposed to different temperature cycles. *Ann. appl. Biol.* **43** (1), 1–11.

FELDMESSER, J., FEDER, W. A., REBOIS, R. V. and HUTCHINS, P. C. (1960). Longevity of *Radopholus similis* and *Pratylenchus brachyurus* in the greenhouse. *Anat. Rec.* **137** (3), 355.

FENWICK, D. W. and REID, E. (1953). Seasonal fluctuations in the degree of hatching from cysts of the potato root eelworm. *Nature, Lond.* **171**, 47.

FERRIS, J. M. (1960). Effect of storage temperatures on survival of plant parasitic nematodes in soil. *Phytopathology*, **50** (9), 635.

FIELDING, M. J. (1951). Observations on the length of dormancy in certain plant infecting nematodes. *Proc. helm. Soc. Wash.* **18** (2), 110–112.

FRANKLIN, M. T. (1937a). The survival of free larvae of *Heterodera schachtii* in soil. *J. Helminth.* **15** (2), 69–74.

—— (1937b). On the survival of *Heterodera marioni* infection out of doors in England. *J. Helminth.* **15** (2), 75–76.

FRENCH, N. and BARRACLOUGH, R. M. (1962). Survival of *Aphelenchoides ritzemabosi* (Schwartz) in soil and dry leaves. *Nematologica*, **7**, 309–316.

GODFREY, G. H. and OLIVEIRA, J. (1932). The development of the root-knot nematode in relation to root tissues of pineapple and cowpea. *Phytopathology*, **22** (4), 325–348.

GOFFART, H. and HEILING, A. (1962). Beobachtungen über die enzymatische Wirkung von Speicheldrüsensekreten pflanzenparasitärer Nematoden. *Nematologica*, **7**, 173–176.

GOLDEN, A. M. (1956). Taxonomy of the spiral nematodes (*Rotylenchus* and *Helicotylenchus*), and the developmental stages and host-parasite relationships of *R. buxophilus*, n.sp., attacking boxwood. *Univ. Md. agric. Exp. Sta.* Bull. **A-85.**

GOLDEN, A. M. and SHAFER, T. (1960). Survival of emerged larvae of the sugar beet nematode (*Heterodera schachtii*) in water and in soil. *Nematologica*, **5**, 32–36.

GOODEY, T. (1922). A simple method of experimentation for skin infection with hook-worm larvae. *Proc. roy. Soc. Med.* **15**, 19–20.

—— (1925). Observations on certain conditions requisite for skin penetration by the infective larvae of *Strongyloides* and *Ankylostomes*. *J. Helminth.* **3** (2), 51–62.

—— (1931). New hosts of *Anguillulina dipsaci* (Kühn, 1858) Gerv. and v. Ben. 1859, with some notes and observations on the biology of the parasite. *J. Helminth.* **9**, 191–196.

—— (1943). A note on the feeding of the nematode *Anguillulina macrura*. *J. Helminth.* **21** (1), 17–19.

GUNDY, S. D., VAN (1959). The life history of *Hemicycliophora arenaria* Raski (Nematoda; Criconematidae). *Proc. helm. Soc. Wash.* **26** (1), 67–72.

HESLING, J. J. and WALLACE, H. R. (1961). Observations on the biology of chrysanthemum eelworm *Aphelenchoides ritzema-bosi* (Schwartz) Steiner in florists' chrysanthemums. I. Spread of eelworm infestation. *Ann. appl. Biol.* **49**, 195–203.

HOLLIS, J. P. (1957). Cultural studies with *Dorylaimus ettersbergensis*. *Phytopathology*, **47** (8), 468–473.

KENNEDY, J. S. and MITTLER, T. E. (1953). A method of obtaining phloem sap via the mouthparts of aphids. *Nature, Lond.* **171**, 528.

KRUSBERG, L. R. (1959). Investigations on the life cycle, reproduction, feeding habits and host range of *Tylenchorhynchus claytoni* Steiner. *Nematologica*, **4**, 187–197.

KRUSBERG, L. R. and SASSER, J. N. (1956). Host-parasite relationships of the lance nematode in cotton roots. *Phytopathology.* **46** (9), 505–510.

LEUKEL, R. W. (1957). Nematode disease of wheat and rye. *Fmrs' Bull. U.S. Dep. Agric.* **1607**, 16 pp.

LEWIS, G. D. and MAI, W. F. (1960). Overwintering and migration of *Ditylenchus dipsaci* in organic soils of southern New York. *Phytopathology*, **50** (5), 341–343.

LINFORD, M. B. (1937a).   The feeding of some hollow-stylet nematodes. *Proc. helm. Soc. Wash.* **4** (2), 41–47.

——— (1937b).   The feeding of the root-knot nematode in root tissue and nutrient solution.   *Phytopathology,* **27**, 824–835.

——— (1941).   The feeding of nematodes before and during their entry into roots.   *Phytopathology,* **31**, 862.

——— (1942).   The transient feeding of root-knot nematode larvae.   *Phytopathology,* **32** (7), 580–589.

LOEWENBERG, J. R., SULLIVAN, T. and SCHUSTER, M. L. (1960).   Gall induction by *Meloidogyne incognita incognita* by surface feeding and factors affecting the behaviour pattern of the second stage larvae.   *Phytopathology,* **50** (4), 322.

LOWNSBERY, B. F. (1951).   Larval emigration from cysts of the golden nematode of potatoes, *Heterodera rostochiensis* Wollenweber.   *Phytopathology,* **41** (10), 889–896.

MILES, H. W. and MILES, M. (1942).   Investigations on potato root eelworm, *Heterodera rostochiensis* Wollenweber.   On the cyst population of a field over a series of years.   *Ann. appl. Biol.* **29** (2), 109–114.

PALO, A. V. (1962).   Translocation and development of stem eelworm, *Ditylenchus dipsaci* (Kühn) in lucerne, *Medicago sativa* L.   *Nematologica,* **7**, 122–132.

PARRIS, G. K. (1948).   Influence of soil moisture on the growth of the potato plant and its infection by the root-knot nematode.   *Phytopathology,* **38**, 480–488.

PEACOCK, F. C. (1959).   The development of a technique for studying the host-parasite relationship of the root-knot nematode *Meloidogyne incognita* under controlled conditions.   *Nematologica,* **4**, 43–55.

REINMUTH, E. (1929).   Der Kartoffelnematode (*Heterodera schachtii* Schm.) Beiträge zur Biologie und Bekämpfung.   *Z. PflKrankh.* **39**, 241–276.

REUVER, I. (1959).   Untersuchungen über *Paratylenchus amblycephalus* n.sp. (Nematoda: Criconematidae.)   *Nematologica,* **4** (1), 3–15.

RHOADES, H. L. and LINFORD, M. B. (1961a).   A study of the parasitic habit of *Paratylenchus projectus* and *P. dianthus*.   *Proc. helm. Soc. Wash.* **28** (2), 185–190.

——— ——— (1961b).   Biological studies on some members of the genus *Paratylenchus*.   *Proc. helm. Soc. Wash.* **28** (1), 51–59.

ROHDE, R. A. and JENKINS, W. R. (1957).   Host range of a species of *Trichodorus* and its host-parasite relationships on tomato.   *Phytopathology,* **47** (5), 295–298.

SASSER, J. N. and TAYLOR, A. L. (1952).   Studies on the entry of larvae of root knot nematodes into roots of susceptible and resistant plants.   *Phytopathology,* **42** (9), 474.

SAYRE, R. M. and MOUNTAIN, W. B. (1962).   The bulb and stem nematode (*Ditylenchus dipsaci*) on onion in Southwestern Ontario.   *Phytopathology,* **52** (6), 510–516.

SLEDGE, E. B. (1959).   The extrusion of saliva from the stylet of the spiral nematode, *Helicotylenchus nannus*.   *Nematologica,* **4** (4), 356.

SPRAU, F. and SÜSS, A. (1962).   Uber die Möglichkeit eines Nachweises des parasitischen charakters freilebender Nematoden für bestimmte Wirtspflanzenarten mit Hilfe von Radioisotopen.   *Nematologica,* **7**, 301–304.

STANDIFER, M. S. and PERRY, V. G. (1960). Some effects of sting and stubby root nematodes on grapefruit roots. *Phytopathology*, **50** (2), 152–156.

STEINER, G. and ALBIN, F. E. (1946). Resuscitation of the nematode *Tylenchus polyhypnus* n.sp. after almost 39 years dormancy. *J. Wash. Acad. Sci.* **36** (3), 97–99.

STREU, H. T., JENKINS, W. R. and HUTCHINSON, M. T. (1961). Nematodes associated with carnations. *New Jersey Agric. Exp. Sta. Rutgers*, Bull. **800**.

TAMURA, I. and KEGASAWA, K. (1958). (II. On the parasitic ability of rice nematodes and their movement into hills.) *Jap. J. Ecol.* **8** (1), 37–42 (in Japanese).

TARJAN, A. C. (1960). Longevity of the burrowing nematode, *Radopholus similis*, in host free soil. *Phytopathology*, **50** (9), 656.

THOMAS, H. A. (1959). On *Criconemoides xenoplax* Raski, with special reference to its biology under laboratory conditions. *Proc. helm. Soc. Wash.* **26** (1), 55–59.

THORNE, G. (1923). Length of the dormancy period of the sugar-beet nematode in Utah. *U.S. Dep. Agric. Circ.* **262**, 1–5.

TRIFFITT, M. J. (1930). Observations on the life-cycle of *Heterodera schachtii*. *J. Helminth.* **8** (4), 185–196.

WALLACE, H. R. (1959). Movement of eelworms. V. Observations on *Aphelenchoides ritzema-bosi* (Schwartz, 1912). Steiner, 1932 on florists' chrysanthemums. *Ann. appl. Biol.* **47** (2), 350–360.

WALLACE, H. R. and GREET, D. N. (1963). Observations on the taxonomy and biology of *Tylenchorhynchus macrurus* (Goodey, 1932) Filipjev, 1936 and *Tylenchorhynchus icarus* n.sp. *Parasitology* (in press).

WIDDOWSON, E., DONCASTER, C. C. and FENWICK, D. W. (1958). Observations on the development of *Heterodera rostochiensis* Woll. in sterile root culture. *Nematologica*, **3**, 308–314.

WINSLOW, R. D. (1956). Seasonal variations in the hatching responses of the potato root eelworm, *Heterodera rostochiensis* Wollenweber, and related species. *J. Helminth.* **30** (2/3), 157–164.

YUKSEL, H. (1960). Observations on the life cycle of *Ditylenchus dipsaci* on onion seedlings. *Nematologica*, **5**, 289–296.

ZUCKERMAN, B. M. (1960). Parasitism of cranberry roots by *Tetylenchus joctus* Thorne. *Nematologica*, **5**, 253–254.

—— (1961). Parasitism and pathogenesis of the cultivated cranberry by some nematodes. *Nematologica*, **6**, 135–143.

CHAPTER 7

Distribution

VERTICAL DISTRIBUTION IN SOIL

In most agricultural soils plant nematodes tend to concentrate at a particular depth which may vary with soil type, host plant, season and many other factors. Cultivation of the soil may disturb the distribution but eventually the pattern is restored although the nematodes may be concentrated at a different depth. Although it is clear that vertical distribution is influenced by plants and the environment, the main problems are to decide which are the major factors influencing distribution and to understand how the nematodes respond to them.

Various authors (Godfrey, 1924; Nielsen, 1949; Steiner, 1952; Bassus, 1962) have suggested that food, root depth, rainfall, height of water table, soil moisture, soil type, depth of subsoil and temperature influence the

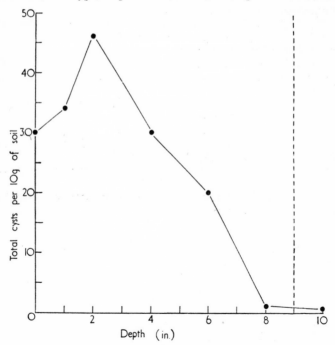

Fig. 50. The vertical distribution in soil of cysts of *Heterodera rostochiensis*. The vertical dotted line indicates the depth of top soil. (From data of Chitwood and Feldmesser, 1948.)

vertical distribution of nematodes in soil. There are several observations on the distribution of nematodes in different soil types and in different seasons; we also know from the soil physicists how physical factors may vary with depth. There is a lack of information from controlled experiments, however, on how nematodes behave in soil under such conditions.

Theoretically, it might be expected that vertical gradients of root concentration, oxygen, temperature, moisture, texture, etc., would influence nematode migration and produce a vertical drift in the population leading to aggregation in a particular zone. This is the dynamic concept of distribution. However, similar distribution patterns could arise if

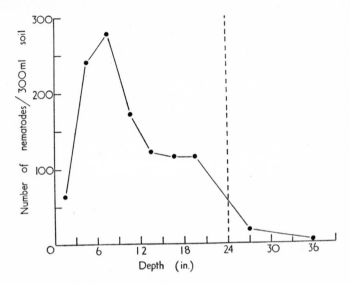

FIG. 51. The vertical distribution of *Xiphinema diversicaudatum* in soil. The vertical dotted line indicates the depth of top soil. (From data of Harrison and Winslow, 1961.)

there was a differential reproductive rate with depth, also dependent on vertical variations of the biotic and physical environment. This is the static concept of distribution. The number of new females of *Heterodera rostochiensis* in the soil around a potato plant is closely related to the amount of root, with a peak of distribution 2 in. (5·1 cm) below soil level (Fig. 50). Reduced numbers at the soil surface are probably caused by low moisture conditions preventing nematode activity. Thus, Peters (1953) found that the population increase of *Heterodera rostochiensis* was least in the top 2 in. of soil. The distribution of *Xiphinema diversicaudatum* also parallels that of the roots with peak population densities at about 3 to 9 in. (7·6 to 22·9 cm), although many nematodes occur below this level (Fig. 51). In young pear tree nurseries the greatest concentration of roots is at a depth of 16 to 24 cm corresponding to the peak of vertical distribution of *Pratylenchus penetrans* (Decker, 1959); *Tylenchulus semipenetrans* may occur as deep as 8 ft (2·44 m) depending on how far the citrus roots penetrate (Baines *et al.*, 1959). The greatest numbers of *Radopholus similis* are found 1 to 5 ft (0·31 to 1·53 m) from the surface but some occur on feeder roots 10 to 12 ft (3·05 to 3·66 m) down (Suit *et al.*, 1953).

Differences in vertical distribution may occur between species. Thus, in coco-nut palm plantations the plant nematodes are concentrated in the upper 60 cm of soil where there are most roots but *Dolichodorus profundus* occurred as deep as 1·2 to 2 m near the water table (Luc and Hoestra, 1960). In soil with spring wheat the freeliving nematodes are concentrated in the upper 10 cm whereas *Rotylenchus robustus* is found 10 to 20 cm below the surface (Witkowski, 1958). *Hemicycliophora similis* may have a different vertical distribution from other parasitic species, for Weischer (1961) found that it was twice as numerous at 50 cm depth as at 10 cm, whereas 90 per cent of the other plant nematodes occurred in the top 30 cm.

The vertical distribution of plant nematodes is, therefore, chiefly related to root distribution. Consequently, where the host has deeply penetrating roots, like citrus and coco-nut palm trees, the range of distribution is correspondingly greater.

Plant nematodes are attracted to roots and congregate there (Chapter 5). Luc (1961), for example, has shown that millet exudes a chemical which attracts *Hemicycliophora paradoxa* 40 cm away. It seems likely, therefore, that the numbers of nematodes attracted to a root zone is a function of the amount of root. Directional movements may also occur in physical gradients (Wallace, 1961). *Ditylenchus dipsaci* (Wallace, 1962) and *Hemicycliophora paradoxa* (Luc, 1961) migrate upwards both to plant roots and in moisture gradients in the absence of roots and there is some evidence (Fig. 52) that the vertical distribution of *Ditylenchus dipsaci* and other soil nematodes is related to rainfall and may show marked changes over short time periods. There is no evidence, however, that movements of nematodes are affected by other physical gradients in the field although Lewis and Mai (1960) suggest that their field sampling data indicate that *Ditylenchus dipsaci* migrates down in the autumn and upwards in the spring. Suggestions that zoo-parasitic nematodes migrate upwards to higher soil moisture levels (Spindler, 1936; Bruns, 1937; Beaver, 1953) also lack experimental evidence.

The rate of reproduction of plant nematodes is closely related to environmental conditions (Chapters 2 and 4), and may therefore, be expected to vary at different soil depths. This is obvious enough at the soil surface where, for example, root knot nematodes may be killed by low moisture and high temperature (Peacock, 1957) and *Ditylenchus dipsaci* by sub-zero temperatures in winter (Lewis and Mai, 1960). However, the association of optimum environmental conditions for reproduction with a particular soil depth has not yet been demonstrated, although this seems likely.

The study of nematode distribution in soil is difficult because of the complexity of the many interrelated factors. Haarløv (1955, 1960) suggests that the vertical distribution of mites and collembola depends on a complex of factors of which size and shape of cavities, their relative

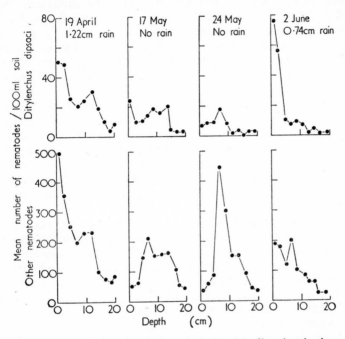

FIG. 52. The vertical distribution of *Ditylenchus dipsaci* and other soil nematodes in soil in an infested oat plot. The amount of rain falling in the week prior to sampling is given. (After Wallace, 1962.)

humidity and the presence of food are the most important. To sum up, root distribution is probably the chief factor influencing plant nematodes although physical factors may play an important secondary role. It also seems likely that vertical distribution patterns are produced by orientation and movement to a particular soil horizon where there are optimal conditions for reproduction.

GEOGRAPHICAL DISTRIBUTION

The factors controlling geographical and vertical distribution of nematodes are quite different. Vertical distribution as we have just seen, is related to the nematodes' own activities whereas the presence of a species in a particular locality often depends on the presence of host plants and on spread (Chapter 5).

The climate of a country may vary widely over short distances according to height above sea-level, and nematode distribution might be expected to vary accordingly. Observations by Krusberg and Hirschmann (1958) in Peru afford a good example of the distribution of phytoparasitic nematodes within a country. Soil samples were taken from the coastal irrigated valleys (altitude 0–700 ft, 0–214 m) the mountains (8,000–14,000 ft, 2,135–4,270 m) and the jungle (1,800–4,800 ft, 549–1,464 m). Although the survey was too restricted to draw definite conclusions about the ecological factors that influence the distribution of different nematode species, several facts emerged. *Meloidogyne* and *Xiphinema* spp. were most frequent on the coast and in the jungle and *Heterodera rostochiensis* in the mountains. The genera *Pratylenchus*, *Tylenchorhynchus*, *Rotylenchus*, *Helicotylenchus* and *Trichodorus* were particularly numerous in the mountains whereas *Helicotylenchus erythrinae* was the most frequent nematode in jungle areas. *Tylenchorhynchus capitatus* was associated with small grain crops in the mountains, *Tylenchulus semipenetrans* with citrus on the coast. Thus, there are obvious distribution differences between species and genera of plant nematodes in Peru but it is difficult to assess whether this is caused by host plant distribution or climate.

The nematode parasite and its host plant are so closely associated that their geographical distribution often coincides. *Tylenchulus semipenetrans*, for example, is closely associated with the citrus growing areas of the world. Distribution within areas of similar climate is also related to crop distribution. In England, *Heterodera schachtii* occurs chiefly in the sugar beet growing areas (Petherbridge and Jones, 1944; Jones, 1951b) and similarly the distribution of *Heterodera rostochiensis* corresponds to to the potato growing areas (Southey and Samuel, 1954).

Soil type may also influence nematode distribution within localised regions, for some species appear to be characteristic of light or heavy soils (Table 4).

Nielsen (1949) and Ward (1960) suggest that the association of a nematode species with a particular soil type may be related to soil moisture. *Ditylenchus dipsaci* may be more prevalent on clay soils because they dry out more slowly at the surface than light soils (Wallace, 1962). The distribution of *Radopholus gracilis* appears to be related to the moisture content of the soil for, with one exception (Norton, 1957), it has only been recorded from very wet environments (Hirschmann, 1955; Golden, 1957). *Dolichodorus heterocephalus* is also associated with swamps, marshes and wet localities (Christie, 1952).

The occurrence of a species in a particular area is not always caused by a previous introduction from another locality; some species appear to be indigenous. Raski (1957) states that in areas of long established agriculture it is difficult to trace infestations of nematodes to their natural habi-

TABLE 4. *Plant parasitic nematodes associated with light soils*

Species	Locality	Author
Belonolaimus gracilis	Florida, U.S.A.	Christie, 1952
Heterodera avenae	England and Wales	Southey, 1956
H. rostochiensis	Germany	Kemper, 1958
Meloidogyne incognita acrita	E. Maryland, U.S.A.	Sasser, 1954
M. hapla	,, ,,	,, ,,
M. incognita	,, ,,	,, ,,
M. incognita acrita	California, U.S.A.	Thomason and Lear, 1959
Meloidogyne sp.	U.S.A.	Anon, 1957
Meloidogyne sp.	U.S.A.	Burton *et al.*, 1946
Nacobbus batatiformis	Nebraska, U.S.A.	Thorne and Schuster, 1956
Pratylenchus penetrans	New York, U.S.A.	Parker and Mai, 1956
P. penetrans	Ontario, Canada	Mountain and Boyce, 1958
P. penetrans	Netherlands	Kleyburg and Oostenbrink, 1959
P. pratensis	,,	,, ,,
Trichodorus christiei	California, U.S.A.	Thomason, 1959
T. pachydermus	Netherlands	Sol and Seinhorst, 1961
Trichodorus sp.	Florida, U.S.A.	Christie, 1952
Tylenchorhynchus dubius	Netherlands	Kleyburg and Oostenbrink, 1959
Xiphinema americanum	New York, U.S.A.	Ward, 1960
Xiphinema sp.	Togo	Luc and Hoestra, 1960

Plant parasitic nematodes associated with heavy soils

Species	Locality	Author
Ditylenchus dipsaci	Netherlands	Seinhorst, 1956
Dolichodorus heterocephalus	Florida, U.S.A.	Christie, 1952
Pratylenchus hexincisus	Texas, U.S.A.	Norton, 1959
P. minyus	Netherlands	Kleyburg and Oostenbrink, 1959
P. thornei	,,	,, ,,
Tylenchorhynchus brevidens	Texas, U.S.A.	Norton, 1959.

tats but, if nematodes are found on indigenous plants in land with no agricultural history, then the nematodes themselves may be indigenous. He suggests that *Meloidogyne hapla* is, therefore, a native of California. Chitwood and Birchfield (1957) suggest that *Tylenchulus semipenetrans* is indigenous to Florida because they found it on the roots of climbing hempweed on land in which no records of cultivation were known.

Several species of *Meloidogyne* may be indigenous to South Africa for they have been found on plants in virgin regions of the Veldt (van der Linde, 1956).

Heterodera rostochiensis was first discovered in Rostock, Germany, in 1913, from where it has spread all over Europe. Oostenbrink (1950) suggested that its sudden appearance was by mutation from a *Heterodera* species already existing in Europe, although the possibility of introduction from a country such as South America was not excluded. Jones (1951a) suggested that this nematode probably originated in the Andes of S. America and was imported with potatoes from that region. With the discovery of *H. rostochiensis* in the mountains of Peru (Wille and Segura, 1952) this hypothesis is now generally accepted. *H. rostochiensis* now occurs widely over Europe and its presence in such countries as India, Israel and the U.S.A. are probably introductions from Europe.

Heterodera rostochiensis occurs chiefly in cooler climates and several authors have suggested that this is because of the low temperature requirements of this species. Kämpfe (1958) found that the optimum temperature for root invasion was 15 to 20°C for *H. rostochiensis* and 25 to 30°C for *H. schachtii*. The larval activity of *H. rostochiensis* was greatest between 10 to 15°C whereas it was about 30°C for *H. schachtii*. Fenwick (1951) also found that temperatures above 20°C reduced penetration of *H. rostochiensis* larvae into potato roots. Mai (1952) studied the survival of encysted larvae of *H. rostochiensis* at temperatures corresponding to those at 6 in. (15·2 cm) depth in Long Island, New York and in Florida. Temperatures ranged from 1 to 23°C for Long Island and 21 to 30°C for Florida. Fewer larvae survived in the higher Florida temperature range. Kämpfe (1958) showed that the distribution of *H. rostochiensis* in Peru lay between the 5 and 10°C isotherms, and it has been recorded from a similar climatic region in India (Jones, 1961).

Heterodera schachtii occurs widely over Europe wherever sugar beet is grown. The sugar beet areas lie mainly between the 20 to 30°C isotherms (Kämpfe, 1958), so *H. schachtii* may be able to tolerate a warmer climate than *H. rostochiensis*.

Minz (1956b) found many species of *Heterodera* in soil in Israel, including *H. rostochiensis* in a citrus nursery where potatoes had previously been grown for more than 10 years. That this species occurs in such a warm country as Israel indicates that correlations between climate and experimental observation on nematode reactions must be treated with caution.

A distinction must be made, however, between a direct effect of climate on the nematode and an indirect effect via the plant. For example, the distribution of the potato and sugar beet growing areas of Europe are more or less similar but potatoes require cooler conditions for growth than sugar beet, consequently, the frequency and distribution of *H. schachtii* and *H. rostochiensis* in Europe may depend on how well the host grows as well as on climate.

The geographical distribution of the root knot nematode is also instructive. Godfrey (1926) suggested that climate was one of the limiting factors in the distribution of this nematode and that temperature was the most important single factor. The most common species in the U.S.A. south of a latitude through Washington D.C. are *Meloidogyne incognita* and *M. incognita acrita*. North of this latitude *M. hapla* occurs most frequently (Taylor and Buhrer, 1958). *M. incognita acrita* has not been found in Hokkaido, the most northerly island of Japan, although *M. hapla* occurs there (Ichinohe, 1955). The only species of *Meloidogyne* found out of doors in England are *M. hapla* (Brown, 1955) and *M. artiellia* (Franklin, 1961). These observations suggest that *M. hapla* occurs more frequently in colder climates than other species; in fact, in the U.S.A. it is called the Northern root knot nematode. World distribution maps of *Meloidogyne* spp. (Gillard, 1961) provide little information on this aspect because there is no indication of the relative frequency of species nor of the particular localities in which they are found. Minz (1956a) has recorded several species, including *M. hapla*, from Israel, where climatic conditions may be very dry and hot, so he concludes that the hypothesis of differential geographical distribution of *Meloidogyne* spp. is tenuous.

The geographical distribution of nematodes is clearly a vague concept and although there appear to be close relationships between climate and the occurrence of some species, this may simply be a reflection of crop distribution. World maps of nematode distribution are of little ecological value because they only indicate the areas which have been surveyed (they also show the world distribution of plant nematologists). More information would be obtained from maps of restricted areas showing the frequencies of different species in relation to cropping and to physical and climatic features, of which the survey of Krusberg and Hirschmann (1958) in Peru is an example.

REFERENCES

ANON (1957). A study of the incidence of nematodes in sugar beet production. *Beet Sugar Development Foundation, Fort Collins, Colorado.*

BAINES, R. C., VAN GUNDY, S. D. and SHER, S. A. (1959). Citrus and avocado nematodes. *Calif. Agric.* **13** (9), 16–18.

BEAVER, P. C. (1953). Persistence of hookworm larvae in soil. *Amer. J. trop. Med. Hyg.* **2**, 102–108.

BROWN, E. B. (1955). Occurrence of the root knot eelworm, *Meloidogyne hapla*, out of doors in Great Britain. *Nature, Lond.* **175**, 430.

BRUNS, W. (1937). Das Verhalten der invasionsfahigen Larven der Pferdestrongyliden in verschiedenen Bodenarten. *Inaugural Dissertation*, Berlin.

BURTON, G. W., McBETH, C. W. and STEPHENS, J. L. (1946). The growth of kobe lespedeza as influenced by the root-knot nematode resistance of the Bermuda grass strain with which it is associated. *J. Amer. Soc. Agron.* **38**, (7), 651–656.

CHITWOOD, B. G. and BIRCHFIELD, W. (1957). Citrus-root nematode, a native to Florida soils. *Plant Dis. Reptr.* **41** (6), 525.

CHITWOOD, B. G. and FELDMESSER, J. (1948). Golden nematode population studies. *Proc. helm. Soc. Wash.* **15** (2), 43–55.

CHRISTIE, J. R. (1952). Some new nematode species of critical importance to Florida growers. *Proc. Soil Sci. Soc. Fla.* **12**, 30–39.

DECKER, H. (1959). *Pratylenchus penetrans* als ursache von mudigkeitser-scheinungen in Baumschulen der DDR. *Nematologica,* Suppl. **2**, 68–75.

FENWICK, D. W. (1951). The effect of temperature on the development of the potato-root eelworm, *Heterodera rostochiensis.* *Ann. appl. Biol.* **38** (3), 615–617.

FRANKLIN, M. T. (1961). A British Root-knot nematode, *Meloidogyne artiellia* n.sp. *J. Helminth.,* R. T. Leiper Suppl. 85–92.

GILLARD, A. (1961). Onderzoekingen omtrent de biologie, de verspreiding ende bestrijding van wortelknobbelaaltjes (*Meloidogyne spp.*). *Meded. LandbHoogesch. Gent,* **26** (2), 515–646.

GODFREY, G. H. (1924). The depth distribution of the root-knot nematode, *Heterodera radicicola* in Florida soils. *J. agric. Res.* **29**, 93–98.

—— (1926). Effect of temperature and moisture on nematode root-knot. *J. agric. Res.* **33** (3), 223–254.

GOLDEN, A. M. (1957). Occurrence of *Radopholus gracilis* (Nematoda: Tylenchidae) in the United States. *Plant Dis. Reptr.* **41** (2), 91.

HAARLØV, N. (1955). Vertical distribution of mites and collembola in relation to soil structure. In; *Soil Zoology,* edited by D. K. McE. Kevan, pp. 167–179. London: Butterworths Scientific Publications.

—— (1960). Microarthropods from Danish soils, ecology, phenology. *Oikos,* Suppl. **3**, 1–176.

HARRISON, B. D. and WINSLOW, R. D. (1961). Laboratory and field studies on the relation of arabis mosaic virus to its nematode vector *Xiphinema diversicaudatum* (Micoletzky). *Ann. appl. Biol.* **49**, 621–633.

HIRSCHMANN, H. (1955). *Radopholus gracilis* (De Mann, 1880) n.comb. (Synonym-*Tylenchorhynchus gracilis*) (De Mann, 1880) Filipjev, 1936. *Proc. helm. Soc. Wash.* **22** (2), 57–63.

ICHINOHE, M. (1955). Two species of the root-knot nematodes in Japan. *Jap. J. appl. Zool.* **20** (1/2), 75–82 (in Japanese).

JONES, F. G. W. (1951a). In discussion of '*Heterodera rostochiensis*: Distribution in relation to climatic and geographical conditions', by O. Ahlberg. *Proc. Int. Nematology Symp. Rothamsted Exp. Sta. Sept. 1951.*

—— (1951b). Further observations on the distribution of the beet eelworm. *J. Helminth.* **25** (3/4), 223–230.

—— (1961). The potato root eelworm (*Heterodera rostochiensis*) in India. *Current Science,* **30**, 187.

KÄMPFE, L. (1958). Physiologische Befunde zur Arttrennung und zum Hertunfrsnachweis in der Gattung *Heterodera* Schmidt. *Verh. dtsch. zool. Ges.* **25**, 383–391.

KEMPER, A. (1958). Kann eine weitere Ausbreitung des Kartoffelnematoden verhindert werden? *Anz. Schädlingsk.* **31** (11), 165–170.

KLEYBURG, P. and OOSTENBRINK, M. (1959). Nematodes in relation to plant growth. I. The nematode distribution pattern of typical farms and nurseries. *Neth. J. agric. Sci.* **7** (4), 327–343.

KRUSBERG, L. R. and HIRSCHMANN, H. (1958). A survey of plant parasitic nematodes in Peru. *Plant Dis. Reptr.* **42** (5), 599–608.

LEWIS, G. D. and MAI, W. F. (1960). Overwintering and migration of *Ditylenchus dipsaci* in organic soils of southern New York. *Phytopathology*, **50** (5), 341–343.

LINDE, W. J., VAN DER (1956). The *Meloidogyne* problem in South Africa. *Nematologica*, **1** (3), 177–183.

LUC, M. (1961). Note préliminaire sur le déplacement de *Hemicycliophora paradoxa* Luc (Nematoda, Criconematidae) dans le sol. *Nematologica*, **6**, 95–106.

LUC, M. and HOESTRA, H. (1960). Les nématodes phytoparasites des sols de cocoteraie du Togo. Essai d'interprétation du peuplement. *L'Agronomie Tropicale*, **15** (5), 497–512.

MAI, W. F. (1952). Temperature in relation to retention of viability of encysted larvae of the golden nematode of potato, *Heterodera rostochiensis* Wollenweber. *Phytopathology*, **42** (2), 113.

MINZ, G. (1956*a*). The root-knot nematode, *Meloidogyne* spp. in Israel. *Plant Dis. Reptr.* **40** (9), 798–801.

—— (1956*b*). Cyst-forming nematodes in Israel. *Plant Dis. Reptr.* **40** (11), 971–973.

MOUNTAIN, W. B. and BOYCE, H. R. (1958). The peach replant problem in Ontario. 5. The relation of parasitic nematodes to regional differences in severity of peach replant failure. *Canad. J. Bot.* **36**, 125–134.

NIELSEN, C. O. (1949). Studies on the soil microfauna. 2. The soil inhabiting nematodes. *Natura Jutlandica*, **2**, 1–131.

NORTON, D. C. (1957). *Radopholus gracilis* in a dry subhumid environment. *Plant Dis. Reptr.* **41** (7), 599.

—— (1959). Relationship of nematodes to small grains and native grasses in north and central Texas. *Plant Dis. Reptr.* **43** (2), 227–235.

OOSTENBRINK, M. (1950). Het aardappelaaltje (*Heterodera rostochiensis* Wollenweber), een gevaarlijke parasiet voor de eenzijdige aardappelcultuur. *Versl. PlZiekt. Dienst, Wageningen*, **115**, 1–230.

PARKER, K. G. and MAI, W. F. (1956). Damage to tree fruits in New York by root lesion nematodes. *Plant Dis. Reptr.* **40** (8), 694–699.

PEACOCK, F. C. (1957). Studies on root-knot nematodes of the genus *Meloidogyne* in the Gold Coast. Part 2. *Nematologica* **2** (2), 114–122.

PETERS, B. G. (1953). Changes in potato root eelworm population with time and depth. *J. Helminth.* **27** (3/4), 113–118.

PETHERBRIDGE, F. R. and JONES, F. G. W. (1944). Beet eelworm (*Heterodera schachtii* Schm.) in East Anglia, 1934–1943. *Ann. appl. Biol.* **31** (4), 320–382.

RASKI, D. J. (1957). New host records for *Meloidogyne hapla* including two plants native to California. *Plant Dis. Reptr.* **41** (9), 770–771.

SASSER, J. N. (1954). Identification and host-parasite relationships of certain root-knot nematodes (*Meloidogyne* sp.) *Univ. Md. agric. Exp. Sta. Bull.* A-77.

SEINHORST, J. W. (1956). Population studies on stem eelworms (*Ditylenchus dipsaci*). *Nematologica*, **1** (2), 159–164.

SOL, H. H. and SEINHORST, J. W. (1961). The transmission of rattle virus by *Trichodorus pachydermus*. *T. Pl.-ziekten.* **67**, 307–311.

SOUTHEY, J. F. (1956). National survey work for cereal root eelworm, (*Heterodera major* (O. Schmidt) Franklin). *Nematologica*, 1 (1), 64–71.

SOUTHEY, J. F. and SAMUEL, G. G. (1954). Potato root eelworm. 1. A review of the situation. 2. Research in progress. *Min. agric. fish. Nat. advisory service.*

SPINDLER, L. A. (1936). Effects of various physical factors on the survival of eggs and infective larvae of the swine nodular worm, *Oesophagostomum dentatum. J. Parasit.* 22, 529.

STEINER, G. (1952). The soil in its relationship to plant nematodes. *Proc. Soil Sci. Soc. Fla.* 12, 24–29.

SUIT, R. F., DUCHARME, E. P., BROOKS, T. L. and FORD, H. W. (1953). Factors in the control of the burrowing nematode on citrus. *Proc. Fla. State hort. Soc.* 66, 46–49.

TAYLOR, A. L. and BUHRER, E. M. (1958). A preliminary report on distribution of root-knot nematode species in the United States. *Phytopathology,* 48, 464.

THOMASON, I. J. (1959). Influence of soil texture on development of the stubby-root nematode. *Phytopathology,* 49 (9), 552.

THOMASON, I. J. and LEAR, B. (1959). Field and vegetable crops. *Calif. Agric.* 13 (9), 8–12.

THORNE, G. and SCHUSTER, M. L. (1956). *Nacobbus batatiformis* n.sp. (Nematoda; Tylenchidae) producing galls on the roots of sugar beets and other plants. *Proc. helm. Soc. Wash.* 23 (2), 128–134.

WALLACE, H. R. (1961). The orientation of *Ditylenchus dipsaci* to physical stimuli. *Nematologica,* 6, 222–236.

—— (1962). Observations on the behaviour of *Ditylenchus dipsaci* in soil. *Nematologica,* 7, 91–101.

WARD, C. H. (1960). Dagger nematodes associated with forage crops in New York. *Phytopathology,* 50 (9), 658.

WEISCHER, B. (1961). Pflanzenparasitäre Nematoden im Möhrenbau. *NachrBl. dtsch. PflSchDienst Berl.* 13 (9), 134–140.

WILLE, J. E. and SEGURA, C. B. (1952). La anguilula dorada, *Heterodera rostochiensis*, una plaga del cultivo de las papas, recien descubierto en el Peru. *Centro Nac. de invest. y Exper. Agric. 'La Molina' Boletin,* 48.

WITKOWSKI, T. (1958). Pionowe rozmieszczenie nicieni w glebie trzech roznych upraw rolniczych. *Zesz. Nauk. Uniw. Torun. Nauk. Mat.-Przyr.* 3 *Biol.* 61–101.

CHAPTER 8

Host-Parasite Relations

The reaction of plants to attack by nematodes varies greatly with different nematode and plant species. At present, next to nothing is known of the mechanisms involved in this complex phenomenon, and the frequently quoted statement that biochemical principles are involved is merely a truism. There is enough descriptive information, however, to emphasise the importance of the study of host-parasite relations, for it forms the basis for recognition and diagnosis of diseases in the field and for control by crop rotation and breeding for resistance.

SYMPTOMS

Symptoms of nematode-infested plants are mostly non-specific and the superficial examination of crops seldom permits an unequivocal diagnosis of nematodes as the causative agent of disease. Thus, poor growth, stunting, patchiness in a crop and discoloured foliage may be produced by organisms other than nematodes or by nutritional and soil physical effects. Furthermore, in a complex environment like the soil, it is likely that no one single factor or organism is responsible for loss of yield in a crop, although some may play a supreme role. While some nematodes are primary pathogens others, by feeding on the host plant, may allow bacteria or fungi to enter the plant without themselves causing major damage; in other diseases there is a closer relationship between the nematode and bacteria, fungi or viruses, for together they cause greater damage than when they are acting alone.

Above ground, species like *Ditylenchus dipsaci, Aphelenchoides ritzema-bosi* (see Plate VI) and *Anguina tritici* produce specific symptoms by direct feeding on aerial parts of the plant, but most of the phytoparasitic nematodes are root feeders and any symptoms which appear in the plant above ground are mostly secondary and non-specific. Wilting, stunting and poor growth, for example, are often the result of root damage which may be caused by a variety of organisms, although the very absence of symptoms accompanied by a slow decline in crop growth is often indicative of nematode attack. Below ground, symptoms on the roots such as galling or discoloured lesions may indicate nematode activity but once again a sure diagnosis is often difficult.

The recognition of such symptoms is, nevertheless, important because it provides a warning that nematodes may be causing damage, but only further critical examination will suggest whether nematodes are really implicated.

163

Above-ground symptoms

1. REDUCED GROWTH. Stunting and slow growth are common in nematode attacks and are often seen as patches in a field. Symptoms such as these are produced, for example, by *Pratylenchus penetrans* and *Pratylenchus pratensis* in various crops (Oostenbrink, 1954), *Heterodera rostochiensis* in potatoes (Oostenbrink, 1950), *H. göttingiana* in peas (Oostenbrink, 1951), *Ditylenchus dipsaci* in lucerne (Brown, 1957) and *H. glycines* in soybean (Ichinohe, 1955). The small areas of stunted plants may be caused by a non-random distribution of nematodes over the field so that

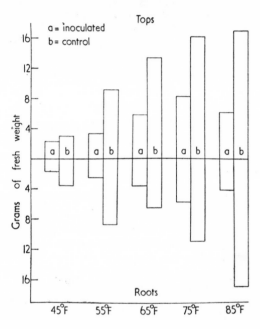

FIG. 53. The influence of *Pratylenchus penetrans* on the growth of apple seedlings at different temperatures. (a) infested, (b) controls. (After Mai, 1960.)

where high-nematode populations occur, disease symptoms are most pronounced. The introduction of nematode-infested seed into uninfested soil might also produce isolated pockets of infestation in a field.

Species of *Pratylenchus* produce poor growth in plants without any other clear-cut symptoms above ground. *P. penetrans* causes such an effect in cherry trees (Parker and Mai, 1956), fruit trees (Kirkpatrick and Mai, 1958) and in apple seedlings (Fig. 53). Similar symptoms are produced in celery by *P. hamatus* (Lownsbery *et al.*, 1952) and in peanuts by *P. brachyurus* (Good *et al.*, 1958). This type of nematode infestation is particularly insidious because reductions in yield are not always apparent from a visual inspection of the crop in the field. Nevertheless losses may be economically important.

The retarded growth of peach trees (Fig. 54) in replanted areas in the U.S.A. and Canada has been attributed to a variety of causes. Koch (1955) described the stunted appearance of the trees but it is only recently that Mountain and Patrick (1959) showed that *Pratylenchus penetrans* was probably the primary pathogen. Chitwood (1949) suggested that *Criconemoides simile* caused symptoms in peach plantations and he

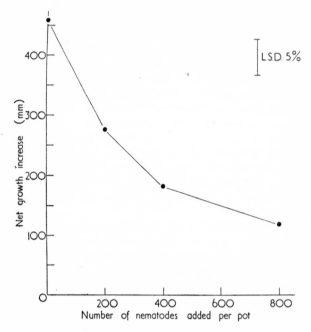

FIG. 54. The influence of *Pratylenchus penetrans* on the growth of peach seedlings. (From data of Mountain and Patrick, 1959.)

emphasised that many organisms and environmental conditions may cause similar disease syndromes. It should not be assumed, therefore, that the same pathogen is involved in all areas where peach replant problems occur.

Stunting and die back in walnut trees are somewhat similar to the peach replant problem and Lownsbery (1956) states that *Pratylenchus vulnus* is the primary cause of this disease.

Seinhorst and Sauer (1956) observed poor growth and stunting in vines in Australia. The absence of specific symptoms and the slow decline of of the vines suggested that nematodes were responsible and on examination of the roots they found symptoms which were attributed to *Meloidogyne incognita, Meloidogyne javanica, Pratylenchus vulnus* and *Pratylenchus scribneri.* Here is an example in which several species may together produce a general syndrome of decline in a crop.

Decline and die-back in banana plantations may be caused by *Radopholus similis* (Loos, 1959) or *Helicotylenchus multicinctus* (Minz *et al.*, 1960). Retarded growth in cotton has been attributed to *Belonolaimus gracilis* (Graham and Holdeman, 1953) and to *Rotylenchulus reniformis* (Birchfield and Jones, 1961). Decline in citrus may be produced by *Radopholus similis* (Suit and Ducharme, 1957), see Plate VII) and by *Tylenchulus semipenetrans* (Reynolds and O'Bannon, 1958). Thus, each case of decline in a crop in a particular area is a problem on its own requiring its own separate investigation to find the primary pathogen.

The same nematode species may cause decline in different types of crop; *Radopholus similis*, for example, affects pepper in much the same way as citrus (Christie, 1957). Oostenbrink and Hoestra (1961) have also shown that poor growth in rose, apple and laburnum trees may be caused by a non-specific infestation of *Pratylenchus penetrans* or by specific fungal pathogens for each of the three plant species. These few examples help to illustrate the non-specific nature of poor growth in crops.

Nematode infestations do not always cause a growth reduction; at low population levels they may even produce an increase (Chitwood and Buhrer, 1946; Chitwood and Feldmesser, 1948; Chitwood and Esser, 1957; Peters, 1961). For example, *Ditylenchus dipsaci* may produce multiple crowns in sugar beet (Dunning, 1954a) and increased tillering in oats. Increased tillering in tall fescue has been attributed to infestations of *Paratylenchus projectus* (Coursen and Jenkins, 1958). However, there is little evidence that such growth changes are important or that nematodes should be considered as beneficial to crop growth.

2. DISCOLOURATION OF FOLIAGE. Die-back in plantations of peach, walnut, citrus, apple, banana, etc., is sometimes accompanied by leaf chlorosis. This is indicative of a nutritional deficiency and, with nematode infestations, the cause often lies in root destruction. Such symptoms have also been observed in celery infested with *Dolichodorus heterocephalus* (Tarjan *et al.*, 1952) and in coffee infested with *Meloidogyne exigua* and *Pratylenchus coffeae* (Chitwood and Berger, 1960). Iris attacked by *Ditylenchus destructor* (J. B. Goodey, 1951b) and narcissus by *Ditylenchus dipsaci* (Thomas, 1958) also show leaf discolouration.

In a more extreme form discolouration may appear as premature yellowing of the leaves as in narcissus infested with *Pratylenchus* sp. (Jensen *et al.*, 1951), peanuts with *Criconemoides* sp. (Machmer, 1953) and cotton with *Hoplolaimus coronatus* (Krusberg and Sasser, 1956).

Discolouration may be less striking as in *Scabiosa caucasica* attacked by *Aphelenchoides blastophthorus*, where the leaves appear a darker green (Franklin, 1952). In some infestations of potatoes by *Heterodera rostochiensis*, on the other hand, the foliage appears to be a lighter green (Chitwood, 1951). Infestations of *Ditylenchus dipsaci* in strawberries (J. B. Goodey, 1951a), *Aphelenchoides ritzemabosi* in chrysanthemums

(Greet and Wallace, 1962) and *Pratylenchus* spp. in boxwood (Tarjan, 1950) may cause bronzing and reddening of the leaf.

Such symptoms are clearly unspecific; discolouration may range from light yellow to deep red, purple and even black and at best this symptom can only serve as a warning of possible nematode infestations.

Some species may produce quite distinctive and specific symptoms, however. *Aphelenchoides oryzae* produces pale yellow or white tips to leaves of rice (Yoshii and Yamamoto, 1950; Cralley, 1949). *Aphelenchoides ritzemabosi* produces clear cut interveinal discolouration in strawberries (Brown, 1959) and in chrysanthemums (Hesling and Wallace, 1961). *Ditylenchus dipsaci* causes similar symptoms in aster leaves (Brown, 1958). Early symptoms of *Anguina graminophila* in *Calamagrostis canadensis* are light yellow-green specks on the leaves (Goto and Gibler, 1951); *Tylenchulus semipenetrans* is reported to induce a fine mottle on the leaves of orange and lemon trees (Baines and Clarke, 1953); discolouration of the leaf tips of boxwood is probably caused by an infestation of *Pratylenchus* sp. (Tarjan, 1948).

Except for interveinal symptoms caused by direct nematode feeding on leaves, discolouration is probably caused by some upset in the nutritional supply of the plant. Edwards (1935) suggests that *Heterodera avenae* in oats produces a foliage discolouration resembling a potash deficiency and Christie and Perry (1951) state that yellowing in vegetables attacked by *Trichodorus* sp. is possibly a mineral deficiency. Strawberries and sweet corn attacked by *Belonolaimus gracilis* show discoloured leaves but the green was restored after spraying with ferrous sulphate, suggesting that the diseased plants had an iron deficiency (Christie *et al.*, 1952). *Pratylenchus vulnus* in roses causes chlorosis and a reduction of iron, copper and potassium in the leaves (Sher, 1957). The influence of *Meloidogyne incognita acrita* and *Trichodorus christiei* on the nutrient status of tomato has also been studied by Maung and Jenkins (1959).

3. DISTORTION AND ABNORMAL GROWTH. Distortion in the aerial parts of nematode infested plants is caused chiefly by the stem and leaf feeding nematodes, *Ditylenchus* spp., *Aphelenchoides* spp, and *Anguina* spp. It is possible that enzymes secreted by the nematodes during feeding disrupt normal growth and so produce irregular-shaped foliage, but there is little evidence for this. Distortion induced by *D. dipsaci* has been recorded in many hosts, including onions (Chitwood *et al.*, 1940), strawberry (J. B. Goodey, 1951a), sugar beet (Dunning, 1954b), red clover (Dijkstra, 1957), lucerne (Brown, 1957), annual aster and sweet sultan (Brown, 1958), narcissus (Thomas, 1958) and tulips and other bulbs (Courtney, 1961). *Aphelenchoides blastophthorus* causes distortion in *Scabiosa caucasica* (Franklin, 1952), *A. oryzae* in rice (Yoshii and Yamamoto, 1950) and *A. ritzemabosi* in chrysanthemums (Hesling and Wallace, 1961). Infestations of *Anguina graminophila* in *Calamagrostis canadensis* produce striking symptoms of twisting and distortion of the leaf (Goto and Gibler, 1951).

Abnormal growth in stems and leaves in the form of hypertrophy and hyperplasia produces swellings, puffiness and gall formation. Such symptoms are typical of *Ditylenchus dipsaci* infestations in numerous hosts and provide one of the few reliable diagnostic features of nematode attack (see Plate VIII). Swollen and puffy tissues also occur in chrysanthemum leaves infested with *Aphelenchoides ritzemabosi*. *Anguina agrostis* forms galls in the inflorescences of several species of grass and their resemblance to ergot has sometimes led to their wrong identification (T. Goodey, 1952). The destruction of the flowers leads to reduced seed production (Courtney and Howell, 1952). *Anguina graminis* and *Ditylenchus graminophilus* form galls on the leaves of grasses and J. B. Goodey (1959) has suggested that such galls are an interaction product between plant and parasite whereby the parasite tends to be isolated from the rest of the plant, so lessening more extensive invasion. In many respects nematode galls resemble those produced by insects.

Below-ground symptoms

1. REDUCED ROOT SYSTEM. It is apparent from the numerous records of the effects of nematodes on the subterranean parts of plants that depletion of the root system is a very common symptom. It would be pointless to review the many nematode parasites and plant hosts associated with this effect but it may be useful to consider the ways in which a reduced root system occurs.

Some nematodes like *Trichodorus* spp. (Christie, 1952) and *Tylenchorhynchus claytoni* (Graham, 1954) can apparently inhibit root growth without producing any other recognisable symptoms. In many other cases, however, the roots appear to be short, stubby, and malformed, e.g. *Belonolaimus gracilis* (Christie *et al.*, 1952) and *Dolichodorus heterocephalus* (Tarjan *et al.*, 1952) on celery, *Tylenchorhynchus* spp. on sugar cane (Birchfield and Martin, 1956), *Xiphinema diversicaudatum* on soybean (Schindler, 1957), *Hemicycliophora typica* on carrots (Kuiper, 1959). Feeder roots may be reduced in number as in sugar cane infested by *Tylenchorhynchus* and *Pratylenchus* spp. (Birchfield, 1953), peppermint by *Longidorus sylphus* (Jensen and Horner, 1956), citrus by *Radopholus similis* (Suit and Ducharme, 1957) and seedless grape by *Xiphinema index* (Raski and Radewald, 1958).

Necrotic lesions are often visible on the roots of plants infested by *Pratylenchus* spp. and in the later stages more general necrosis and root rot may occur so that the plant eventually has a poorly developed, brown root system. Such symptoms have been described for a variety of plants by Taylor and Loegering (1953), Oostenbrink (1954), Parker and Mai (1956), Seinhorst and Sauer (1956), Kirkpatrick and Mai (1958) and Mountain and Patrick (1959) and many others.

Radopholus similis causes similar symptoms on citrus (Feder and Ford,

1957), and in banana (see Plate IX) this species produces lesions which girdle the root, thereby weakening their anchoring power so that at a later stage the trees tend to be uprooted (Loos, 1959; Loos and Loos, 1960; Blake, 1961). Lesions are also visible on banana roots attacked by *Helicotylenchus multicinctus* (Minz *et al.*, 1960).

Intensive attacks by plant nematodes produce cracking and splitting (Doncaster, 1953; Feder and Feldmesser, 1955; Lownsbery, 1956; Krusberg and Nielsen, 1958; Chitwood and Berger, 1960) until eventually the roots become blackened (Perry, 1958) and assume a generally rotten appearance (Goheen and Smith, 1956). Such symptoms are not usually the result of nematodes alone for breakdown of the cortex allows other pathogens to enter and contribute to the general decay of the root system (see Plate X).

2. ROOT PROLIFERATION. Some species of plant nematodes do not produce general root decay, and lesions are often hard to detect. In these circumstances the host plant often responds to nematode attack by increased root growth. *Heterodera* spp. in particular induce such symptoms. For example, root proliferation has been recorded in oats attacked by *H. avenae* (Edwards, 1935), potatoes by *H. rostochiensis* (Chitwood, 1951), soybean by *H. glycines* (Ichinohe, 1955) and sugar beet by *H. schachtii* (Savary, 1960). *Trichodorus christiei*, *Belonolaimus gracilis*, *Dolichodorus heterocephalus*, *Paratylenchus projectus* and *Meloidogyne* spp. also cause increased root growth in numerous hosts. Some species of *Pratylenchus* may induce such symptoms on certain hosts, Boxwood trees for example (Tarjan, 1948), and Seinhorst and Sauer (1956) found that *Pratylenchus scribneri* caused extensive root proliferation in vines although the roots did not spread very far and their tips were damaged. The formation of numerous small roots at the expense of the larger more deeply penetrating roots often renders plants more susceptible to wilting and uprooting and ability to absorb nutrients is also impaired.

3. GALL FORMATION. *Meloidogyne* spp. form characteristic galls on the roots of host plants (see Plate XI). The size, number and shape of the galls vary, however, for different species and for different host plants. Reynolds (1955), for example, found little evidence of galling on lucerne roots containing *Meloidogyne* although there was a decrease in the length and number of roots. Conversely, galls may reach an enormous size; Steiner and his colleagues (1934) found *Meloidogyne* galls up to 2 ft in diameter at the base of stems of the ornamental plant, *Thunbergia laurifolia*. The knotted, swollen and distorted root system is usually diagnostic of *Meloidogyne* infestations and has earned them the name of root knot nematodes. Not all galls are the result of *Meloidogyne* activity, however. *Ditylenchus radicicola* produces small galls on grass roots. These are usually more or less spherical but Kuiper (1953) records spiral shaped galls. *Heterodera rostochiensis* may produce swellings on black nightshade (Doncaster, 1953) and also on tomato roots where they may

reach a size resembling galls (Widdowson *et al.*, 1958). *Nacobbus batati-formis* (Thorne and Schuster, 1956) and *Nacobbus serendipiticus* (Franklin, 1959) produce large galls on beet and tomatoes respectively and these may be easily mistaken for root knot galls. Galls and distorted roots may also appear in strawberries and soybean attacked by *Xiphinema diversicaudatum* (Schindler and Braun, 1957; Schindler, 1957), and in seedless grape *Xiphinema index* produces malformation, abnormal bending and swelling of the roots (Raski and Radewald, 1958). *Hemicycliophora similis* (Zuckerman, 1961) and *Hemicycliophora* sp. (van Gundy, 1957) induce galling in cranberry and lemon roots respectively.

Root swelling and galling is therefore a common feature of plant nematode infestations and is a useful diagnostic symptom. It is not specific to nematodes, however, for bacteria, fungi and insects may produce galls, swellings and cankers on plant roots.

4. CONCLUSIONS. The chief symptoms of nematode infestations have now been described and illustrated by a few examples of particular host-parasite reactions. Lack of specificity and the indefinite nature of many of the symptoms makes diagnosis difficult. Furthermore, the syndrome of an infested crop may be affected by external factors such as rainfall (Chitwood and Feldmesser, 1948), drought and temperature (Tarjan, 1948; Mai, 1960) and varietal differences in the host may introduce further heterogeneity (Feder and Ford, 1957; Dropkin, 1959). First examination of a crop may reveal one or more symptoms of poor growth, reduced yield, premature death, leaf fall, wilting or low resistance to drought and temperature extremes, etc. The crop is obviously diseased in some way. Closer examination of the plants may reveal irregularities which suggest that a plant pathogen is responsible for this debility, and soil samples may indicate an association between certain plant nematodes and the severity of the disorder. There is still no reliable evidence, however, to implicate nematodes although the apparent absence of symptoms caused by other pathogens and the presence of nematodes within the plant may increase suspicion that a nematode problem is involved. Only controlled experiments will reveal whether the nematode could be the primary cause of the crop failure and whether it is associated with a fungus, bacterium or virus in a disease complex. The principles establishing pathogenicity have now to be applied. Even if experiments show that nematodes can cause such damage to the crop, it is still not established that they are, in fact, the real cause of the problem in the field. Field experiments, using nematicide treatments as controls, may show that disease symptoms are worse when nematodes are associated with the crop and that increased yields are obtained when nematodes are killed. Such experiments may clearly show the beneficial effects of nematicide treatment on crop growth but that they indicate the identity of the pathogen is sometimes open to question; to solve these problems more information is needed on the effects of nematicides on other soil pathogens, on the plant and on the nutritional status of the soil.

PRINCIPLES OF PATHOGENICITY

How can we establish that disease in a crop is caused primarily by a particular nematode? To establish such a relationship we must follow the strict scientific principles known as Koch's postulates. These entail four stages in proving pathogenicity: (1) constant association of the suspected organism with the disease, (2) isolation and study of the organism in pure culture, (3) production of the disease by inoculation of the host with a pure culture of the organism and (4) re-isolation of the organism from the inoculated diseased host and confirmation of its identity with the original inoculant.

In nematode problems it is often impossible to adhere rigidly to these concepts which were used initially to establish the pathogenicity of bacteria in man and animals. Thus, no-one has yet succeeded in culturing plant parasitic nematodes in media of known chemical composition. Oostenbrink (1956) considers that in most nematode infestations of plants, pure populations of some nematode species are difficult to obtain because they are weakened or killed during collection, cleaning and inoculation. Furthermore, with such symptoms as growth reduction in a host plant, it is difficult to obtain enough sterile nematodes with present techniques and to maintain a plant and its growth medium in a sterile condition long enough to show such symptoms (Lownsbery and Thomason, 1959). Many diseases are caused by a complex of organisms, consequently the results of the activities of the primary parasite may be completely modified or obscured (Mountain, 1960a).

Although plant nematodes cannot yet be cultured on artificial media, there are several techniques for obtaining aseptic monocultures of nematodes (Mountain, 1955; Pitcher and Crosse, 1958; Peacock, 1959; Mountain and Patrick, 1959; Krusberg, 1961; Ducharme and Hanks, 1961). Thus, in some species, at any rate, we can satisfy Koch's second law, and recent advances in the study of plant parasitic nematodes on seedlings and tissue cultures under sterile conditions should make it possible to apply the principles of pathogenicity to many nematode associations. So far, however, this has been done for only a few such associations. As Dropkin (1955) points out, the pathogenicity of such a well known nematode as *Heterodera schachtii*, the sugar beet nematode, has not been established. Much of the data, in fact, does not get past the stage of showing an association between host and parasite.

Several alternative methods have been suggested for indicating pathogenicity in those nematode associations where Koch's postulate cannot be applied. Oostenbrink (1956), for example, suggests that distinct improvement of plant growth in soil, treated with a specific nematicide like DD, indicates that nematodes are the chief cause of the disease. However, such methods do not permit identification of the particular nematode species responsible and the role of the other soil organisms. Oostenbrink also suggests that reproducing the disease symptoms in soil in which the crop has not previously been grown, but where the nematode species has increased on other crops, is a reliable way of determining the nematode primarily responsible for the disease.   Oostenbrink points out that such methods are complementary to Koch's postulates and are useful when the postulates cannot be applied.   Lownsbery and Thomason (1959) suggest that if (*a*) suspensions of the nematodes and associated microorganisms are pathogenic, (*b*) final plant weights are inversely proportional to the numbers of nematodes added and (*c*) the control plants with associated microorganisms alone are not diseased, then the nematodes are clearly key participants in pathogenesis, although their precise role remains to be proved.   There are also methods where plant growth is compared in soil with and without nematodes but although it is certainly useful to have other methods which indicate possible nematode-plant relationships, these can only establish tentative hypotheses on pathogenicity.   Mountain (1960a, b, c), quite rightly, is adamant on this point.   He states that the only way we can discover what a nematode is really doing to the plant is to use a microbiologically-sterile population containing a single nematode species.   If we don't know exactly what is added in an inoculum then the role of the nematode in the etiology of the disease will never be known and any conclusions developed from such an approach will be unsound.

There is no escape from the logic of this argument, for there can be no compromise with the scientific method as laid down in the laws of pathogenicity.   It has to be accepted that, with our present limited knowledge, proof of pathogenicity for some nematode problems cannot be established and tentative hypotheses have to be accepted instead. This situation is analogous to the problem of cause and effect in studies of the influence of environmental factors on nematode activity discussed in Chapter 4.

The peach replant problem in Canada is an excellent example of the kind of problem facing the plant nematologist.   In Ontario, it was found that the replacement of peach trees in old orchards was difficult. The young peach tree replants often failed to grow satisfactorily and showed symptoms of chlorosis.   The roots showed varying degrees of discolouration and necrosis; brown lesions could be seen on the white lateral roots and root proliferation was evident by the end of the growing season (Koch, 1955).   Peach replant failure in the past had been ascribed to insects, nutritional factors, toxic agents, fungi and nematodes and it was thought that a complex of several factors was responsible.

Patrick (1955) investigated the importance of soil toxins produced by the interaction of microorganisms and peach root residues in old orchards.   He found that such substances were produced and that they inhibited the respiration of peach roots.   It was concluded that microbial action on the amygdalin fraction of the roots was mainly responsible for the toxic factor frequently found in orchards, and Patrick suggested that any organisms that produced root lesions, such as fungi, insects and nematodes, would help to produce the toxins. Patrick's hypothesis was supported by Ward and Durkee (1956) who demonstrated that the highest concentration of amygdalin occurred in the root bark.

At this stage in the problem, therefore, it seemed that hydrolysis of amygdalin in peach roots was initiated by root destroying organisms, resulting in the production of toxins which inhibited growth of newly-planted young peach trees. Further information was provided by Wensley (1956) who studied the fungi associated with replant failure. He found fourteen species of fungi which were facultative parasites on peach roots and by applying fumigants to the soil he showed that increased root growth was associated with reduction in the numbers of the pathogenic fungi. Some fumigants were effective even though they were only slightly fungicidal and the fact that they were highly nematicidal led Wensley to the conclusion that nematodes were a possible primary contributory factor to peach failure. He therefore suggested that the combined action of nematodes and fungi might be the answer to the problem.

Mountain and Boyce (1958a) now entered the picture to examine the problem from the nematode aspect and from the very beginning their investigations were based on Koch's rules of proof of pathogenicity. They analysed soil samples from 167 peach orchards and isolated and identified the plant parasitic nematodes. Twenty-five genera were found, all of which were considered as potential factors in the peach replant problem, but only *Pratylenchus penetrans* showed consistent association with the disease, thus satisfying the first postulate of close association. Later work by Mountain and Boyce (1958b) provided confirmatory evidence. It was shown that control of *P. penetrans* with nematicides produced increased growth in peach trees; *P. penetrans* was the first nematode to attack newly developing peach roots; the soils of all commercial peach orchards in Ontario contained *P. penetrans*.

The way was now open to try to establish the pathogenicity of *P. penetrans* by applying the remaining three postulates. Mountain and Patrick (1959) succeeded in obtaining numbers of sterile, active and infective *P. penetrans* by immersion of the nematodes in a bactericide-fungicide solution. Sterile peach seeds were also obtained by chemical treatment and grown in sterile culture medium in test tubes. Sterile nematodes were then added to tubes containing a sterile, well developed peach root system and sterile sand. Subsequent effects on the roots were observed by direct microscopic examination. Lesions were visible within 90 min. and their development was followed at intervals thereafter. Isolations from the necrotic areas on the roots failed to show the presence of fungi and bacteria in the tissues and microscopic examination of incipient lesions invariably showed at least one *P. penetrans* buried in the tissue. Mountain and Patrick showed, therefore, that *P. penetrans* could invade and kill peach root tissues in the absence of bacteria and fungi. They also demonstrated in other experiments that this nematode could reduce the growth of peach seedlings, so their results satisfied the rules of proof of pathogenicity and *P. penetrans* was described as a true plant pathogen.

These experiments, however, do not establish the role of the nematode in peach replant failure under natural conditions. They only suggest that *P. penetrans* by its own pathogenic properties, probably plays a primary role in the etiology of the disease. Mountain and Patrick (1959) suggest that *P. penetrans* incites root degeneration through the formation of extensive infection sites which allow bacteria and fungi to increase the extent of the root rot. The presence of toxic substances in the soil by the hydrolysis of amygdalin in the infested roots is an additional factor in the disease complex although Hine (1961) has shown that amygdalin breakdown is so rapid in soil that it is probably unimportant.

It can be concluded that the chances of success in solving problems of this kind are enhanced by the combined activities of scientists of varied disciplines and by adhering to the principles of proof of pathogenicity.

HISTOPATHOLOGY

The cellular reactions of plants to nematode invasion vary widely from the unspecific cell necrosis in lesions produced by *Pratylenchus* spp. to specific cell hypertrophy and hyperplasia in the galls of *Anguina* spp.

Lesions are often formed on the surface of roots during the feeding and invasion of plant nematodes. Damage of this kind may be caused by nematodes such as *Criconemoides curvatum* forcing their way into the cortex where they remain embedded two to three cells deep (Streu *et al.*, 1961). The destruction of cells often produces a cavity in the root which may extend as far as the stele. *Belonolaimus gracilis*, for example, produces lesions on bean roots which extend into the stele destroying cells of xylem and phloem (Standifer, 1959). Sometimes lesions are very small and hard to detect. *Rotylenchus buxophilus* produces numerous small brown wounds on the roots of boxwood; several cells leading well into the cortex may be discoloured suggesting that the nematode injects some diffusible chemical substance into the plant (Golden, 1956). *Helicotylenchus nannus* produces a similar effect in roses (Davis and Jenkins, 1960). Discolouration of the root may be so extensive as to be termed root rot. Lesions on peach roots infested by *Pratylenchus penetrans* may enlarge to a length of 2 cm in 4 days (Mountain and Patrick, 1959) and *Pratylenchus scribneri* causes similar symptoms in amaryllis bulbs (Christie and Birchfield, 1958). *Ditylenchus destructor* also causes extensive necrosis and rotting in iris and potato (J. B. Goodey, 1951b) but other organisms are undoubtedly involved in such extensive breakdown of plant tissues.

In pine seedlings infested with *Hoplolaimus tylenchiformis*, cells in the roots collapse following the migration of nematodes through the cortical tissues (Ruehle and Sasser, 1960). *Aphelenchoides ritzemabosi* also leaves tracks of brown necrotic cells in chrysanthemum leaves (Wallace, 1961b).

Tracks of *Radopholus similis* in banana roots are initially a pink-red colour but these subsequently turn black. This nematode may also form brown to black lesions with slightly shrunken centres and longitudinal cracks up to 4 in. long, which girdle the root (Loos and Loos, 1960). The type and extent of plant lesions probably depends on the distribution of certain chemicals in the plant root. Thus, in apple seedlings infested by *Pratylenchus penetrans* the epidermis and endodermis become brown but not the intervening parenchyma. Pitcher and his colleagues (1960) showed that the necrosis and discolouration was related to distribution of phenolic substances in the root. These substances were absent in the cortex but occurred in the epidermis and endodermis. It was suggested that the nematode enzymes reacted with the phenols releasing products which were toxic to invaded and adjacent cells. It has also been suggested that browning of infested tissues is caused by mechanical damage to cells during nematode feeding; polyphenols and polyphenol oxidase come together and oxidation proceeds to give the familiar brown end products of such a chemical reaction (Wallace, 1961a).

Lesion formation and necrosis may be accompanied by other effects. Infestations of *Rotylenchus coheni* in *Hippeastrum* roots, for example, induce meristematic cell formation in cortical cells near the lesion, so forming a suberised periderm around the wound (J. B. Goodey, 1952). Cell elongation may be inhibited in lemon roots infested by *Hemicycliophora arenaria* (van Gundy and Rackham, 1961). Apical growth is retarded in sweet potato roots parasitised by *Meloidogyne incognita incognita* (Krusberg and Nielsen, 1958) and in lucerne shoots containing *Aphelenchoides ritzemabosi* (Krusberg, 1961). General maturation of the root tip occurs in bean roots infested with *Belonolaimus longicaudatus* (Standifer, 1959), in grapefruit with *Trichodorus christiei* (Standifer and Perry, 1960) and in tomato with a *Trichodorus* sp. (Rohde and Jenkins, 1957). Vascular tissue extends to the root tip and the region of cell elongation disappears.

Cell hypertrophy and hyperplasia, the formation of tyloses and abnormal cell division have also been observed in nematode infested plants. Brief descriptions of the histopathology of plants associated with infestations of a few selected genera will help to illustrate these phenomena.

Meloidogyne

Krusberg and Nielsen (1958) describe the histopathology of sweet potato infested by *Meloidogyne incognita acrita*. After invasion the second stage larvae migrate intercellularly and intracellularly to the site of feeding and subsequent nematode growth. Most larvae are found in the stele in the region of cell elongation, in the cambial region or in the parenchyma. The first reaction of the plant to nematode feeding is giant-cell formation (see Plate XII). The protoplasm in parenchymatous cells around the head of the larvae becomes granular and the nuclei swell.   Each larva is associated with about four to nine giant cells which are multinucleate, containing from 50 to several hundred nuclei, either scattered or in masses.   The enlargement of the giant cells appears to be caused by the dissolution of adjacent parenchyma cell walls, with fusion and multiplication of protoplasm and subsequent deposition of a wall around the enlarged lumen.   Nematode feeding also stimulates division of the parenchyma cells bordering giant cells.   Cork cells are formed around nematode infestations and seem to be an injury response.   Hypertrophy of cortical parenchyma cells sometimes occurs but usually in regions where nematodes have died or necrotic cells are present.   The overall reaction of these effects is a swelling of the entire root caused by hypertrophy and hyperplasia of cells.   Heavy larval infections inhibit apical growth and cause swelling of root tips whereas single nematode infections cause small galls to form.

Dropkin and Nelson (1960) studied the histological responses of nineteen soybean varieties infected with *M. incognita incognita* and *M. incognita acrita*.   Giant cell development in roots of susceptible varieties began with intense multiplication followed by hypertrophy of cells about the larval head.   Dissolution of the walls of hypertrophied cells resulted in several large multinucleate cells; nuclear division within giant cells was rare.

Enlargement of giant cells in tomato and cucumber roots infested by *M. incognita incognita* arises by a combination of turgor pressure and cell wall digestion (Owens and Novotny, 1960).   The multinucleate condition was produced from the accumulation of nuclei from several cells and from divisions without cytokinesis.   Cellulose, free sugars, phosphorylated intermediates and keto acids decreased in galls and starch disappeared.   Total free amino acids and amides increased about four-fold.   Protein, nucleic acids, phosphorus and nitrogen were doubled and enzyme activity was much greater in galls than in healthy roots.   Amino acids accumulated principally in the giant cells.   Myuge (1956b) also found increased amino acid concentrations in the giant cells and he suggested that the nematodes break down the proteins faster than they can absorb the resultant products.   Myuge (1956a) also considered that the amino acids were the primary cause of gall formation.

Giant cell formation appears to be associated with successful nematode growth and development.   Crittenden (1958), for example, showed that in susceptible varieties of soybean infested by *M. incognita acrita*, numerous large giant cells with many enlarged nuclei were formed.   In resistant varieties, however, there were only a few relatively small giant cells and each contained only a few nuclei.   Dropkin (1959), studying the same parasite and host plant, found a correlation between giant-cell size and structure and egg production.   In susceptible varieties, where reproduction was high, the giant cells were large whereas in resistant varieties they were small.   Dropkin (1955) also makes the point that giant cell formation and gall formation are two distinct responses to

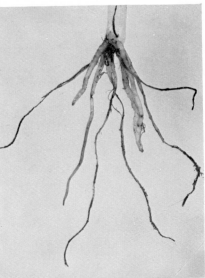

VIII. *Above:* Influence of *Ditylenchus dipsaci* on oats. Left hand plant un-infested; right hand plant infested, showing swelling of the shoot bases and increased tillering. *See* page 168. (Re-produced by permission of Rothamsted Experimental Station.)

IX. *Top right:* Destruction of roots of a young banana seedling by *Radopholus similis*. *See* page 169. (Reproduced by permission of New South Wales Dept. of Agriculture.)

X. *Bottom right:* Lesions on cotton roots caused by *Belonolaimus gracilis*. *See* page 169. (Reproduced by per-mission of T. W. Graham.)

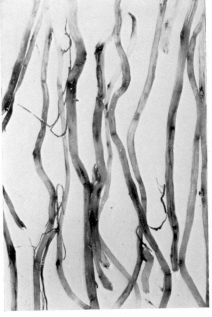

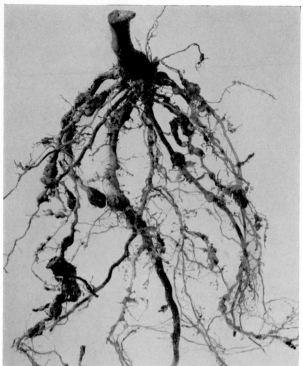

XI. *Left:* Galls on the roots of tomato caused by *Meloidogyne incognita.* *See* page 169. (Reproduced by permission of Rothamsted Experimental Station.)

XII. *Below:* Transverse section of tomato root showing female *Meloidogyne* sp. Darkly stained giant cells are grouped near the head of the nematode. *See* page 175. (Reproduced by permission of Rothamsted Experimental Station.)

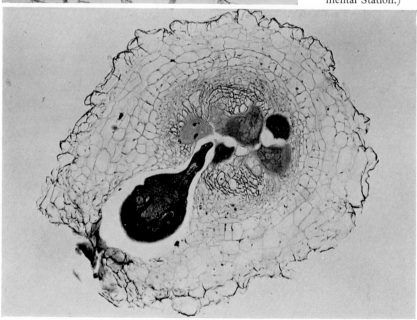

XIII. *Opposite:* Transverse section of lucerne roots showing effects of *Ditylenchus dipsaci.* (A) 1 week after inoculation—no apparent symptoms; (B) 4 weeks after inoculation showing cell destruction with nematodes in the cavities. *See* page 177. (Reproduced by permission of L. R. Krusberg.)

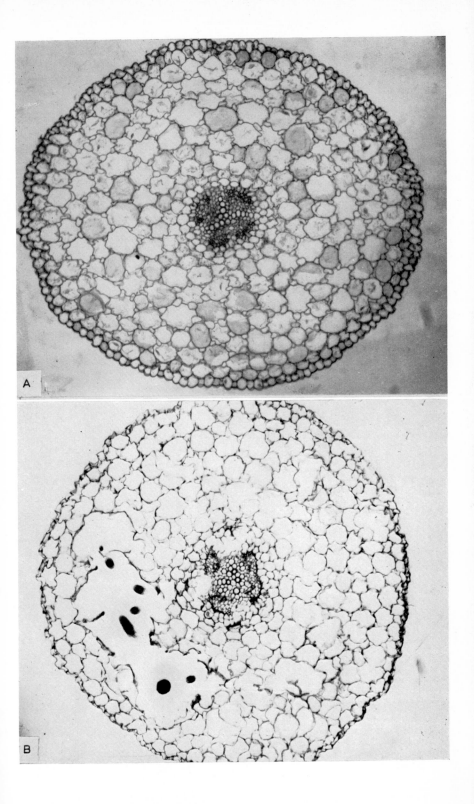

XIV. *Right:* Transverse section of a citrus rootlet containing a cavity formed by and filled with *Radopholus similis.* *See* page 179. (Reproduced by permission of E. P. Ducharme.)

XV. *Top left:* Transverse section of a citrus root showing the stele girdled by a cavity formed by *Radopholus similis.* *See* page 179. (Reproduced by permission of E. P. Ducharme.)

XVI. *Bottom:* Transverse section of a citrus root infested with *Radopholus similis* showing hypertrophy and hyperplasia of pericycle. *See* page 179. (Reproduced by permission of E. P. Ducharme.)

Meloidogyne infection and Loewenberg and colleagues (1960) found that galls could be formed without the nematode entering the plant. In such cases a larva had been feeding at the site of the gall for some hours before moving away, suggesting that the substances secreted into the cell during nematode feeding induced the cellular changes.

Heterodera

Němec (1911) made a detailed study of the histopathology of sugar beet roots infested by *H. schachtii*. Groups of giant cells were formed by the breakdown of longitudinal and transverse cell walls giving multinucleate syncytia. The giant cells occurred near the head of a larva in tissues external to the endodermis and subsequently developed thickened walls. Triffitt (1931) found similar responses in potato roots attacked by *H. rostochiensis*. Feldmesser (1953) observed that giant cells were evident during the third larval stage of *H. rostochiensis* in tomato. The giant cells developed in the cortex and stele causing discontinuity of some vascular elements and retarded differentiation of others. Giant cells were formed by the dissolution of cell walls, coalescence of the cytoplasmic masses and aggregation of nuclei from the previously intact cells. Cole and Howard (1958) state that giant cells may be formed in the cortex, endodermis, pericycle and parenchyma cells of the central vascular strand. In this last site, giant cell formation inhibits cambium formation and hence no secondary xylem is produced. The multinucleate and granular appearance of giant cells was also observed. *H. rostochiensis* in susceptible potatoes causes formation of giant cells but in resistant potatoes these are replaced by necrotic cells (Kühn, 1958). Susceptible and resistant varieties of soybean and sugar beet react in a similar way to infestation by *H. glycines* (Ross, 1958) and *H. schachtii* (Bergman, 1958) respectively.

Ditylenchus

Most *Ditylenchus* spp. inhabit the intercellular spaces of parenchymatous and cortical tissues of leaves and stems (see Plate XIII) where they cause swelling by hypertrophy and hyperplasia of the cells. The middle lamella of cell walls is dissolved so that cells which were once elongate become almost spherical. The swellings also contain large air spaces. Localised swellings or galls formed on the leaves of *Plantago lanceolata* by *D. dipsaci* are caused by hypertrophy and hyperplasia especially in the spongy mesophyll (J. B. Goodey, 1939) and *D. graminophilus* produces similar reactions in leaves of bent grass (T. Goodey, 1933). The formation of galls or spikkels and giant cells by *D. dipsaci* is considered by Feder and Feldmesser (1953) to be analogous to gall formation by *Meloidogyne*.

Seinhorst (1956b) considers that dissolution of the middle lamella is associated with the ability of *D. dipsaci* to reproduce in the host plant.

12

In resistant varieties of red clover, for example, necrosis develops around the invading nematodes and they die or fail to mature, whereas in susceptible varieties the tissues swell with the breakdown of the middle lamella and rounding-off of the cells (Bingefors, 1957).   The histopathology of oats infested by *D. dipsaci* has been studied in detail by Blake (1962). In susceptible varieties parenchyma cells around the nematode enlarge and separate soon after invasion, with the subsequent formation of large air-spaces.   The separated cells are loose and their cytoplasmic contents decrease.   There is no increase in the number of nuclei but they appear to be misshapen.   When most of the cytoplasm is withdrawn, the cell walls collapse and a cavity forms in the tissue around each nematode. In resistant oat varieties, cavities are also formed by collapse of the cell walls but they are fewer and smaller and there is no cell separation or hypertrophy.

Aphelenchoides

The reaction of chrysanthemums to infestation by *Aphelenchoides ritzemabosi* has been described by Hesling and Wallace (1961).   The first reaction of the leaf is the production of patches of an opaque brown substance within the cells near the eelworms.   Browning then becomes more extensive and the number of chloroplasts in the cells is reduced. Eventually browning extends to the epidermis, few chloroplasts remain and cells in the mesophyll are ruptured, producing large cavities.   During necrosis the mesophyll and palisade tissue are equally affected but only in the final stages of decay do the vascular bundles and collenchyma break down.   There was no indication of hyperplasia or hypertrophy in infested mature leaves but leaves on young cuttings were often puffy and swollen, suggesting that such reactions were occurring.

Anguina

Anguina spp. produce well defined galls in leaves, stems and inflorescences.   T. Goodey's (1934) description of the galls of *Anguina cecidoplastes* on *Andropogon pertusus* provides a good example of these highly organised structures.   The galls are small, pronounced, localised swellings arising steeply from the leaf.   The first signs of swelling in the tissues occur in the mesophyll and in the two epidermal layers, but the xylem and phloem cells are unaffected.   The mesophyll cells show marked hypertrophy, their cytoplasm is granular and the plastids are grouped around the periphery of the cell.   The epidermal cells immediately above the gall undergo some multiplication and enlargement forming a layer two to three cells deep, whereas those of the lower epidermis become enlarged and stretched.   In older galls there is an innermost layer, two to three cells deep, lining an inner cavity.   These cells are thin-walled, greatly enlarged and rounded, with finely granular protoplasm but few chloroplasts.   Outside this zone is another layer, three to six cells deep, made up of elongate cells with thickened walls, each cell containing a large nucleus. Goodey suggests that such galls bear a close resemblance to those formed by cynipid wasps and with this resemblance in mind he suggests that the cells lining the central cavity form a nutritive zone. There is no evidence, however, to indicate the possible function of this cell layer.

Radopholus

The histopathology of citrus roots invaded by *Radopholus similis* has been described by Ducharme (1959). As the nematodes move through the roots, tunnels and cavities are formed in the cortex and stele (see Plate XIV). The nematodes enter the stele through the passage cells of the endodermis to reach the phloem-cambium ring, where they accumulate in large numbers. The phloem-cambium ring is often destroyed by necrosis so that the stele is girdled by a nematode-filled cavity separating the remains of the stele from the cortex (see Plate XV). Wound gum accumulates next to the stele in the invaded area giving an amber colour to the older parts of the lesion. Some cells near the nematode show hypertrophy and hyperplasia (see Plate XVI). Tumour formation from the pericycle occurs when the nematodes pass through the endodermis.

Blake (1961) studied the effects of *R. similis* in banana roots. He found that lesions originated as a puncture in the epidermis of the root. The nematodes were mostly in advance of the necrotic region as it spread from the original puncture. Cells near the nematodes were enlarged and often ruptured and those bounding the lesion showed evidence of mild hypertrophy. The lesions, which resembled those described by Ducharme (1959) on citrus roots, were extended into the cortex of banana roots by tunnelling of the nematodes but the stele was not invaded. Loos and Loos (1960) also described the tracks and lesions formed by *R. similis* in banana roots.

Conclusions

The cellular changes that occur in plants infested by nematodes have been described in detail by several authors and although wide gaps still remain in our knowledge of this aspect of nematology, at least we have a good idea of the range of possible plant reactions. Little is known, however, of how these reactions occur.

Hypotheses have been advanced suggesting that enzymes in nematode saliva induce changes in cell division and morphology. Sayre (in Mountain, 1960), for example, suggests that *Meloidogyne* larvae secrete a proteolytic enzyme which makes available essential amino-acids for nematode growth and at the same time releases indolacetic acid in root tissues. Indolacetic acid might also be released by proteolytic activity on structural protein. The splitting of peptide bonds of the protein chain would release a number of different amino-acids including trypto-phane which is a precursor of indolacetic acid. Thus a high level of indolacetic acid would accumulate in the tissues around the nematode and induce cellular changes and gall formation. This is an attractive hypothesis for there is evidence that nematodes can secrete proteolytic enzymes, that amino-acids do accumulate in *Meloidogyne* galls, and, as Krusberg (1961) has shown, free tryptophane occurs in lucerne galled by *Ditylenchus dipsaci* but not in healthy plants. Krusberg suggests that tryptophane could easily be converted to indolacetic acid by nematode or plant enzymes and so induce the galling reaction. Further weight is added to the hypothesis by the fact that plant growth hormones induce symptoms in plants similar to those associated with nematode invasion and that indole compounds are present in the galled tissues of *Abelmoschus esculentus* infested with *Meloidogyne javanica* (Balasubramanian and Rangaswami, 1962). Hypotheses have also been advanced to explain other plant reactions to nematode infestation and, as Dropkin (1955) has pointed out, histochemical methods and enzyme analysis will help to give the necessary information. It is along such lines that future work on histopathology will move.

ASSOCIATIONS WITH OTHER MICROORGANISMS

Previous mention has been made of the difficulty of studying host-parasite relations where nematodes are associated with other micro-organisms in the etiology of a disease. Such associations may be more prevalent than is realised at present, a view also expressed by Steiner (1953).

Species which produce large lesions in the plant root allow other organisms to enter the plant. There then follows a succession of secon-dary invaders which aggravate the initial nematode damage and may even assume a dominant role in the subsequent root rot (Perry, 1958; Mountain and Patrick, 1959). This may not always happen, however, as Seinhorst (1961) has pointed out. Ducharme (1957), for example, showed that in sterile root cultures of citrus, *Radopholus similis* caused cigar-shaped tumours to appear in the pericycle. Tumours were smaller and less frequent in roots in the field, however, owing to rapid root decomposition by other microorganisms. The sterile roots contained larger nematode populations and were more seriously damaged than non-sterile roots. Thus, the secondary invaders did not aggravate the nematode-induced disease, in fact, they appeared to inhibit the nematodes which were causing the major part of the root damage.

Such associations between nematodes and other organisms are fortui-tous but there may be a closer relationship between a nematode species and a species of fungus, bacterium or virus. The nematode may simply provide a means of entry into the host plant, or there may be a synergistic effect, and there is even some evidence of obligate relationships.

Fungi

Holdeman and Graham (1952, 1953) found that varieties of cotton, resistant to *Fusarium* wilt, succumbed to wilt only when the sting nematode, *Belonolaimus gracilis*, was present in the soil. *Meloidogyne* spp. may cause similar effects. Smith (1954), for example, showed that the effects of *Fusarium* wilt in cotton increased when the plants were attacked by these nematodes. Smith suggested that in addition to providing openings in the root for the fungus, *Meloidogyne* also increased the susceptibility of the host in the later stages of development. Smith and Dick (1960) state that breeding varieties of cotton resistant to *Fusarium* wilt is complicated by the relationships of the nematode (*Meloidogyne* spp.) to the disease. Thus, nematodes may lower resistance, so part of the wilt resistance may be attributed to resistance to nematodes. Wilt resistance in Upland cotton, *Gossypium hirsutum*, was controlled by a major dominant gene with modifying genes determining *Meloidogyne* resistance. Post-emergence damping-off of cotton by the fungus *Rhizoctonia solani* is increased in the presence of *Meloidogyne incognita acrita* (Reynolds and Hanson, 1957). Losses were reduced by controlling the nematodes with soil fumigants. Plant nematodes may not aggravate all kinds of cotton wilt, however. The application of ethylene dibromide to soil and control of nematodes did not decrease the amount of *Verticillium* wilt of cotton (McClellan *et al.*, 1956).

Symptoms of black-shank, a fungal disease of tobacco, are also increased by nematodes. Sasser and his colleagues (1955) grew two varieties of black-shank resistant tobacco in steam sterilised soil to which *Phytophthora parasitica var. nicotianae* and *Meloidogyne* spp. were added alone and in combination. Where the inoculum contained fungus and nematodes together, the black-shank symptoms developed earlier and were more severe than in soil with the fungus alone. The nematodes appeared to do more than simply wound the tissues because plant roots, cut artificially and inoculated with fungus showed no increased symptoms. It was suggested that the nematode altered the host cells biochemically thereby providing a more congenial substratum for the fungus. Increased resistance to black-shank was achieved by crossing known resistant varieties with other varieties known to be tolerant to infestations of *Meloidogyne*, *Pratylenchus* and *Tylenchorhynchus claytoni* (Moore *et al.*, 1956). Root knot resistance incorporated into plants with black-shank resistance reduced the losses from this disease (Powell and Nusbaum, 1958). Wilt symptoms in tobacco caused by *Fusarium oxysporum var. nicotianae* were greater when *Tylenchorhynchus claytoni* was present in the soil, but the fungus was not dependent on the nematode for invasion of the host (Holdeman, 1956).

Jenkins and Coursen (1957) found that *Fusarium* wilt in tomatoes was increased by root knot nematodes. In resistant varieties, the nematodes shortened the time for wilt symptoms to appear. Artificial wounding did not affect suceptibility, so Jenkins and Coursen concluded that nematodes lowered the natural resistance in some tomato varieties in addition to providing a means of entry for the fungus. These results were supported by Cohn and Minz (1960) who showed that *Meloidogyne hapla* and *Meloidogyne incognita* break resistance to *Fusarium* wilt in tomatoes. They also found that different *Meloidogyne* spp. did not produce this effect to the same degree and that artificial wounding failed to break resistance. They concluded that the mechanism of resistance-breakdown was not understood and that it was not caused by wounding of the tissues by nematodes. Binder and Hutchinson (1959) repeated some of the work of Jenkins and Coursen (1957), just described. They found that although the wilt resistant tomato, Chesapeake, was heavily galled by *Meloidogyne incognita acrita* the resistance to *Fusarium* was not impaired. Binder and Hutchinson concluded that the breaking of resistance in tomatoes was influenced by the race of nematode used in experiments and by the number of nematodes in the inoculum.

Increased severity of *Fusarium* diseases has also been reported in lucerne infested with *Meloidogyne* (McGuire *et al.*, 1958), in bananas with *Radopholus similis* (Newhall, 1958), in grapefruit with *Radopholus similis* (Feder and Feldmesser, 1961) and in carnation with *Meloidogyne* spp. (Schindler *et al.*, 1961). There is, therefore, considerable evidence of the importance of plant parasitic nematodes in *Fusarium* wilt disease in various crops. Furthermore, the nematode does not always act simply as an incitant by providing a means of entry into the host. It exercises more profound effects but little is known of this aspect; biochemical changes may be involved but there is no evidence for this yet. There is also little evidence of an obligate relationship between nematodes and fungi. Labruyère *et al.* (1959) showed that early yellowing of peas was caused by extensive decay of the root cortex. The nematode *Hoplolaimus uniformis* and the fungus *Fusarium oxysporum* did not produce these symptoms alone but together they often caused complete destruction of the cortex.

Synergistic relationships between nematodes and fungi have also been recorded on wheat. Benedict and Mountain (1956) found that the fungus *Rhizoctonia solani* and the nematode *Pratylenchus minyus* were closely and consistently associated with naturally occurring infections of winter wheat. In greenhouse and field experiments the combined effect of the fungus and nematode on the growth of wheat was almost twice that of either pathogen alone. Pure culture techniques did not reveal the dependence of the fungus on the nematode for host penetration although they were closely associated in the disease. Similar observations were made on an association between *Verticillium albo-atrum* and *Pratylenchus penetrans* in egg plant by McKeen and Mountain (1960), who emphasise the importance of assessing the effects of other parasitic microorganisms in interpreting the population dynamics of nematodes and the etiology of the diseases they cause. They, too, suggest that plant nematodes may provide an entry into host plants by mechanical damage and, by secreting enzymes during feeding, provide a substrate for fungal growth.

Later work by Mountain and McKeen (1962) showed that *Verticillium dahliae*, added to a field soil infested with *Pratylenchus penetrans*, increased the rate of reproduction of the nematode in the roots of egg plant and tomato, but not in pepper. The rate of reproduction of *Tylenchorhynchus capitatus* was also increased on tomato roots with the fungus added. Mountain and McKeen point out that there is a direct association between the incidence of wilt and the suitability of the plant as a host for *P. penetrans*. In addition, some relationship exists between the incidence of wilt and the increase in numbers of *P. penetrans* in the presence of the fungus. Both of these observations suggest complex interrelationships between the plant, the fungus and the nematode.

Bacteria

Stewart and Schindler (1956) studied wilting of carnation cuttings infected with the bacterium *Pseudomonas caryophylli* in association with different phytoparasitic nematodes. Cuttings were inoculated with either *Meloidogyne* spp., *Helicotylenchus nannus*, *Xiphinema diversicaudatum* or *Ditylenchus* sp. followed by inoculations with the bacterium. Treatments with and without root wounds were included as well as parallel treatments without bacteria. The results of the experiments indicated that root wounding, *Meloidogyne* spp. and *Helicotylenchus nannus* increased the rate of wilting in the presence of bacteria. *Xiphinema diversicaudatum* showed no effect with or without bacteria and with the *Ditylenchus* inoculum the rate of wilting even decreased. Stewart and Schindler conclude that endoparasitic and ectoparasitic nematodes aggravate the bacterial wilt in carnations by wounding the roots and allowing the bacteria to enter the plant.

Symptoms of bacterial wilt caused by *Pseudomonas solanacearum* in tobacco are also increased by the plant nematode *Meloidogyne incognita acrita* (Lucas et al., 1955). Thus to obtain maximum benefit from wilt resistant varieties it was suggested that the root knot nematodes should be controlled. Similar symptoms were obtained with inocula of bacterium plus nematode as with a bacterial suspension poured on to freshly cut roots, thus the nematode probably contributes to the disease by allowing bacteria to enter the roots. Lucas and his colleagues draw a distinction between the bacterial wilt disease in which the pathogen is essentially a wound invader and black-shank disease of tobacco in which the pathogen *Phytophthora parasitica nicotianae* is capable of penetrating uninjured tissues directly. Lucas and Krusberg (1956), however, found that *Tylenchorhynchus claytoni* did not increase the severity of bacterial wilt from *Xanthomonas solanacearum* in wilt resistant tobacco plants grown in soil infested with both pathogens, in fact the symptoms were sometimes reduced. Lucas and Krusberg suggest that weakening of the tobacco roots by the nematode provides a less suitable environment for the bacterium which develops best in vigorous, actively growing plants. They also point out that *Tylenchorhynchus claytoni* does not penetrate to the xylem tissues of the tobacco root during feeding, hence bacterial infections are less likely to occur with this species than with *Meloidogyne* spp. which reach the xylem.

It is therefore clear that in disease complexes it is essential to understand the ecology and behaviour of the pathogens involved if their role in disease production is to be interpreted.

Schuster (1959) suggests that root knot nematodes may provide entry for the bacterial wilt *Corynebacterium flaccumfaciens* into beans but the results are inconclusive. Crosse and Pitcher (1952), on the other hand, state that cauliflower disease of strawberries fails to appear if the two pathogens involved, *Corynebacterium fascians* and *Aphelenchoides ritzema-bosi* are inoculated separately into the plant. There is therefore an obligate relationship between the bacterium and the nematode. Later experiments (Pitcher and Crosse, 1958) confirmed the role of the two pathogens in the disease but some of the original views were modified. The disease was now considered to be primarily a hyperplastic bacterial symptom modified by nematode activity. Nevertheless, the nematode was essential as a vector of the bacterium. Two distinct but related diseases in nematode infested field strawberries were, therefore, distinguished: those caused by nematodes in association with the bacterium and those caused by nematodes alone. Cheo (1946) also claimed that bacterial disease of wheat was the result of an obligate relationship between a bacterium *Bacterium tritici* and the nematode *Anguina tritici*.

Viruses

It was suspected for some time that nematodes might transmit viruses (Christie, 1951) and virologists were aware that a living soil organism was probably acting as a vector in such virus diseases as Scottish raspberry curl (Cadman, 1956) and beet ring spot (Harrison, 1957) but none had isolated a nematode vector or even suggested the kinds of nematodes which could act as vectors.

Hewitt, Raski and Goheen (1958) were the first to show that nematodes could be vectors of soil borne viruses. Experiments in vineyards and in containers under controlled conditions, demonstrated that fan leaf disease of grapevines in California was soil-borne and not air-borne and that it was transmitted by *Xiphinema index*. Screenings containing nematodes from fan leaf soil transmitted fan leaf virus to healthy *Vitis vinifera* var. Mission. *X. index* hand-picked from the screenings transmitted the virus to healthy Mission plants and to *V. rupestris* var. St. George. *X. index* from the root zone of healthy Tokay grapes and figs in separate tests also transmitted the virus from diseased to healthy St.

George vines growing in the same clay pots. No transmission occurred in the absence of nematodes.

This provided unequivocal proof that nematodes could act as virus vectors. It opened up a completely new field in plant pathology and little time elapsed before there were further reports of other nematode virus associations.

Harrison and Cadman (1959) found that *Arabis* mosaic virus was closely associated with the presence of a *Xiphinema* sp. and they suggested that this nematode was a possible vector. Breece and Hart (1959) showed that healthy peach seedlings developed yellow bud mosaic virus in the presence of *Xiphinema americanum*. No symptoms appeared in the absence of nematodes, so they concluded that *X. americanum* was a vector. Frazier and Maggenti (1962) showed eventually that peach yellow bud mosaic was transmitted to healthy *Fragaria vesca* by populations of *X. americanum*, thus agreeing with Breece and Hart's observations. Fulton's (1962) observations showed that *X. americanum* was also a vector of tobacco ring spot virus. Jha and Posnette (1959) found that it was necessary for a *Xiphinema* sp. to be present in soil for raspberry yellow dwarf virus to be transmitted to healthy strawberry plants. Sol and his colleagues (1960) showed that when nematodes from rattle virus soil were transferred to nematode and virus free soil, tobacco plants grown in the soil became heavily infected with rattle virus. It was suggested that *Trichodorus pachydermus* was probably the vector and subsequent work confirmed this (Sol and Seinhorst, 1961). Of four dorylaimoid species tested, rattle virus was transmitted by only one, *T. pachydermus*; even one specimen of this species could infect a tobacco plant. The American strain of tobacco rattle virus is also transmitted by a *Trichodorus* species, *T. christiei* (Walkinshaw *et al.*, 1961).

Harrison and his colleagues (1961) found that *Longidorus elongatus* was closely associated with soil from patches in raspberry and strawberry plantations where plants were infected with the beet ring spot strain of tomato black ring virus. *Longidorus elongatus* from soil containing the virus transmitted it to sugar beet, turnips and spinach seedlings. Non-infective nematodes acquired and subsequently transmitted the virus from infected cucumber and potato plants. When adults and larvae were used separately only the larvae transmitted the virus.

The study of nematodes as virus vectors is still in the early stages and little attempt has been made yet to investigate the mechanism of virus transmission. Raski and Hewitt (1960), however, have shown that the fan leaf virus persists in its vector for at least 30 days during which time the nematodes can survive free of host plants and still remain capable of transmitting the virus. They conclude that the fan leaf virus is not carried on the nematode stylet but is intimately associated with the nematode's digestive system. Transmission of the virus may occur within 24 hr. of the nematodes being introduced to roots of healthy plants.

There is also some evidence that the virus is not passed from one generation to the next via the egg.

Harrison, Mowat and Taylor (1961) point out that all the nematodes so far implicated as virus vectors belong to the order Enoplida and they fall into two major groups which correspond to the two major groups of viruses they transmit. The viruses with polyhedral particles cause symptoms of the ring spot type and have vectors belonging to two closely related genera in the superfamily Dorylaimoidea, *Xiphinema* and *Longidorus*. The rod-shaped tobacco rattle virus is transmitted by *Trichodorus* spp. in the superfamily Diphtherophoroidea. Observations on crops and soils suggest that the spread of each major antigenic variant of these viruses depends on the presence of a specific nematode, but this apparent specificity needs confirmation by experiment.

Information on the ecology and physiology of the nematode virus vectors is an important aspect of this problem. Harrison and Winslow (1961) have approached this subject by laboratory and field studies on the relation of arabis mosaic virus to its vector *Xiphinema americanum*. They found that patches of plants infested with the virus in a range of crops, including some, like celery and marrow, not before known to be hosts, coincided with patches of soil infested with *X. diversicaudatum*. Adult nematodes transmitted the virus more readily than larvae but none, transferred when moulting, infected healthy plants. *X. diversicaudatum* was still infective after 24 days in moist peat, with no plants. Hedgerow trees appeared to be the hosts of the nematode and at least one, elder, was also a host of the virus. Harrison and Winslow also found that *X. diversicaudatum* occurred at soil depths of 3 ft but most were 3 to 9 in. deep. They suggest that *X. diversicaudatum* and arabis mosaic virus probably occur commonly in natural woodland in Britain and that their incidence has decreased as the land has been turned over to agriculture.

These are the sort of problems which have to be studied in future work on nematode-virus associations, the whole subject is full of unanswered and fascinating questions: Where does the virus occur in the nematode? How does it pass from nematode to plant? How long can it persist in the nematode? Is there a close specificity between a virus and its nematode vector? What nematode species are capable of acting as vectors? These questions and the equally important subject of the ecology of the nematode vectors await serious consideration.

The association of nematodes with other microorganisms in plant diseases is obviously a fruitful field for research. In fact it may be no exaggeration to say that such investigations may change many of our ideas on host-parasite relations and the etiology of diseases in which plant parasitic nematodes are involved.

BIOLOGICAL RACES

Races of nematodes are of obvious importance to the plant breeder who is trying to produce plants resistant to nematode attack and to the nematologist who relies to some extent on the pathological reactions of the plant to identify the nematode. Successful nematode control by crop rotation also depends on knowing which crops a particular nematode will attack. A consideration of races in host-parasite relations is therefore important, especially in control problems.

A biological or physiological race can only be distinguished by its specific physiological characteristics such as pathogenicity. Races often comprise several biotypes, each of which is capable of a change in virulence by genetic mutation or recombination to give rise to new biotypes and new races but this is probably a rare occurrence in plant nematodes. New biological races could also arise by selection among different biotypes within a race. Thus, a few individuals in a race may be able to develop and reproduce on a variety of host plants resistant to the nematode race. These individuals may then produce a new nematode population of different virulence capable of multiplying on the formerly resistant host plant. In this way a new race would arise. These principles are well illustrated in experiments by Riggs and Winstead (1959). They recovered females of *Meloidogyne incognita incognita, M. incognita acrita* and *M. arenaria arenaria* which had matured on resistant Hawaii 5,229 tomatoes. Larvae from the females were transferred to other plants of this resistant variety and in this way they obtained populations which were as virulent in the resistant tomatoes as the parents were on the susceptible varieties. The new race was physiologically distinct from the parent population and had the inherent genetic ability to develop in the presence of the Mi gene, a single incompletely dominant gene controlling resistance. The specialised nature of the new races was indicated by their inability to parasitise resistant varieties of other crop plants.

There are numerous examples where races are known or suspected to occur. Thus Martin (1954) found differences ranging from no parasitism to severe parasitism within isolated egg masses of *Meloidogyne incognita incognita* and *M. incognita acrita*. Lider (1954) found evidence of racial differences in *M. incognita acrita* in the ability to produce galls on vines. Four species of *Meloidogyne* have been found in Queensland, Australia, *M. javanica, M. arenaria, M. hapla* and *M. incognita* and Colbran (1958) states that there are distinct physiological races in all of them. Goplen and his colleagues (1959) tested the virulence of twenty collections of *Meloidogyne* spp. on five varieties of lucerne. Three races were found in *M. incognita acrita*, two in *M. javanica javanica* and two in *M. hapla*. Dropkin (1959) studied the host-parasite interaction between soybeans and four *Meloidogyne* spp. so that he could establish a bioassay method for distinguishing races. Galling and egg mass production varied as parasite or host was changed. A Californian population of *M. incognita acrita* could be distinguished from a Maryland population by differential behaviour on soybean varieties.

Biological races of *Ditylenchus dipsaci* have been known for at least 50 years and suggestions (Steiner, 1956) that they are morphologically distinct have not been substantiated. Seinhorst (1957), however, distinguished eleven biological races by their pathogenicity on nine plant species. Southey (1957) tested the tulip, narcissus and hyacinth races of *D. dipsaci* on thirteen plant species and his results agreed with those of Seinhorst. Barker (1959) using Seinhorst's (1957) technique with nine plant species, found that the teasel race of *D. dipsaci* did not reproduce in lucerne nor the lucerne race in teasel. There are indications, however, that further races of *D. dipsaci* occur. Bingefors (1957), for example, states that different populations of the red clover race of *D. dipsaci* differ in their ability to attack different red clover varieties. Goodey and Hooper (1958) found that *D. dipsaci* from oats failed to cause any noticeable damage to wheat in England, contrary to observations in Italy. They, therefore, suggest that the *D. dipsaci* race on wheat in Italy is different from that in England. Differences between populations of the lucerne race on various host plants have also been observed by Barker and Sasser (1959).

In Holland, *Ditylenchus radicicola* is usually found on the roots of several grasses in old meadows but it has not yet been found on cereals. In Scandinavia, however, this nematode parasitises barley. Inoculation tests showed that the Dutch population attacked *Poa annua* heavily but barley only slightly whereas for the Scandinavian population the heaviest attacks were on barley and least on *Poa annua*. No morphological differences were found between the populations (s'Jacob, 1962).

Raski (1952) investigating the host range of *Heterodera schachtii* found variations between populations from different localities. Andersen (1961) found that populations of *H. avenae* from different districts of Denmark behaved differently to different varieties of oats; two biological races were distinguished. Shepherd (1959a) tested eight populations of *H. schachtii* from different parts of England on *Beta patellaris* which is resistant to this nematode. A few cysts were found and Shepherd suggests that this may indicate that 'resistance-breaking-biotypes' occur as in *H. rostochiensis*. The occurrence of a race of *H. rostochiensis* capable of reproducing on resistant varieties of potato has been recorded by van der Laan and Huysman (1957) and Dunnett (1957). Jones (1957) confirmed these findings and suggested that if 'resistance-breaking' behaved as a simple dominant, the increase of the new race would be rapid, if recessive, very slow at first. He further suggested that whatever the mode of inheritance, the rate of increase of this race would be slower than with new strains of pathogens such as potato blight because of lack of mobility and slow rate of reproduction in nematodes. Later work by Jones (1958) showed that of twenty populations of *H. rostochiensis* fourteen contained the 'resistance-breaking' race.

Ducharme and Birchfield (1956) state that field observations indicated the existence of three biological races of *Radopholus similis*. Laboratory experiments confirmed the existence of two races; one race parasitised banana roots, the other race roots of both banana and citrus. Slootweg

(1956) has also suggested that *Pratylenchus penetrans* may comprise several different races.

It is clear that biological races in species of plant nematodes are by no means a rarity, in fact it is possible that they may occur in most species. If this is so, some present concepts of host-specificity and pathogenicity may have to be modified. Studies on the host-parasite relations of a nematode species and host-plant species may necessitate the use of as many different populations of the nematode and varieties of the host-plant as possible. There is also a need for research on the genetics of plant nematode races. Cultures of individual nematodes on plant tissue cultures accompanied by pathogenicity tests may help to solve this problem.

HOST SPECIFICITY

Different species and races of plant nematodes only attack a certain number of plant species; this number may be very large for such polyphagous species as *Ditylenchus dipsaci* or very small for nematodes like *Heterodera rostochiensis*. Some indication of this can be obtained from the books by Goodey, T. (1956) and by Goodey, J. B., Franklin and Hooper (1959) who list the records of plant-nematode associations in the literature. It should be pointed out, however, that many of these are only associations and not definite indications that plants are hosts. To establish this, it is necessary to show that the nematode can reproduce in its host.

Meloidogyne is a good example of the variation of host-specificity and reaction within a genus. Thus, Tarjan (1952) states that valid differences exist in the reactions of snapdragon to infestation by five species of *Meloidogyne*. Similarly, Sasser (1952) using different host plants, distinguished five species. Identification was based on the susceptibility of the host plants and the types of galls produced on the roots. Van der Linde (1956) states, however, that on applying Sasser's host reaction test in South Africa, he found that *M. incognita incognita* parasitised *Lycopersicon peruvianum*. According to the test the nematode would be identified as *M. incognita acrita*. There are two possibilities here. Either van der Linde's morphological identification was wrong or the Sasser test can only be used on populations within a localised area. Further light is thrown on the problem by Triantaphyllou and Sasser (1960) who propagated fourteen single egg mass or larval isolates from twelve populations of *M. incognita* from nine states in the U.S.A. The nematodes were propagated on tomato for twelve generations. The perineal patterns, on which identification of *Meloidogyne* spp. is partly based, ranged from typical *incognita* to typical *acrita* types within individual isolates. They concluded that since distinction between the two sub-species is often uncertain, the division of the species into two sub-species serves no practical purpose. So van der Linde's *M. incognita incognita* might well have been *M. incognita acrita*. Triantaphyllou and

Sasser further suggest that stable morphological characteristics may nevertheless be found which can be correlated with physiological behaviour such as host specificity. They consider that such correlations may be found easily in populations from localised areas and that *Meloidogyne* problems of this sort are essentially local problems.

In the genus *Meloidogyne* where identification of species is often difficult and where races may occur within a species, it would be dangerous to discuss host-specificity except in localised areas. Even in the genus *Heterodera* where taxonomy is possibly on a firmer footing, variations in host range between populations from different localities may occur (Raski, 1952; Oostenbrink, 1955). Once again, however, it is essential to know the exact identity of host and parasite in studying host specificity. Thus, Oostenbrink (1955) comments that *Solanum nigrum* is a good host of *H. rostochiensis* in the U.S.A. but no such infections have been found in England or Holland. Doncaster (1957) found that, in England, *S. nigrum* was a poor host of *H. rostochiensis* whereas Prummel (1958) showed that a Dutch population of this nematode produced fully mature cysts on a *S. nigrum* variety from Mecklenburg in Germany but not on a Dutch variety. Thus, the identity of the host as well as the parasite must be established and even the possibility of nematode races has to be considered. Host specificity is not, therefore, a clear-cut phenomenon in plant nematology, consequently host-lists will continually change and may be expected to differ between localities.

There is little evidence to suggest that host specificity is determined by the plant's influence on hatching and moulting or on the ability of the nematode to find the plant and invade it. Winslow (1955) suggests that emergence of larvae from cysts of *Heterodera* spp. tends to occur in the root exudates from their own hosts and not in the exudates from non-hosts. Host-specificity could, therefore, be influenced by chemicals external to the plant. Golden (1958), however, found that root diffusates from three species of wild beet stimulated larval emergence in *H. schachtii* although the plants were non-hosts. Lownsbery and Viglierchio (1961) and Viglierchio (1961) state that root diffusates do not govern host selection rigorously as nematodes are attracted to numerous agents. The unspecific nature of attraction to roots has already been discussed (Chapter 4) and Rhoades and Linford (1959) have also shown that there is imperfect agreement between the suitability of plants as hosts and their production of active root diffusate for moulting of preadult nematodes of *Paratylenchus projectus* and *Paratylenchus dianthus*. Shepherd (1959b) found that the presence of host plant roots did not affect the number of *Heterodera* larvae invading adjacent non-host roots, suggesting that chemical exudates were not specifically involved in attraction to and invasion of roots. Moreover, many non-hosts were invaded, although usually by relatively few larvae.

The factors which determine whether a plant will be a suitable host for a nematode or not are largely unknown. Some plants appear to produce toxins on invasion and so inhibit development; others possibly lack some chemical essential for the nutrition of the parasite, but this is only speculation. Whatever the factors, however, it appears that they operate within the plant.

RESISTANCE

To feed, develop and reproduce, nematodes must penetrate the cells of the host plant. Endoparasitic nematodes invade and develop within the plant whereas ectoparasitic nematodes feed externally; with both types, any characteristic of the host which inhibits these activities is termed resistance but if nematode reproduction occurs the plant is said to be susceptible. There are various categories of host status from extreme susceptibility to immunity. Peacock (1957), for example, states that groundnuts are immune to a *Meloidogyne* sp. in the Gold Coast; no larvae entered the roots of the host plant although several different populations were used. Furthermore, plants which succumb to nematode attack are also said to be susceptible, those that withstand the attack are resistant. Finally, a plant which is infested by a high number of actively reproducing nematodes but which shows little indication of injury is said to be tolerant. Dropkin (1955) points out that difficulties in terminology arise because there are two separate factors in resistance. One is the suitability of the host plant for the life of the parasite, the other is the effect of the parasite on the well-being of the host. Hence, resistance can be measured by the plant's reaction to the parasite as well as the effect of the plant on nematode reproduction. Consequently numbers of nematodes in a plant may not give a satisfactory indication of resistance, because low populations may indicate either resistance or extreme susceptibility if the nematodes cannot persist in severely injured tissues (Rohde, 1960). The situation is well summed up by Dropkin and Nelson (1960) who constructed a table to show the variations in host-parasite reaction:

		Host growth	
		Good	Poor
Parasite growth {	Good	tolerant	susceptible
	Poor	resistant	intolerant

Some reference has already been made (page 176) to the histopathology of resistant and susceptible varieties of host plant species but the following examples will help to emphasise these differences.

Varieties and species of citrus infested by *Radopholus similis* fall into three categories: (1) tolerant plants which made good growth had undamaged vigorous root systems and carried a high nematode infestation, (2) susceptible plants which made poor growth, had moderate to severely damaged root systems and carried a medium to high nematode population, (3) resistant plants which made good growth, had vigorous root systems showing little or no damage and contained few nematodes (Feder and Ford, 1957).

Dropkin and Nelson (1960) studied the histological response to infection in nineteen soybean varieties infested with *Meloidogyne incognita incognita* and *M. incognita acrita*. Four host reactions were observed: (1) a hypersensitive reaction in which cells immediately around the larvae die, (2) cells near the larvae undergo moderate fusion and show great numbers of peculiar cell inclusions, (3) cells enlarge, contain many nuclei and contain diffuse highly vacuolated cytoplasm. These three types of cell reaction are always associated with poor nematode development and so indicate resistance. (4) Giant cells are formed with thickened walls, many nuclei and dense cytoplasm. This reaction occurred in susceptible varieties where it was associated with rapid nematode growth and abundant egg production. Ross (1958) found similar reactions in soybeans infested with *Heterodera glycines*; in resistant varieties the feeding areas were necrotic whereas, in sucseptible varieties, giant cells were formed. Resistance of cotton varieties to *Meloidogyne incognita acrita* is related to conditions within the roots that prevent or delay larval development and not to the failure of the larvae to invade the host. Resistant varieties show increased root necrosis, reduced hypertrophy and hyperplasia, reduced tissue disorganisation and gall formation and the nematodes do not mature (Minton, 1962).

Plants susceptible to *Ditylenchus dipsaci* become swollen because of hypertrophy and dissolution of the middle lamella between cells, and the rate of nematode reproduction is high. Resistant plants often show a hypersensitive reaction to invasion for necrotic areas appear, there is less swelling and reproduction is inhibited (Seinhorst, 1956b; Dijkstra, 1957; Bingefors, 1957; Barker, 1959). Resistance in lucerne to *Ditylenchus dipsaci* may be a hypersensitive reaction which inhibits meristematic growth but necrotic areas are not diagnostic of resistance. The critical phase in the completion of the nematode's life cycle in resistant lucerne varieties is egg production (Grundbacher, 1962).

There are numerous other references in the literature to histopathological differences between resistant and susceptible varieties and the list of plants resistant to different nematode species is even more extensive. Franklin and Hooper (1959) for example, have listed more than 300 species and varieties of plant recorded as resistant to *Meloidogyne* spp.

The environment may also influence the plant and modify its resistance. Plants growing in well fertilised soil, for example, are often more resistant to nematodes than undernourished plants.

The type of resistance varies between different plant species. Thus, Sasser (1954) found four different types of interaction between *Meloidogyne* spp. and various plants: (1) no larvae penetrated the roots, (2) few larvae invaded and none developed, (3) many invaded and a few developed, (4) many invaded and many developed. Resistance may, therefore, operate outside the plant, at the plant surface and within the plant. These aspects will now be considered.

Resistance outside the host

Rohde (1960) suggests that failure to produce a hatching factor by plants may confer resistance in the presence of *Heterodera* spp. He also considers that repulsion or lack of attraction by plants would increase resistance. There is little evidence to support these views, but Rohde is correct in pointing out that so few studies have been made on immune plants that the possibility of repulsion by the plant cannot be ruled out. There is good evidence, however, that some plants may inhibit nematode activity by the secretion of toxic substances into the soil. Oostenbrink and his colleagues (1957) showed that when *Tagetes patula* was grown as a main crop, *Pratylenchus* populations in the soil were reduced by 90 per cent. This effect was not caused by decay of haulms or roots but was apparently a direct nematicidal effect. *Tylenchorhynchus dubius* was also suppressed but *Rotylenchus robustus*, a number of Tylenchida and saprozoic nematodes were unaffected. Cultivation of *Tagetes* between the rows or around the foot of other plants reduced the *Pratylenchus* populations in their roots as well as in the soil, giving better growth of perennials in the second year or in the succeeding crop. Uhlenbroek and Bijloo (1958, 1959, 1960) isolated active nematicidal principles from the *Tagetes* roots. These compounds were found to be derivatives of 2,2′-bithienyl.

Rohde and Jenkins (1958) found that the asparagus variety Mary Washington was resistant to *Trichodorus christiei*. Populations of this nematode declined more rapidly in soil containing asparagus roots than in soil without roots and nematode numbers did not increase on a suitable host if its roots were intermingled with those of asparagus. Rohde and Jenkins thought that some compound was present in the rhizosphere of asparagus which either killed the nematodes or inhibited their reproduction. Such a compound was found in the soil and it was shown to have originated in the asparagus roots where it occurred in high concentrations, especially in storage roots. Examination of the compound indicated that it was composed of carbon, hydrogen and oxygen and contained alcohol and ether linkage groups. It was concluded that the compound was a glycoside with a low molecular weight aglycone. This toxic compound secreted from asparagus roots was also toxic to *Paratylenchus projectus*, *Tylenchorhynchus claytoni*, *Helicotylenchus nannus*, *Belonolaimus gracilis*, *Tylencholaimus striatus* and *Diphtherophora* sp. Rohde (1960) later showed that the toxicity of this compound was related to interference with acetylcholinesterase in the nematode. Cholinesterase was found in several species and it appeared to be concentrated chiefly in the nervous system. No staining reaction for the enzyme was obtained after pretreatment of the nematodes with asparagus extract, indicating that the enzyme had been inactivated.

Luc (1961) has shown that some unknown chemical compound from millet roots inhibits movement of *Hemicycliophora paradoxa* and it is possible that plants, especially those which appear to be immune to nematode attacks, may produce such chemicals.

Resistance at the plant surface

Evidence for this type of resistance is often unsatisfactory because it is usually based on the number of nematodes found in the roots of resistant and susceptible plant varieties. Nematodes in resistant plant roots may die and disappear quickly, especially where there is a necrotic reaction to invasion. Furthermore, it is possible that nematodes may invade and then leave a resistant root whereas in a susceptible root they may tend to stay. Direct observations of repulsion or inability to penetrate the epidermis are needed.

Dijkstra (1957) states that larvae of *Ditylenchus dipsaci* invaded resistant varieties of red clover at a slower rate than susceptible ones but he did not consider resistance to invasion to be important. Williams (1958) found that fewer *Heterodera rostochiensis* larvae invaded the more resistant species of *Solanum*. Similarly, Sasser (1954) showed that plants resistant to *Meloidogyne* spp. were invaded to a lesser degree than susceptible plants. The root systems of resistant tomatoes were invaded by fewer larvae of *Meloidogyne incognita*, usually one-half or less, than those of susceptible varieties (Dean and Struble, 1953). Nematodes entering resistant roots produced extensive necrosis within 48 hr., and 2 weeks after inoculation most of the invading larvae had died and disappeared. Dean and Struble found no difference between the numbers of larvae entering resistant and susceptible sweet potato varieties however.

Ichinohe and Asai (1956) found no relationship between the rate of larval invasion of *Heterodera glycines* and the degree of varietal resistance in soybean, although many of the larvae invading resistant plants died quickly. Similarly, Feder and Ford (1957) did not attribute resistance in citrus varieties attacked by *Radopholus similis* to impeded penetration. Golden (1958) came to the same conclusion in his work on resistance in beet species to *Heterodera schachtii*. De Guiran (1960) found that equal numbers of *Meloidogyne javanica* and *M. incognita acrita* invaded roots of resistant *Crotalaria* and susceptible tomatoes. Riggs and Winstead (1959) counted the numbers of larvae of *M. incognita* that invaded resistant and susceptible varieties of tomato seedlings. The seedlings were placed on damp filter paper and 100 larvae were introduced into sterile soil covering the roots. Counts were made after 24, 48, 96 and 144 hr. but no difference was found between the numbers of larvae invading the susceptible and resistant varieties. Resistant plants showed necrosis and larvae were dead in 96 hr. after inoculation. These results emphasise that in experiments like these it is necessary to make counts within a day or two of inoculation otherwise death and decay of larvae in resistant plants may be interpreted as reduced invasion.

Resistance within the plant

Rohde (1960) states that, in general, in most resistant plants, attraction and penetration occur readily. Once penetration occurs there is often a change in the host tissues which is necessary for the parasite to continue development. These changes may involve gall formation, giant-cell development or cell breakdown. He further states that failure of the parasite to mature is directly related to failure of the host to react to the presence of the parasite. There is little evidence to support the hypothesis that some essential nutrient is withheld from the parasite.

Dropkin and Nelson (1960) agree with Rohde for they consider that resistance in soybeans to root knot nematodes is associated with a failure to respond to larval secretions by hyperplasia. Numerous other authors have also stated that absence of swelling in plants infested with *Ditylenchus dipsaci* or absence of giant-cell formation in the presence of *Heterodera* and *Meloidogyne* spp. are indicative of resistance.

Riggs and Winstead (1958) consider that resistance factors are inherent within individual cells and are not translocated within the plant. Peacock (1959) also states that resistance in the root does not depend on downward transmission from the stem. Forster (1956), on the other hand, found that while there was no transference of susceptibility from a susceptible tomato scion to a resistant *Lycopersicon peruvianum* root-stock, a scion of *Lycopersicon peruvianum* increased the resistance of a tomato root-stock to attack by larvae of *Meloidogyne incognita*.

At present, however, the evidence is in favour of the hypothesis that resistance is localised within individual cells and is of a chemical nature. Peacock (1959) lists ways in which such a chemical factor could determine resistance. Attempts to find chemical differences between resistant and susceptible varieties have largely failed, however, and even if they were successful it would only establish a correlation. There would be no evidence that the chemical differences were necessarily involved in resistance at all. Shibuya (1952) suggests that proteins in resistant and susceptible varieties of sweet potato may be related to giant-cell formation and Swink and Finkner (1956) think that high galactinol content in sugar beet may indicate susceptibility. But there is little evidence for these hypotheses. Chemical analyses of non-infected oat varieties, resistant or susceptible to *Meloidogyne incognita acrita*, failed to show any difference in amino acid or sugar content (Ferver and Crittenden, 1958). When leaves of chrysanthemum varieties, resistant and susceptible to *Aphelenchoides ritzemabosi*, were tested for polyphenols, no differences were found (Wallace, 1961b). Mountain and Patrick (1959), however, found that peach seedlings of the variety Shalil supported high root populations of *Pratylenchus pene-trans* without discernible stunting, whereas seedlings of the variety Lovell grown under identical conditions contained smaller root popula-tions of the nematode and were markedly stunted. Shalil contained less of the chemical amygdalin than Lovell. Mountain and Patrick suggest, therefore, that resistance in a variety like Shalil may be associated with the low amygdalin content. It is possible, however, that the low nema-tode population in Lovell is indicative of resistance caused by a hyper-sensitive reaction. The population might eventually die leaving the plant to grow vigorously. In the variety Shalil, however, tissue destruc-tion might increase slowly and eventually produce a malformed tree. Pitcher (private communication) disagrees with this interpretation. He states that by the time the nematode numbers decline the roots would have already suffered a severe check and growth would continue to be limited by the combined effects of the residual nematode population, secondary pathogens and toxic root residues.

Nevertheless, hypersensitivity may determine resistance in chrysanthe-mums infested with *Aphelenchoides ritzemabosi* (Wallace, 1961b). Leaves of resistant varieties brown quickly and there is no nematode multiplica-tion, so the initial infestation is isolated and does not spread to the other leaves of the plant. Leaves of susceptible varieties, however, brown slowly, the nematodes reproduce and spread over the plant. Infested leaves of resistant and susceptible varieties brown at different rates because, in resistant varieties, the gravid females move about in the leaf, piercing hundreds of cells which subsequently turn brown. In suscep-tible varieties the females do not move, they pierce few cells and lay many eggs. This difference in behaviour was attributed to the absence of a nutritional factor in leaves of resistant varieties because no difference was found between varieties in the concentration of polyphenols or polyphenol oxidase which are responsible for browning. Such a hypothesis has no supporting evidence, however, and there are several other possible explanations for the differential browning rate of resistant and susceptible chrysanthemum varieties.

Hypersensitive reactions resulting in the formation of necrotic cells may also confer resistance to plants infested with sedentary nematodes like *Heterodera* and *Meloidogyne* because the nematodes are unable to feed on such cells. If the nematode can migrate through the tissues however and so escape from necrotic areas, the hypersensitive reaction may produce susceptibility. It is only when the number of host cells killed is great and the rate of reproduction begins to fall that hypersensi-tivity will have any obvious adverse effect upon the parasite. Mountain (private communication) found an example of this in varieties of Burley tobacco infested with *Pratylenchus minyus*. The root cells of the ex-tremely susceptible variety Harrow Velvet were hypersensitive to the parasite and after some weeks the population in the roots dropped drastically; by then the plant was almost dead. In contrast, the root cells of Green Briar were not killed as rapidly, there was no noticeable effect on reproduction and no measurable effect on growth. Mountain concludes that in this host-parasite relationship, hypersensitivity resulted in extreme susceptibility and tolerance in apparent resistance.

The rapid appearance of necrotic cells in plant tissues invaded by nematodes may therefore confer resistance if the plant is able to survive this drastic reaction but, if the plant succumbs, this hypersensitivity makes it susceptible.

The phenomenon of resistance in peach, tobacco and chrysanthemum emphasises that no generalisation can be applied to resistance in a particular host-parasite relationship. It also helps to underline some of the problems associated with resistance, in particular:

(1) The isolation and identification of enzymes secreted by nematodes during feeding and their influence on plant tissues.

(2) Elucidation of the biochemical differences between resistant and susceptible varieties, associated with differences in cellular response to nematode feeding.

(3) Identification of the chemicals in plant cells which promote and inhibit nematode development and reproduction.

All these problems involve the culture of plant nematodes in media of known chemical composition.

There are, of course, many other questions to be answered. For example, if we refer to Rohde's remarks at the beginning of this section (page 195) we might ask if giant cell formation etc. in host tissues are essential for nematode development or whether they are just symptoms of a successful host-parasite relationship. But in answering such questions we are always brought back to these same basic biochemical problems.

REFERENCES

ANDERSEN, S. (1961). Resistens mod Havreål, *Heterodera avenae*. *Medd. VetHøjsk. Landb. Plantenkultur. Kbh.* **68**, 1–179.

BAINES, R. C. and CLARKE, O. F. (1953). Some effects of the citrus root nematode on the growth of orange and lemon trees. *Phytopathology*, **42**, 1.

BALASUBRAMANIAN, M. and RANGASWAMI, G. (1962). Presence of indole compounds in nematode galls. *Nature, Lond.* **194**, 774–775.

BARKER, K. R. (1959). Studies on the biology of the stem nematode. *Phytopathology*, **49** (5), 315.

BARKER, K. R. and SASSER, J. N. (1959). Biology and control of the stem nematode *Ditylenchus dipsaci*. *Phytopathology*, **49** (10), 664–670.

BENEDICT, W. G. and MOUNTAIN, W. B. (1956). Studies on the etiology of a root rot of winter wheat in south-western Ontario. *Canad. J. Bot.* **34**, 159–174.

BERGMAN, B. H. H. (1958). Sugar beet eelworm and its control. 5. Some microscopic observations on the development of larvae of *Heterodera schachtii* in the roots of susceptible and resistant plants. *Meded. Inst. Suikerbeit. Bergen-o-Z*, **28** (3), 151–168.

BINDER, E. and HUTCHINSON, M. T. (1959).   Further studies concerning the effect of the root knot nematode. *Meloidogyne incognita acrita* on the susceptibility of the Chesapeake tomato to Fusarium wilt.   *Plant Dis. Reptr.* **43** (9), 972–978.

BINGEFORS, S. (1957).   *Studies on breeding red clover for resistance to stem nematodes.* Uppsala: Almquist & Wiksells Boktryckeri AB.

BIRCHFIELD, W. (1953).   Parasitic nematodes associated with diseased roots of sugar cane.   *Phytopathology*, **43**, 289.

BIRCHFIELD, W. and JONES, J. E. (1961).   Distribution of the reniform nematode in relation to crop failure of cotton in Louisiana.   *Plant Dis. Reptr.* **45** (9), 671–673.

BIRCHFIELD, W. and MARTIN, W. J. (1956).   Pathogenicity on sugarcane and host plant studies of species of *Tylenchorhynchus*.   *Phytopathology*, **46**, 277.

BLAKE, C. D. (1961).   Root rot of bananas caused by *Radopholus similis* (Cobb) and its control in New South Wales.   *Nematologica*, **6**, 295–310.

—— (1962).   The etiology of tulip root disease in susceptible and resistant varieties of oats infested by the stem nematode, *Ditylenchus dipsaci* (Kühn) Filipjev.   II. Histopathology of tulip root and development of the nematode.   *Ann. appl. Biol.* **50**, 713–722.

BREECE, J. R. and HART, W. H. (1959).   A possible association of nematodes with the spread of peach yellow bud mosaic virus.   *Plant. Dis. Reptr.* **43** (9), 989–990.

BROWN, E. B. (1957).   Lucerne stem eelworm in Great Britain.   *Nematologica*, Suppl. **2**, 369–375.

—— (1958).   Observations on a race of *Ditylenchus dipsaci* attacking annual aster and sweet sultan.   *Plant Pathology*, **7** (4), 150–151.

—— (1959).   Eelworms on strawberries.   *Plant Pathology*, **8** (4), 152.

CADMAN, C. H. (1956).   Studies on the etiology and mode of spread of Scottish raspberry leaf curl disease.   *J. Hort. Sci.* **31** (2), 111–118.

CHEO, C. (1946).   A note on the relation of nematodes (*Tylenchus tritici*) to the development of the bacterial disease of wheat caused by *Bacterium tritici*.   *Ann. appl. Biol.* **33**, 447–449.

CHITWOOD, B. G. (1949).   Ring nematodes (Criconematinae).   A possible factor in decline and replanting problems of peach orchards.   *Proc. helm. Soc. Wash.* **16** (1), 6–7.

—— (1951).   The golden nematode of potatoes.   *U.S. Dept. Agric. Circ.* **875**.

CHITWOOD, B. G. and BERGER, C. A. (1960).   Preliminary report on nemic parasites of coffee in Guatemala; with suggested *ad interim* control measures.   *Plant Dis. Reptr.* **44** (11), 841–847.

CHITWOOD, B. G. and BUHRER, E. M. (1946).   Further studies on the life history of the golden nematode of potatoes, *Heterodera rostochiensis* Wollenweber.   *Proc. helm. Soc. Wash.* **13** (2), 54–56.

CHITWOOD, B. G. and ESSER, R. P. (1957).   Pathogenicity tests involving *Meloidodera floridensis*, a nematode associated with slash pine.   *Plant Dis. Reptr.* **41** (7), 603–604.

CHITWOOD, B. G. and FELDMESSER, J. W. (1948).   Golden nematode population studies.   *Proc. helm. Soc. Wash.* **15** (2), 43–55.

CHITWOOD, B. G., NEWHALL, A. G. and CLEMENT, R. L. (1940).   Onion bloat or eelworm rot a disease caused by the bulb or stem nematode, *Ditylenchus dipsaci* (Kühn) Filipjev.   *Proc. helm. Soc. Wash.* **7** (1), 44–51.

CHRISTIE, J. R. (1951). The feeding habits of plant parasitic nematodes. *Proc. Fla. State hort. Soc.* **64**, 120–122.

—— (1952). Some new nematode species of critical importance to Florida growers. *Proc. Soil Sci. Soc. Fla.* **12**, 30–39.

—— (1957). The yellows disease of pepper (*piper*) and spreading decline of citrus. *Plant Dis. Reptr.* **41** (4), 267–268.

CHRISTIE, J. R. and BIRCHFIELD, W. (1958). Scribner's lesion nematode, a destructive parasite of *Amaryllis*. *Plant Dis. Reptr.* **42** (7), 873–875.

CHRISTIE, J. R., BROOKS, A. N. and PERRY, V. G. (1952). The sting nematode, *Belonolaimus gracilis*, a parasite of major importance on strawberries, celery and sweet corn in Florida. *Phytopathology*, **42**, 173–176.

CHRISTIE, J. R. and PERRY, V. G. (1951). A root disease of plants caused by a nematode of the genus *Trichodorus*. *Science*, **113** (2937), 491–493.

COHN, E. and MINZ, G. (1960). Nematodes and resistance to *Fusarium* wilt in tomatoes. *Hassadeh*, **40**, 1347–1349.

COLBRAN, R. C. (1958). Studies of plant and soil nematodes. 2. Queensland host records of root knot nematodes (*Meloidogyne* spp.). *Qd. J. agric. Sci.* **15** (3), 101–136.

COLE, C. S. and HOWARD, H. W. (1958). Observations on giant cells in potato roots infected with *Heterodera rostochiensis*. *J. Helminth.* **32** (3), 135–144.

———— (1959). The effect of growing resistant potatoes on a potato root eelworm (*Heterodera rostochiensis* Woll.) population. *Nematologica*, **4** (4), 307–316.

COURSEN, B. W. and JENKINS, W. R. (1958). Host-parasite relationships of the pin nematode, *Paratylenchus projectus*, on tobacco and tall fescue. *Plant Dis. Reptr.* **42** (7), 865–872.

COURTNEY, W. D. (1961). Nematodes infecting narcissi and tulips in the Pacific northwest. *The Daffodil and Tulip Yearbook 1961*.

COURTNEY, W. D. and HOWELL, H. B. (1952). Investigations on the bent grass nematode, *Anguina agrostis* (Steinbuch, 1799) Filipjev, 1936. *Plant Dis. Reptr.* **36** (3), 78–83.

CRALLEY, E. M. (1949). White tip of rice. *Phytopathology*, **39**, 5.

CRITTENDEN, H. W. (1958). Histology and cytology of susceptible and resistant soybeans infested with *Meloidogyne incognita acrita*. *Phytopathology*, **48**, 461.

CROSSE, J. E. and PITCHER, R. S. (1952). Studies in the relationship of eelworms and bacteria to certain plant diseases. I. The etiology of strawberry cauliflower disease. *Ann. appl. Biol.* **39**, 475–486.

DAVIS, R. A. and JENKINS, W. R. (1960). Nematodes associated with roses. *Univ. Md. agric. Expt. Sta.* Bull. **A-106**.

DEAN, J. L. and STRUBLE, F. B. (1953). Resistance and susceptibility to root knot nematodes in tomato and sweet potato. *Phytopathology*, **43**, 290.

DIJKSTRA, J. (1957). Symptoms of susceptibility and resistance in seedlings of red clover attcked by the stem eelworm, *Ditylenchus dipsaci* (Kühn) Filipjev. *Nematologica*, **2** (3), 228–237.

DONCASTER, C. C. (1953). A study of host-parasite relationships. The potato root eelworm (*Heterodera rostochiensis*) in Black Nightshade (*Solanum nigrum*) and tomato. *J. Helminth.* **27** (1/2), 1–8.

—— (1957). Growth, invasion and root diffusate production in tomato and black nightshade inoculated with potato root eelworm. *Nematologica*, **2,** 7–15.

DROPKIN, V. H. (1955). The relations between nematodes and plants. *Exp. Parasitol.* 4 (3), 282–322.

—— (1959). Varietal response of soybeans to *Meloidogyne*—a bioassay system for separating races of root knot nematodes. *Phytopathology*, **49** (1), 18–23.

DROPKIN, V. H. and NELSON, P. E. (1960). The histopathology of root-knot nematode infections in soybeans. *Phytopathology*, **50** (6), 442–447.

DUCHARME, E. P. (1957). How burrowing nematodes affect citrus roots. *Proc. Fla. hort. Soc.* **70,** 58–60.

—— (1959). Morphogenesis and histopathology of lesions induced on citrus roots by *Radopholus similis*. *Phytopathology*, **49** (6), 388–396.

DUCHARME, E. P. and BIRCHFIELD, W. (1956). Physiological races of the burrowing nematode. *Phytopathology*, **46** (11), 615–616.

DUCHARME, E. P. and HANKS, R. W. (1961). Gnotobiotic techniques and the study of *Radopholus similis* on citrus. *Plant Dis. Reptr.* 45 (9), 742–744.

DUNNETT, J. M. (1957). Variation in pathogenicity of the potato root eelworm (*Heterodera rostochiensis* Woll.) and its significance in potato breeding. *Euphytica*, **6,** 77–89.

DUNNING, R. A. (1954a). Beet stem eelworm, some results of preliminary work. *Brit. Sugar Beet Rev.* **22** (4), 161–166.

—— (1954b). Beet stem eelworm. *Plant Pathology*, 3 (4), 133–134.

EDWARDS, E. E. (1935). On *Heterodera schachtii*, with special reference to the oat race in Britain. *J. Helminth.* **13** (2), 129–138.

FEDER, W. A. and FELDMESSER, J. (1953). The structure and cytology of *Ditylenchus dipsaci* induced 'spikkels' in lesions of *Narcissus pseudonarcissus*. *Phytopathology*, **43,** 471.

—— —— (1955). Progress report on studies on the reproduction of the burrowing nematode. *Radopholus similis* (Cobb) Thorne, on citrus seedlings growing in petri dishes. *Plant Dis. Reptr.* **39** (5), 395–396.

—— —— (1961). The spreading decline complex: the separate and combined effects of *Fusarium* spp. and *Radopholus similis* on the growth of Duncan grapefruit seedlings in the greenhouse. *Phytopathology*, **51** (10), 724–726.

FEDER, W. A. and FORD, H. W. (1957). Susceptibility of certain citrus varieties to the burrowing nematode. *Proc. Fla. hort. Soc.* **70,** 60–63.

FELDMAN, A. W., DUCHARME, E. P. and SUIT, R. F. (1961). N, P and K in leaves of citrus trees infected with *Radopholus similis*. *Plant Dis. Reptr.* 45 (7), 564–568.

FELDMESSER, J. (1953). A cytological study of the effects of the golden nematode, *Heterodera rostochiensis*, on tomato. *Phytopathology*, **43,** 471.

FERVER, A. F. and CRITTENDEN, H. W. (1958). Host-parasite relationships of *Avena sativa* and a root knot nematode *Meloidogyne incognita acrita*. *Phytopathology*, **48,** 461.

FORSTER, A. R. (1956). The development of *Heterodera rostochiensis* and *Meloidogyne incognita* in cross-grafted solanaceous plants with different susceptibilities. *Nematologica*, **1** (4), 283–289.

FRANKLIN, M. T. (1952). A disease of *Scabiosa caucasica* caused by the nematode *Aphelenchoides blastophthorus* n.sp. *Ann. appl. Biol.* **39** (1), 54–60.

FRANKLIN, M. T. (1959). *Nacobbus serendipiticus* n.sp. a root-galling nematode from tomatoes in England. *Nematologica*, **4**, 286–293.

FRANKLIN, M. T. and HOOPER, D. J. (1959). *Plants recorded as resistant to root-knot nematodes (Meloidogyne spp.)*. Comm. agric. Bur., Farnham Royal, England.

FRAZIER, N. W. and MAGGENTI, A. R. (1962). Nematode transmission of yellow bud mosaic virus to strawberry. *Plant Dis. Reptr.* **46** (5), 303–304.

FULTON, J. P. (1962). Transmission of tobacco ringspot virus by *Xiphinema americanum*. *Phytopathology*, **52** (4), 375.

GOHEEN, A. C. and SMITH, J. B. (1956). Effects of inoculation of strawberry roots with meadow nematodes, *Pratylenchus penetrans*. *Plant Dis. Reptr.* **40** (2), 146–149.

GOLDEN, A. M. (1956). Taxonomy of the spiral nematodes (*Rotylenchus* and *Helicotylenchus*) and the developmental stages and host-parasite relationships of *R. buxophilus* n.sp. attacking boxwood. *Univ. Md. agric. Exp. Sta. Bull.* **A-85**.

—— (1958). Interrelationships of certain *Beta* species and *Heterodera schachtii*, the sugar beet nematode. *Plant Dis. Reptr.* **42** (10), 1157–1162.

GOOD, J. M., BOYLE, L. W. and HAMMONS, R. O. (1958). Studies of *Pratylenchus brachyurus* on peanuts. *Phytopathology*, **48** (10), 530–535.

GOODEY, J. B. (1939). The structure of the leaf galls of *Plantago lanceolata* L. induced by *Anguillulina dipsaci* (Kühn) Gerv. and v. Ben. *J. Helminth.* **17** (4), 183–190.

—— (1951a). Observations on the attack by the stem eelworm, *Ditylenchus dipsaci*, on strawberry. *Ann. appl. Biol.* **38** (3), 618–623.

—— (1951b). The potato tuber nematode, *Ditylenchus destructor* Thorne, 1945; the cause of eelworm disease in bulbous iris. *Ann. appl. Biol.* **38** (1), 79–90.

—— (1952). *Rotylenchus coheni* n.sp. (Nematoda: Tylenchida) parasitic on the roots of *Hippeastrum* sp. *J. Helminth.* **26** (2/3), 91–96.

—— (1959). Gall-forming nematodes of grasses in Britain. *J. Sports Turf Res. Inst.* **10** (35), 1–7.

GOODEY, J. B., FRANKLIN, M. T. and HOOPER, D. J. (1959). *Supplement to the nematode parasites of plants catalogued under their hosts. 1955–1958.* Comm. agric. Bur., Farnham Royal, England.

GOODEY, J. B. and HOOPER, D. J. (1958). Observations on the effects of *Ditylenchus dipsaci* and *Anguina tritici* on certain wheat and barley varieties. *Nematologica*, **3**, 24–29.

GOODEY, T. (1933). *Anguillulina graminophila* n.sp., a nematode causing galls on the leaves of fine bent grass. *J. Helminth.* **11** (1), 45–56.

—— (1934). *Anguillulina cecidoplastes* n.sp., a nematode causing galls on the grass *Andropogon pertusus* Willd. *J. Helminth.* **12** (4), 225–236.

—— (1952). Eelworm galls mistaken for ergot in flowers of Canadian grasses. *Nature, Lond.* **169**, 456.

—— (1956). *The nematode parasites of plants catalogued under their hosts.* Revised edition by J. B. Goodey and M. T. Franklin; Comm. agric. Bur., Farnham Royal, England.

GOPLEN, B. P., STANFORD, E. H. and ALLEN, M. W. (1959). Demonstration of physiological races within three root-knot nematode species attacking alfalfa. *Phytopathology*, **49** (10), 653–656.

GOTO, S. and GIBLER, J. W. A leaf gall forming nematode on *Calamagrostis canadensis* (Michx.) Beauv. *Plant Dis Reptr.* **35** (4), 215–216.

GRAHAM, T. W. (1954). Recent developments with ectoparasitic nematodes. *Plant Dis. Reptr.* Suppl. **227**, 80.

GRAHAM, T. W. and HOLDEMAN, Q. L. (1953). The sting nematode *Belonolaimus gracilis* Steiner: a parasite on cotton and other crops in South Carolina. *Phytopathology*, **43** (8), 434–439.

GREET, D. N. and WALLACE, H. R. (1962). Diagnosis of eelworm attack in chrysanthemum. *Plant Pathology*, **11** (1), 43.

GRUNDBACHER, F. J. (1962). Testing alfalfa seedlings for resistance to the stem nematode *Ditylenchus dipsaci* (Kühn) Filipjev. *Proc. helm. Soc. Wash.* **29**, 152–158.

GUIRAN, G., DE (1960). Étude comparative de la pénétration des larves de *Meloidogyne javanica* (Treub, 1885) Chitwood 1949 et de *Meloidogyne incognita acrita* Chitwood 1949 dans les racines des plantes hotes et non hotes. Resultats préliminaires. *Meded. LandbHoogesch. Gent.* **25** (3/4), 1047–1056.

GUNDY, S. D., VAN (1957). The first report of a species of *Hemicycliophora* attacking citrus roots. *Plant Dis. Reptr.* **41** (12), 1016–1018.

GUNDY, S. D., VAN and RACKHAM, R. L. (1961). Studies on the biology and pathogenicity of *Hemicycliophora arenaria*. *Phytopathology*, **51** (6), 393–397.

HARRISON, B. D. (1957). Studies on the host range, properties and mode of transmission of beet ring-spot virus. *Ann. appl. Biol.* **45** (3), 462–472.

HARRISON, B. D. and CADMAN, C. H. (1959). Role of dagger nematode (*Xiphinema* sp.) in outbreaks of plant diseases caused by arabis mosaic virus. *Nature, Lond.* **184** (4699), 1624–1626.

HARRISON, B. D., MOWAT, W. P. and TAYLOR, C. E. (1961). Transmission of a strain of tomato black ring virus by *Longidorus elongatus* (Nematoda). *Virology*, **14**, 480–485.

HARRISON, B. D. and WINSLOW, R. D. (1961). Laboratory and field studies on the relation of arabis mosaic virus to its nematode vector *Xiphinema diversicaudatum* (Micoletzky). *Ann. appl. Biol.* **49**, 621–633.

HESLING, J. J. and WALLACE, H. R. (1961). Observations on the biology of chrysanthemum eelworm, *Aphelenchoides ritzema-bosi* (Schwartz) Steiner in florists' chrysanthemums. II. Symptoms of eelworm infestation. *Ann. appl. Biol.* **49**, 204–209.

HEWITT, W. B., RASKI, D. J. and GOHEEN, A. C. (1958). Nematode vector of soil-borne fan leaf virus of grapevines. *Phytopathology*, **48** (11), 586–595.

HINE, R. B. (1961). The role of amygdalin breakdown in the peach replant problem. *Phytopathology*, **51** (1), 10–13.

HOLDEMAN, Q. L. (1956). The effect of tobacco stunt nematode on the incidence of *Fusarium* wilt in flue-cured tobacco. *Phytopathology*, **46** (2), 129.

HOLDEMAN, Q. L. and GRAHAM, T. W. (1952). The association of the sting nematode with some persistent cotton wilt spots in north eastern South Carolina. *Phytopathology*, **42**, 283.

—— —— (1953). The sting nematode breaks resistance to cotton wilt. *Phytopathology*, **43**, 475.

ICHINOHE, M. (1955). Studies on the morphology and ecology of the soybean nematode. *Hokkaido agric. Exp. Sta. Rept.* **48**.

ICHINOHE, M. and ASAI, K. (1956). Studies on the resistance of soybean plants to the nematode *Heterodera glycines*. 1. Varieties 'Daiichi-hienuki' and 'Nangun-takedate'. *Hokkaido Nat. agric. Exp. Sta. Res. Bull.* **71**.

s'JACOB, J. J. (1962). Beobachtungen an *Ditylenchus radicicola* (Greeff). *Nematologica*, **7**, 231–234.

JENKINS, W. R. and COURSEN, B. W. (1957). The effect of root knot nematodes *Meloidogyne incognita acrita* and *M. hapla* on *Fusarium* wilt of tomato. *Plant Dis. Reptr.* **41** (3), 182–186.

JENSEN, H. J., ANDERSON, C. G. and WIEMAN, J. (1951). A root-lesion nematode disease of narcissus. *Plant Dis. Reptr.* **35** (12), 522–523.

JENSEN, H. J. and HORNER, C. E. (1956). A decline of peppermint caused by an ectoparasitic nematode, *Longidorus sylphus*. *Phytopathology*, **46**, 637.

JHA, A. and POSNETTE, A. F. (1959). Transmission of a virus to strawberry plants by a nematode (*Xiphinema* sp.). *Nature, Lond.* **184** (4691), 962–963.

JONES, F. G. W. (1957). Resistance breaking biotypes of the potato root eelworm (*Heterodera rostochiensis* Woll.). *Nematologica*, **2**, 185–192.

—— (1958). Resistance breaking populations of potato root eelworm. *Plant Pathology*, **7** (1), 24–25.

KIRKPATRICK, J. D. and MAI, W. F. (1958). *Pratylenchus penetrans*, serious pest of fruit tree roots. *Farm Research*, June.

KOCH, L. W. (1955). The peach replant problem in Ontario. 1. Symptomatology and distribution. *Canad. J. Bot.* **33**, 450–460.

KRUSBERG, L. R. (1961). Studies on the culturing and parasitism of plant parasitic nematodes in particular *Ditylenchus dipsaci* and *Aphelenchoides ritzema-bosi* on alfalfa tissues. *Nematologica*, **6** (3), 181–200.

KRUSBERG, L. R. and NIELSEN, L. W. (1958). Pathogenesis of root knot nematodes to the Porto Rico variety of the sweet potato. *Phytopathology*, **48** (1), 30–39.

KRUSBERG, L. R. and SASSER, J. N. (1956). Host parasite relationships of the lance nematode in cotton roots. *Phytopathology*, **46** (9), 505–510.

KÜHN, H. (1958). Uber die Abwehrnekrose eines Kartoffelbastardes gegen den Kartoffelnematoden (*Heterodera rostochiensis* Wr. in *Solanum tuberosum* subsp. *andigena* (Juz. et Buk.) Hwk. × *Solanum tuberosum* L.). *Z. Pfl. Krankh.* **65**, 465–472.

KUIPER, J. (1953). Waarnemingen betreffende *Ditylenchus radicicola* (Greeff, 1872) Filipjev, 1936. *Tijdschr. Pl. Ziekt.* **59** (4), 143–148.

KUIPER, K. (1959). Inoculatieproeven met *Hemicycliophora typica*. *Meded. LandbHoogesch. Gent*, **24** (3/4), 619–627.

LAAN, P. A., VAN DER and HUYSMAN, C. A. (1957). Een eerste aanwijzing voor het bestaan van biotypen van het aardappelcystenaaltje, welke zich sterk kunnen vermeerderan in resistente nakomelingen van *Solanum tuberosum* subsp. *andigena*. *Tijdschr. Pl. Ziekten*, **63**, 365–368.

LABRUYÈRE, R. E. DEN OUDEN, H. and SEINHORST, J. W. (1959). Experiments on interaction of *Hoplolaimus uniformis* and *Fusarium oxysporum* F. *pisi* race 3 and its importance in 'Early Yellowing' of peas. *Nematologica*, **4**, 336–343.

LIDER, L. A. (1954). Inheritance of resistance to a root knot nematode (*Meloidogyne incognita* var. *acrita* Chitwood) in *Vitis* spp. *Proc. helm. Soc. Wash.* **21** (1), 53–60.

LINDE, W. J., VAN DER (1956). The *Meloidogyne* problem in South Africa. *Nematologica*, **1** (3), 177–183.

LOEWENBERG, J. R., SULLIVAN, T. and SCHUSTER, M. L. (1960). Gall induction by *Meloidogyne incognita incognita* by surface feeding and factors affecting the behaviour pattern of the second stage larvae. *Phytopathology*, **50** (4), 322.

LOOS, C. A. (1959). Symptom expression of Fusarium wilt disease of the Gros Michel banana in the presence of *Radopholus similis* (Cobb, 1893) Thorne, 1949 and *Meloidogyne incognita acrita* Chitwood, 1949. *Proc. helm. Soc. Wash.* **26** (2), 103–111.

LOOS, C. A. and LOOS, S. B. (1960). The black-head disease of bananas (*Musa acuminata*). *Proc. helm. Soc. Wash.* **27** (2), 189–193.

LOWNSBERY, B. F. (1956). *Pratylenchus vulnus*, primary cause of the root lesion disease of walnuts. *Phytopathology*, **46** (7), 376–379.

LOWNSBERY, B. F., STODDARD, E. M. and LOWNSBERY, J. W. (1952). *Paratylenchus hamatus* pathogenic in celery. *Phytopathology*, **42** (12), 651–653.

LOWNSBERY, B. F. and THOMASON, I. J. (1959). Progress in nematology related to horticulture. *Proc. Amer. Soc. hort. Sci.* **74**, 730–746.

LOWNSBERY, B. F. and VIGLIERCHIO, D. R. (1961). Importance of response of *Meloidogyne hapla* to an agent from germinating tomato seeds. *Phytopathology*, **51** (4), 219–222.

LUC, M. (1961). Note préliminaire sur le déplacement de *Hemicycliophora paradoxa* Luc (Nematoda, Criconematidae) dans le sol. *Nematologica*, **6**, 95–106.

LUCAS, G. B. and KRUSBERG, L. R. (1956). The relationship of the stunt nematode to Granville wilt resistance in cotton. *Plant Dis. Reptr.* **40** (2), 150–152.

LUCAS, G. B., SASSER, J. N. and KELMAN, A. (1955). The relationship of root knot nematodes to Granville wilt resistance in tobacco. *Phytopathology*, **45**, 537.

MACHMER, J. H. (1953). *Criconemoides* spp. a ring nematode associated with peanut 'yellows'. *Plant Dis. Reptr.* **37** (3), 156.

MAI, W. F. (1960). Growth of apple seedlings in relation to soil temperature and inoculation with *Pratylenchus penetrans*. *Phytopathology*, **50** (3), 237–238.

MARTIN, W. J. (1954). Parasitic races of *Meloidogyne incognita* and *M. incognita* var. *acrita*. *Plant Dis. Reptr.* Suppl. **227**, 86–88.

MAUNG, O. and JENKINS, W. R. (1959). Effects of root knot nematode, *Meloidogyne incognita acrita* Chitwood, 1949 and a stubby root nematode *Trichodorus christiei* Allen, 1957 on the nutrient status of tomato, *Lycopersicon esculentum* hort. var. Chesapeake. *Plant Dis. Reptr.* **43** (7), 791–796.

McCLELLAN, W. D., WILHELM, S. and GEORGE, A. (1956). Incidence of *Verticillium* wilt in cotton not affected by root knot nematodes. *Plant Dis. Reptr.* **39** (3), 226–227.

McGUIRE, J. M., WALTERS, H. J. and SLACK, D. A. (1958). The relationship of root-knot nematodes to the development of *Fusarium* wilt in alfalfa. *Phytopathology*, **48**, 344.

McKEEN, C. D. and MOUNTAIN, W. B. (1960). Synergism between *Pratylenchus penetrans* (Cobb) and *Verticillium albo-atrum* R & B in eggplant wilt. *Canad. J. Bot.* **38**, 789–794.

MINTON, N. A. (1962). Factors influencing resistance of cotton to root knot nematodes (*Meloidogyne* spp.). *Phytopathology*, **52** (3), 272–279.

MINZ, G., ZIV, D. and STRICH-HARARI, D. (1960). Decline of banana plantations caused by spiral nematodes in the Jordan valley and its control by DBCP. *Ktavim. Quart. J. Nat. Univ. Inst. agric.*, **10**, 147–157.

MOORE, E. L., DROLSOM, P. N., TODD, F. A. and CLAYTON, E. E. (1956). Black shank resistance in flue cured tobacco as influenced by tolerance to certain parasitic nematodes. *Phytopathology*, **46**, 545.

MOUNTAIN, W. B. (1955). A method of culturing plant parasitic nematodes under sterile conditions. *Proc. helm. Soc. Wash.* **22** (1), 49–52.

—— (1960a). Theoretical considerations of plant nematode relationships. In: *Nematology, fundamentals and recent advances with emphasis on plant parasitic and soil forms.* Edited by J. N. Sasser and W. R. Jenkins. Chapter 37. Chapel Hill: Univ. N. Carolina Press.

—— (1960b). Acceptable standards of proof and approaches for evaluating plant-nematode relationships. In: *Nematology, fundamentals and recent advances with emphasis on plant and soil forms.* Edited by J. N. Sasser and W. R. Jenkins. Chapter 38. Chapel Hill: Univ. N. Carolina Press.

—— (1960c). Mechanisms involved in plant nematode relationships. In: *Nematology, fundamentals and recent advances with emphasis on plant and soil forms.* Edited by J. N. Sasser and W. R. Jenkins. Chapter 39. Chapel Hill. Univ. N. Carolina Press.

MOUNTAIN, W. B. and BOYCE, H. R. (1958a). The peach replant problem in Ontario. 5. The relation of parasitic nematodes to regional differences in severity of peach replant failure. *Canad. J. Bot.* **36**, 125–134.

—— —— (1958b). The peach replant problem in Ontario. 6. The relation of *Pratylenchus penetrans* to the growth of young peach trees. *Canad. J. Bot.* **36**, 135–151.

MOUNTAIN, W. B. and McKEEN, C. D. (1962). Effect of *Verticillium dahliae* on the population of *Pratylenchus penetrans*. *Nematologica*, **7**, 261–266.

MOUNTAIN, W. B. and PATRICK, Z. A. (1959). The peach replant problem in Ontario. 7. The pathogenicity of *Pratylenchus penetrans* (Cobb, 1917) Filip. & Stek. 1941. *Canad. J. Bot.*, **37**, 459–470.

MYUGE, S. G. (1956a). (A contribution to the study of the physiology of nutrition of the gall nematode.) In Russian. *Dokladi Akademi Nauk. S.S.S.R.* **108**, 164–165.

—— (1956b). (The trophic characteristics of *Meloidogyne incognita*.) In Russian. *Zhurnal Obshchei Biologii*, **17** (5), 396–399.

NĚMEC, B. (1911). Uber die Nematodenkrankheit der Zuckerrube. *Z. Pfl. Krankh.* **21** (1/2), 1–10.

NEWHALL, A. G. (1958). The incidence of Panama disease of banana in the presence of the root knot and the burrowing nematodes (*Meloidogyne* and *Radopholus*). *Plant Dis. Reptr.* **42** (7), 853–856.

OOSTENBRINK, M. (1950). Het aardappelaaltje (*Heterodera rostochiensis* Wollenweber), een gevaarlijke parasiet voor de eenzijdige aardappelcultuur. *Versl. PlZiekt. Dienst Wageningen*, **115**, 230 pp.

—— (1951). Het erwtencystenaaltje, *Heterodera göttingiana* Liebscher, in Nederland. *Tijdschr. Pl. Ziekt.* **57**, 52–64.

—— (1954). Over de betekenis van vrijlevende wortelaaltjes in Land- en tuinbouw. *Versl. Pl. Ziekt. Dienst Wageningen*, **124**, 196–233.

—— (1955). Over de waardplanten van het bietencystenaaltje *Heterodera schachtii* Schmidt. *Versl. Pl. Ziekt. Dienst Wageningen*, **127**, 186–193.

—— (1956). De postulaten van Koch en einige andere mogelijdcheden van bewijsvoering in de nematologie. *Meded. LandbHoogesch. Gent*, **21** (3), 1–8.

OOSTENBRINK, M. and HOESTRA, H. (1961). Nematode damage and 'specific sickness' in *Rosa, Malus* and *Laburnum*. *Tijdschr. Pl. Ziekt.* **67**, 264–272.

OOSTENBRINK, M., KUIPER, K. and S'JACOB, J. J. (1957). *Tagetes* als feind-pflanzen von *Pratylenchus*- arten. *Nematologica*, Suppl. **2**, 424–433.

OWENS, R. G. and NOVOTNY, H. M. (1960). Physiological and biochemical studies on nematode galls. *Phytopathology*, **50** (9), 650.

PARKER, K. G. and MAI, W. F. (1956). Damage to tree fruits in New York by root lesion nematodes. *Plant Dis. Reptr.* **40** (8), 694–699.

PATRICK, Z. A. (1955). The peach replant problem in Ontario. 2. Toxic substances from microbial decomposition products of peach root residues. *Canad. J. Bot.* **33**, 461–486.

PEACOCK, F. C. (1957). Studies on root knot nematodes of the genus *Meloidogyne* in the Gold Coast. Part 1. *Nematologica*, **2** (1), 76–84.

—— (1959). The development of a technique for studying the host-parasite relationship of the root-knot nematode *Meloidogyne incognita* under controlled conditions. *Nematologica*, **4**, 43–55.

PERRY, V. G. (1958). Parasitism of two species of dagger nematode (*Xiphinema americanum* and *X. chambersi*) to strawberry. *Phytopathology*, **48** (8), 420–423.

PETERS, B. G. (1961). *Heterodera rostochiensis* population density in relation to potato growth. *J. Helminth. R. T. Leiper* Suppl. 141–150.

PITCHER, R. S. and CROSSE, J. E. (1958). Studies on the relationship of eelworms and bacteria to certain plant diseases. *Nematologica*, **3** (3), 244–256.

PITCHER, R. S., PATRICK, Z. A. and MOUNTAIN, W. B. (1960). Studies on the host parasite relations of *Pratylenchus penetrans* (Cobb) to apple seedlings. 1. Pathogenicity under sterile conditions. *Nematologica*, **5**, 309–314.

POWELL, N. T. and NUSBAUM, C. J. (1958). The effect of root knot nematode resistance on the incidence of black shank in tobacco. *Phytopathology*, **48**, 344.

PRUMMEL, W. (1958). *Solanum nigrum* L. als waardplant voor het aardappel-cystenaaltje *Heterodera rostochiensis* Wollenw. *Tijdschr. Pl. Ziekt.* **64**, 142–143.

RASKI, D. J. (1952). On the host range of the sugar beet nematode in California. *Plant Dis. Reptr.* **36** (1), 5–7.

RASKI, D. J. and HEWITT, W. B. (1960). Experiments with *Xiphinema index* as a vector of fanleaf virus of grapevines. *Nematologica*, **5**, 166–170.

RASKI, D. J. and RADEWALD, J. D. (1958). Reproduction and symptomatology of certain ectoparasitic nematodes on roots of Thompson seedless grape. *Plant Dis. Reptr.* **42** (8), 941–943.

REYNOLDS, H. W. (1955). Varietal susceptibility of alfalfa to two species of root knot nematodes. *Phytopathology*, **45** (2), 70–72.

REYNOLDS, H. W. and HANSON, R. G. (1957). *Rhizoctonia* disease of cotton in presence and absence of the cotton root knot nematode in Arizona. *Phytopathology*, **47** (5), 256–261.

REYNOLDS, H. W. and O'BANNON, J. H. (1958). The citrus nematode and its control on living citrus in Arizona. *Plant Dis. Reptr.* **42** (11), 1288–1292.

RHOADES, H. L. and LINFORD, M. B. (1959). Molting of preadult nematodes of the genus *Paratylenchus* stimulated by root diffusates. *Science*, **130** (3387), 1476–1477.

RIGGS, R. D. and WINSTEAD, N. N. (1958). Attempts to transfer root-knot resistance in tomato by grafting. *Phytopathology*, **48**, 344.

—— (1959). Studies on resistance in tomato to root-knot nematodes and on the occurrence of pathogenic biotypes. *Phytopathology*, **49**, 716–724.

ROHDE, R. A. (1960). Mechanisms of resistance to plant parasitic nematodes. In: *Nematology fundamentals and recent advances with emphasis on plant and soil forms*. Edited by J. N. Sasser and W. R. Jenkins. Chapter 43. Chapel Hill: Univ. N. Carolina Press.

ROHDE, R. A. and JENKINS, W. R. (1957). Host range of a species of *Trichodorus* and its host parasite relationships on tomato. *Phytopathology*, **47** (5), 295–298.

—— —— (1958). Basis for resistance of *Asparagus officinalis* var. *altilis* L. to the stubby root nematode *Trichodorus christiei* Allen, 1957. *Univ. Md. agric. Expt. Sta.* Bull. **A-97**, June.

ROSS, J. P. (1958). Host parasite relationship of the soybean cyst nematode in resistant soybean roots. *Phytopathology*, **48**, 578.

RUEHLE, J. L. and SASSER, J. N. (1960). The relationship of plant parasitic nematodes to the growth of pines in outplantings. *Phytopathology*, **50** (9), 652.

SASSER, J. N. (1952). Identifications of root-knot nematodes (*Meloidogyne* spp.) by host reactions. *Plant Dis. Reptr.* **36** (3), 84–86.

—— (1954). Identification and host parasite relationships of certain root knot nematodes (*Meloidogyne* sp.). *Univ. Md.* Bull. **A-77**, 31 pp.

SASSER, J. N., LUCAS, G. B. and POWERS, H. R. (1955). The relationship of the root knot nematodes to black shank resistance in tobacco. *Phytopathology*, **45** (8), 459–461.

SAVARY, A. (1960). Les nématodes de la betterave. *Rev. rom. Agric.* **16** (6), 57–60 and **16** (7), 62–67.

SAYRE, R. M. (1960). Mechanisms involved in plant nematode relationships. In: *Nematology fundamentals and recent advances with emphasis on plant and soil forms*. Edited by J. N. Sasser and W. R. Jenkins. Chapter 39. Chapel Hill: Univ. N. Carolina Press.

SCHINDLER, A. F. (1957). Parasitism and pathogenicity of *Xiphinema diversicaudatum*, an ectoparasitic nematode. *Nematologica*, **2**, 25–31.

SCHINDLER, A. F. and BRAUN, A. J. (1957). Pathogenicity of an ectoparasitic nematode, *Xiphinema diversicaudatum* on strawberries. *Nematologica*, **2**, 91–93.

SCHINDLER, A. F., STEWART, R. N. and SEMENIUK, P. (1961). A synergistic *Fusarium*-nematode interaction in carnations. *Phytopathology*, **51** (3), 143–146.

208   *Plant Parasitic Nematodes*

SCHUSTER, M. L. (1959). Relation of root knot nematodes and irrigation water to the incidence and dissemination of bacterial wilt of bean. *Plant Dis. Reptr.* **43** (1), 27–32.

SEINHORST, J. W. (1956a). Population studies on stem eelworms (*Ditylenchus dipsaci*). *Nematologica*, **1** (2), 159–164.

—— (1956b). Biologische rassen van het stengelaaltje *Ditylenchus dipsaci* (Kuhn) Filipjev en hun waardplanten. 1. Reacties van vatbare en resistente planten op aantasting en verschillende vormen van resistentie. *Tijd. Pl. Ziekt.* **62**, 179–188.

—— (1957). Some aspects of the biology and ecology of stem eelworms. *Nematologica*, Suppl. **2**, 355–361.

—— (1961). Plant- nematode inter-relationships. *Ann. Rev. Microbiol.* **15**, 177–196.

SEINHORST, J. W. and SAUER, M. R. (1956). Eelworm attacks on vines in the Murray valley irrigation area. *J. Austral. Inst. Agric. Sci.* **22** (4), 296–299.

SHEPHERD, A. M. (1959a). Testing populations of beet eelworm, *Heterodera schachtii* Schmidt for resistance-breaking biotypes using wild beet (*Beta patellaris* Moq.) as indicator. *Nature, Lond.* **183**, 1141–1142.

—— (1959b). The invasion and development of some species of *Heterodera* in plants of different host status. *Nematologica*, **4**, 253–267.

SHER, S. A. (1957). A disease of roses caused by a root lesion nematode, *Pratylenchus vulnus*. *Phytopathology*, **47**, 703.

SHIBUYA, M. (1952). Studies on the varietal resistance of sweet potato to the root knot nematode injury. *Mem. Faculty Agric.* (*Kagoshima*) **1**, (1).

SLOOTWEG, A. F. G. (1956). Root rot of bulbs caused by *Pratylenchus* and *Hoplolaimus* spp. *Nematologica*, **1** (3), 192–201.

SMITH, A. L. (1954). Resistance to *Fusarium* wilt and root knot nematode in Upland cotton varieties. *Phytopathology*, **44**, 333,

SMITH, A. L. and DICK, J. B. (1960). Inheritance of resistance to *Fusarium* wilt in Upland and Sea Island cottons as complicated by nematodes under field conditions. *Phytopathology*, **50** (1), 44–48.

SOL, H. H., HEUVEN, J. C. and SEINHORST, J. W. (1960). Transmission of rattle virus and *Atropa belladonna* mosaic virus by nematodes. *Tijdschr. Pl. Ziekt.* **66**, 228–231.

SOL, H. H. and SEINHORST, J. W. (1961). The transmission of rattle virus by *Trichodorus pachydermus*. *Tijdschr. Pl. Ziekt.* **67**, 307–311.

SOUTHEY, J. F. (1957). Observations on races of *Ditylenchus dipsaci* infesting bulbs. *J. Helminth.* **31** (1/2), 39–46.

STANDIFER, M. S. (1959). The pathologic histology of bean roots injured by sting nematodes. *Plant Dis. Reptr.* **43** (9), 983–986.

STANDIFER, M. S. and PERRY, V. G. (1960). Some effects of sting and stubby root nematodes on grapefruit roots. *Phytopathology*, **50** (2), 152–156.

STEINER, G. (1953). Plant nematodes the grower should know. *4th Proc. Soil Soc. Fla.*

—— (1956). The problem of the taxon in the nematode genus *Ditylenchus* and its agricultural implications. *Proc. 14th Int. Congr. Zool. Copenhagen, 1953*, 377–379.

STEINER, G., BUHRER, E. M. and RHOADS, A. S. (1934). Giant galls caused by the root-knot nematode. *Phytopathology*, **24** (2), 161–163.

STEWART, R. N. and SCHINDLER, A. F. (1956). The effect of some ectoparasitic and endoparasitic nematodes on the expression of bacterial wilt in carnations. *Phytopathology*, **46** (4), 219–222.

STREU, H. T. (1960). Parasitism and pathogenicity of the ring nematode *Criconemoides curvatum* on greenhouse carnation var. White Sim. *Phytopathology*, **50**, 656.

STREU, H. T., JENKINS, W. R. and HUTCHINSON, M. T. (1961). Nematodes associated with carnations. *New Jersey agric. Exp. Sta. Rutgers*, Bull. **800**.

SUIT, R. F. and DUCHARME, E. P. (1957). Spreading decline of citrus. *State Plant Board Fla.* **2**, Bull. 2.

SWINK, J. F. and FINKER, R. E. (1956). Galactinol weight relationships in breeding for resistance to the sugar beet nematode. *J. Amer. Soc. Sugar Beet Technol.* **9** (1), 70–73.

TARJAN, A. C. (1948). The meadow nematode disease of boxwood. *Phytopathology*, **38**, 577.

—— (1950). Investigations of meadow nematodes attacking boxwood and the therapeutic value of sodium selenate as a control. *Phytopathology*, **40**, 1111–1124.

—— (1952). Pathogenic behaviour of certain root-knot nematodes *Meloidogyne* spp., on snapdragon, *Antirrhinum majus* L. *Phytopathology*, **42**, 637–641.

TARJAN, A. C., LOWNSBERY, B. F. and HAWLEY, W. O. (1952). Pathogenicity of some plant nematodes from Florida soils. 1. The effect of *Dolichodorus heterocephalus* Cobb on celery. *Phytopathology*, **42**, 131–132.

TAYLOR, A. L. and LOEGERING, W. Q. (1953). Nematodes associated with root lesions in Abaca. *Tirrialba*, **3** (1–2), 8–13.

THOMAS, P. R. (1958). Severe eelworm (*Ditylenchus dipsaci* (Kuhn) Filipjev) infestation on the narcissus variety Soleil d'Or. *Nematologica*, **3**, 73–78.

THORNE, G. and SCHUSTER, M. L. (1956). *Nacobbus batatiformis* n.sp. (Nematoda: Tylenchidae) producing galls on the roots of sugar beets and other plants. *Proc. helm. Soc. Wash.* **23** (2), 128–134.

TRIANTAPHYLLOU, A. C. and SASSER, J. N. (1960). Variation of perineal patterns and host specificity of *Meloidogyne incognita*. *Phytopathology*, **50** (10), 724–735.

TRIFFITT, M. J. (1931). On the pathogenicity of *Heterodera schachtii* to potatoes and mangolds. *J. Helminth.* **9** (1), 1–16.

UHLENBROEK, J. H. and BIJLOO, J. D. (1958). Investigations on nematicides. 1. Isolation and structure of a nematicidal principle occurring in *Tagetes* roots. *Rec. Trav. chim. Pays-Bas.* **77** (11), 1004–1009.

—— —— (1959). Investigations on nematicides. 2. Structure of a second nematicidal principle isolated from *Tagetes* roots. *Rec. Trav. chim. Pays-Bas.* **78** (5), 382–390.

—— —— (1960). Investigations on nematicides. 3. Polythienyls and related compounds. *Rec. Trav. chim. Pays-Bas.* **79** (11), 1181–1196.

VIGLIERCHIO, D. R. (1961). Attraction of parasitic nematodes by plant root emanations. *Phytopathology*, **51** (3), 136–143.

WALKINSHAW, C. H., GRIFFIN, G. D. and LARSON, R. H. (1961). *Trichodorus christiei* as a vector of potato ring spot (tobacco rattle) virus. *Phytopathology*, **51** (11), 806–808.

WALLACE, H. R. (1961a). Browning of chrysanthemum leaves infested with *Aphelenchoides ritzemabosi*. *Nematologica*, **6**, 7–16.

WALLACE, H. R. (1961b). The nature of resistance in chrysanthemum varieties to *Aphelenchoides ritzemabosi*. *Nematologica*, **6**, 49–58.

WARD, G. M. and DURKEE, A. B. (1956). The peach replant problem in Ontario. 3. Amygdalin content of peach tree tissues. *Canad. J. Bot.* **34**, 419–422.

WENSLEY, R. N. (1956). The peach replant problem in Ontario. 4. Fungi associated with replant failure and their importance in fumigated and non-fumigated soils. *Canad. J. Bot.* **34**, 967–981.

WIDDOWSON, E., DONCASTER, C. C. and FENWICK, D. W. (1958). Observations on the development of *Heterodera rostochiensis* Woll. in sterile root cultures. *Nematologica*, **3**, 308–314.

WILLIAMS, T. D. (1958). Potatoes resistant to root eelworm. *Proc. Linn. Soc. Lond. 169 session, 1956–1957*, Pts. 1 and 2, April 1958, 93–104.

WINSLOW, R. D. (1955). The hatching responses of some root eelworms of the genus *Heterodera*. *Ann. appl. Biol.* **43** (4), 19–36.

YOSHII, H. and YAMAMOTO, (1950). A rice nematode disease, 'Senchu Shingare Byo'. 1. Hibernation of *Aphelenchoides oryzae*. *J. Fac. agric. Kyushu Univ.* **9**, 209–222.

ZUCKERMAN, B. M. (1961). Parasitism and pathogenesis of the cultivated cranberry by some nematodes. *Nematologica*, **6** (2), 135–143.

CHAPTER 9

Populations

The study of plant nematode populations has so far made little contribution to the fundamentals of animal population dynamics; it has only tended to confirm previously established hypotheses. This is perhaps understandable in so young a science as plant nematology. Nevertheless, nematode population dynamics is an important subject because it is so closely related to the incidence of crop injury and forms the basis of advisory work on cropping programmes in agriculture. In this chapter, therefore, stress will be laid on those factors controlling the growth and size of populations.

In general, population changes are determined by factors which favour population increase and those favouring population decrease. Both sets of factors may be either density-dependent or density-independent, a concept which in the present context will be adopted more for convenience than for scientific reasons, in view of the controversial nature of this topic in animal ecology.

There is, in fact, little information on the influence of density-dependent factors on nematode populations. One clear-cut example, however, is the relationship between population size and the sex ratio (Chapter 2). It has been shown that, in *Heterodera rostochiensis* (Ellenby, 1954), in *Heterodera avenae* (Lindhardt, 1961) and in *Meloidogyne* spp. (Triantaphyllou, 1960), the ratio of males to females increases with increase in population size. Such a change would tend to reduce the rate of reproduction as the numbers of nematodes increased. Kort's (1962) experiments also suggest that at low population levels, the rate of population increase of *Heterodera rostochiensis* is inhibited because in this species mating is essential and the chances of it occurring decrease. Kort's data show an optimum inoculum level of 0·5 eggs/g for maximum reproduction rate. Competition for food is also an obvious density-dependent factor which is often said to reduce the reproductive rate in dense populations but there is little firm evidence to support this. Triantaphyllou and Hirschmann (1960) suggest that variation in the growth rate of *Meloidogyne incognita* is caused by competition for food and by crowding; they also observed that development was retarded where numerous larvae entered the root. It is possible, however, that factors other than the lack of food inhibit development in concentrated populations. The factors influencing populations containing more than one species are, likewise, unknown. Chapman (1959), for example, found that the

211

growth of red clover and lucerne was reduced by *Pratylenchus penetrans* and *Tylenchorhynchus martini*. When both species occurred together *Pratylenchus penetrans* reproduced as well as it did when alone. *Tylenchorhynchus martini* on the other hand increased only 10 to 25 per cent as much as it did when alone. In mixed populations of *Meloidogyne* some species are dominant to others (Minz and Strich-Harari, 1959). Interspecific and intra-specific competition in the host plant undoubtedly occur but what the nematodes are competing for, and how they affect each other, is unknown.

More is known about density-independent factors, in fact the sections describing the influence of environmental factors on nematodes (Chapters 4, 5, 6), host specificity (Chapter 8) and resistance (Chapter 8) provide numerous examples of how the environment can affect the rate of reproduction and population growth. It must be emphasised at the outset, however, that these are only superficial associations; it is one matter to associate population increase with a period of rainfall, and quite another to show how rainfall modifies the soil environment so that the rate of nematode reproduction is increased. Similarly, population increase of a nematode species may vary with the type of host crop, but is this because of differences in nematode nutrition, density of the root system or root distribution? Field population studies can only give the final picture of the influence of all the interdependent factors in the environment and should not attempt to show the influence of particular factors.

THE INFLUENCE OF THE ENVIRONMENT

As population growth is determined by the rate of reproduction which is in turn influenced by the environment, it is not surprising that nematode populations in the field show wide fluctuations throughout the year and that changes in population density vary from one year to another. Thus, Oostenbrink (1961b) remarks that although there is a linear relationship between the log of initial population of *Pratylenchus penetrans* and growth reduction in susceptible crops, the relationship varies greatly with crop, soil, year and other factors affecting growth of the plant.

Thomason (1960) found that soil temperatures from November to May in California were too low for development of *Meloidogyne javanica*, the increase of larvae in the soil in May being due to egg hatch at warmer temperatures. Some species like *Heterodera avenae* appear to cause most damage in Germany when high rainfall and low temperatures occur in April and May (Goffart, 1932). The greatest injury to peach trees in California by *Criconemoides xenoplax* occurs in winter and spring, however, when the nematode populations are most dense. During summer and autumn the higher temperatures and dry conditions appear to inhibit population increases (Lownsbery, 1959). In the Netherlands populations of *Paratylenchus* and *Pratylenchus*, on the other hand, may increase from a low level in the soil during June and July to a peak in August to November, following high soil temperatures and heavy rain (Cichorius, 1960).

Marked changes in population density are often associated with periods of rainfall. Parris (1948) considered that increased root knot nematode activity and increased galling on potatoes was related to rainfall. According to Frandsen (1951) the severity of *Ditylenchus dipsaci* attacks on red clover were associated with the amount of rainfall in May and June and he attributed this to the greater spread of the nematode and more vigorous plant growth in wet conditions. Similarly, onions attacked by *D. dipsaci* appear to show heavier losses in years with heavy rainfall in May (Nolte, 1957). It seems likely that high rainfall and soil moisture are associated with increased activity of *D. dipsaci* (Seinhorst, 1950) as well as greater spread and emergence from infested plants into the soil (Wallace, 1962). Hence, if this occurs in spring when the plants are young and more susceptible to nematode attack, greater losses will occur. Similarly, populations of *Paratylenchus projectus*, *Tylenchorhynchus brevidens* and *Aphelenchus avenae* were at a low level during dry periods and only increased in density after rainfall when eggs in the soil hatched (Norton, 1959). Seasonal fluctuations in populations of *Tylenchorhynchus* spp. in soybeans and *T. martini* in rice were also closely correlated with rainfall (Hollis and Fielding, 1958). With these species, however, high rainfall was associated with low population levels and greatest numbers of *T. martini* occurred following periods when the land had not been flooded.

These examples emphasize that no generalisations can be made about the relationship between population fluctuations in the soil and the amount of rainfall or temperature; there are too many other complicating factors. It is difficult to distinguish between the direct influence these factors have on the nematodes and their effect through the plant. Illumination is a good example of this. Increasing day length appears to be associated with increased numbers of cysts of *Heterodera rostochiensis* on potato plants (Ellenby, 1958). It is likely that such light conditions favour increased plant growth and this in turn favours higher nematode reproduction. It might also induce the production of more active root diffusate which would increase the rate of hatching. In fact Winslow and Ludwig (1957) found that short days (8 to 10 hr.) favoured production of more active root diffusate than did long days (14 to 16 hr.). High illumination (1,200 ft. candles) increased populations of *Pratylenchus* sp. on wheat and *Paratylenchus* sp. on soybean more than low illumination (300 ft candles) and this may be a rhizosphere effect related to bacterial growth and amino acid production (Henderson and Katznelson, 1961). Light may therefore influence nematode populations but only through its effect on the plant.

The same can be said of fertilisers and plant nutrients added to the soil. Thus, with low population levels of *Meloidogyne incognita* the rate of reproduction increased with the level of potassium in the host plant (Oteifa, 1952, 1953). Populations of *Xiphinema americanum* and *Pratylenchus penetrans*, on the other hand, were significantly lower under trees receiving high rates of potassium (Kirkpatrick *et al.*, 1959a). Soil counts of *Xiphinema americanum* and *Paratylenchus* sp. increased as leaf nitrogen increased and leaf potassium decreased; there was no relationship between population levels and soil analysis (Kirkpatrick *et al.*, 1959b). The addition of high nitrogen rates to soybeans increased the population of *Heterodera glycines*. This response was attributed to stimulation of root growth which provided more multiplication sites for the nematodes (Ross, 1959). Bird (1960), however, showed that at low infestation levels the growth of *Meloidogyne javanica* was more rapid in plants deficient in nitrogen than in healthy plants on full nutrient. Nematode population responses to potassium and nitrogen levels in the plant vary, therefore, with the species of host plant and nematode and no general conclusions can be drawn.

In countries with a temperate climate, nematode populations often increase in the spring. For example, *Heterodera humuli* larvae increase in number in the soil during April and May (Simon, 1958); increased larval emergence of *H. rostochiensis* occurs mostly during the spring (Bijloo and Boogaers, 1956; Den Ouden, 1960); larvae emerge from cysts of *H. avenae* in greater numbers during March to July (Hesling, 1958) and similar observations are recorded by Wallace (1956), who suggests that dry conditions in late spring inhibit further emergence. Nolte (1960) considers that high rainfall in April and May increases attacks of *Ditylenchus dipsaci* on garlic. It is unwise, however, to attribute such behaviour to any single factor; it is more likely that a combination of factors such as temperature, soil moisture, aeration and increased plant growth contribute to the increase in nematode population density and activity in the spring.

Dieter (1959) considers that climatic conditions in the spring are not of primary importance; he suggests that the degree of development of the host plant determines the infestation level of *Heterodera avenae* in the host crop, at a time when environmental conditions are optimal for larval hatch. There is little doubt that the damage caused by nematode populations is related to the age of the plant, in fact this has provided a possible means of reducing yield losses. Raski and Johnson (1959), for example, showed that if sugar beet was planted early and was established before temperatures reached the optimum for activity of *H. schachtii*, economic yields were obtained. Southey (1955, 1956), however, found no evidence that winter or spring sowing of oats had any influence on *H. avenae* attacks; 48 per cent of spring sown crops and 50 per cent of winter sown crops were infested and there was no relationship between infestation level and time of sowing. It is likely that where young plants or seedlings are subjected to a mass invasion in the spring and succumb, nematode populations in the soil decrease. Furthermore, although early sowing may help young plants to escape the spring invasion, nematode populations may increase later in the season. Nematode population changes are also associated with plant growth. Thus, Wehunt (1957) showed that maximal plant growth of white clover in Louisiana coincided with maximum nematode populations. Edwardo (1961) studied soil populations of *Pratylenchus penetrans* in strawberry beds and found that numbers of nematodes reached a maximum in the soil in June and in the roots in July. At the end of July the concentration of nematodes per unit volume of root decreased because of increased root growth but increased in September with the invasion of new roots.

The influence of the environment on nematode populations is evident in the experiments of Dolliver (1961) who showed that the ability of *Pratylenchus penetrans* to reproduce in peas was related to the physiological status of the plant attacked. Treatments that reduced plant dry weight moderately, such as less favourable light and temperature, excision of plant parts and limitation of the nutrient supply, increased populations. On the other hand, treatments that reduced dry weight considerably reduced nematode numbers. Dolliver concluded that population increases in the various treatments indicated the intimate interaction between the parasite, host and the environment.

THE INFLUENCE OF THE HOST CROP

The rate of reproduction of a nematode depends on the species of plant it is parasitising. In resistant varieties and non-host species there may be no reproduction, consequently the population density falls. In some host-plants the reproductive rate may be insufficient to compensate for mortality losses, hence there would be a population decline here as well. An increase in population density occurs when the plant permits a reproduction rate in excess of the mortality rate. Such increases clearly depend on the level of the initial population and length of growing season. A few examples will illustrate these points.

A population of *Heterodera avenae* increased on oats but declined under crops of rye and autumn sown wheat until it reached a level which permitted a good oat crop three years later. Wheat, barley and rye sown in the autumn also caused greater population decreases than when sown in the spring (Hesling, 1959). Jones and Moriarty (1956b) showed, in microplot experiments, that oats and barley caused greater population increases of *H. avenae* than did wheat. Highest populations followed the barley variety Herta, whereas a slight decline occurred with the barley variety Kron and the wheat variety Bersée. Similar experiments showed that the number of both cysts and eggs of *H. göttingiana* increased with a crop of peas; with vetch, however, the cyst population was doubled, although there was only a small increase in the number of eggs (Jones and Moriarty, 1956a). Populations of *Meloidogyne hapla* increased under potatoes, beets, carrots and some leguminous crops whereas they were suppressed under cereals (s'Jacob, 1960). To obtain information about the rate of multiplication of *Paratylenchus projectus* on different hosts, Rhoades and Linford (1961) added 100 individuals of mixed stages to pots containing various plants. The total number of nematodes per pot was determined after 105 days, with the following results: 38,000 with red clover, 147,000 with Timothy, 181,000 with celery and 2,637,000 with jasmine tobacco.

The population density of nematodes in soil is often determined by the last grown crop. Thus, Kleyburg and Oostenbrink (1959) found marked qualitative and quantitative differences in nematode infestations on various farms and nurseries in Holland. Farmland was characterised by the presence of *Heterodera avenae* and *Heterodera trifolii*, which were absent in nurseries, probably because of overcropping of cereals on farms. The influence of cropping on nematode populations is well illustrated by Oostenbrink's (1961a) three-year rotation experiment in Holland. The main facts which emerged from this work were: negligible populations of *Heterodera* and *Paratylenchus* spp. may rise to a high level in 1 or 2 years, given an efficient host crop; the influence of this population may persist for at least two years in later crops which are less efficient hosts; growing the same crop on the same land for several years produces distinctive populations of *Heterodera* spp. Cultivated soil nearly always contains a complex of plant nematodes and Oostenbrink and his colleagues (1956) emphasise that unless crop rotation is practised, populations of particular nematode species will build up and eventually cause damage.

Studies on nematode populations, however, have been mainly concerned with individual species rather than mixed populations and so it is to this kind of work that we will now turn for further information.

HETERODERA POPULATIONS

Chitwood and Feldmesser (1948) computed an empirical rate of increase for *Heterodera rostochiensis* based on field observations. They claimed that a small isolated infestation in a potato field originated from a single cyst dropped from a cultivator, four years previously. Soil samples suggested that the number of cysts in the isolated area was about 2,551. By taking the fourth root of this figure, i.e. 7·11, they arrived at the annual rate of increase. Subsequent experiments, however, revealed that reproductive rate varied between 0·5 and 23·2 and depended on the size of the original population. Chitwood and Feldmesser expressed their data graphically and indicated that there was an intermediate inoculum level for maximum reproductive rate. Their data do not permit such a conclusion, however, although there is little doubt that the rate of reproduction decreased with increase in inoculum size. The data also showed that the number of new females first increased and then levelled off with increase in inoculum size.

Jones (1956) studied the effect of different host plants on populations of *Heterodera schachtii*. He suggested that host, soil, season and enemies were the principal factors influencing population change and, of these, he was primarily concerned with the host effect. Microplots (Jones, 1955a, 1955b, 1955c) were used to compare the efficiency of host and non-host crops as well as fallows. Cruciferae caused greater increases in the nematode populations than Chenopodiaceae when the initial population was low and greater decreases when it was high. Non-hosts and inefficient hosts caused reductions of the same order as host plants

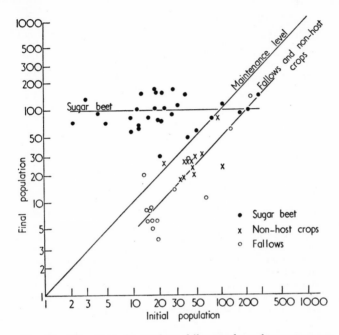

Fig. 55. The effect of sugar beet, fallows and non-host crops on a population of *Heterodera schachtii*. Initial population levels ranged from 2 to 252 hatchable larvae per g soil. Ceiling level 100 hatchable larvae per g or 140·4 egg/g soil. (After Jones, 1956.)

in the same families. When sugar beet was grown at different initial nematode population levels, the final population tended to rise to about the same level, although this varied with soil and season. Thus, a comparison of the effect of initial population in plots of sugar beet, non-host crops and fallow soil showed that populations in all beet plots rose to a ceiling level of about 100 hatchable larvae per g of soil. Fallows and non-host crops caused decreases to about half the initial level (Fig. 55). The effect of growing host crops of different efficiencies was then summarised diagrammatically (Fig. 56).

The ceiling effect also occurs in the field. Jones (1956) took soil samples from a series of transects through a field heavily infested with

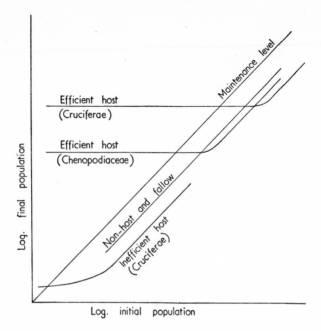

FIG. 56. Graph summarising the effects on final nematode population of the cultivation of host and non-host crops. The Cruciferae appear to exert a greater effect on the population of *Heterodera schachtii* than do the Chenopodiaceae. Host plants from the former usually cause greater increases at low initial levels and greater decreases at high initial levels. Non-hosts and inefficient hosts in the Cruciferae also appear to cause greater decreases in population than do similar plants from the Chenopodiaceae. (After Jones, 1956.)

Heterodera schachtii (Fig. 57). The nematode population tended to fluctuate around a level of 200 eggs/g of soil. Goffart's (1952) experiments on population increase of *H. schachtii* also showed that populations rise to more or less the same level whatever the initial population and Chitwood and Feldmesser's experiments described previously also tend to support this hypothesis. Winslow (1955) showed that the ceiling level of *H. göttingiana* populations depended on the host crop. Broad bean and lentils supported lower populations than other leguminous crops. Such differences may be an inherent feature of the plant species but less subtle factors such as volume of the root system may also be involved. Apel and Kämpfe (1957a), for example, found that high population densities of *H. schachtii* were associated with slow growth in root length in various hosts. They, too, showed that each host species had a population density which was not often exceeded (Apel and Kämpfe, 1957b).

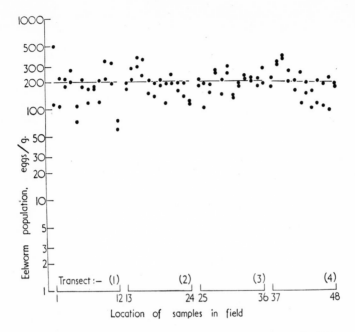

FIG. 57. The ceiling effect of *Heterodera schachtii* in an English field soil 2 years after the cultivation of a crop of cress seed. Pairs of 100 g soil samples were taken at 14 yd intervals in four parallel transects from an area of 2 acres, 12 points in each transect. (After Jones, 1956.)

The ceiling phenomenon is familiar in animal populations and it is generally supposed that the environment exerts an increasing resistance to population increase as the size of the population grows. Jones (1956) considers that, with plant parasites, change in the sex-ratio, predators and disease could contribute but that the most likely factor is intra-specific competition within roots. So far, however, little attempt has been made to identify the actual density-dependent factors which control nematode populations.

The annual decline of *Heterodera* populations under non-host crops and in fallow soils, on the other hand, appears to be independent of population level. Jones (1956) found with *H. schachtii* that it was about 20 per cent for cysts, 40 per cent for cysts with contents and 50 per cent for eggs. The annual decline of *H. avenae* larval populations is about 60 per cent (Hesling, 1958). Such data form the basis for the planning of crop rotations. For if the size of the nematode population which the crop will support without showing serious losses in yield is known, and if the population level in a field has been estimated, it is possible to calculate how long the field should be rested from host crops to bring the population down to an economically safe level (Fig. 58). This economic zero will vary with different soils, crops and localities but Jones (1945) has suggested a tentative level of 10 eggs of *H. schachtii* per g of air-dried soil, above which it is unsafe to grow sugar beet. Jones (1956) stresses that because of differences between localities and crops, standardised 3 or 4 year rotations cannot be expected to work satisfactorily in every case, especially as more fields become generally infested. The control of cropping should, therefore, be based on soil samples taken from individual fields and the period of rest calculated.

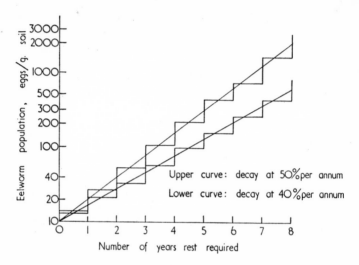

FIG. 58. A step scale from which the approximate number of years rest from host plants can be read off to ensure a satisfactory crop of sugar beet. The scale assumes that the soil population of beet eelworm is known in terms of eggs/g air dried soil, and that the average annual rate of decay of *Heterodera schachtii* populations is between 40 and 50 per cent. The scale starts at the economic zero, assumed to be 10 eggs/g. (After Jones, 1956.)

The economic importance of *Heterodera* spp. and the ease with which their cysts can be recovered and counted probably explains why most of the critical work on nematode populations has been done with this genus. Population estimates based on cyst counts alone, however, are sometimes unreliable because of the variability of egg numbers within the cyst. Hence, populations are usually expressed as viable cysts, eggs or hatchable larvae per g of soil. Hesling (1957) considers that the best criterion of population increase in *Heterodera* spp. is the ratio of number of new eggs produced at the end of the season to the original number of eggs. This criterion obviates errors caused by variation in cyst size which may not be reflected in egg numbers. In later work Hesling (1961) used

Heterodera rostochiensis cysts of three different size grades to give different inoculum levels on *Solanum demissum*. Similar infestation levels in terms of eggs per g of soil, but with different numbers of cysts of different size, produced similar final nematode populations. This appears to substantiate Hesling's point that eggs not cysts should be used in measuring *Heterodera* populations but, it is also possible that a uniform final population would have been obtained even if different egg-inoculum levels had been used because nematode populations tend to reach a ceiling level.

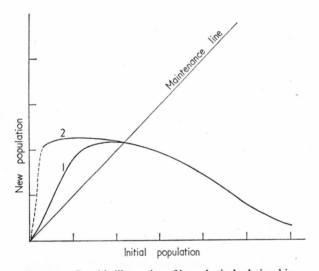

FIG. 59. Graphic illustration of hypothetical relationship between the initial and new populations produced in *Heterodera* spp. for one (1) and two (2) generations, after cultivation of a host crop. The maintenance line represents those points at which old and new populations are equal; points to the left and right represent increase and decrease respectively. The broken line portions are conjectural. (After Jones, 1959.)

The principles involved in the population dynamics of *Heterodera* are well summarised in the three graphs by Jones (1959). The first (Fig. 59) shows the relationship between initial population and final population of new individuals. The greatest rate of increase occurs at low initial levels but as the initial population increases the rate of increase becomes less and ultimately tends towards zero. There are therefore many pairs of initial population levels which produce the same final population of new nematodes, a fact also observed by Hague and Hesling (1958) who suggest that to avoid ambiguity in experiments, infestation levels should be used lower than those giving the maximum final nematode population.

Jones' second graph (Fig. 60) shows the decline in the initial population
under fallow or neutral crops.   The annual rate of decline appears to be
about 50 per cent for several species and occurs chiefly in the early part
of the growing season.   A host crop, or a non-host crop with a root
diffusate causing hatch, increases larval emergence from the cyst and this
hypothetical effect is shown by the dotted curve in the graph.   The third

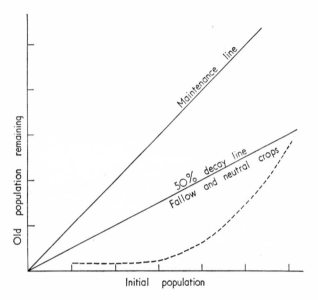

FIG. 60.   Graphic illustration of hypothetical relationship
between the initial population level of *Heterodera* spp. and
the fraction remaining (i.e. the old population) after fallow
and neutral crops, and the conjectural level (broken line)
after crop producing an active diffusate.   (After Jones,
1959.)

graph (Fig. 61) is the summation of the first two and gives some idea of
the final population consisting of the new individuals plus the old ones
from the original population.   The result is a curve which is relatively
flat over most initial population levels and explains the ceiling effect
described previously.

   The relationships between yield and nematode population density vary
with host plant.   A tolerant plant variety, for example, may withstand
heavy infestations and show little loss in yield, a susceptible variety may
succumb at much lower infestation levels.   Lownsbery and Peters (1955)
showed in an outdoor pot experiment that height and final weight of
plants of Connecticut 15 shade tobacco were inversely proportional to the
logarithm of the initial density of viable encysted larvae of *H. tabacum* in
soil in which the plants were grown.   This was true over the range 50 to

3,200 larvae per g of soil. Every ten-fold increase in density led to a loss in plant weight of 139 g for normally fertilised plants and 25 g for smaller, unfertilised plants. The highest density which maintained itself was 1,000 larvae per g of soil. At this density reduction in weight of normally infested plants was 25 per cent. Jones (1956) obtained a similar

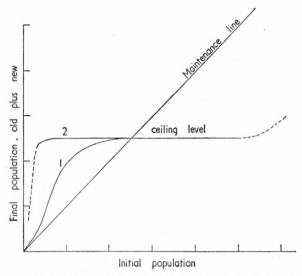

FIG. 61. Graphic illustration of the hypothetical relationship between initial and final populations of *Heterodera* spp. after cultivation of a host crop. Summation of the new population (Fig. 59) and the relict of the old population (dotted curve of Fig. 60) gives a curve more or less flat over a considerable range of initial populations, i.e. a ceiling level. (After Jones, 1959.)

result in experiments on the effect of initial population density of *H. schachtii* on yield of tops and roots of sugar beet. The relationship between yield and initial population was not linear but linear regressions were obtained when yield was plotted against the logarithm of the initial population. There was no evidence of a disturbance of sugar metabolism by the nematode infestations.

Very low initial population levels may increase yields, as Jones (1957) has shown for sugar beet infested with *H. schachtii*. At higher population levels there was a significant inverse linear regression of total yield upon log. inoculation level. Peters (1961) exposed potato plants in pots to a graded series of inocula of cysts of *H. rostochiensis* and found that high inocula reduced the growth of shoots and tubers. But, like Jones, he found that with very low nematode inocula the plants showed greater growth than the uninfested controls. Peters' experiments also indicated that multiplication was highest with the lowest inocula but that the highest net population resulted from a moderate inoculum. Ichinohe

(1955) found a similar effect in soybean infested with *H. glycines*. Most females were counted on the roots of plants moderately affected by nematode attack. Kort and s'Jacob (1956) on the other hand, state that there is a positive correlation between the degree of infestation of *H. avenae* and damage to oat crops in the field.

DITYLENCHUS DIPSACI POPULATIONS

Population changes of *Ditylenchus dipsaci* differ considerably from those of *Heterodera* spp. Seinhorst (1957) studied the influence of various crops on the soil population of the rye and onion races of *D. dipsaci*. Apart from rye and onions there was little indication of differences between hosts or non-host plants on the subsequent level of soil infestation. On heavy soils, low degrees of infestation, i.e. less than 100 nematodes per 500 g of soil, generally increased during the summer and decreased in the winter whether a host or non-host was grown. On light soils, however, there was a consistent decrease in the nematode population to a level of about 5 nematodes or lower per 500 g of soil, except when rye, oats or onions were grown. Damage occurred in many crops at infestation levels as low as 10 nematodes per 500 g of soil, a similar level to that found by Palo (1962). Hence the rotation of susceptible crops is of little use on heavy soils, whereas on infested light soils, onions can be grown once in 3 or 4 years and rye from once in 2 to once in 4 years. Seinhorst suggests that populations of *D. dipsaci* can increase in the absence of a host crop because many weeds are host plants.

Thus, whereas population increases of *Heterodera* are related to the growth of host crops, *D. dipsaci* fluctuates between rather narrow limits, depending chiefly on soil type and little on the host plants. The close relationship between soil type and the occurrence of *D. dipsaci* in onions (Seinhorst, 1956) strongly supports this hypothesis. As Seinhorst points out, little is known of the factors influencing the mortality of *D. dipsaci* in soil, although they appear to be specific because sandy soils containing few *D. dipsaci* often contain large numbers of other nematodes —10,000 to 30,000 per 500 g of soil. These factors may be chemical in some soils (Seinhorst, 1950) but in others the effect of soil type may be related to the vertical movement of *D. dipsaci* and its ability to survive and invade in the surface layers of the soil (Wallace, 1962).

The relationship between initial soil population of *D. dipsaci* and injury to crops may be similar to that of *Heterodera* spp. Thus, injury to onion seedlings is linear for a range of 10 to 1,000 nematodes/lb (453·6 g) of soil (Sayre and Mountain, 1962), and Palo (1962) found a similar relationship for *D. dipsaci* on lucerne.

PRATYLENCHUS POPULATIONS

Changes in populations of *Pratylenchus* spp. probably resemble those of *Ditylenchus dipsaci*. *Pratylenchus* appears to be widely distributed over large areas and whether it causes damage depends on the crops grown. Oostenbrink (1956), for example, grew potatoes, oats, rye, beet and woody perennials and found that their roots contained various stages of *P. penetrans* and *P. pratensis* thus indicating the polyphagous nature of these species. *P. pratensis* reached its highest population density in the roots of cereals which also increased the soil population far more than potatoes, beet or woody perennials. Oostenbrink attributes this to the extensive development of the root system in cereals. Edwardo (1960, 1961) has also stressed the importance of root growth and concentration on the population size of *P. penetrans*. Good and his colleagues (1954) compared the effect of continuous cropping with two- and three-year rotations on populations of *Pratylenchus leiocephalus*. The largest populations occurred when maize was grown continuously but when grown in rotation with peanuts the numbers decreased. More nematodes were found in the soil following lupin than after oats.

There is little information on the influence of population density on the increase in numbers of *Pratylenchus* spp. Oostenbrink (1961b), however, has demonstrated significant linear regressions between the logarithm of initial soil population density or root population density and the reduction in growth of susceptible crops. The relationship varies with crop, soil, year and different extraction techniques may also give different results.

CONCLUSIONS

Nematode population increase and reductions in yield of crops are clearly influenced by the initial density of nematodes in the soil. Moreover these effects, as we have seen, depend not only on the type of crop but on the nematode species. Seinhorst (1960) states that measurable damage only occurs when the population density exceeds a certain limit—2,000 to 5,000 eggs of *Heterodera schachtii* in 500 g of soil for sugar beet, 1 to 5 *Ditylenchus dipsaci* in 500 g of soil for onions, about 1 *Pratylenchus penetrans* in 500 g of soil for daffodils and 500 *P. penetrans* in 500 g of soil for potatoes; Ferris (1962) states that more than 5 *P. penetrans* in 500 g of soil resulted in injury to onions. In other words, the presence of a plant nematode species in a soil does not necessarily indicate that there will be a reduction of crop yield; it all depends on the size of the nematode population and the species of host plant.

There is some evidence of a linear relationship between yield and the logarithm of the population density of several nematode species and Justesen and Tammes (1960) have studied this phenomenon by considering four hypothetical models representing natural conditions. They show how competitive forces act, and limit the effect of increasing numbers of injurious organisms. They suggest that the harmful effect of the individual decreases as their numbers increase and that competition affects the sex ratio as well as causing the death of individuals. Hollis and Fielding (1955) suggest that this environmental resistance factor can

15

be assessed by comparing the theoretical reproductive rate of a species and its actual numbers on the host plant. The theoretical population size after a given time is calculated from the equation $(a-x)^n$ where a = the initial number of nematodes, x = the number of eggs laid per generation and n the number of generations. What are needed now are more data on the factors which limit multiplication at high population densities.

Nematode populations fluctuate widely even in the same crop in the same season, as Sasser and Nusbaum (1955) showed for root knot nematodes in two-year tobacco rotation experiments. Such population changes are often caused by weather conditions and may affect the number of plant parasitic nematodes in the soil as well as in the host tissues. Chapman (1960), for example, found that the numbers of larvae of *Meloidogyne arenaria* in the soil relative to those in red clover roots, increased during the season. Such an effect may be caused by nematodes leaving the host plant in greater numbers under the influence of some environmental factor. In fact, the number of nematodes in the soil and in the plant at any one time may be the result of a two way movement into and out of the plant. *Ditylenchus dipsaci* leaves oat plants in large numbers during wet weather, for example, hence the numbers in the soil increase rapidly (Wallace, 1962); during subsequent dry periods fresh invasion may then reduce the soil population.

It is now clear that studies in population dynamics and the relationships between population levels and crop yields demand some control of the environment if valid interpretations of field observations are to be made. The best approach to such problems is probably to study the influence of single factors alone and in combination, to progress from there to pot experiments where some measure of environmental control can still be achieved, thence to microplots where population levels and distribution in the soil, soil type and crop density can be controlled. Hypotheses explaining nematode population changes in the field should also be based on a wide variety of observations in different years from different localities, soil types, nematode population levels, etc.

REFERENCES

APEL, A. and KÄMPFE, L. (1957a). Beziehungen zwischen wirt und parasit in infektionsverlauf von *Heterodera schachtii* Schmidt in Kurzfristigen topfversuchen. 1. Infektionsgang bei verschiedenen Wirtspflanzen. *Nematologica*, **2**, 131–143.

—— —— (1957b). Beziehungen zwischen wirt und parasit in infektionsverlauf von *Heterodera schachtii* Schmidt in Kurzfristigen topfversuchen. 2. Haupt- und Nebenwurzelbefall, Geschlechtsver- haltnis der Adulten und Lagerichtung der Larven. *Nematologica*, **2**, 215–227.

BIJLOO, J. D. and BOOGAERS, P. A. M. (1956). Population decrease of *Heterodera rostochiensis* after DD treatment of the soil. *Nematologica*, **1** (1), 20–30.

BIRD, A. F. (1960). The effect of some single element deficiencies on the growth of *Meloidogyne javanica. Nematologica,* **5** (2), 78–85.

CHAPMAN, R. A. (1959). Development of *Pratylenchus penetrans* and *Tylenchorhynchus martini* on red clover and alfalfa. *Phytopathology,* **49** (6), 357–359.

—— (1960). Population development of *Meloidogyne arenaria* in red clover. *Phytopathology,* **50** (9), 631.

CHITWOOD, B. G. and FELDMESSER, J. (1948). Golden nematode population studies. *Proc. helm. Soc. Wash.* **15** (2), 43–55.

CICHORIUS, H. D. (1960). Uber das Auftreten freilebender Wurzelnematoden in Rheinischen Boden unter besonderer Berucksichtigung der Standortver hältnisse. *Nematologica,* **5** (4), 231–252.

DIETER, A. (1959). Beobachtungen uber *Heterodera major* O. Schmidt an Hafer. *NachrBl. dtsch. PflSchDienst. Berl.* **14** (3), 43–48.

DOLLIVER, J. S. (1961). Population levels of *Pratylenchus penetrans* as influenced by treatments affecting dry weight of Wando pea plants. *Phytopathology,* **51** (6), 364–368.

EDWARDO, A. A., DI (1960). Population variation of *Pratylenchus penetrans* and other nematodes associated with roots. *Phytopathology,* **50** (9), 633.

—— (1961). Seasonal population variations of *Pratylenchus penetrans* in and about strawberry roots. *Plant Dis. Reptr.* **45** (1), 67–71.

ELLENBY, C. (1954). Environmental determination of the sex ratio of a plant parasitic nematode. *Nature, Lond.* **174,** 1016.

—— (1958). Day length and cyst formation in the potato root eelworm, *Heterodera rostochiensis* Wollenweber. *Nematologica,* **3** (2), 81–90.

FERRIS, J. M. (1962). Some observations on the number of root lesion nematodes necessary to cause injury to seedling onions. *Plant Dis. Reptr.* **46** (7), 484–485.

FRANDSEN, K. J. (1951). Studies on the clover stem nematode (*Tylenchus dipsaci* Kühn). *Acta Agriculturae Scandanavica,* **1** (3), 203–270.

GOFFART, H. (1932). Untersuchungen am Hafernematoden *Heterodera schachtii* Schm. unter besonderer Berucksichtigung der schleswigholsteinischen Verhaltnisse I. 111. Beitrag zu: Rassenstudien an *Heterodera schachtii.* Schm. *Arb. biol. Abt. (Anst.-Reichsanst) Berl.* **20** (1), 1–26.

—— (1952). Austeigen und Abklingen die Nematoden versenchung und ihre Bewertung im Rubenanbau. *Zucker,* **14,** 315–317.

GOOD, J. M., ROBERTSON, W. K. and THOMPSON, L. G. (1954). Effect of crop rotation on the populations of meadow nematode, *Pratylenchus leiocephalus* in Norfolk loamy fine sand. *Plant Dis. Reptr.* **38** (3), 178–180.

HAGUE, N. G. and HESLING, J. J. (1958). Population studies on cyst-forming nematodes of the genus *Heterodera. Proc. Linn. Soc. Lond. 169 sessions, 1956–1957,* Pts. 1 and 2, April 1958, 86–92.

HENDERSON, V. E. and KATZNELSON, H. (1961). The effects of plant roots on the nematode population of the soil. *Canad. J. Microbiol.* **7,** 163–167.

HESLING, J. J. (1957). *Heterodera major* O. Schmidt 1930 on cereals—a population study. *Nematologica,* **2,** 285–299.

—— (1958). *Heterodera major* O. Schmidt (1930). Population changes in the field and in pots of fallow soil. *Nematologica,* **3,** 274–282.

—— (1959). Some observations on the cereal root eelworm population of field plots of cereals with different sowing times and fertiliser treatment. *Ann. appl. Biol.* **47** (3), 402–409.

HESLING, J. J. (1961). *Heterodera rostochiensis* (Woll. 1923) on *Solanum demissum*—a population study. *Ann. appl. Biol.* **49** (2), 350–359.

HOLLIS, J. P. and FIELDING, M. J. (1955). Studies on the population dynamics of plant nematodes. *Ann. Rep. La. Agric. Exp. Sta. 1954–1955*, 161.

—— —— (1958). Population behaviour of plant parasitic nematodes in soil fumigation experiments. *La. State Univ. agric. Exp. Sta.* Bull. **515**.

ICHINOHE, M. (1955). A study on the population of the soybean nematodes (*Heterodera glycines*). 1. An observation on the relation between the crop damage and the female infestation. *Hokkaido Nat. agric. Exp. Sta. Res.* Bull. **68**.

S'JACOB, J. J. (1960). Der Einfluss Einiger gewachse auf die Population von *Meloidogyne hapla*. *Nematologica*, Suppl. **2**, 141–143.

JONES, F. G. W. (1945). Soil populations of beet eelworm (*Heterodera schachtii* Schm.) in relation to cropping. *Ann. appl. Biol.* **32** (4), 351–380.

—— (1955a). Quantitative methods in nematology. *Ann. appl. Biol.* **42**, 372–381.

—— (1955b). A microplot technique for the study of soil populations of cyst forming root eelworm of the genus *Heterodera*. In: *Soil Zoology*, edited by D. K. McE. Kevan, pp. 390–393.

—— (1955c). Quantitative methods for the estimation of cyst forming nematodes (*Heterodera* spp.) in soil. In: *Soil Zoology*, edited by D. K. McE. Kevan, pp. 394–402.

—— (1956). Soil populations of beet eelworm (*Heterodera schachtii* Schm.) in relation to cropping. 2. Microplot and field plot results. *Ann. appl. biol.* **44** (1), 25–56.

—— (1957). Soil populations of beet eelworm (*Heterodera schachtii* Schm.) in relation to cropping. 3. Further experiments with microplots and pots. *Nematologica*, **2**, 257–272.

—— (1959). Ecological relationships of nematodes. In: *Plant pathology, problems and progress 1908–1958*. Edited by C. S. Holton, G. W. Fisher, R. W. Fulton, H. Hart and S. E. A. McCallan. Chapter 35. Madison: Univ. Wisconsin Press.

JONES, F. G. W. and MORIARTY, F. (1956a). Further observations on the effects of peas and vetch upon soil population levels of pea root eelworm, *Heterodera göttingiana* Liebscher. *Nematologica*, **1** (3), 268–273.

—— —— (1956b). A preliminary experiment on the effect of various cereals on the soil population of cereal root eelworm, *Heterodera major* O. Schmidt. *Nematologica*, **1** (4), 326–330.

JUSTESEN, S. H. and TAMMES, P. M. L. (1960). Studies of yield losses. 1. The self-limiting effect of injurious or competitive organisms on crop yield. *Tijdschr. Pl. Ziekt.* **66**, 281–287.

KIRKPATRICK, J. D., MAI, W. F., FISHER, E. G. and PARKER, K. G. (1959a). Population levels of *Pratylenchus penetrans* and *Xiphinema americanum* in relation to potassium fertilisation of Montmorency sour cherries on Mazzard root stock. *Phytopathology*, **49**, 543.

—— —— —— —— (1959b). Relation of nematode populations to nutrition of sour cherries. *Phytopathology*, **49**, 543.

KLEYBURG, P. and OOSTENBRINK, M. (1959). Nematodes in relation to plant growth. 1. The nematode distribution pattern of typical farms and nurseries. *Neth. J. agric. Sci.* **7** (4), 327–343.

KORT, J. (1962). Effect of population density on cyst production in *Heterodera rostochiensis* Woll. *Nematologica*, **7**, 305–308.

KORT, J. and S'JACOB, J. J. (1956). Een orienterend onderzoek naar het voorkomen ven en de schade veroorzaakt door het havercystenaaltje. *Tijdschr. Pl. Ziekt.* **62**, 7–11

LINDHARDT, K. (1961). Nogle undersøgelser over infektionsgradens indflydelse pa havrealens køn. (*Heterodera major* O. Schmidt 1930). *Tidsskr. Planteavl.* **64** (5), 889–896.

LOWNSBERY, B. F. (1959). Studies of the nematode *Criconemoides xenoplax* on peach. *Plant Dis. Reptr.* **43** (8), 913–917.

LOWNSBERY, B. F. and PETERS, B. G. (1955). The relation of the tobacco cyst nematode to tobacco growth. *Phytopathology*, **45** (3), 163–167.

MINZ, G. and STRICH-HARARI, D. (1959). Inoculation experiments with a mixture of *Meloidogyne* spp. on tomato roots. *Ktavim.* **9** (3/4), 275–279.

NOLTE, H. W. (1957). *Ditylenchus dipsaci* an zwiebeln in Mittel Deutschland. *Nematologica*, **2**, Suppl. (1957) 376–381.

—— (1960). *Ditylenchus dipsaci* (Kühn) an Knoblauch (*Allium sativum* L.). *Nematologica*, Suppl. **2**, 61–63.

NORTON, D. C. (1959). Relationship of nematodes to small grains and native grasses in north central Texas. *Plant Dis. Reptr.* **43** (2), 227–235.

OOSTENBRINK, M. (1956). Over de invloed van verschillende gewassen op de vermeerdering van en de schade door *Pratylenchus penetrans* (Vermes, Nematoda). *Tijdschr. Pl. Ziekt.* **62**, 189–203.

—— (1961a). Nematodes in relation to plant growth. 2. The influence of the crop on the nematode population. *Neth. J. agric. Sci.* **9** (1), 55–60.

—— (1961b). Nematodes in relation to plant growth. 3. *Pratylenchus penetrans* (Cobb) in tree crops, potatoes and red clover. *Neth. J. agric. Sci.* **9** (3), 188–209.

OOSTENBRINK, M., S'JACOB, J. J. and KUIPER, K. (1956). An interpretation of some crop rotation experiences based on nematode surveys and population studies. *Nematologica*, **1**, 202–215.

OTEIFA, B. A. (1952). Effect of potassium nutrition and amount of inoculum on rate of reproduction of the root knot nematode *Meloidogyne incognita*. *Phytopathology*, **42**, 15.

—— (1953). Development of the root knot nematode *Meloidogyne incognita* as affected by potassium nutrition of the host. *Phytopathology*, **43** (4), 171–174.

OUDEN, H., DEN (1960). Periodicity in spontaneous hatching of *Heterodera rostochiensis* in the soil. *Nematologica*, Suppl. **2**, 101–105.

PALO, A. V. (1962). Translocation and development of stem eelworm, *Ditylenchus dipsaci* (Kühn) in lucerne, *Medicago sativa* L. *Nematologica*, **7**, 122–132.

PARRIS, G. K. (1948). Influence of soil moisture on the growth of the potato plant and its infection by the root knot nematode. *Phytopathology*, **38**, 480–488.

PETERS, B. G. (1961). *Heterodera rostochiensis* population density in relation to potato growth. *J. Helminth. R. T. Leiper Suppl.* 141–150.

RASKI, D. J. and JOHNSON, R. T. (1959). Temperature and activity of the sugar beet nematode as related to sugar beet production. *Nematologica*, **4**, 136–141.

RHOADES, H. L. and LINFORD, M. B. (1961). Biological studies on some members of the genus *Paratylenchus*. *Proc. helm. Soc. Wash.* **28** (1), 51–59.

ROSS, J. P. (1959). Nitrogen fertilisation on the response of soybeans infected with *Heterodera glycines*. *Plant Dis. Reptr.* **43** (12), 1284–1286.

SASSER, J. N. and NUSBAUM, C. J. (1955). Seasonal fluctuations and host specificity of root knot nematode populations in two year tobacco rotation plots. *Phytopathology*, **45**, 540.

SAYRE, R. M. and MOUNTAIN, W. B. (1962). The bulb and stem nematode (*Ditylenchus dipsaci*) on onion in Southwestern Ontario. *Phytopathology*, **52** (6), 510–516.

SEINHORST, J. W. (1950). De betekenis van de toestand van de grond voor het optreden van aantasting door het stengelaaltje (*Ditylenchus dipsaci* (Kühn) Filipjev). *Tijdschr. Pl. Ziekt.* **56** (5/6), 289–348.

—— (1956). Population studies on stem eelworms (*Ditylenchus dipsaci*). *Nematologica*, **1** (2), 159–164.

—— (1957). Some aspects of the biology and ecology of stem eelworms. *Nematologica*, **2** (Suppl. 1957), 355–361.

—— (1960). Over het bepalen van door aaltjes veroorzaakte opbrenstvermindering bij culturgewassen. *Meded. LandbHoogesch. Gent.* **25** (3/4), 1026–1039.

SIMON, L. (1958). Nematologische untersuchungen an Hopfen. 2. Zur Morphologie und Biologie von *Heterodera humuli* Filipjev 1934. *Nematologica*, **3** (4), 269–273.

SOUTHEY, J. F. (1955). Survey of cereal root eelworm in England and Wales 1954. *Plant Pathology*, **4** (3), 98–102.

—— (1956). National survey work for cereal root eelworm (*Heterodera major* (O. Schmidt) Franklin). *Nematologica*, **1** (1), 64–71.

THOMASON, I. J. (1960). The effect of winter cereals on the population level of *Meloidogyne javanica*. *Phytopathology*, **50** (9), 657.

TRIANTAPHYLLOU, A. C. (1960). Sex determination in *Meloidogyne incognita* Chitwood, 1949 and intersexuality in *M. javanica* (Treub, 1885) Chitwood, 1949. *Ann. Inst. Phytopath. Benaki N.S.*, **3**, 12–30.

TRIANTAPHYLLOU, A. C. and HIRSCHMANN, H. (1960). Post infection development of *Meloidogyne incognita* Chitwood, 1949. *Ann. Inst. Phytopath. Benaki N.S.* **3**, 1–11.

WALLACE, H. R. (1956). The seasonal emergence of larvae from cysts of the beet eelworm, *Heterodera schachtii* Schmidt. *Nematologica*, **1**, 227–238.

—— (1962). Observations on the behaviour of *Ditylenchus dipsaci* in soil. *Nematologica*, **7**, 91–101.

WEHUNT, E. J. (1957). Population trends of nematodes associated with white clover in Louisiana. *Phytopathology*, **47** (1), 36.

WINSLOW, R. D. (1955). The effect of some leguminous crops on the soil population level of pea root eelworm. *Plant Pathology*, **4** (3), 86–88.

WINSLOW, R. D. and LUDWIG, R. A. (1957). Studies on hatching stimulation in the beet nematode, *Heterodera schachtii* Schmidt. *Canad. J. Bot.* **35**, 619–634.

CHAPTER 10

Control

Many accounts have been published of attempts to control plant nematodes in different countries and climates. As much of this information is of a local nature, however, it is difficult to draw general conclusions on the most efficient way of applying control measures. Consequently no attempt will be made to review the literature, instead emphasis will be placed on the principles of control.

CHEMICALS

Many chemicals are recommended by commercial firms to control nematodes in soil. Of these the halogenated hydrocarbons are probably the most widely used, including methyl bromide, D-D (1,3-dichloro-propene-1,2-dichloropropane), ethylene dibromide, Nemagon (1,2-di-bromo-3-chloropropane), Telone (1,3-dichloropropene) and related chlorinated C_3 hydrocarbons. Vapam (sodium N-methyl dithiocarba-mate) has also proved useful, especially in preplanting treatments. Various methods of applying the chemicals to the soil have been tried and rates of application and the use of surface seals have been studied. Christie (1959) gives a useful account of this side of the problem, but (1) different species may react differently to the same nematicide, (2) the same species may react differently to different nematicides. Thus, in chemical control problems, both the nematodes and the chemicals are variables. The following examples illustrate this.

Holdeman (1956) did three years of field trials to control *Belonolaimus gracilis* in a deep sandy soil of low fertility in the northeastern region of S. Carolina. He showed that ethylene dibromide was more effective than D-D when applied in the rows; reinfestation was also quicker in the D-D treated plots. Endo and Sasser (1957) compared the efficiency of D-D, ethylene dibromide, methyl bromide, Nemagon and Telone in controlling *Heterodera glycines* in N. Carolina. Methyl bromide and Telone were the most effective. Lear and his colleagues (1952), on the other hand, found that ethylene dibromide failed to control *Heterodera rostochiensis* on Long Island, New York, whereas a mixture of dichloro-butenes and D-D were effective. Anderson (1956) also showed that the best kills of *Rotylenchulus reniformis* were obtained with D-D; Nemagon was less effective and ethylene-dibromide least efficient of all. Nusbaum (1955) applied three nematicides on sixteen tobacco farms in twelve counties in central and eastern N. Carolina. Root and soil samples for nematode assays were collected from each plot in mid-season and after

231

harvest. All three nematicides gave satisfactory control of root knot nematodes but D-D was better than the others in two tests located on coarse sandy soils. The other two nematicides, both formulations of ethylene dibromide, markedly reduced *Tylenchorhynchus claytoni* and almost eliminated *Helicotylenchus* spp. and *Xiphinema americanum*. Ethylene dibromide was much less effective than D-D against *Pratylenchus* spp. but D-D was inferior to the other chemicals in the control of *Tylenchorhynchus claytoni*.

Such differences which occur through interaction of the environment, the nematode and the chemical, pose several fundamental questions: (1) How do different chemicals kill nematodes? (2) Why are some species resistant to certain chemicals? (3) How does the soil environment affect the dispersion of the chemical, its ability to reach the nematode and its persistence in soil? (4) What are the best methods for assaying the efficacy of nematicides? These problems will now be considered, although there is an obvious lack of information on all these aspects of plant nematode biology.

The reaction of nematodes to chemicals

Penetration of the nematode by the chemical is a necessary prerequisite to the physiological reactions associated with death. As Chitwood (1952) points out, the nematode egg is chitinoid and permeable to water, gases and chemicals although a mucoid covering opposes drying out and the penetration of chemicals such as fat solvents. Inside the egg shell, the waxy vitelline membrane provides a further barrier to chemical penetration. Chemicals may enter nematode larvae through the mouth, anus or vulva as well as through the cuticle; they are, therefore, probably less resistant to nematicides than eggs. The impermeability of the larval and adult cuticle to chemicals is attributed to the presence of lipids (Chitwood, 1952) but if nematicides can enter via natural apertures then the cuticle may not be very important as a barrier. Research is needed on the composition of the egg membranes, adult and larval cuticles, their permeability to different chemicals and the sites of entry of nematicides. Cuticular structure has been discussed very briefly in Chapter 1, it now remains to be seen whether comparative studies for different nematode species can explain differences in resistance to nematicides.

Chitwood (1952) suggests that the nitro group increases the toxicity of halogenated hydrocarbons although the halogen is essential for penetration, and that they kill the nematodes by precipitating proteins, blocking nerve endings and by destroying nerve sheaths and cellular membranes. This is also a fruitful field for further research.

Factors influencing the efficacy of nematicides

Allen and Raski (1950) applied D-D to cans of soil at 2·15 ml per single injection point. Root knot nematode larvae and *Heterodera schachtii* eggs were killed at least 8 in. (19·3 cm) laterally from, and 12 in. (30·5 cm) below the point of injection in sandy loam soils. In these and other soil types the fumigant was least effective at depths of 3 in. (7·6 cm) from the surface. The lateral and downward movement of the fumigant was less in soils having a relatively high moisture equivalent. Allen and Raski suggest that inability to control *Heterodera schachtii* in California with D-D is caused partly by the failure of the fumigant to diffuse through soils containing clay and much organic matter. Thus, D-D was about 100 times as effective in a sandy loam as in clay or organic loam.

McBeth (1954) suggests five factors which affect the activity of soil fumigants: (*a*) Temperature; chemicals with a boiling point of 150 to 200°C are most effective at soil temperatures of 27°C or higher; at 10°C they are almost ineffective. Hence D-D in a sandy soil diffuses 6 in. in less than 24 hr. at 24°C whereas at 7°C it takes 96 hr. (*b*) Soil moisture; in sandy loam or clay loam soils the moisture should not be more than 85 per cent nor less than 50 per cent of field capacity. (*c*) Soil type; heavy clay soils are unsuitable for fumigation owing to sorption on the increased active surface area of the soil particles and the blocking of pore spaces by soil moisture. Where soils have a moisture equivalent of 25 per cent or more, the dosage of fumigants must be increased. (*d*) Compaction; the soil should be in seed bed condition for most efficient nematicide treatment. (*e*) Sorption; chemicals are sorbed more in dry than in moist soils. Peat soils are not favourable for fumigation because of the high level of sorption on the organic matter.

Holdeman (1954) supports McBeth's recommendations and he gives the essential conditions necessary for successful fumigation, which are: (*a*) sandy soils can be treated more successfully than clay or peat soils, (*b*) the soil should be in good tilth, (*c*) plant roots of the previous crop should be decomposed, (*d*) moisture should be 'moderate' and 'uniform', (*e*) soil temperature is not critical between 10 and 30°C, although efficiency increases with rise in temperature and (*f*) the soil surface should be sealed after treatment with D-D and ethylene dibromide.

Van den Brande and colleagues (1954, 1956) stressed the importance of the water content of the soil when fumigating with D-D for the control of *Heterodera rostochiensis*. The optimum soil moisture level was poorly defined, however, although it was probably somewhat less than field capacity. Their experiments showed that between 2·5 and 16·5°C there was no significant difference in nematode kill, hence soil treatments could be given in spring, summer or autumn as long as the soil moisture was favourable.

Soil fumigants with a high vapour pressure diffuse rapidly through the soil and so build up quickly to a lethal concentration. Thus, Apt and Gould (1961) showed that populations of *Pratylenchus penetrans* were reduced more by fumigants with a high vapour pressure such as D-D, ethylene dibromide and methyl bromide than by dibromochloropropane, which has a low vapour pressure. It is clear from these few examples that the behaviour of a nematicide in a particular soil depends on the properties of the chemical and the environment in which it occurs. The problem thus involves not only the biologist and soil physicist, but the physical chemist as well. Wade and Call have contributed to the knowledge of soil fumigation from the physical-chemical angle. Their results with ethylene dibromide can be briefly summarised as follows. Sorption of ethylene dibromide by soils is rapid, most of the amount sorbed being taken up within half an hour. Over the usual field range of moisture content, the amount of ethylene dibromide held by the soil remains

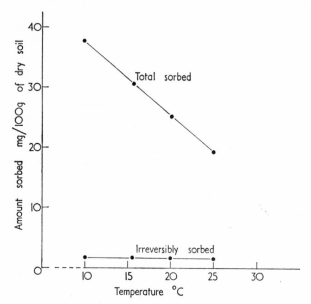

Fig. 62. Effect of temperature on the amount of ethylene-dibromide sorbed by a soil at a moisture content of 10·84 per cent. (After Wade, 1954a.)

constant although there is an increase with increase in moisture content, owing to solution of the fumigant in the soil water. The amount of ethylene dibromide sorbed is proportional to the organic carbon content of the soil (Wade, 1954a) and decreases with increase in temperature (Fig. 62). Once in the soil, liquid ethylene dibromide remains stable, over the field range of moisture for at least one week (Wade, 1954b). In dry soils below the field range of moisture content, sorptive capacity increases as the soils get drier (Wade, 1955).

Call (1957a) showed that the effects of moisture and carbon dioxide on the diffusion of ethylene dibromide in air were small but definite. Thus the diffusion coefficient in the upper 12 to 15 in. (30·5 to 38·1 cm) of normal field soils is reduced by 1 to 2 per cent as the carbon dioxide content is usually between 1 and 4 per cent in this region. Call (1957b) also studied the sorption of ethylene dibromide on twenty different soils at their field capacity. In all the soils, which ranged from coarse sands to heavy peats, the sorption coefficient was correlated with surface area, organic matter content, moisture content (Figs. 63 and 64) and less closely with clay content. Call found that he could predict the sorption coefficient with reasonable accuracy from moisture content alone. The

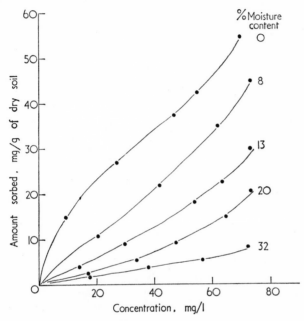

Fig. 63. Sorption isotherms of ethylene-dibromide on Black Fen soil at different moisture contents at 20°C. (After Wade, 1955.)

diffusion of ethylene dibromide was also studied in different soil types (Call, 1957c). Blocked pores were an important factor and sorption had a great influence on the unsteady-state diffusion coefficient. Call suggests that owing to the dynamic equilibrium between vapour and sorbed phases, the sorbed phase forms a reservoir of material available for transfer as the vapour diffuses away through the soils. Call (1957d) then showed that diffusion is the most important factor controlling the distribution of ethylene dibromide vapour in soil. Low concentrations near the surface are caused by loss of fumigant into the air; the only way to prevent this is to seal the soil surface with water or with an impervious covering, or to decrease the porosity by rolling. Concentration-time products (C.T.)

were calculated at various distances from the injection point and the median lethal dose was derived from C.T.-distance curves. (The LD 50 of ethylene dibromide for nematodes was assumed to be a C.T. product of 300 μg h/ml). The LD 50 ranges had a linear relationship to soil porosity for all soils at two temperatures (10 and 20°C). Thus, Call suggests that, contrary to usual practice, fields should be fumigated when the soil is well compacted before cultivation as a seed bed. The reduction of porosity in the soil surface layers following rainfall may be

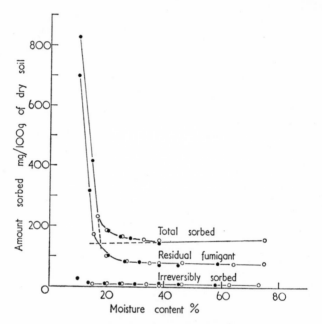

FIG. 64. Effect of moisture content of Black Fen soil on the amount of ethylene-dibromide sorbed. (After Wade, 1954a.)

advantageous for fumigation but such a practice is of doubtful value in countries like Great Britain where rainfall is erratic. Call and Hague (1962) later confirmed the importance of porosity in controlling the spread of fumigants in soil. The C.T. product at any point in the soil varied inversely as the soil porosity and directly as the dosage of the fumigant.

Wade's and Call's data mostly confirm what was suspected already, nevertheless, their data are based on objective experiments and help to explain the influence of the soil environment on the efficacy of fumigants. It seems likely that future research on the fundamentals of chemical control must follow similar lines if the subject is not to be overburdened by a mass of conflicting data dealing with local nematode problems.

Methods of assaying nematicides

Because of the wide variation in the physical and chemical properties of nematicides, there is no single technique for determining their efficacy. McBeth and Bergeson (1953) have adopted the following screening methods to ensure that as few materials as possible are discarded: (1) Water screen; chemicals are tested in aqueous solution or emulsion. (2) Soil injection; volatile materials are injected into either sealed or open containers of root knot nematode infested soil depending on the volatility of the material. Effectiveness is measured with indicator plants such as tomato, tobacco, cucumber, lettuce, etc. (3) Soil mix; relatively non-volatile materials are impregnated on a solid carrier and mixed intimately with root knot infested soil. The same plants again are used as indicators of effectiveness. (4) Field tests; chemicals are tested in small replicated plots under field conditions.

A rapid method of screening nematicides has been suggested by Klein and Allison (1957). A sand-loam-peat mixture is infested with adults, larvae and eggs of *Meloidogyne* spp. from knotted roots. The infested soil is treated by adding the various chemicals and then placed in containers which are covered for a short time when fumigants are used. Four-day old cucumber seedlings are transplanted into treated and untreated soils and root knot severity is assessed about 7 days later by determining the percentage of the root system which is knotted.

Rapid methods have their drawbacks, however. Ichikawa and his colleagues (1955), for example, found that Nemagon showed no nematicidal effects on *Meloidogyne* when soil samples were taken 1 week after treatment. The nematicidal effect increased from 2 to 9 weeks, however. The time lag between treatment and sampling is thus an important factor for some chemicals.

Hague and Omidvar (1962) advocate that in work with *Heterodera rostochiensis*, the final nematode population should be used as a criterion of the efficacy of nematicides because it allows for the effects of delayed hatch, for mortality at all stages after treatment as well as for reduction in viability of hatched larvae. Such a procedure would take longer than the usual *in vitro* tests and is influenced by the growth of the crop and the incidence of other diseases, etc. Furthermore, the final nematode populations, even at the lowest concentrations of nematicides which could be measured, were too high for a reliable statistical treatment to test nematicidal efficacy (Call and Hague, 1962). 100 per cent kills in nematicide experiments are, therefore, to be avoided because they yield little information on the relationship between chemical C.T. products and nematode kill. To overcome this problem larger samples of soil air will have to be taken or some other means of chemical estimation must be used, such as radio-tracer techniques. It should also be emphasised that in testing the effects of nematicides, or in any other experiments for that matter, the validity of the experimental method must be determined before it is

applied.   The fact that a technique yields results which appear to con-
form to preconceived hypotheses is no indication of the efficiency of the
technique.

In the routine testing of chemicals for nematicidal properties it is
obviously useful to use an organism which can be easily cultured in large
numbers.   Peters (1952) used the vinegar eelworm, *Turbatrix aceti*, so
that inactive substances could be quickly eliminated leaving the active
ones for full-scale trials.   Tarjan and Hopper (1954) selected *Panagrellus
redivivus* as a test organism because of its large size, ease of culture, short

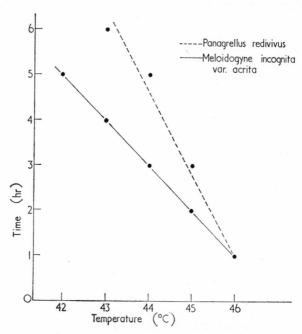

FIG. 65.   A comparison of the thermal death time of *Panagrellus redivivus* and *Meloidogyne incognita acrita*. (After
Santmyer, 1955.)

life cycle and high activity.   In comparing the effects of solutions or
emulsions of various chemicals they also found little difference between
the reactions of this species and many other free-living and plant parasitic
nematodes.   Santmyer (1955), however, suggests that some physiological
similarities must exist between the test nematode and the plant parasitic
species or the test organism must be rejected as unsatisfactory.   Santmyer then goes on to show that *Panagrellus redivivus* is more heat resistant than *Meloidogyne* spp. and he concludes that greater physiological
differences exist between these two nematodes than had been previously
assumed (Fig. 65).   Santmyer (1956) showed that only a small propor-

ion of the metabolic energy is consumed during nematode movement. Thus starved nematodes had a much lower metabolic rate than fresh nematodes, although their motility was the same. Consequently, nema- icides might reduce metabolic activity but this would not influence motility until the nematodes were almost dead. Thus, loss of motility only shows gross effects and is an inefficient criterion for assessing the efficacy of nematicides. Similarly, staining techniques only distinguish living and dead nematodes; chemical treatments may seriously impair the infectivity of nematodes without inactivating or killing them, hence the importance of screening methods with plants in soil.

Conclusions

It can be concluded, then, that in testing for nematicidal efficiency it is necessary to aim at closer control of the soil environment especially soil moisture and porosity, in preliminary screening experiments, and various concentrations and periods of treatment should be used. It should also be remembered that the reactions of free-living nematodes to chemicals may be different from those of plant nematodes. Finally, the ultimate criterion of the efficacy of a nematicide must always be based on field observations.

It has previously been stated (Chapter 8) that it is invalid to implicate nematodes as the primary pathogen in a diseased crop on the basis of comparisons between nematicide treated and untreated plots. Similarly, it is questionable whether increased yields on nematicide treated plots are caused entirely by the killing of plant nematodes; chemical treatment kills other disease organisms as well. Furthermore, soil fumigation may influence plant nutrients in the soil thereby increasing yields, although Reynolds and Evans (1953) state that increased growth in tobacco occurs by control of *Tylenchorhynchus dubius* and not through such a soil amend- ment effect. Nevertheless, this may be an important factor in some field problems. The influence of nematicides on the soil population generally and on the plant itself needs further study.

Chemicals, other than toxic substances, may also be used for nematode control. Lownsbery (1951), for example, suggests that a synthetic chemical which would stimulate hatching of *Heterodera* spp. in soil would be a useful method of control. A substance which would act at concentrations low enough to make application practicable and which would not break down too rapidly in the soil has yet to be found, however. The same can be said of nematode repellents, which Davis and Deak (1960) suggest may be applied to the soil in the plant rows. At present, chemical control depends chiefly on nematicidal or nematistatic chemi- cals applied either to the soil or directly to the plant by soaking it in a solution prior to planting. The discovery of efficient stimulants or repellents and especially of systemic nematicides will be the next major step forward.

PHYSICAL METHODS

Plant parasitic nematodes can easily be killed in the laboratory by the application of heat, irradiation, osmotic pressure, etc. It is more difficult, however, to employ such methods to large quantities of soil, especially if plants are present. The soil acts as a gigantic 'buffer', absorbing all excessive treatments and affording excellent protection for the nematodes. Daulton and Stokes (1952), for example, claimed that a pulsating electrostatic field, set up by a simple induction coil across suitably spaced electrodes, destroyed root knot nematodes in dry or damp soil and in water. Only a comparatively small voltage was needed to kill the larvae but this had to be increased for other nematode stages. Lear and Jacob (1955), however, found that high voltage, non-thermal, electrical soil treatments were completely impracticable. In their tests, the maximum electrical treatment was so modified by voltage breakdown by the soil and by temperature rise from the dissipated electrical energy, that there was no discernable reduction in nematode numbers.

Irradiation

There is good evidence that nematodes are killed or seriously affected by irradiation. Fassuliotis and Sparrow (1955) demonstrated that irradiation of potato tubers with X-rays inhibited sprouting and also inhibited development of *Heterodera rostochiensis*. Cysts of this nematode exposed to 20,000 roentgens contained only brown and dead eggs, at 40,000 r. the eggs lost their contents completely. Fassuliotis (1957) later repeated some of this work and found that cysts of *H. rostochiensis* were more resistant to irradiation than the preliminary observations suggested. Emergence of larvae from the cysts was only delayed at 160,000 r. and a dosage of 360,000 r. was needed to suppress emergence by 85 per cent. Infectivity of irradiated larvae was inversely proportional to the dosage. Wood and Goodey (1957) found that a dose of 48,000 to 96,000 r. was needed to inactivate *Ditylenchus destructor* and *Rhabditis* spp. Weischer (1957) used low dosage rates of 400 r/hr. when he irradiated *H. rostochiensis* and *H. schachtii* with radium for different periods. Treatments for less than 72 hr. had no apparent effect on the nematodes and Weischer points out that nematodes appear to have a higher resistance than other animals to such treatment. Myers (1960) examined the sensitivity of various plant parasitic and free-living nematodes to gamma and X-irradiation. He found that cell maturation occurred after all doses up to 500,000 r, gonad development occurred in all genera up to 320,000 r and in *Tylenchorhynchus claytoni* up to 400,000 r. Few *Panagrellus silusiae* survived doses up to 1,500,000 r for 24 hr., although some survived for three weeks in culture after a dose of 960,000 r. Most species survived 2 months without serious decrease in population level at doses up to 320,000 r. To irradiate nematodes in the field is difficult, however. In fact, Myers and Dropkin (1959) state that it is impracticable because of the length of time needed to irradiate even small areas and because damage to plant roots occurs at levels of irradiation below those required to disrupt the nematodes' life cycle.

Ultrasonics

Kämpfe (1962) treated *Heterodera* spp. and free-living nematodes with ultrasonics. Intact cysts of *Heterodera* were little affected by the treatment and *Heterodera* larvae appeared to be more resistant than other nematode species. The intensity of the ultrasonics appeared to be more important than the duration of the treatment. Kämpfe concludes from his experiments that the use of ultrasonics as a practical control measure is not feasible at present.

Osmotic pressure

Machmer (1958) found that *Tylenchulus semipenetrans* and *Meloidogyne incognita acrita* not only survived but increased in numbers at a high soil salinity. The nematodes appeared to tolerate salts in soils when host plants were injured. Feder (1960), however, claimed that up to 100 per cent of the nematodes were killed when sucrose or dextrose was added to nematode infested soil at the rate of 1 to 5 per cent by weight. Feder suggests that his data show that the quantitative addition of these carbohydrates to nematode infested soils of known moisture content gives predictable percentages of nematode kill and that these effects can be readily repeated in the field. Dextrose, Feder states, would be a safe and simple material which could be applied easily at a minimum risk to human beings or animals and it is harmless to the plants it protects. Later work by Feder and his colleagues (1962) showed that the osmotic effect was enhanced by the addition of 1 ton/acre of mono-sodium-lauryl-sulphate detergent to sugar soil mixtures; with this, the exposure time for kill was reduced by 25 per cent. There are several objections to this procedure, however. Blake (1961a), for example, calculated the changes in the total potential (osmotic potential plus suction potential) of soil after adding dextrose at the rate of 1 to 5 per cent by weight as Feder suggested. Even with 0·1 per cent dextrose, the total potential would retard plant growth but not inferere with nematode movement. Furthermore, Blake states that the potential at which nematodes are killed by exosmosis approximates to that at which plants permanently wilt. Thus, sugar cannot be applied to the soil to control nematodes when the plants are there and even if the soil were treated while fallow, the addition of such large amounts of carbohydrate might render nitrogen temporarily unavailable and induce profound changes in the populations of soil microorganisms. Concentrated sugar solutions fail to inhibit completely the subsequent emergence of *Heterodera schachtii* from cysts in beet root

16

diffusate and so the addition of sugar to soil to control this species is considered by Steele (1962) to be impracticable. Feder's hypothesis has yet to be tested under wide variations in the field, so it would be unwise to reject this approach out of hand. Nevertheless, it is valid to ask whether a field treatment which advocates the application of some 20 or 30 tons/acre of dextrose to soil is practicable and economical, when the yield of sugar from beets is of the order of 2 to 4 tons/acre.

Heat

Heat treatment is probably the most successful physical control measure developed so far. It is widely used for the killing of nematodes within plant tissues before planting and has proved useful with nematode-infested bulbs, corms and tubers, and roots of plants such as chrysanthemums, strawberries, bananas and citrus (Staniland, 1959; Christie, 1959; Jenkins, 1960). The basis of all these problems is the same. First, the time-temperature-mortality curves of the nematode have to be determined. This entails immersing the nematodes (contained in as small a volume of water as possible) into thermostatically controlled water baths at different temperatures for different lengths of time. After such treatment the nematodes are examined for activity, stained to see if they are dead or introduced into soil containing host plants to assess their ability to invade, develop and reproduce. Although the relationship between exposure-time at different temperatures and nematode mortality has been described previously (Chapter 4) it should be emphasised that no generalisations can be made for genera or different stages of a species. For example, Walker (1960, 1962) found marked differences between species of *Meloidogyne* in their reaction to high temperatures and Sherman (1934) and Cairns (1953) showed that quiescent fourth stage larvae of *Ditylenchus dipsaci* are more resistant to heat than other stages. Information must also be obtained on the plants' reaction to temperature because if the treatment is to be successful the plants must be able to tolerate temperatures lethal to nematodes.

The next stage is to assess the heat penetrability of the plant tissues. If nematodes live in the middle of plant tissues it is necessary to know the time required for the lethal temperature to build up there. Staniland (1953) used copper-nickel thermocouples to measure temperatures inside strawberry runners. Observations were made on runners of various sizes and Staniland found that the large ones required 3 to 4 min. and the smaller ones 2 to 3 min. to reach equilibrium with the temperature of the water in which they were immersed. This was taken into account when determining the time to kill *Ditylenchus dipsaci*. Thus 46·1°C for 4 min. killed the nematode, so the runners were immersed in water at this temperature for 7 to 8 min. This technique gave good control of *Ditylenchus dipsaci* with only slight loss of plants. Blake (1961b) measured the rate of penetration of heat through banana corm tissue during hot water treatment. He found that the size of the corms considerably affected heat penetration. Thus in a bath at 55°C, a temperature of 42°C was recorded after about 16 min. in spearpoints of 12·7 cm diameter or less, and in quartered corms. In larger spearpoints and in halved and whole corms, 42°C was not reached in 30 min. With such information on the time needed to kill *Radopholus similis* at different temperatures in water, Blake suggested that banana sets less than 13 cm diameter should be immersed in water at 55°C for 20 min.

The most efficient way of heat-treating quantities of plant material is mainly an engineering problem. Blake (1961b) treated banana sets in a tank of 1,000 gal. (4,546 l) capacity in which the water was heated by low pressure steam and circulated by a centrifugal pump. The quantity of steam entering the tank was thermostatically controlled. Eight wire baskets each holding 40 to 70 sets were placed in the tank. Hesling (1961) discusses problems in the routine hot water treatment of chrysanthemum stools. He states that the short treatment of 46·1°C for 5 min. is impracticable because of the difficulty in maintaining close control of the water temperature and the large amount of electrical power needed. Hesling suggests that a capillary type thermostat in direct control of the electrical supply to the heater should be used. Agitation of the stools and circulation of the water by an impeller type of pump is also advocated and finally a treatment of 43·3°C for 20 min. may be more practicable.

A new approach to heat treatment is the application of 'dry heat' (Thomason *et al.*, 1960). Sweet potato seed roots were treated at 45°C for 30 hr. and this gave complete control of root knot nematodes, with 68 per cent of the roots surviving.

Campbell and Courtney (1960) state that some soil-borne organisms can be controlled by momentary treatment of the soil mass with steam, super-heated to 427 to 454°C, while the soil is being agitated and pulverised. This differs from the conventional soil sterilisation techniques in that the microorganisms were apparently killed by selective absorption of heat, while the temperature of the treated soil was not significantly raised. A machine was designed to treat the soil in the field so that nematodes could be controlled.

BIOLOGICAL CONTROL

Biological control aims at increasing the parasites and predators of nematodes in the soil, to increase the mortality of plant nematodes. This can be done by changing the environment, by addition of organic amendments or by introducing other organisms directly. However, as has been stated before, the soil with its flora and fauna is an efficient 'buffer' and this term can be used in a biological as well as a chemical sense. An organism introduced into the soil will reach a population level determined by the edaphic and biotic factors in the environment. Consequently, it would be unrealistic to suppose, for example, that predatory nematodes introduced into a plot of soil would reach numbers greatly in excess of those usually encountered elsewhere. Christie (1960) is more optimistic for he considers that such an approach might be of enormous practical importance and an attractive and unexplored field awaiting investigation.

To increase the concentration of nematode-destroying organisms in the soil it is necessary to alter the environment so that some of the forces restraining multiplication of the organisms are weakened. The only serious attempt at the biological control of plant nematodes has been concerned with the use of nematode trapping fungi (Chapter 4). In almost all these experiments a soil amendment was used thereby altering the environment in favour of the nematode trapping fungi. The results are mostly negative (Duddington, Jones and Williams, 1956; Duddington Jones and Moriarty, 1956). Mankau (1960, 1961a) found no evidence that *Arthrobotrys arthrobotryoides* or *Dactylaria thaumasia* controlled the numbers of *Meloidogyne incognita* even with soil amendments, and he concluded (Mankau, 1961b) that it was probably impossible to give immediate protection to crops highly susceptible to root knot nematodes by the application of predacious fungi.

Duddington and Duthoit (1960), however, obtained statistically significant reductions in the mean number of larvae of *Heterodera avenae* in 2 ft (0·61 m) square plots to which 1·5 lb (680 g) of chopped cabbage had been added, compared with untreated plots. Duddington, Everard and Duthoit (1961), in later experiments, obtained further evidence that *Dactylaria thaumasia* reduced the invasion of oat seedlings by *Heterodera avenae*. There is some doubt, of course, whether the fungi are entirely responsible for such reductions.

Van der Laan (1956) found that organic manure in the soil reduced the infestation level of *Heterodera rostochiensis* in potato roots more than artificial fertilisers did. Mankau and Minteer (1962) also showed that of eight organic materials added to soil infested with *Tylenchulus semipenetrans*, only cattle manure failed to cause substantial reductions in numbers of larvae in 84 days. Castor pomace, a by-product of castor oil extraction, eliminated all the larvae of *Tylenchulus semipenetrans* from soil but was apparently non-toxic to nematodes. There was increased activity of microorganisms in the soil following these treatments but the factors responsible for killing the nematodes were not determined. In somewhat similar experiments, Johnson (1962) determined the effect of adding organic amendments to soil in relation to the influence of temperature, moisture and pH on the incidence of *Meloidogyne incognita*. Johnson suggests that the nematodes may be adversely affected by changes in the physical environment of soil receiving organic amendments although he does not rule out the importance of predacious fungi. The influence of several organic additives on the microorganisms in the soil has also been studied by Mankau (1962). Numbers of saprophytic nematodes increased, but not the predacious *Dorylaimus* spp. Dung and green manure appeared to promote the greatest activity of predacious fungi.

Such results are encouraging but there is clearly a need for research on the basic principles governing changes in the populations of micro-organisms and in the physico-chemical environment in the soil after the addition of soil amendments. The early and somewhat optimistic view that plant nematodes could be controlled by the direct application of parasites and predators is now being replaced by a more realistic approach, namely the analysis of physical and biological changes in the soil in relation to nematode numbers.

CROP ROTATION

We have already seen in the chapter on populations that the numbers of nematodes in the soil are profoundly affected by the types of crops which are grown, and that yields are reduced as nematode population size increases. Crop rotation attempts to keep such populations to a level at which crop damage is reduced to a minimum. By growing non-host crops, the numbers of plant nematodes are reduced, the number of years for this to occur depending on the initial population and the rate of population decrease.

The value of crop rotation has long been recognised in the control of *Heterodera* spp. Thus, continuous cropping with potatoes increases the cyst population of *H. rostochiensis* more than 3-year rotations with corn, green beans, red clover or perennial rye-grass (Mai and Lownsbery, 1952). In Northern Ireland, the potato root eelworm order restricts the growing of potatoes, in areas where infections are known to occur, to not more than twice in 8 years and then only in fields which have first been sampled and found to be free from *H. rostochiensis* (Chamberlain, 1955). Brown (1961) gives some idea of the effect of crop rotation on yields of potatoes growing in soil infested with *H. rostochiensis*. Potato yield after 3 years' continuous cropping was 1,631 kg/hectare, and with a non-host in the second year it was 4,515 kg/hectare. After 2 years' continuous potatoes the yield was 8,780 kg/hectare and with a non-host in the first year 12,544 kg/hectare. In the early days of the sugar beet industry in Great Britain, beet was grown without rotation. The first control measure against *Heterodera schachtii* was the introduction of a clause into contracts forbidding the growing of beet after beet or mangolds. In 1939 control measures stipulated that: (1) in uninfested fields within a scheduled area, beet could not be grown until the land had been free from susceptible crops for 2 years; (2) for infested fields with a low nematode population this time was extended to 3 years; (3) with high nematode populations beet could not be grown for 5 years following a host. In 1941 the growing of sugar beet was restricted to not more than once in every 3 years in large areas of peat fen soil in East Anglia (Petherbridge and Jones, 1944). That the beet eelworm problem has been contained in Great Britain seems to be due in no small measure to crop rotation. There is no legislation in the U.S.A. for cropping programmes to comba Heterodera schachtii, although it is recognised there that crop rotation are essential. Golden and Jorgenson (1961), for example, recommendec that there should be 3-year rotations in fields where the nematode has not been found, 4-year rotations where some crop injury is visible, anc 5- or 6-year rotations if there are noticeable reductions in crop yield Lucerne, clover, beans, peas, potatoes and maize are suggested as usefu non-host crops to use in such rotations with infestations of *Heteroderc glycines*. Ross (1960) tried fourteen cropping sequences with soybeans grown every year, and every second, third or fourth year. He used cow-peas, maize and cotton as non-host crops. The average soybean yields for the continuous, 2-year and 3-year rotations were 1·3, 6·7 and 12·8 bushels/acre in 1958 and 1·9, 5·8 and 14·0 bushels/acre in 1959. Soy-bean yields with the 4-year rotation were no different from the 3-year rotation. Crittenden (1956) states that the best results for controlling *Meloidogyne incognita* were obtained by growing the non-host crops for 2 consecutive years followed by the host crop. Similarly, infestations of *Pratylenchus leiocephalus* can be reduced by growing a non-host crop of peanuts in rotation with maize (Good *et al.*, 1954). Studies in five rotation and fumigation experiments, and additional surveys showed that *Pratylenchus penetrans* was a major cause of sickness in many crops of woody plants, potatoes and red clover (Oostenbrink, 1961a). On the basis of these trials, Oostenbrink suggested that: (1) the cultivation of potatoes, oats, rye and red clover in infested nurseries should be avoided; (2) beet or mangold should be grown before potatoes or red clover on heavily infested arable land; and (3) cultivation of red clover should be avoided on soil infested with *Pratylenchus penetrans*.

Advice given to growers on crop rotations is the culmination of much research into the host specificity, distribution, population dynamics and general biology of particular nematode species. The problem is far more difficult, however, when several species of nematodes are involved in damage to a crop. Oostenbrink (1954) emphasises the importance of migratory root nematodes in agriculture and horticulture. He suggests that their distribution and damage to crops is widespread and that the old rotational system of rye, oats and potatoes was successful in the past because it checked the population increase of such nematodes. Oosten-brink and his colleagues (1956) consider, in fact, that a dynamic noxious population occurs in nearly all cultivated soil and that there is a close relationship between cropping sequence and the composition of and damage by the nematode complex. Some rotations may therefore increase some species at the expense of others. Beet following potatoes, for example, produced a decrease in *Pratylenchus* spp. whereas potatoes following beet decreased *Paratylenchus* populations. Potatoes always seemed to decrease populations of migratory plant parasitic nematodes whereas clover-grass and winter wheat increased them (Cichorius, 1960).

The influence of crop rotations on populations of several species is still imperfectly understood. With some nematodes, for example *Tricho-dorus* spp., crop rotation may even be impracticable because of their very wide host range. Rohde and Jenkins (1957) could only find Jimson-weed, asparagus, poinsettia and crotalaria as non-hosts of these species. In organising crop rotation programmes for a given area it is, therefore, necessary to identify the nematodes present in the soil, to determine their host specificity and to study the relationship between nematode numbers and crop damage. It has been mentioned previously that host specificity is essentially a local problem which is determined by the species and races of nematodes present; it follows, therefore, that crop rotation systems should also be based on local information. This is particularly true for *Meloidogyne* spp. Sasser (1954), for example, found that the predominant species in Maryland, U.S.A., were *M. hapla* and *M. incognita acrita* and he was able to suggest rotational programmes based on host-specificity tests with these species. To apply these suggestions to other states in the U.S.A. or in other countries would be dangerous, however, as subsequent research has shown (van der Linde, 1956).

Crop rotation programmes must be acceptable to the farmer, of course. Non-host crops must be worth growing; it is unlikely that a grower will willingly consent to insert some useless or uneconomic crop into his rotations. Van der Linde (1956) states that in S. Africa farmers are only willing to include cash crops in a rotation and are reluctant to grow the non-host *Crotalaria* even though the land is heavily infested with root knot nematodes. It really amounts to how much the grower is aware of the danger of plant nematodes and of injudicious cropping programmes. Thus, sugar beet growers in California, Colorado and Michigan appear to be unenlightened in this respect, for Caveness (1958) states that only 10 per cent of the infested fields studied received the necessary 4 years' rest from susceptible crops to control *Heterodera schachtii*. It would be pointless to pursue the reasons for this attitude because we would enter into the field of economics and psychology. Nevertheless, it is clear that considerable responsibility is placed on the shoulders of those nematologists whose task it is to advise farmers on crop rotations. It is important to ensure that non-host crops really are non-hosts. Thus, Golden and Shafer (1959) point out that tomatoes, an economically important crop in many beet growing areas of the U.S.A., should not be used as a non-host crop in rotations for the control of *Heterodera schachtii* because tomato is a host of certain populations of this species. They suggest however that *Hesperis matronalis* could be used as a trap plant as it is a non-host of *Heterodera schachtii* and root knot nematodes (Golden and Shafer, 1958). Den Ouden (1956) made a similar suggestion, but he was doubtful whether it would be practicable in Dutch agriculture.

Some plants appear to be antagonistic to nematodes for they reduce populations to a greater extent than non-hosts. *Crotalaria* is a good example of this. Ochse and Brewton (1954) grew twenty-one varieties of this plant in rows on two plots of soil heavily infested with root knot nematodes. Soil from around seven of the varieties contained negligible numbers of nematodes. Ochse and Brewton suggest that this indicates that the *Crotalaria* root system has a toxic effect on nematodes and that, planted in advance of a crop, they may reduce subsequent damage. Birchfield and Bistline (1956) also found that *Crotalaria spectabilis* and *Crotalaria striata* inhibited the reproduction and survival of *Radopholus similis* in inoculation experiments. They suggest that these plants may be a better cover crop for cleared and treated spreading-decline areas than the more commonly used hairy-indigo (*Indigofera hirsuta*), which is a host. Colbran (1957) states that Sudan grass (*Andropogon sorghum* v. *sudanensis*) and *Crotalaria* spp. were the most suitable cover crops for reducing populations of *Meloidogyne javanica*. A note of doubt is introduced by Ford and Hannon (1958), however, for they state that *Radopholus similis* is capable of penetrating the roots of *Crotalaria spectabilis* and laying viable eggs. They suggest that although *Crotalaria* is a poor host the nematode may, nevertheless, be able to complete its life cycle and therefore this plant has doubtful value as a cover crop. The efficacy of *Crotalaria* as a cover or trap crop therefore depends on the species or variety of the main crop plant and the species of nematode being studied. It should be emphasised, however, that the presence of a few females in the roots does not preclude the use of a plant as a trap crop; information on soil populations are needed before this conclusion can be reached.

There is evidence from Dutch nematologists that *Tagetes* spp. may reduce populations of some plant parasitic nematodes. Oostenbrink and his colleagues (1957) tested sixteen varieties of *Tagetes patula* and *Tagetes erecta* placed between the rows or round the feet of other plants. They found that all varieties suppressed populations of *Pratylenchus* in the roots of other plants as well as in the soil, resulting in better growth of perennials in the second year, or of the succeeding crop. The *Tagetes* had to be grown for 3 to 4 months and it was suggested that the roots had a nematicidal action. Later work (Meijneke and Oostenbrink, 1958) showed that populations of *Pratylenchus, Tylenchorhynchus, Paratylenchus* and *Rotylenchus robustus* were also reduced, giving better growth of crops. Some doubt was expressed about the effect on *Meloidogyne* and no data were available for *Heterodera* and *Ditylenchus*. Oostenbrink (1959) considers that *Tagetes* is a good preceding crop to one susceptible to *Pratylenchus penetrans* and is also a good green manure. In fact he suggests (Oostenbrink, 1960c) that this plant increases the yield of most crops on sandy and peaty soils, usually by 10 to 40 per cent. Oostenbrink concludes that this is caused by a direct suppression of root infesting nematodes.

Visser and Vythilingham (1959) state that *Tagetes erecta* and *Tagetes patula* considerably reduce *Pratylenchus coffeae* and *Meloidogyne javanica* populations in tea plantations but Tarjan (1960) found no evidence from field tests that *Tagetes* reduced the numbers of *Radopholus similis* in grapefruit roots or in the soil.

There are three points of criticism. First, the effect of *Tagetes* has been tested on only a few species, so it may not be entirely unspecific, as is assumed in some quarters of the popular agricultural and horticultural press. For example, the cultivation of *Tagetes* in soil infested with *Heterodera rostochiensis* is of negligible value (Omidvar, 1962). Second, little is known of the relationship between *Tagetes*, nematodes and crop plant growth, thus how much of the increased yields after *Tagetes* is caused by the killing of nematodes or from other effects is unknown. Third, the fact that *Tagetes* reduces the numbers of a particular plant nematode in soil does not necessarily mean that this plant will show increased yields. It is necessary to establish that numbers of the nematode are sufficient to cause damage in the first place. It is quite possible that many naturally-occurring populations of plant nematodes have no deleterious effect on a crop at all. In spite of these criticisms the use of cover-, trap- or enemy-crops provides a potentially useful control measure in crop rotations. Such an opinion is supported by the evidence that *Asparagus* (Rohde and Jenkins, 1958) exudes a nematicidal chemical from its roots. Trap crops may be useful when conventional crop rotations have apparently failed to control a nematode attack, e.g. *Heterodera göttingiana* (Stemerding, 1960). Nevertheless, Shepherd (1962), who has reviewed the subject, considers that in the control of *Heterodera* spp., there has been little success.

Although crop rotation is probably the most effective control measure in most nematode problems at present, it is by no means completely effective. In fact, where such cropping programmes are forced on a grower because of nematode attacks it may almost be considered as a last resort. The nematode is dictating agricultural practice and although crop rotation may be considered beneficial now, it is to be hoped that future research, in nematology and in agriculture generally, will eventually permit the growth of crops without any regard to sequence.

BREEDING FOR RESISTANCE

To produce plants resistant to parasitic nematodes involves several stages in research. First, the nematode must be defined as clearly as possible because different races or species may produce different symptoms in the same species of plant. In any case, it is always advisable to assess resistance with several nematode populations from different localities to see if racial differences occur. The status of the plant itself must likewise be known.

Second, it is necessary to ensure that laboratory or greenhouse techniques for the assessment of resistance provide maximum opportunity for the plants to react to the nematodes. Thus, physical conditions should be optimal for hatch, movement, invasion and development.

Where tests have to be done initially on a field scale, the problem is more difficult, because uniformity of infection and control of the environment is almost impossible. In these cases well randomised and statistically designed plot experiments seem to be the only answer.

Third, valid criteria for the assessment of resistance must be devised which allow only the minimum of subjective appraisal. Data on nematode pathogenicity and symptoms of the infested plant provide such information and nematode population studies will indicate whether the plant is immune, tolerant or resistant.

Fourth, different varieties or closely related species of the plant being studied are then tested for resistance and some idea is obtained of the genetics of heritable resistance, so that a plant breeding programme can be started.

Fifth, crosses and backcrosses are made with potentially useful plant material until a variety is obtained which appears to fulfil the requirements of a nematode-resistant plant and which still has commercially desirable qualities.

Sixth, the resistant plant is tested under field conditions in different localities and soil types to assess the influence of environment on resistance. The population dynamics of the nematode under the resistant crop should also be studied because it may not be advisable to grow the resistant types continuously if there is a danger that other races or closely related species will be selected out and multiply.

Such an approach for the breeding of nematode-resistant plants is obviously idealistic and in many breeding programmes one or more of these stages may be omitted or modified. Some nematode problems have already been largely solved by the breeding of resistant varieties but in most cases results are still undergoing the test of time in field trials. The following examples illustrate the principles and briefly indicate the problems associated with such work.

Meloidogyne

One of the problems in breeding strains of root-knot resistant tobacco was the apparent closely bound linkage between factors controlling resistance and narrow leaves (Wallace, 1954; Graham, 1954). Studies on the inheritance of resistance in tobacco were made by crossing susceptible and resistant plants in various combinations. F_1, F_2, F_3 and backcross progenies were grown in soil infested with *M. incognita acrita* and their responses indicated that a single dominant factor controlled resistance (Drolsom *et al.*, 1958). A collection of 970 tobaccos from Mexico, Central and Southern America was made by Clayton and his co-workers (1958a, 1958b) and tested for resistance to *M. incognita acrita*. All but the strain TI 706 were eliminated. After a series of backcrosses to a flue-cured variety, lines were selected giving highly resistant plants with most of the commercially desirable characters but with narrower leaves and lower yields than the best varieties; however, subsequent crosses eliminated the linkage between resistance and small leaves. Resistance was due to a single dominant gene pair but modifier genes apparently affected its expression. Graham (1960) then stated that a new flue-cured tobacco breeding line PD 611 resistant to *M. incognita acrita* had been released to tobacco breeders for further variety development. Thus the breeding of resistant tobacco has made good progress. Graham (1961), however, found that although selected breeding lines were consistently resistant to *M. incognita acrita* they were susceptible to *M. javanica* and *M. arenaria*. These last two species are not common in the tobacco growing areas of North Carolina, South Carolina and Georgia but there is always the possibility that they will spread and increase. Hence it is necessary, as Graham suggests, to develop a wider range of resistance that would include other species of *Meloidogyne*. Breeding for resistance is never static, the research for new resistant lines must continue as the proportions of races and species in a population change.

In cotton the degree of galling and the percentage of plants suffering from *Fusarium* wilt are closely correlated. Smith (1954a) suggests that root knot nematodes not only provide an entrance for the fungus but increase the susceptibility of the host in the later stages of development. To improve root knot resistance in cotton would therefore increase resistance to *Fusarium* wilt, and Smith (1954b) considers that breeding programmes should be organised on this basis to provide the greatest immediate benefit to the cotton crop. When a nematode is the primary incitant of a disease, the breeding of nematode resistant plants is clearly of great importance. It is also essential to study the pathogenicity of the organisms in a disease so that plant breeding programmes can be directed against the primary pathogen.

Thomason and Smith (1957) derived a line of tomato, HES 4875, from a cross of *Lycopersicon esculentum* and *Lycopersicon peruvianum*. This line was highly resistant to *Meloidogyne incognita acrita* and resistance was governed by a single dominant gene. Furthermore, a backcross of HES 4875 and a commercial tomato was resistant to *M. javanica* as well. Winstead and Barham (1957) also developed a tomato line, Hawaii 5229, resistant to *M. incognita*, *M. incognita acrita*, *M. javanica* and *M. arenaria*. The same gene appeared to control resistance to each of these four species; resistance was incompletely dominant. These varieties would be valuable for growing in soil infested with these species but even if no other species appeared there is always the danger that a race may be selected to which the plant would not be resistant. Riggs and Winstead (1959), in fact, showed that this occurred in *M. incognita incognita*, *M. incognita acrita* and *M. arenaria* parasitising the resistant tomato strain Hawaii 5229.

Hare's work on the breeding of pepper resistant to root knot nematodes indicates some of the stages involved in this method of control. 162 lines of pepper were tested for resistance to a population of gall-producing nematodes, the species of which were undetermined. Resistance was evaluated by grading the plants according to number and size of galls and the amount of root destruction (Hare, 1951). Further refinements were made when pure cultures of *Meloidogyne* spp. were introduced into sterile soil containing various varieties of pepper (Hare, 1953). The reaction of seven selected pepper varieties to five different *Meloidogyne* spp. was then studied and it was apparent that there were great differences in the susceptibility of the varieties to the different species, suggesting that several different genes or sets of genes were responsible for resistance to *Meloidogyne* (Hare, 1956a). In tests with a single species, *M. incognita acrita*, Hare (1956b) found four highly resistant varieties of pepper. The inheritance of this resistance was then determined (Hare, 1957). The resistant variety Santanka X S was crossed with three commercial varieties and the resistance of the F_1, F_2 and F_3 generations assessed. The resistant variety 405 B Mexico was crossed with two commercial varieties and the F_1, F_2, F_3 and backcross generations were also examined. The evidence suggested that resistance to *M. incognita* and *M. incognita acrita* was controlled by a single dominant gene. All of the parents in the crosses were resistant to *M. arenaria* and *M. javanica*. The way was now open to breed strains of commercial peppers resistant to these four *Meloidogyne* spp. and Hare suggested that the parents should consist of a variety containing the dominant gene resistant to *M. incognita* and a commercial variety selected for resistance to *M. arenaria* and *M. javanica*.

Numerous other workers have succeeded in breeding resistant lines to *Meloidogyne* in other crops. The chief problem lies in the difficulty of obtaining resistance to several species. In many areas, however, a single species is often dominant, so the introduction of a crop resistant to that species would confer immediate if not everlasting benefit on the crop.

Heterodera rostochiensis

The first step in the process of breeding resistant lines of potato was made by Ellenby (1945, 1954) who screened many *Solanum* spp. and found that *S. vernei* and *S. tuberosum* ssp. *andigena* were resistant to *Heterodera rostochiensis*. Mai and Peterson (1952) confirmed these results and in addition stated that *S. sucrense* also had resistant properties. Toxopeus and Huijsman (1952) also stated that resistant varieties of *andigena* offered a good basis for a breeding programme and in crosses between resistant *andigena* seedlings and between these seedlings and *tuberosum* varieties they showed that resistance was inherited by a single dominant gene (Toxopeus and Huijsman, 1953). Subsequent work by Jones (1954), Goffart and Ross (1954) and Dunnett (1957) also confirmed that some lines of *andigena* were resistant to *Heterodera rostochiensis*.

This monogenic dominance is somewhat complicated because *andigena* and *tuberosum* are tetraploid. Thus if H is the dominant gene, resistant seedlings can have the following genotypes: (1) Hhhh, simplex giving 50 per cent resistant progeny when crossed with a susceptible variety (hhhh); (2) HHhh, duplex giving 83 per cent resistant progeny when crossed with a susceptible variety; (3) HHHh, triplex; and (4) HHHH, quadruplex, both giving 100 per cent resistant progeny when crossed with a susceptible variety (Huijsman, 1956). It was easy, therefore, to raise large numbers of resistant seedlings but to combine this with the commercial characters of existing potato varieties was much more difficult. Huijsman (1956) found some mature cysts on the roots of resistant plants and he suggested that physiological races might develop which would break down the resistance of the breeding material. Toxopeus (1956) also stressed the importance of new biotypes developing on resistant plants and he advocated the search for more resistant material of a different genetical background as a safeguard for future unfavourable developments.

These warnings were well founded, for van der Laan and Huijsman (1957) found that resistant lines of potato were not resistant to *Heterodera rostochiensis* from Peru. In the same year Dunnett (1957) reported that a population from an Edinburgh garden (Duddingston population) developed and produced cysts on resistant *andigena* and some hybrids from *andigena × tuberosum* crosses. Resistance in *Solanum vernei* was retained, however. In a survey of H. *rostochiensis* populations from soils in Great Britain, Dunnett assessed that about 10 per cent of the populations sampled were capable of developing on resistant plants. Jones (1957) made a more detailed survey on samples of infested soil from twenty localities and confirmed Dunnett's findings. Jones suggested that research was needed on the mode of inheritance of 'resistance-breaking' in H. *rostochiensis* because this would influence the rate at which the proportion of the biotypes in natural populations would increase when resistant potatoes were grown. If 'resistance-breaking' behaved as a simple dominant, increase would probably be rapid, if recessive, slow at first. Jones and Pawelska (1962) tested the ability of forty-seven British populations to form cysts on plants with resistance derived from several species of *Solanum*. The potato variety Arran Banner was used as a standard susceptible host. Cyst production on *andigena* hybrids ranged from less than 1 per cent of those on Arran Banner to slightly over 100 per cent. About half the populations produced 10 per cent or less, and populations of this type, against which *andigena* resistance would be effective, were especially common in S.E. England and Northern Ireland (Fig. 66). Jones and Pawelska's data also indicate that there is much variability in cyst production on different types of resistant potato suggesting that many biotypes of H. *rostochiensis* exist. Breeding work must clearly use a wide range of nematode populations.

In spite of these difficulties it may be possible to use resistant potatoes in certain localised areas where the population has been studied. Thus,

Jones and Pawelska (1962) suggest that resistance derived from *andigena* would be immediately useful in about half the potato fields in England and Wales and would be effective in most fields in S.E. England and Northern Ireland.   Similarly, resistant potatoes could probably be used on Long Island, U.S.A., for Harrison (1960) found no indication of 'resistance-breaking' biotypes there.

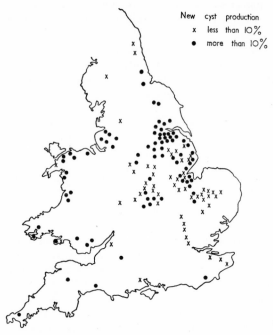

FIG. 66.   The distribution of resistance-breaking biotypes of *Heterodera rostochiensis* in England and Wales.   Production of new cysts expressed as a percentage of those developing on the susceptible variety Arran Banner.   (After Jones and Pawelska, 1962.)

What is the effect of growing resistant potatoes on populations of *Heterodera rostochiensis*?   Cole and Howard (1959) showed that a greater decrease in the nematode population occurred under resistant potatoes than in fallow soil.   They state, however, that it would take many crops on a fen type soil to reduce the population to a level where two crops of a susceptible variety would not raise it again to a dangerous level.   This may be an effect of soil type, however; bigger reductions may occur on sandy soils.   The continuous growing of potatoes resistant to 'non-resistance-breaking' biotypes of the nematodes can change the population to one consisting largely of a 'resistance-breaking' biotype

(Cole and Howard, 1962a). When the nematode population consists mostly of the non-aggressive or 'non-resistance-breaking' biotype, however, then resistant potatoes may considerably reduce the nematode population without causing much increase in the aggressive biotype (Cole and Howard, 1962b). Huijsman (1961) grew resistant potatoes in a sandy soil for 6 years and found that even after that time the soil was still noticeably infested. There was an indication that after three generations of such varieties the level of infestation remained at a constant level at which the crop was not much damaged. Huijsman concluded

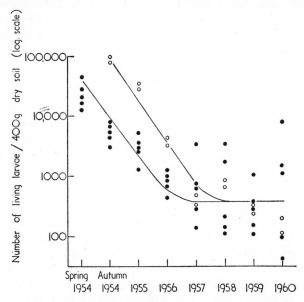

FIG. 67. Changes in a population of *Heterodera rostochiensis* in terms of living eggs/400 g dried soil when resistant potato varieties were grown continuously. Open circles indicate heavily infested plots, closed circles—moderately infested plots. (After Huijsman, 1961.)

that it was impossible to eradicate *Heterodera rostochiensis* completely by growing resistant potato varieties (Fig. 67).

What, then, is the value of growing resistant potatoes? Cole and Howard (1962b) suggest that as well as reducing the nematode population it would also be possible to avoid lengthening rotations or giving land a long rest from potatoes. It might even be possible to return to growing susceptible varieties after one or two crops of resistant potatoes.

There seems to be no alternative to this approach until potato varieties have been bred which are resistant to aggressive biotypes. Dunnett (1960) concludes that until immunity to *Heterodera rostochiensis* or a type of resistance which always suppresses cyst formation can be incorporated in new varieties of potato, the problem of controlling the nematode by varietal resistance is a problem of nematode strains. The answer to these problems, Dunnett says, is an appropriate rotation of different resistant varieties at suitable intervals in particular fields. Although there appears to be no lack of resistance in the tuber bearing Solanums, it may be many years before a range of different types of resistance is available to commercial varieties of potato. For the plant breeder future developments will include the search for new resistance material and the breeding of new resistant strains. The nematologist, however, will probably be concerned with further studies on the distribution of biotypes, the population dynamics of mixed populations and the study of the mode of inheritance of 'resistance breaking' with all its physiological implications.

Ditylenchus dipsaci

Red clover suffers serious damage from this nematode in Sweden but strains selected for their resistance on heavily infested soil have helped to contain the disease. Merkur and Resistenta are two such resistant strains which are grown in the south of Sweden. However, their lack of winter-hardiness prevents their cultivation in the north of that country. Bingefors investigated the possibility of breeding other resistant strains and he studied the nature of resistance in red clover to *Ditylenchus dipsaci*. Bingefors (1951) found that resistance prevented development and reproduction in red clover. Correlation between resistance of clover strains in field trials and their inability to reproduce was good. By crossing resistant and susceptible red clover strains Bingefors (1956) hoped to obtain some idea of the mode of inheritance of resistance. The results did not indicate any simple inheritance by one, two or three genes but there were indications that a few genes had a major influence. Bingefors (1957) also showed that a red clover variety which was highly resistant in the south of Sweden was also resistant in other parts of the country. In preliminary tests of nematode populations from different parts of Sweden it was found that there were differences in their ability to attack different red clover varieties. Nevertheless the resistant variety Merkur was highly resistant to all the populations tested. This situation is therefore different from that with *Heterodera rostochiensis* where breeding for resistance has been complicated by variations in resistance to different biotypes. Bingefors (1960) concludes that breeding red clover strains for resistance to *Ditylenchus dipsaci* in Sweden has depended on selection in heavily infested fields. With the increasing amount of resistance in red clover material, however, this method is no longer reliable because yield differences are not very clear in fields with a low infestation. Thus the selection method must be replaced by artificial infection methods and early diagnosis of resistance on plant symptoms. A simple and highly efficient technique for infesting red clover seedlings has been described by Bingefors (1957), who inoculated seedlings enclosed in rolled-up cylinders of filter paper. The close correlation between necrosis and resistance in red clover enabled the material to be rapidly screened. Grundbacher (1962) tested lucerne seedlings for resistance by assessing the amount of nematode reproduction in the shoot apex region. Eggs and nematodes were counted in stained plant tissues.

Oats are also severely attacked by *Ditylenchus dipsaci*, and T. Goodey (1937) showed that some varieties were resistant to attack, resistance being due to the inability of the nematode to develop in the plant. Thus the material for a breeding programme was already known and the techniques of Seinhorst (1952) enabled oat seedlings to be easily and efficiently infected. Seinhorst's (1945) observations on symptoms of infested resistant and susceptible varieties of rye also provided a ready means of assessing resistance in the oat seedling stage. Plants without the typical swelling of the hypocotyl were diagnosed as being resistant to *D. dipsaci*. Jones and his colleagues (1955) tested oat varieties for resistance to *D. dipsaci* in heavily infested soil. They found several suitable varieties which they suggested make it possible to cultivate oats successfully on infested land and to incorporate resistance to the nematode into future oat breeding programmes. In a study of some 250 forms of oats, Griffiths and his colleagues (1957) found new sources of resistance in cultivated and wild species. The varietal tests revealed no lack of resistance in the hexaploid group of oat species but in tracing the pedigree and origin of the small group of resistant varieties belonging to *Avena sativa* it was observed that those developed in England and Wales all stemmed from the variety Grey Winter. Those of Irish and European origin also seemed to be derived from a variety like Grey Winter, suggesting that they all carried the same factor for resistance. No evidence was found of biotypes in the *D. dipsaci* populations and the fact that the Grey Winter type of resistance was still effective in spite of continuous cultivation in areas containing the nematode, is further evidence of a lack of biotypes. Goodey and Hooper (1962), however, found differences in the severity of attack on oats by populations from different localities in England and they suggest that biotypes of *D. dipsaci* may exist. They point out, however, that differences in viability of the various inocula could account for this. Goodey and Hooper also state that the genes for resistance are to be found only in the older 'wild types' of oats, *Avena sterilis* and *A. ludoviciana*, that some unimproved *A. byzantina* populations still retain them but that *A. sativa* has lost them through breeding from a restricted number of genotypes with improved cropping capacity and grain quality which unfortunately did not carry the resistance factors.

The control of *Ditylenchus dipsaci* by the cultivation of resistant plants is therefore an accomplished fact in several host crops. The success is largely due to the absence of biotypes so enabling the resistance to persist wherever the crop is grown.

17

Other plant nematode species

Breeding for resistance to other plant parasitic nematodes has no progressed as far as those just described. Nevertheless, it is interesting that *Heterodera avenae* may have biotypes. Andersen (1959) found non-aggressive and aggressive biotypes in populations attacking barley; in oats, resistant varieties were resistant to both biotypes. Andersen (1961) designated these biotypes as 1 and 2. Many barley varieties were resistant to biotype 1 but only two varieties were highly resistant to both biotypes. Andersen found that resistance in the barley varieties Drost and Alfa to biotype 1 and resistance in no. 191 to both biotypes depended on one dominant gene. Partial resistance to both biotypes occurred in the variety Kron.

Ford and Feder (1958) devised a technique for screening seedlings of citrus varieties to *Radopholus similis* and later work (Ford et al., 1959) produced several varieties which were tolerant or resistant to this nematode. Results from field tests will eventually indicate the value of these varieties.

Nelson (1956) demonstrated that inbred lines of corn differed in their reaction to *Tylenchorhynchus claytoni*. Some lines were highly susceptible whereas others appeared to be resistant because the numbers of nematodes decreased. Crosses between resistant and susceptible plants suggested that susceptibility was dominant to resistance.

Hardly any work has been done on the breeding of lines resistant to ectoparasitic plant nematodes. This is perhaps not surprising because the evidence for the pathogenicity and for the amount of damage they cause is somewhat tenuous for many species.

REFERENCES

ALLEN, M. W. and RASKI, D. J. (1950). Chemical control of nematodes. Soil type important limiting factor in control of certain plant parasitic nematodes with volatile soil fumigants. *Calif. Agric.* 4 (10), 5.

ANDERSEN, S. (1959). Resistance of barley to various populations of the cereal root eelworm (*Heterodera major*). *Nematologica*, 4 (2), 91–98.

—— (1961). Resistens mod Havreál. *Heterodera avenae. Medd. VetHøjsk. afdeling for Landbrugets Plantekultur Kbh.* 68, 1–179.

ANDERSON, E. J. (1956). Comparison of initial kills and subsequent increase of nematode populations following soil fumigation. *Phytopathology*, 46, 634.

APT, W. J. and GOULD, C. J. (1961). Control of root lesion nematode, *Pratylenchus penetrans* on narcissus. *Plant Dis. Reptr.* 45 (4), 290–295.

BINGEFORS, S. (1951). The nature of resistance to stem nematode, *Ditylenchus dipsaci* (Kühn) Filipjev, in red clover, *Trifolium pratense* L. *Acta. agric. Scand.* 1, 180–189.

—— (1956). Inheritance of resistance to stem nematodes in red clover. *Nematologica*, 1, 102–108.

BINGEFORS, S. (1957). *Studies on breeding red clover for resistance to stem nematodes.* Uppsala: Almquist and Wiksells Boktryckeri AB, 123 pp.

—— (1960). Stem nematodes in clovers and lucerne and their control by breeding for resistance. *Proc. 8th Int. Grassland congr.*, Paper 2A/5, pp. 78–81.

BIRCHFIELD, W. and BISTLINE, F. (1956). Cover crops in relation to the burrowing nematode, *Radopholus similis*. *Plant Dis. Reptr.* **40** (5), 398–399.

BLAKE, C. D. (1961a). Importance of osmotic potential as a component of the total potential of the soil water on the movement of nematodes. *Nature, Lond.* **192** (4798), 144–145.

—— (1961b). Root rot of bananas caused by *Radopholus similis* (Cobb) and its control in New South Wales. *Nematologica*, **6**, 295–310.

BRANDE, J., VAN DEN, KIPS, R. H. and D'HERDE, J. (1954). Veldproeven in verband met de invloed van het watergehalte van de bodem en van de bodentemperatuur bij de scheikundige bestrijding van het aardappelcystenaaltje *Heterodera rostochiensis* Woll. *Meded. LandbHoogesch. Gent.* **19** (4), 765–776.

—— —— (1956). Survey of the results of four years experiments on the chemical control of the potato root eelworm. *Nematologica*, **1**, 81–86.

BROWN, E. B. (1961). A rotational experiment on land infested with potato root eelworm, *Heterodera rostochiensis* Woll. *Nematologica*, **6**, 201–206.

CAIRNS, E. J. (1953). Relationship of the environmental moisture conditions of the mushroom-spawn nematode, *Ditylenchus* sp. to its control by heat. *Mushroom Science II, Gembloux 1953*, 161–164.

CALL, F. (1957a). The diffusion of ethylene dibromide vapour in air. *J. Sci. Food Agric.* **8**, 86–89.

—— (1957b). Soil fumigation. IV. Sorption of ethylene dibromide on soils at field capacity. *J. Sci. Food Agric.* **8**, 137–142.

—— (1957c). Soil fumigation. V. Diffusion of ethylene dibromide through soils. *J. Sci. Food Agric.* **8**, 143–150.

—— (1957d). Soil fumigation. VI. The distribution of ethylene dibromide round an injection point. *J. Sci. Food Agric.* **8**, 591–596.

CALL, F. and HAGUE, N. G. M. (1962). The relationship between the concentration of ethylene dibromide and nematicidal effects in soil fumigation. *Nematologica*, **7**, 186–193.

CAMPBELL, L. and COURTNEY, W. D. (1960). Effect of high temperature water vapour on soil organisms. *Plant Dis. Reptr.* **4** (10), 804–805.

CAVENESS, F. E. (1958). Status of crop sequences related to *Heterodera schachtii* on sugar beets. *J. Amer. Soc. Sugar Beet Tech.* **10** (4), 283–285.

CHAMBERLAIN, R. (1955). Potato root eelworm prevention in Northern Ireland. *Sci. Hort.* **11**, 118–123.

CHITWOOD, B. G. (1952). Nematocidal action of halogenated hydrocarbons. *Advances in Chemistry*, Series 7, 91–99.

CHRISTIE, J. R. (1959). *Plant nematodes, their bionomics and control.* Agricultural Experiment Stations, University of Florida, Gainesville, Florida.

—— (1960). Biological control—Predacious nematodes. In: '*Nematology fundamentals and recent advances with emphasis on plant parasitic and soil forms.*' Edited by J. N. Sasser and W. R. Jenkins. Chapter 46. Chapel Hill: Univ. N. Carolina Press.

CICHORIUS, H. D. (1960). Uber das Auftreten freilebenden Wurzelnematoden in Rheinischen Böden unter besonderer Berücksichtigung der Standortver hältnisse. *Nematologica*, **5**, 231–252.

CLAYTON, E. E., GRAHAM, T. W., TODD, F. A., GAINES, J. G. and CLARK, F. A. (1958a). Resistance to the root-knot disease of tobacco. Part I. *Tobacco*, **146** (18), 20–25.

—— —— —— —— (1958b). Resistance to the root knot disease of tobacco. Part II. *Tobacco*, **146** (19), 20–24.

COLBRAN, R. C. (1957). Nematode control in pumpkins. *Queensland Agr. J.* **83** (9), 499–501.

COLE, C. S. and HOWARD, H. W. (1959). The effect of growing resistant potatoes on a potato root eelworm (*Heterodera rostochiensis* Woll.) population. *Nematologica*, **4**, 307–316.

—— —— (1962a). Further results from a field experiment on the effect of growing resistant potatoes on a potato root eelworm (*Heterodera rostochiensis*) population. *Nematologica*, **7**, 57–61.

—— —— (1962b). The effect of growing resistant potatoes on a potato root eelworm population—a microplot experiment. *Ann. appl. Biol.* **50**, 121–127.

CRITTENDEN, H. W. (1956). Control of *Meloidogyne incognita acrita* by crop rotations. *Plant Dis. Reptr.* **40** (11), 977–980.

DAULTON, R. A. C. and STOKES, W. M. (1952). The destruction or inhibition of root knot nematodes by exposure to an electrostatic field. *Emp. J. Exp. Agr.* **20** (80), 271–273.

DAVIS, D. and DEAK, J. E. (1960). An assay for the detection of nematode repellants. *Plant Dis. Reptr.* **44** (8), 622–624.

DROLSOM, P. N., MOORE, E. L. and GRAHAM, T. W. (1958). Inheritance of resistance to root knot nematodes in tobacco. *Phytopathology*, **48**, 686.

DUDDINGTON, C. L. and DUTHOIT, C. M. G. (1960). Green manuring and cereal root eelworm. *Plant Pathology*, **9**, 7–9.

DUDDINGTON, C. L., EVERARD, C. O. R. and DUTHOIT, C. M. G. (1961). Effect of green manuring and a predacious fungus on cereal root eelworm in oats. *Plant Pathology*, **10** (3), 108–109.

DUDDINGTON, C. L., JONES, F. G. W. and MORIARTY, F. (1956). The effect of predacious fungus and organic matter upon the soil population of beet eelworm, *Heterodera schachtii* Schm. *Nematologica*, **1**, 344–348.

DUDDINGTON, C. L., JONES, F. G. W. and WILLIAMS, T. D. (1956). An experiment on the effect of a predacious fungus upon the soil population of potato root eelworm, *Heterodera rostochiensis* Woll. *Nematologica*, **1**, 341–343.

DUNNETT, J. M. (1957). Variation in pathogenicity of the potato root eelworm (*Heterodera rostochiensis* Woll.) and its significance in potato breeding. *Euphytica*, **6**, 77–89.

—— (1960). Potato breeder's strains of root eelworm (*Heterodera rostochiensis* Woll.). *Nematologica*, Suppl. 2, 84–94.

ELLENBY, C. (1945). Susceptibility of South American tuber-forming species of *Solanum* to the potato root eelworm (*Heterodera rostochiensis* Wollenweber). *Emp. J. Agric.* **13**, 158–168.

—— (1954). Tuber forming species and varieties of the genus *Solanum* tested for resistance to the potato root eelworm, *Heterodera rostochiensis* Wollenweber. *Euphytica*, **3**, 195–202.

ENDO, B. Y. and SASSER, J. N. (1957). The effectiveness of various soil fumigants for control of the soybean cyst nematode. *Phytopathology*, **47**, 9.

FASSULIOTIS, G. (1957). X-ray studies on the golden nematode, *Heterodera rostochiensis*. *Phytopathology*, **47**, 520.

FASSULIOTIS, G. and SPARROW, A. H. (1955). Preliminary report of X-ray studies of the golden nematode. *Plant Dis. Reptr.* **39** (7), 572.

FEDER, W. A. (1960). Osmotic destruction of plant parasitic and saprophytic nematodes by the addition of sugars to soil. *Plant Dis. Reptr.* **44** (12), 883–885.

FEDER, W. A., EICHHORN, J. L. and HUTCHINS, P. C. (1962). Sugar-induced osmotic dehydration of nematodes enhanced by the addition of detergents. *Phytopathology*, **52** (1), 9.

FORD, H. W. and FEDER, W. A. (1958). Procedure used for rapid evaluation of citrus for resistance to certain endoparasitic nematodes. *Amer. J. Hort. Sci.* **71**, 278–284.

FORD, H. W., FEDER, W. A. and HUTCHINS, P. C. (1959). Promising root stocks that tolerate the burrowing nematode. *Proc. Fla. State hort. Soc.* **965**, 96–102.

FORD, H. W. and HANNON, C. I. (1958). The burrowing nematode, *Radopholus similis* in roots of *Crotalaria spectabilis*. *Plant Dis. Reptr.* **42** (4), 461–463.

GOFFART, H. and ROSS, H. (1954). Untersuchungen zur Frage der Resistenz von Wildarten der Kartoffel gegen den Kartoffelnematoden (*Heterodera rostochiensis* Wr.). *Der Züchter*, **24** (7/8), 193–201.

GOLDEN, A. M. and JORGENSON, E. C. (1961). The sugar beet nematode and its control. *U.S. Dep. Agric.* leaflet **486**.

GOLDEN, A. M. and SHAFER, T. (1958). Unusual response of *Hesperis matronalis* L. to root knot nematodes (*Meloidogyne* spp.). *Plant Dis. Reptr.* **42** (10), 1163–1166.

—— —— (1959). Susceptibility of tomato (*Lycopersicon esculentum*) to the sugar beet nematode (*Heterodera schachtii*). *Plant Dis. Reptr.* **43** (11), 1196–1197.

GOOD, J. M., ROBERTSON, W. K. and THOMPSON, L. G. (1954). Effect of crop rotation on the populations of meadow nematode, *Pratylenchus leiocephalus*, in Norfolk loamy fine sand. *Plant Dis. Reptr.* **38** (3), 178–180.

GOODEY, J. B. and HOOPER, D. J. (1962). Observations on attack by *Ditylenchus dipsaci* on varieties of oats. *Nematologica*, **8**, 33–38.

GOODEY, T. (1937). Observations on the susceptibility of certain varieties of oats to 'tulip-root' caused by the stem eelworm, *Anguillulina dipsaci*. *J. Helminth.* **15**, 203–214.

GRAHAM, T. W. (1954). Problems in breeding for resistance to nematodes in tobacco. *Plant Dis. Reptr.* Suppl. **227**, 89.

—— (1960). A root-knot resistant tobacco breeding line released to breeders. *Phytopathology*, **50** (8), 575.

—— (1961). Responses of tobacco breeding lines to three species of root knot nematodes in greenhouse tests. *Plant Dis. Reptr.* **45** (9), 692–695.

GRIFFITHS, D. J., HOLDEN, J. H. W. and JONES, J. M. (1957). Investigations on resistance of oats to stem eelworm, *Ditylenchus dipsaci* Kühn. *Ann. appl. Biol.* **45**, 709–720.

GRUNDBACHER, F. J. (1962).   Testing alfalfa seedlings for resistance to the stem nematode *Ditylenchus dipsaci* (Kühn) Filipjev.   *Proc. helm. Soc. Wash.* **29**, 152–158.

HAGUE, N. G. M. and OMIDVAR, A. M. (1962).   Techniques for determining the efficacy of fumigants against the potato root eelworm, *Heterodera rostochiensis* Woll.   *Nematologica*, **7**, 219–230.

HARE, W. W. (1951).   Resistance to nematodes in pepper.   *Phytopathology*, **41**, 16.

—— (1953).   Nematode resistance in pepper.   *Phytopathology*, **43**, 474.

—— (1956a).   Comparative resistance of seven pepper varieties to five root knot nematodes.   *Phytopathology*, **46**, 669.

—— (1956b).   Resistance in pepper to *Meloidogyne incognita acrita*.   *Phytopathology*, **46**, 98.

—— (1957).   Inheritance of resistance to root knot nematodes in pepper.   *Phytopathology*, **47**, 455.

HARRISON, M. B. (1960).   The reactions of three golden nematode populations to resistant and susceptible potato selections.   *Phytopathology*, **50** (9), 638.

HESLING, J. J. (1961).   Problems in the routine hot-water treatment of chrysanthemum stools.   *Plant Pathology*, **10** (4), 139–141.

HOLDEMAN, Q. L. (1954).   Nematodes as possible members of disease complexes involving other plant pathogens.   *Plant Dis. Reptr.* Suppl. **227**, 77–79.

—— (1956).   Effectiveness of ethylene dibromide, D-D, and Nemagon in controlling the sting nematode on sandy soils in South Carolina.   *Phytopathology*, **46**, 15.

HUIJSMAN, C. A. (1956).   Breeding for resistance to the potato root eelworm in the Netherlands.   *Nematologica*, **1**, 94–99.

—— (1961).   The influence of resistant potato varieties on the soil population of *Heterodera rostochiensis* Woll.   *Nematologica*, **6** (3), 177–180.

ICHIKAWA, S. T., GILPATRICK, J. D. and MCBETH, C. W. (1955).   Soil diffusion pattern of 1,2-dibromo-3-chloropropane.   *Phytopathology*, **45**, 576–578.

JENKINS, W. R. (1960).   Control of nematodes by physical methods.   In *Nematology fundamentals and recent advances with emphasis on plant parasitic and soil forms*.   Edited by J. N. Sasser and W. R. Jenkins.   Chapter 42.   Chapel Hill: Univ. N. Carolina Press.

JOHNSON, L. F. (1962).   Effect of addition of organic amendments to soil on root knot of tomatoes.   11. Relationship of soil temperature, moisture and pH.   *Phytopathology*, **52** (5), 410–413.

JONES, F. G. W. (1954).   First steps in breeding for resistance to potato root eelworm.   *Ann. appl. Biol.* **41** (2), 348–353.

—— (1957).   Resistance-breaking biotypes of the potato root eelworm (*Heterodera rostochiensis* Woll.).   *Nematologica*, **2**, 185–192.

JONES, F. G. W. and PAWELSKA, K. (1962).   The behaviour of populations of potato root eelworm (*Heterodera rostochiensis* Woll.) towards some resistant tuberous and other *Solanum* species.   *Ann. appl. Biol.* **51**, 277–294.

JONES, J. M., GRIFFITHS, D. J. and HOLDEN, J. H. W. (1955).   Varietal resistance in oats to attacks by the stem and bulb eelworm.   *Plant Pathology*, **4**, 35–43.

KÄMPFE, L. (1962). Zur Wirkung von Ultraschall auf Cystenbildende und freilebende Nematoden. *Nematologica*, **7**, 164–172.

KLEIN, H. H. and ALLISON, C. C. (1957). A rapid method of screening of nematocides in the greenhouse. *Phytopathology*, **47**, 21.

LAAN, P. A., VAN DER (1956). The influence of organic manuring on the development of the potato root eelworm, *Heterodera rostochiensis*. *Nematologica*, **1** (2), 112–125.

LAAN, P. A., VAN DER and HUYSMAN, C. A. (1957). Een eerste aanwijzing voor het bestaan van biotypen van het aardappelcystenaaltje, welke zich sterk kunnen vermeerderan in resistente nakomelingen van *Solanum tuberosum* subsp. *andigena*. *Tijdschr. PlZiekt.* **63**, 365–368.

LEAR, B. and JACOB, F. C. (1955). Results of laboratory tests with high voltage, non-thermal electrical treatments for control of root knot nematodes. *Plant Dis. Reptr.* **39** (5), 397–399.

LEAR, B., MAI, W. F., FELDMESSER, J. and SPRUYT, F. J. (1952). Soil fumigation experiments on Long Island, New York, to control golden nematode of potatoes. *Phytopathology*, **42**, 193–196.

LINDE, W. J., VAN DER (1956). The *Meloidogyne* problem in South Africa. *Nematologica*, **1**, 177–183.

LOWNSBERY, B. F. (1951). Larval emigration from cysts of the golden nematode of potatoes, *Heterodera rostochiensis* Wollenweber, *Phytopathology*, **41** (10), 889–896.

MACHMER, J. H. (1958). Effect of soil salinity on nematodes in citrus and papaya plantings. *J. Rio Grande Valley Hort. Soc.* **12**, 57–60.

MAI, W. F. and LOWNSBERY, B. F. (1952). Crop rotation in relation to the golden nematode population of the soil. *Phytopathology*, **42** (7), 345–347.

MAI, W. F. and PETERSON, L. C. (1952). Resistance of *Solanum ballsii* and *S. sucrense* to the golden nematode, *Heterodera rostochiensis* Wollenweber. *Sci.* **116** (3009), 224–225.

MANKAU, R. (1960). The use of nematode-trapping fungi to control root knot nematodes. *Phytopathology*, **50** (9), 645.

—— (1961a). An attempt to control root knot nematode with *Dactylaria thaumasia* and *Arthrobotrys arthrobotryoides*. *Plant Dis. Reptr.* **45** (3), 164–166.

—— (1961b). The use of nematode-trapping fungi to control root knot nematodes. *Nematologica*, **6**, 326–332.

—— (1962). The effect of some organic additives upon a soil nematode population and associated natural enemies. *Nematologica*, **7**, 65–73.

MANKAU, R. and MINTEER, R. J. (1962). Reduction of soil populations of the citrus nematode by the addition of organic materials. *Plant Dis. Reptr.* **46** (5), 375–378.

MCBETH, C. W. (1954). Some practical aspects of soil fumigation. *Plant Dis. Reptr.* Suppl. **227**, 95–97.

MCBETH, C. W. and BERGESON, G. B. (1953). Methods of assaying nematicides. *Phytopathology*, **43**, 264–267.

MEIJNEKE, C. A. R. and OOSTENBRINK, M. (1958). *Tagetes* ter bestrijding van aaltjesaantastingen. *Meded. Directeur van de Tuinbouw*, **21**, 283–290.

MYERS, R. (1960). The sensitivity of some plant parasitic and free-living nematodes to gamma and X-irradiation. *Nematologica*, **5**, 56–63.

MYERS, R. and DROPKIN, V. H. (1959). Impracticability of control of plant parasitic nematodes with ionising radiations. *Plant Dis. Reptr.* **43** (3), 311–313.

NELSON, R. R. (1956). Resistance to the stunt nematode in corn. *Plant Dis. Reptr.* **40** (7), 635–639.

NUSBAUM, C. J. (1955). Variable effects of nematocides on parasitic nematode populations in row-fumigated tobacco plots. *Phytopathology*, **45**, 349.

OCHSE, J. J. and BREWTON, W. S. (1954). Preliminary report on *Crotalaria* versus nematodes. *Proc. Fla. Hort. Soc.* **67**, 218–219.

OMIDVAR, A. M. (1962). The nematicidal effects of *Tagetes* spp. on the final population of *Heterodera rostochiensis* Woll. *Nematology*, **7**, 62–64.

OOSTENBRINK, M. (1954). Over de betekenis van vrijlevende wortelaaltjes in land- en tuinbouw. *Versl. Pl. Ziekt. Dienst. Wageningen*, **124**, 196–233.

—— (1959). Einige Gründüngungsfragen im Hinblick auf pflanzenparasitäre Nematoden. *Ver. IV Internationalen Pflanzenschutz-Kongresses Hamburg 1957*. Bd. 1 (Braunschweig, 1959) S. 575–577.

—— (1960). *Tagetes patula* L. als voorvrucht van enkele land- en tuinbouwgewassen op zand- en dalgrond. *Meded. LandbHoogesch. Gent.* **25** (3/4), 1065–1075.

—— (1961). Nematodes in relation to plant growth. III. *Pratylenchus penetrans* (Cobb) in tree crops, potatoes and red clover. *Neth. J. agric. Sci.* **9** (3), 188–209.

OOSTENBRINK, M., S'JACOB, J. J. and KUIPER, K. (1956). An interpretation of some crop rotation experiences based on nematode surveys and population studies. *Nematologica*, **1**, 202–215.

OOSTENBRINK, M., KUIPER, K. and S'JACOB, J. J. (1957). *Tagetes* als feindpflanzen von *Pratylenchus*-arten. *Nematologica*, **2**, Suppl. (1957) 424–433.

OUDEN, H., DEN (1956). The influence of hosts and non-susceptible hatching plants on populations of *Heterodera schachtii*. *Nematologica*, **1**, 138–144.

PETERS, B. G. (1952). Toxicity tests with vinegar eelworm. 1. Counting and culturing. *J. Helminth.* **26** (2/3), 97–110.

PETHERBRIDGE, F. R. and JONES, F. G. W. (1944). Beet eelworm (*Heterodera schachtii* Schm.) in East Anglia, 1934–1943. *Ann. appl. Biol.* **31** (4), 320–332.

REYNOLDS, H. W. and EVANS, M. E. (1953). The stylet nematode, *Tylenchorhynchus dubius*, a root parasite of economic importance in the southwest. *Plant Dis. Reptr.* **37** (11), 540–544.

RIGGS, R. D. and WINSTEAD, N. N. (1959). Studies on resistance in tomato to root knot nematodes and on the occurrence of pathogenic biotypes. *Phytopathology*, **49**, 716–724.

ROHDE, R. A. and JENKINS, W. R. (1957). Host range of a species of *Trichodorus* and its host parasite relationships on tomato. *Phytopathology*, **47** (5), 295–298.

—— —— (1958). Basis for resistance of *Asparagus officinalis* var. *altilis* L. to the stubby root nematode *Trichodorus christiei* Allen 1957. *Univ. Md. agric. Exp. Sta. Bull.* **A-97**.

ROSS, J. P. (1960). Soy bean cyst nematode control by crop rotation. *Phytopathology*, **50** (9), 652.

SANTMYER, P. H. (1955). A comparison of the thermal death time of two dissimilar species of nematodes: *Panagrellus redivivus* (Linn. 1767) Goodey

1945 and *Meloidogyne incognita* var. *acrita* Chitwood 1949. *Proc. helm. Soc. Wash.* **22** (1), 22–25.

——— (1956). Studies on the metabolism of *Panagrellus redivivus* (Nematoda, Cephalobidae). *Proc. helm. Soc. Wash.* **23** (1), 30–36.

SASSER, J. N. (1954). Identification and host-parasite relationships of certain root knot nematodes (*Meloidogyne* sp.). *Univ. Md.* Bull. **A-77**.

SEINHORST, J. W. (1945). Een laboratoriummethode voor de bepaling van de vatbaarheid van rogge voor aantasting door het stengelaaltje (*Ditylenchus dipsaci* (Kühn) Filipjev). *Tijdschr. PlZiekt.* **51**, 39–52.

——— (1952). Een nieuwe methode voor de bepaling van de vatbaarheid van roggeplanten voor aantasting door stengelaaltjes (*Ditylenchus dipsaci* (Kühn) Filipjev). *Tijdschr. Pl. Ziekten.* **58**, 103–108.

SHEPHERD, A. M. (1962). The emergence of larvae from cysts in the genus *Heterodera*. Comm. agric. Bur., Farnham Royal, England. viii + 90 pp.

SHERMAN, G. W. (1934). Survival and revival of *Anguillulina dipsaci* from narcissus material. *Proc. helm. Soc. Wash.* **1** (1), 19–20.

SMITH, A. L. (1954a). Resistance to *Fusarium* wilt and root knot nematode in Upland cotton varieties. *Phytopathology*, **44**, 333.

——— (1954b). Problems on breeding cotton for resistance to nematodes. *Plant Dis. Reptr.* Suppl. **227**, 90–91.

STANILAND, L. N. (1953). Hot water treatment of strawberry runners. *Plant Pathology*, **2** (2), 44–48.

——— (1959). The principles of the hot water treatment of plants. *Plant Pathology, Tech. Bull. Minist. Agric. Lond.*, No. **7**, H.M.S.O. Pp. 147–156.

STEELE, A. E. (1962). Effects of pretreatment of *Heterodera schachtii* cysts with sugar solutions on emergence of larvae in sugar-beet root diffusate. *Plant Dis. Reptr.* **46** (1), 43–44.

STEMERDING, S. (1960). The influence of different rotations on a population of pea cyst eelworm, *Heterodera göttingiana* Liebscher. *Nematologica*, Suppl. **2**, 97–100.

TARJAN, A. C. (1960). Some effects of African marigold on the citrus burrowing nematode, *Radopholus similis*. *Phytopathology*, **50** (8), 577.

TARJAN, A. C. and HOPPER, B. E. (1954). Suitability of *Panagrellus redivivus* as a test organism for contact nematicide evaluation. *Phytopathology*, **44**, 112.

THOMASON, I. J., VAN GUNDY, S. D. and McKINNEY, H. E. (1960). Thermotherapy for root knot nematodes *Meloidogyne* spp. of sweet potato and Tarragon propagating stocks. *Plant Dis. Reptr.* **44** (5), 354–358.

THOMASON, I. J. and SMITH, P. G. (1957). Resistance in tomato to *Meloidogyne javanica* and *M. incognita acrita*. *Plant Dis. Reptr.* **41** (3), 180–181.

TOXOPEUS, H. J. (1956). Some remarks on the development of new biotypes in *Heterodera rostochiensis* that might attack resistant potato clones. *Nematologica*, **1**, 100–102.

TOXOPEUS, H. J. and HUIJSMAN, C. A. (1952). Genotypical background of resistance to *Heterodera rostochiensis* in *Solanum tuberosum* var. *andigenum*. *Nature, Lond.*, **170**, 1016.

——— ——— (1953). Breeding for resistance to potato root eelworm. 1. Preliminary data concerning the inheritance of the nature of resistance. *Euphytica*, **2**, 180–186.

18

VISSER, T. and VYTHILINGHAM, M. K. (1959). The effect of marigolds and some other crops on the *Pratylenchus* and *Meloidogyne* populations in tea soil. *Tea Quart.* **30**, 30–38.

WADE, P. (1954a). Soil fumigation. I. The sorption of ethylene dibromide by soils. *J. Sci. Food Agric.* **5**, 184–192.

—— (1954b). Soil fumigation. II. The stability of ethylene dibromide in soil. *J. Sci. Food Agric.* **6**, 288–291.

—— (1955). Soil fumigation. III. The sorption of ethylene dibromide by soils at low moisture content. *J. Sci. Food Agric.* **1**, 1–3.

WALKER, J. T. (1960). The effect of hot water at different temperatures on larvae of various species of *Meloidogyne*. *Phytopathology*, **50** (9), 658.

—— (1962). The sensitivity of larvae and eggs of *Meloidogyne* species to hot water treatments. *Nematologica*, **7**, 19–24.

WALLACE, A. T. (1954). An association between narrow leaves and root knot nematode resistance in flue-cured tobacco. *Agron. J.* **46** (10), 468–469.

WEISCHER, B. (1957). Die wirkung ionisierender strahalen auf die entwicklung von *Heterodera rostochiensis* und *H. schachtii*. *Nematologica*, **2**, 300–305.

WINSTEAD, N. N. and BARHAM, W. S. (1957). Inheritance of resistance in tomato to root knot nematodes. *Phytopathology*, **47**, 37.

WOOD, F. C. and GOODEY, J. B. (1957). Effects of gamma-ray irradiation on nematodes infesting cultivated mushroom beds. *Nature, Lond.* **180**, 760–761.

Index